JOHNSON'S DICTIONARY

A MODERN SELECTION

JOHNSON'S DICTIONARY

A MODERN SELECTION

BY

E.L. McADAM
& GEORGE MILNE

CASSELL

This paperback edition 1995 by
Cassell
Wellington House
125 Strand
London WC2R 0BB

First published 1963 by Victor Gollancz Ltd

Distributed in the United States
by Sterling Co., Inc.
387, Park Avenue South, New York, NY 10016–8810

Distributed in Australia
by Capricorn Link (Australia) Pty Ltd
2/13 Carrington Road
Castle Hill, NSW 2154

British Library Cataloguing-in-Publication Data
A catalogue record for this book is available from the British Library

ISBN 0-304-34705-1

Printed and bound in Great Britain by Biddles Ltd

Contents

Introduction

If SHAKESPEARE had wanted to use an English dictionary, he would have had to compile his own. In the year of his death, however, a beginning was made with an *English Expositour*, and a *Guide into Tongues* appeared in 1617. Cockeram's *English Dictionarie: or, an Interpreter of Hard English Words* (1623), is just what it advertises: only hard words are included. *Take* is not there, or *want*, though you will find *suaviloquus*, "Hee which speakes Rhetorically," the Englishness of which may be doubted. Cockeram's is a very small book, 195 pages in a modern reprint, without etymologies or examples. The next hundred years saw a large advance both in the number of dictionaries and in their comprehensiveness. Milton's nephew, Edward Phillips, published *A New World of English Words* in 1658, and his world was greatly enlarged by Bailey's *Universal Etymological English Dictionary* in 1721. But even an improved Bailey in 1736 could not be considered a standard dictionary—it was far behind those produced by the academies of France and Italy.

Samuel Johnson, wholly unknown to the public, because all his work had been published anonymously, set out in 1746 to produce such a dictionary, and did. When it appeared in 1755, in two large folio volumes, each the size of a lectern Bible, it swept the field, and maintained its position in England for nearly a century. It is the most famous English dictionary before Webster, and perhaps the best before the eleven-volume *Oxford English Dictionary*. But, except for some quotations in Bartlett and in Boswell's *Johnson,* it is unread and unknown, for a simple reason: it has been out of print for about a hundred years. A modern reprint of the whole *Dictionary* might fill ten large volumes, and would be both impressive and unread. We have therefore decided to make a selection, the nature of which has been determined by the basic character of Johnson's *Dictionary*.

Although Johnson had the help of six copyists, his *Dictionary* is essentially a one-man book, essentially if not quite literally, because the compiler of the first word-list must have been an inventor comparable to the man who devised the wheel, and both have been imitated ever after, though the lexicographers have been blamed oftener than praised. There are only three ways, plus combinations, of making word-lists: recording words heard, using those in earlier dictionaries, or listing those in other books. Johnson mentions the first in his Preface, but dismisses it as too much work. He used the second, acknowledging his predecessors. All lexicographers use earlier dictionaries, if only to avoid the danger of omitting some words by inadvertence. But Johnson also saw the other danger, of including words invented by lexicographers which might never have been used by anyone else. The third method is perhaps the best: read all the books, pamphlets, magazines, and newspapers in the language. Then record all the words, sort, define, and exemplify.

Johnson simplified this impossibility in two ways: he decided to begin with Sir Philip Sidney (about 1580) and to end just before his contemporaries. He modified this a little by using Chaucer occasionally, and a few of his own friends, as well as some of his own works, though not over his name. Secondly, he used what books were easily at hand. He read these, underlined words, put initials in the margins as cues, and his copyists put the words and the sentences in which they occurred on slips of paper. Some of these marked volumes survive. The same method, expanded to thousands of books, hundreds of readers, and millions of cards, is still used.

As far as we know, Johnson did not explicitly exclude any class of words. He omitted some obscene words, but those he omitted were not common in print. (He had no prejudice against merely vulgar words, and may have enjoyed them, as his two examples under *fart* suggest.) He recorded a large amount of slang, often with disapprobation. Curiously enough, technical dictionaries were often more comprehensive and accurate than general dictionaries at that time, and Johnson drew heavily on such works for legal, medical, and ecclesiastical terms. For physics he used Newton, but botany and zoology had not settled down to a logical nomenclature, and he had to use second-rate authorities. (Later on, he helped introduce Linnaeus's method to England.) He used what books were available for agriculture and building. Electricity excited him: he refers to the *Transactions* of the Royal Society, and is aware of what Franklin is experimenting on in the colonies.

In part, Johnson's attitude toward science is typical of his era. He still looks back at the almost medieval view of alchemy, physiology, and medicine, when the transmutation of base metals into gold, the excess of one body fluid over another, and the use of "mummy" as a drug were worth serious consideration. But he constantly quotes that great seventeenth-century physician and debunker, Sir Thomas Browne, to deflate these, and often adds a bit of eighteenth-century common sense as well. It is typical that Johnson had some chemical apparatus in his rooms for many years and performed experiments on the weight-loss of leaves by drying.

It is hard to remember, after having had the *Encyclopaedia Britannica* for nearly two centuries, that we have not always had it. There were English encyclopedias, but none had reached the status of an institution. Dictionaries, therefore, in Johnson's time often included material which now would be put into an encyclopedia. Such are the articles on *amber, camel,* and *electricity* which we reprint.

Outside of a fairly general dislike of slang in polite writing, and an equally general acceptance of scientific and technical terms, Johnson's attitude toward "standard English" is complex. There had been a vocal but not large movement in England to establish an academy on the French model to determine and stabilize the language. Swift was a strong adherent of the plan. To this Johnson was utterly opposed. When he began his *Dictionary*, he thought stability desirable and possible, though not by a government agency. He adhered to a cyclical theory of language, after the model of the gold-silver-bronze ages of Latin literature. He thought that English should adhere to its Old English origins, and avoid Latin ("I do not love Latin originals" under *ferry*), and he particularly objected to what he considered unnecessary importation of French words (see *role*). But by the time he had reached the end of his compilation, Johnson had learned a great deal. When he wrote his Preface he was clear in his own mind that language was in a state of constant change. Indeed, in his statement that the change was least in isolated communities and most in great centers of commerce he was very close to modern theory.

It will by now be obvious that this was not only a one-man but a very personal dictionary. Johnson feels that he is not only required to record and to exemplify but to judge. Hundreds of times he objects to the use of a word, whether by Shakespeare, Milton, Dryden, Pope, or Addison, all of whom are the objects of his almost unlimited admiration. His admiration for Spenser and Swift and some others is under greater control. But always there is a man reading, often laughing, finally judging. Yet even here there is no autocrat enjoying his official authority. How many lexicographers have been willing to say, "I don't know"? Johnson does, many times, as under *etch*, "a country word, of which I know not the meaning." It would have been easy, but not scientific, to leave them out. We have provided notes when the meaning is now at least guessed at.

Other personal aspects of the *Dictionary* are many. Some definitions are prejudiced: "*excise*. A hateful tax levied upon commodities, and adjudged not by the common judges of prop-

erty, but wretches hired by those to whom excise is paid";
"*pension*. An allowance made to any one without an equivalent. In England it is generally understood to mean pay given
to a state hireling for treason to his country." The eccentricity
of the first may be explained—but who would want to explain
it away?—by the fact that excise was a relatively new tax, and
therefore of course hateful, and secondly that Johnson's father
had had trouble with the officers charged with collecting the
tax. Pensions, on the other hand, were not new, but none was
awarded for purely literary merit till Johnson got one seven
years after this; he obstinately and characteristically never
changed this definition. *Pastern*, on the other hand, is wrong
and he eventually corrected it. *Whig* and *Tory* tell us after the
fact that Johnson was a Tory, but it is doubtful that the definitions would have seemed particularly tendentious to readers
then. There is really an almost complete absence of political
prejudice in the book. The same may be said of prejudice
against the Scots. The definition of *oats* is the only one we have
noticed to which objection has been made: "A grain, which in
England is generally given to horses, but in Scotland supports
the people." (And this is in fact an innocent expansion of
Bailey's definition, "a grain, food for horses.") There are easily
a hundred remarks about Scottish usage which are colorless.
Twice Johnson honored MacBean, one of his Scottish amanu-
enses, with credit for information about Northern words.

References of an even more personal character are often,
as Gibbon remarked in another connection, veiled in a learned
language. Johnson salutes his birthplace, Lichfield, under *lich*,
"Salve, magna parens." Elsewhere, in Greek, he apparently
laments the recent death of his wife (*rest*). Also in Greek or
Latin he comments ironically on the spiritual home of "writers
of dictionaries" under *grubstreet*, on his poverty under *necessaries*, and on his age under *measure*. Sometimes he uses English. In a slurring reference to Swift, under *tale*, he gives modern biographers new evidence for an old puzzle: why, though
he enjoyed Swift, did he so often malign him? Perhaps the
answer is simple: Swift, a Tory and an Anglican clergyman,

used dirty language; Johnson could have accepted this, perhaps, in one who was not a priest, and, like himself, a Tory and
an Anglican.

The impact of Johnson's *Dictionary* on his contemporaries
was fourfold: first and best, its size. It was two and a half
times as large as Bailey, almost 2300 pages of definitions and
examples, as well as a preface, a history of the language, and
a grammar (the last two of no particular importance). Where
Cockeram in 1623 had given no definitions of *to take*, and
Bailey eighteen, Johnson gave 134. Second, its etymologies.
These were far more elaborate than in any previous dictionary,
and therefore more vulnerable. This was the favorite point of
attack of reviewers who felt that Gothic was the real original
of English or that Johnson just didn't know enough Old Norse.
(No other lexicographer did either.) Third, the definitions.
These were the meat of the book, its glory, and they still are.
Fourth, the examples. Johnson originally intended to give a
kind of anthology of English literature and learning, ranging
from the Elizabethan period at least through the Restoration,
arranged in chronological order. But when his materials were
collected they were far too bulky for publication, and he had
to contract. Furthermore, his references were inexact, and he
seems to have relied too much on his memory or to have lost
some of his notes: "*cream.* Used somewhere by Swift." Never-
theless his definitions and examples are vastly more comprehensive than in any earlier dictionary, and the examples are
more liberal in length than in any later dictionary. He arranged them in rough chronological order.

These characteristics of Johnson's *Dictionary* have determined the nature of our selection. We considered using Johnson's own abridgment, in the Preface to which he very neatly
explained the purpose of the larger work, and the different
purpose and nature of the shorter one:

> Having been long employed in the study and cultivation of
> the English language, I lately published a dictionary like
> those compiled by the academies of Italy and France, for
> the use of such as aspire to exactness of criticism or ele-
> gance of style.

But it has been since considered that works of that kind are by no means necessary to the greater number of readers, who, seldom intending to write or presuming to judge, turn over books only to amuse their leisure, and to gain degrees of knowledge suitable to lower characters, or necessary to the common business of life: these know not any other use of a dictionary than that of adjusting orthography, or explaining terms of science or words of infrequent occurrence, or remote derivation.

But since Johnson omitted from his abridgment a great many definitions and all of the examples, it did not fit our purpose, which is to furnish the modern reader enough of the original work so as to give him some sense of the unique quality of this landmark of literature and learning. There would be no point in repeating ordinary definitions of words found in any modern dictionary, but where such a word is given an unusual sense or definition it is included. A large number of obsolete words are included, and we have given a selection of the examples, not only because they illustrate the words, but in many cases because they are delightful in themselves. We have finally given all of Johnson's entries under Z, so that the reader may see one unabridged section.

We have reprinted Johnson's Preface to the first edition, not only because it is a careful explanation of what his *Dictionary* is, but because it is a noble piece of English prose and, in the end, a moving personal document. Johnson could define *lexicographer* as "a writer of dictionaries, a harmless drudge," but the sad irony of this is not a true index either to his purpose or to his final accomplishment. The *Dictionary* was accepted by both the public and the scholars, including Adam Smith in Scotland, and praised by the French and Italian academies. Johnson was satisfied. Many years later he told Boswell, "I knew very well what I was undertaking,—and very well how to do it,—and have done it very well."

E. L. M. Jr.

G. M.

A note on the text

WE HAVE USED the first edition of the *Dictionary* because in later editions the titles of the works Johnson used were generally omitted, and some of the definitions modified. We have, however, normalized Johnson's spellings of the names of authors quoted (*Jonson, Browne,* instead of *Johnson, Brown*) thinking that the interest of the modern reader is better served thus than in preserving Johnson's indifference to such things. (As far as we know, he never spelled Boswell's name other than *Boswel.*) But, except for expanding his abbreviations, we have left his titles untouched: no reader will fail to recognize *Faerie Queene* in *Fairy Queen.* Spelling and punctuation in definitions and examples remain unchanged, though typographical errors are silently corrected.

We have not followed the eighteenth-century practice of italicizing proper names, and have reduced capitalization to modern usage.

To produce an uncluttered text, we have omitted the names of parts of speech in definitions, except to avoid ambiguity.

Johnson's etymologies are generally of interest only to a specialist, and we have therefore omitted most of them. We have retained those which seem particularly individual or eccentric, or which, perhaps, are spectacularly wrong.

As usual in the period, Johnson mixes I-J and U-V. We have separated these letters in the modern way.

Preface to the Dictionary

———————

BY

SAMUEL JOHNSON

Preface

It is the fate of those who toil at the lower employments of life, to be rather driven by the fear of evil, than attracted by the prospect of good; to be exposed to censure, without hope of praise; to be disgraced by miscarriage, or punished for neglect, where success would have been without applause, and diligence without reward.

Among these unhappy mortals is the writer of dictionaries; whom mankind have considered, not as the pupil, but the slave of science, the pionier of literature, doomed only to remove rubbish and clear obstructions from the paths of Learning and Genius, who press forward to conquest and glory, without bestowing a smile on the humble drudge that facilitates their progress. Every other authour may aspire to praise; the lexicographer can only hope to escape reproach, and even this negative recompense has been yet granted to very few.

I have, notwithstanding this discouragement, attempted a dictionary of the English language, which, while it was employed in the cultivation of every species of literature, has itself been hitherto neglected, suffered to spread, under the direction of chance, into wild exuberance, resigned to the tyranny of time and fashion, and exposed to the corruptions of ignorance, and caprices of innovation.

[3]

When I took the first survey of my undertaking, I found our speech copious without order, and energetick without rules: wherever I turned my view, there was perplexity to be disentangled, and confusion to be regulated; choice was to be made out of boundless variety, without any established principle of selection; adulterations were to be detected, without a settled test of purity; and modes of expression to be rejected or received, without the suffrages of any writers of classical reputation or acknowledged authority.

Having therefore no assistance but from general grammar, I applied myself to the perusal of our writers; and noting whatever might be of use to ascertain or illustrate any word or phrase, accumulated in time the materials of a dictionary, which, by degrees, I reduced to method, establishing to myself, in the progress of the work, such rules as experience and analogy suggested to me; experience, which practice and observation were continually increasing; and analogy, which, though in some words obscure, was evident in others.

In adjusting the *orthography*, which has been to this time unsettled and fortuitous, I found it necessary to distinguish those irregularities that are inherent in our tongue, and perhaps coeval with it, from others which the ignorance or negligence of later writers has produced. Every language has its anomalies, which, though inconvenient, and in themselves once unnecessary, must be tolerated among the imperfections of human things, and which require only to be registred, that they may not be increased, and ascertained, that they may not be confounded: but every language has likewise its improprieties and absurdities, which it is the duty of the lexicographer to correct or proscribe.

As language was at its beginning merely oral, all words of necessary or common use were spoken before they were written; and while they were unfixed by any visible signs, must have been spoken with great diversity, as we now observe those who cannot read to catch sounds imperfectly, and utter them negligently. When this wild and barbarous jargon was first reduced to an alphabet, every penman endeavoured to express, as he could, the sounds which he was accustomed to pronounce or to receive, and vitiated in writing such words as were already vitiated in speech. The powers of the letters, when they were applied to a new language, must have been vague and unsettled, and therefore different hands would exhibit the same sound by different combinations.

From this uncertain pronunciation arise in a great part the various dialects of the same country, which will always be observed to grow fewer, and less different, as books are multiplied; and from this arbitrary representation of sounds by letters, proceeds that diversity of spelling observable in the Saxon remains, and I suppose in the first books of every nation, which perplexes or destroys analogy, and produces anomalous formations, which, being once incorporated, can never be afterward dismissed or reformed.

Of this kind are the derivatives *length* from *long*, *strength* from *strong*, *darling* from *dear*, *breadth* from *broad*, from *dry*, *drought*, and from *high*, *height*, which Milton, in zeal for analogy, writes *highth; Quid te exempta juvat spinis de pluribus una;* ° to change all would be too much, and to change one is nothing.

This uncertainty is most frequent in the vowels, which are so capriciously pronounced, and so differently modified, by accident or affectation, not only in every province, but in every mouth, that to them, as is well known to etymologists, little regard is to be shewn in the deduction of one language from another.

Such defects are not errours in orthography, but spots of barbarity impressed so deep in the English language, that criticism can never wash them away; these, therefore, must be permitted to remain untouched: but many words have likewise been altered by accident, or depraved by ignorance, as the pronunciation of the vulgar has been weakly followed; and some still continue to be variously written, as authours differ in their care or skill: of these it was proper to enquire the true orthography, which I have always considered as depending on their derivation, and have therefore referred them to their

° "What good would it do to remove one out of many errors?" Horace, *Epistles,* 2.2.212.

original languages: thus I write *enchant, enchantment, enchanter,* after the French, and *incantation* after the Latin; thus *entire* is chosen rather than *intire,* because it passed to us not from the Latin *integer,* but from the French *entier.*

Of many words it is difficult to say whether they were immediately received from the Latin or the French, since at the time when we had dominions in France, we had Latin service in our churches. It is, however, my opinion, that the French generally supplied us; for we have few Latin words, among the terms of domestick use, which are not French; but many French, which are very remote from Latin.

Even in words of which the derivation is apparent, I have been often obliged to sacrifice uniformity to custom; thus I write, in compliance with a numberless majority, *convey* and *inveigh, deceit* and *receipt, fancy* and *phantom;* sometimes the derivative varies from the primitive, as *explain* and *explanation, repeat* and *repetition.*

Some combinations of letters having the same power are used indifferently without any discoverable reason of choice, as in *choak, choke; soap, sope; fewel, fuel,* and many others; which I have sometimes inserted twice, that those who search for them under either form, may not search in vain.

In examining the orthography of any doubtful word, the mode of spelling by which it is inserted in the series of the dictionary, is to be considered as that to which I give, perhaps not often rashly, the preference. I have left, in the examples, to every authour his own practice unmolested, that the reader may balance suffrages, and judge between us: but this question is not always to be determined by reputed or by real learning; some men, intent upon greater things, have thought little on sounds and derivations; some, knowing in the ancient tongues, have neglected those in which our words are commonly to be sought. Thus Hammond writes *fecibleness* for *feasibleness,* because I suppose he imagined it derived immediately from the Latin; and some words, such as *dependant, dependent; dependance, dependence,* vary their final syllable, as one or other language is present to the writer.

In this part of the work, where caprice has long wantoned

without controul, and vanity sought praise by petty reformation, I have endeavoured to proceed with a scholar's reverence for antiquity, and a grammarian's regard to the genius of our tongue. I have attempted few alterations, and among those few, perhaps the greater part is from the modern to the ancient practice; and I hope I may be allowed to recommend to those, whose thoughts have been, perhaps, employed too anxiously on verbal singularities, not to disturb, upon narrow views, or for minute propriety, the orthography of their fathers. It has been asserted, that for the law to be *known,* is of more importance than to be *right.* Change, says Hooker, is not made without inconvenience, even from worse to better. There is in constancy and stability a general and lasting advantage, which will always overbalance the slow improvements of gradual correction. Much less ought our written language to comply with the corruptions of oral utterance, or copy that which every variation of time or place makes different from itself, and imitate those changes, which will again be changed, while imitation is employed in observing them.

This recommendation of steadiness and uniformity does not proceed from an opinion, that particular combinations of letters have much influence on human happiness; or that truth may not be successfully taught by modes of spelling fanciful and erroneous: I am not yet so lost in lexicography, as to forget that *words are the daughters of earth, and that things are the sons of heaven.* [*] Language is only the instrument of science, and words are but the signs of ideas: I wish, however, that the instrument might be less apt to decay, and that signs might be permanent, like the things which they denote.

In settling the orthography, I have not wholly neglected the pronunciation, which I have directed, by printing an accent upon the acute or elevated syllable. It will sometimes be found, that the accent is placed by the authour quoted, on a different syllable from that marked in the alphabetical series; it is then to be understood, that custom has varied, or that the authour has, in my opinion, pronounced wrong. Short directions are

---

[*] Paraphrased from a line in Samuel Madden's *Boulter's Monument,* a poem which Johnson was paid to revise before publication.

sometimes given where the sound of letters is irregular; and if they are sometimes omitted, defect in such minute observations will be more easily excused, than superfluity.

In the investigation both of the orthography and significa-tion of words, their *etymology* was necessarily to be considered, and they were therefore to be divided into primitives and de-rivatives. A primitive word, is that which can be traced no further to any English root; thus *circumspect, circumvent, cir-cumstance, delude, concave,* and *complicate,* though com-pounds in the Latin, are to us primitives. Derivatives, are all those that can be referred to any word in English of greater simplicity.

The derivatives I have referred to their primitives, with an accuracy sometimes needless; for who does not see that *re-moteness* comes from *remote, lovely* from *love, concavity* from *concave,* and *demonstrative* from *demonstrate?* but this gram-matical exuberance the scheme of my work did not allow me to repress. It is of great importance in examining the general fabrick of a language, to trace one word from another, by not-ing the usual modes of derivation and inflection; and uniform-ity must be preserved in systematical works, though sometimes at the expence of particular propriety.

Among other derivatives I have been careful to insert and elucidate the anomalous plurals of nouns and preterites of verbs, which in the Teutonick dialects are very frequent, and, though familiar to those who have always used them, interrupt and embarrass the learners of our language.

The two languages from which our primitives have been derived are the Roman and Teutonick: under the Roman I comprehend the French and provincial tongues; and under the Teutonick range the Saxon, German, and all their kindred dia-lects. Most of our polysyllables are Roman, and our words of one syllable are very often Teutonick.

In assigning the Roman original, it has perhaps sometimes happened that I have mentioned only the Latin, when the word was borrowed from the French; and considering myself as em-ployed only in the illustration of my own language, I have not been very careful to observe whether the Latin word be pure or barbarous, or the French elegant or obsolete.

For the Teutonick etymologies I am commonly indebted to Junius and Skinner,° the only names which I have forborn to quote when I copied their books; not that I might appropriate their labours or usurp their honours, but that I might spare a perpetual repetition by one general acknowledgment. Of these, whom I ought not to mention but with the reverence due to instructors and benefactors, Junius appears to have excelled in extent of learning, and Skinner in rectitude of understanding. Junius was accurately skilled in all the northern languages, Skinner probably examined the ancient and remoter dialects only by occasional inspection into dictionaries; but the learning of Junius is often of no other use than to show him a track by which he may deviate from his purpose, to which Skinner always presses forward by the shortest way. Skinner is often ignorant, but never ridiculous: Junius is always full of knowledge; but his variety distracts his judgment, and his learning is very frequently disgraced by his absurdities.

The votaries of the northern muses will not perhaps easily restrain their indignation, when they find the name of Junius thus degraded by a disadvantageous comparison; but whatever reverence is due to his diligence, or his attainments, it can be no criminal degree of censoriousness to charge that etymologist with want of judgment, who can seriously derive *dream* from *drama*, because *life is a drama, and a drama is a dream;* and who declares with a tone of defiance, that no man can fail to derive *moan* from μόνος, *monos*, who considers that grief naturally loves to be *alone.*†

Our knowledge of the northern literature is so scanty, that of words undoubtedly Teutonick the original is not always to be found in any ancient language, and I have therefore inserted

---

° Francis Junius (d. 1677) author of *Etymologicum Anglicanum*, 1743; Stephen Skinner (d. 1667) author of *Etymologicon Linguae Anglicanae*, 1671.

† We have omitted a long footnote in which Johnson gives other examples of Junius's "etymological extravagance."

Dutch or German substitutes, which I consider not as radical but parallel, not as the parents, but sisters of the English.

The words which are represented as thus related by descent or cognation, do not always agree in sense; for it is incident to words, as to their authours, to degenerate from their ancestors, and to change their manners when they change their country. It is sufficient, in etymological enquiries, if the senses of kindred words be found such as may easily pass into each other, or such as may both be referred to one general idea.

The etymology, so far as it is yet known, was easily found in the volumes where it is particularly and professedly delivered; and, by proper attention to the rules of derivation, the orthography was soon adjusted. But to *collect* the *words* of our language was a task of greater difficulty: the deficiency of dictionaries was immediately apparent; and when they were exhausted, what was yet wanting must be sought by fortuitous and unguided excursions into books, and gleaned as industry should find, or chance should offer it, in the boundless chaos of a living speech. My search, however, has been either skilful or lucky; for I have much augmented the vocabulary.

As my design was a dictionary, common or appellative, I have omitted all words which have relation to proper names; such as *Arian, Socinian, Calvinist, Benedictine, Mahometan;* but have retained those of a more general nature, as *Heathen, Pagan.*

Of the terms of art I have received such as could be found either in books of science or technical dictionaries; and have often inserted, from philosophical writers, words which are supported perhaps only by a single authority, and which being not admitted into general use, stand yet as candidates or probationers, and must depend for their adoption on the suffrage of futurity.

The words which our authours have introduced by their knowledge of foreign languages, or ignorance of their own, by vanity or wantonness, by compliance with fashion, or lust of innovation, I have registred as they occurred, though commonly only to censure them, and warn others against the folly of naturalizing useless foreigners to the injury of the natives.

I have not rejected any by design, merely because they were unnecessary or exuberant; but have received those which by different writers have been differently formed, as *viscid,* and *viscidity, viscous,* and *viscosity.*

Compounded or double words I have seldom noted, except when they obtain a signification different from that which the components have in their simple state. Thus *highwayman, woodman,* and *horsecourser,* require an explication; but of *thieflike* or *coachdriver* no notice was needed, because the primitives contain the meaning of the compounds.

Words arbitrarily formed by a constant and settled analogy, like diminutive adjectives in *ish,* as *greenish, bluish,* adverbs in *ly,* as *dully, openly,* substantives in *ness,* as *vileness, faultiness,* were less diligently sought, and many sometimes have been omitted, when I had no authority that invited me to insert them; not that they are not genuine and regular offsprings of English roots, but because their relation to the primitive being always the same, their signification cannot be mistaken.

The verbal nouns in *ing,* such as the *keeping* of the *castle,* the *leading* of the *army,* are always neglected, or placed only to illustrate the sense of the verb, except when they signify things as well as actions, and have therefore a plural number, as *dwelling, living;* or have an absolute and abstract signification, as *colouring, painting, learning.*

The participles are likewise omitted, unless, by signifying rather qualities than action, they take the nature of adjectives; as a *thinking* man, a man of prudence; a *pacing* horse, a horse that can pace: these I have ventured to call *participial adjectives.* But neither are these always inserted, because they are commonly to be understood, without any danger of mistake, by consulting the verb.

Obsolete words are admitted, when they are found in authours not obsolete, or when they have any force or beauty that may deserve revival.

As composition is one of the chief characteristicks of a language, I have endeavoured to make some reparation for the universal negligence of my predecessors, by inserting great numbers of compounded words, as may be found under *after, fore, new, night, fair,* and many more. These, numerous as they are, might be multiplied, but that use and curiosity are here satisfied, and the frame of our language and modes of our combination amply discovered.

Of some forms of composition, such as that by which *re* is prefixed to note *repetition,* and *un* to signify *contrariety* or *privation,* all the examples cannot be accumulated, because the use of these particles, if not wholly arbitrary, is so little limited, that they are hourly affixed to new words as occasion requires, or is imagined to require them.

There is another kind of composition more frequent in our language than perhaps in any other, from which arises to foreigners the greatest difficulty. We modify the signification of many verbs by a particle subjoined; as to *come off,* to escape by a fetch; to *fall on,* to attack; to *fall off,* to apostatize; to *break off,* to stop abruptly; to *bear out,* to justify; to *fall in,* to comply; to *give over,* to cease; to *set off,* to embellish; to *set in,* to begin a continual tenour; to *set out,* to begin a course or journey; to *take off,* to copy; with innumerable expressions of the same kind, of which some appear wildly irregular, being so far distant from the sense of the simple words, that no sagacity will be able to trace the steps by which they arrived at the present use. These I have noted with great care; and though I cannot flatter myself that the collection is complete, I believe I have so far assisted the students of our language, that this kind of phraseology will be no longer insuperable; and the combinations of verbs and particles, by chance omitted, will be easily explained by comparison with those that may be found.

Many words yet stand supported only by the name of Bailey, Ainsworth, Philips,° or the contracted *Dict.* for *Dictionaries* subjoined: of these I am not always certain that they are read in any book but the works of lexicographers. Of such

---

° Nathaniel Bailey (d. 1742) compiled the *English Dictionary,* 1721, which was Johnson's principal reference to check inclusion of words. Robert Ainsworth (d. 1743) was the author of a Latin *Thesaurus,* 1736. Edward Phillips published *A New World of English Words* in 1658.

I have omitted many, because I had never read them; and many I have inserted, because they may perhaps exist, though they have escaped my notice: they are, however, to be yet considered as resting only upon the credit of former dictionaries. Others, which I considered as useful, or know to be proper, though I could not at present support them by authorities, I have suffered to stand upon my own attestation, claiming the same privilege with my predecessors of being sometimes credited without proof.

The words, thus selected and disposed, are grammatically considered: they are referred to the different parts of speech; traced, when they are irregularly inflected, through their various terminations; and illustrated by observations, not indeed of great or striking importance, separately considered, but necessary to the elucidation of our language, and hitherto neglected or forgotten by English grammarians.

That part of my work on which I expect malignity most frequently to fasten, is the *Explanation;* in which I cannot hope to satisfy those, who are perhaps not inclined to be pleased, since I have not always been able to satisfy myself. To interpret a language by itself is very difficult; many words cannot be explained by synonimes, because the idea signified by them has not more than one appellation; nor by paraphrase, because simple ideas cannot be described. When the nature of things is unknown, or the notion unsettled and indefinite, and various in various minds, the words by which such notions are conveyed, or such things denoted, will be ambiguous and perplexed. And such is the fate of hapless lexicography, that not only darkness, but light, impedes and distresses it; things may be not only too little, but too much known, to be happily illustrated. To explain, requires the use of terms less abstruse than that which is to be explained, and such terms cannot always be found; for as nothing can be proved but by supposing something intuitively known, and evident without proof, so nothing can be defined but by the use of words too plain to admit a definition.

Other words there are, of which the sense is too subtle and evanescent to be fixed in a paraphrase; such are all those which are by the grammarians termed *expletives*, and, in dead languages, are suffered to pass for empty sounds, of no other use than to fill a verse, or to modulate a period, but which are easily perceived in living tongues to have power and emphasis, though it be sometimes such as no other form of expression can convey.

My labour has likewise been much increased by a class of verbs too frequent in the English language, of which the signification is so loose and general, the use so vague and indeterminate, and the senses detorted so widely from the first idea, that it is hard to trace them through the maze of variation, to catch them on the brink of utter inanity, to circumscribe them by any limitations, or interpret them by any words of distinct and settled meaning: such are *bear, break, come, cast, full, get, give, do, put, set, go, run, make, take, turn, throw.* If of these the whole power is not accurately delivered, it must be remembered, that while our language is yet living, and variable by the caprice of every one that speaks it, these words are hourly shifting their relations, and can no more be ascertained in a dictionary, than a grove, in the agitation of a storm, can be accurately delineated from its picture in the water.

The particles are among all nations applied with so great latitude, that they are not easily reducible under any regular scheme of explication: this difficulty is not less, nor perhaps greater, in English, than in other languages. I have laboured them with diligence, I hope with success; such at least as can be expected in a task, which no man, however learned or sagacious, has yet been able to perform.

Some words there are which I cannot explain, because I do not understand them; these might have been omitted very often with little inconvenience, but I would not so far indulge my vanity as to decline this confession: for when Tully owns himself ignorant whether *lessus*, in the twelve tables, means a *funeral song*, or *mourning garment;* and Aristotle doubts whether οὐρεύς,* in the Iliad, signifies a *mule*, or *muleteer*, I

---

* Read οὐρεύς; Aristotle, *Poetics*, 25.16. Ordinarily *mule*, the word is used by Homer for *guard*.

may freely, without shame, leave some obscurities to happier industry, or future information.

The rigour of interpretative lexicography requires that *the explanation, and the word explained, should be always reciprocal;* this I have always endeavoured, but could not always attain. Words are seldom exactly synonimous; a new term was not introduced, but because the former was thought inadequate: names, therefore, have often many ideas, but few ideas have many names. It was then necessary to use the proximate word, for the deficiency of single terms can very seldom be supplied by circumlocution; nor is the inconvenience great of such mutilated interpretations, because the sense may easily be collected entire from the examples.

In every word of extensive use, it was requisite to mark the progress of its meaning, and show by what gradations of intermediate sense it has passed from its primitive to its remote and accidental signification; so that every foregoing explanation should tend to that which follows, and the series be regularly concatenated from the first notion to the last.

This is specious, but not always practicable; kindred senses may be so interwoven, that the perplexity cannot be disentangled, nor any reason be assigned why one should be ranged before the other. When the radical idea branches out into parallel ramifications, how can a consecutive series be formed of senses in their nature collateral? The shades of meaning sometimes pass imperceptibly into each other; so that though on one side they apparently differ, yet it is impossible to mark the point of contact. Ideas of the same race, though not exactly alike, are sometimes so little different, that no words can express the dissimilitude, though the mind easily perceives it, when they are exhibited together; and sometimes there is such a confusion of acceptations, that discernment is wearied, and distinction puzzled, and perseverance herself hurries to an end, by crouding together what she cannot separate.

These complaints of difficulty will, by those that have never considered words beyond their popular use, be thought only the jargon of a man willing to magnify his labours, and procure veneration to his studies by involution and obscurity. But every art is obscure to those that have not learned it: this uncertainty of terms, and commixture of ideas, is well known to those who have joined philosophy with grammar; and if I have not expressed them very clearly, it must be remembered that I am speaking of that which words are insufficient to explain.

The original sense of words is often driven out of use by their metaphorical acceptations, yet must be inserted for the sake of a regular origination. Thus I know not whether *ardour* is used for *material heat,* or whether *flagrant,* in English, ever signifies the same with *burning;* yet such are the primitive ideas of these words, which are therefore set first, though without examples, that the figurative senses may be commodiously deduced.

Such is the exuberance of signification which many words have obtained, that it was scarcely possible to collect all their senses; sometimes the meaning of derivatives must be sought in the mother term, and sometimes deficient explanations of the primitive may be supplied in the train of derivation. In any case of doubt or difficulty, it will be always proper to examine all the words of the same race; for some words are slightly passed over to avoid repetition, some admitted easier and clearer explanation than others, and all will be better understood, as they are considered in greater variety of structures and relations.

All the interpretations of words are not written with the same skill, or the same happiness: things equally easy in themselves, are not all equally easy to any single mind. Every writer of a long work commits errours, where there appears neither ambiguity to mislead, nor obscurity to confound him; and in a search like this, many felicities of expression will be casually overlooked, many convenient parallels will be forgotten, and many particulars will admit improvement from a mind utterly unequal to the whole performance.

But many seeming faults are to be imputed rather to the nature of the undertaking, than the negligence of the performer. Thus some explanations are unavoidably reciprocal or circular, as *hind, the female of the stag; stag, the male of the hind:*

sometimes easier words are changed into harder, as *burial* into *sepulture* or *interment, drier* into *desiccative, dryness* into *siccity* or *aridity, fit* into *paroxysm;* for the easiest word, whatever it be, can never be translated into one more easy. But easiness and difficulty are merely relative, and if the present prevalence of our language should invite foreigners to this dictionary, many will be assisted by those words which now seem only to increase or produce obscurity. For this reason I have endeavoured frequently to join a Teutonick and Roman interpretation, as to *cheer* to *gladden,* or *exhilarate,* that every learner of English may be assisted by his own tongue.

The solution of all difficulties, and the supply of all defects, must be sought in the examples, subjoined to the various senses of each word, and ranged according to the time of their authours.

When first I collected these authorities, I was desirous that every quotation should be useful to some other end than the illustration of a word; I therefore extracted from philosophers principles of science; from historians remarkable facts; from chymists complete processes; from divines striking exhortations; and from poets beautiful descriptions. Such is design, while it is yet at a distance from execution. When the time called upon me to range this accumulation of elegance and wisdom into an alphabetical series, I soon discovered that the bulk of my volumes would fright away the student, and was forced to depart from my scheme of including all that was pleasing or useful in English literature, and reduce my transcripts very often to clusters of words, in which scarcely any meaning is retained; thus to the weariness of copying, I was condemned to add the vexation of expunging. Some passages I have yet spared, which may relieve the labour of verbal searches, and intersperse with verdure and flowers the dusty desarts of barren philology.

The examples, thus mutilated, are no longer to be considered as conveying the sentiments or doctrine of their authours; the word for the sake of which they are inserted, with all its appendant clauses, has been carefully preserved; but it may sometimes happen, by hasty detruncation, that the general

[17]

tendency of the sentence may be changed: the divine may desert his tenets, or the philosopher his system.

Some of the examples have been taken from writers who were never mentioned as masters of elegance or models of stile; but words must be sought where they are used; and in what pages, eminent for purity, can terms of manufacture or agriculture be found? Many quotations serve no other purpose, than that of proving the bare existence of words, and are therefore selected with less scrupulousness than those which are to teach their structures and relations.

My purpose was to admit no testimony of living authours, that I might not be misled by partiality, and that none of my cotemporaries might have reason to complain; nor have I departed from this resolution, but when some performance of uncommon excellence excited my veneration, when my memory supplied me, from late books, with an example that was wanting, or when my heart, in the tenderness of friendship, solicited admission for a favourite name.

So far have I been from any care to grace my pages with modern decorations, that I have studiously endeavoured to collect examples and authorities from the writers before the restoration, whose works I regard as *the wells of English undefiled,* as the pure sources of genuine diction. Our language, for almost a century, has, by the concurrence of many causes, been gradually departing from its original Teutonick character, and deviating towards a Gallick structure and phraseology, from which it ought to be our endeavour to recal it, by making our ancient volumes the ground-work of stile, admitting among the additions of later times, only such as may supply real deficiencies, such as are readily adopted by the genius of our tongue, and incorporate easily with our native idioms.

But as every language has a time of rudeness antecedent to perfection, as well as of false refinement and declension, I have been cautious lest my zeal for antiquity might drive me into times too remote, and croud my book with words now no longer understood. I have fixed Sidney's work for the boundary, beyond which I make few excursions. From the authours which rose in the time of Elizabeth, a speech might be formed adequate to all the purposes of use and elegance. If the language of theology were extracted from Hooker and the translation of the Bible; the terms of natural knowledge from Bacon; the phrases of policy, war, and navigation from Raleigh; the dialect of poetry and fiction from Spenser and Sidney; and the diction of common life from Shakespeare, few ideas would be lost to mankind, for want of English words, in which they might be expressed.

It is not sufficient that a word is found, unless it be so combined as that its meaning is apparently determined by the tract and tenour of the sentence; such passages I have therefore chosen, and when it happened that any authour gave a definition of a term, or such an explanation as is equivalent to a definition, I have placed his authority as a supplement to my own, without regard to the chronological order, that is otherwise observed.

Some words, indeed, stand unsupported by any authority, but they are commonly derivative nouns or adverbs, formed from their primitives by regular and constant analogy, or names of things seldom occurring in books, or words of which I have reason to doubt the existence.

There is more danger of censure from the multiplicity than paucity of examples; authorities will sometimes seem to have been accumulated without necessity or use, and perhaps some will be found, which might, without loss, have been omitted. But a work of this kind is not hastily to be charged with superfluities: those quotations which to careless or unskilful perusers appear only to repeat the same sense, will often exhibit, to a more accurate examiner, diversities of signification, or, at least, afford different shades of the same meaning: one will shew the word applied to persons, another to things; one will express an ill, another a good, and a third a neutral sense; one will prove the expression genuine from an ancient authour; another will shew it elegant from a modern: a doubtful authority is corroborated by another of more credit; an ambiguous sentence is ascertained by a passage clear and determinate; the word, how often soever repeated, appears with new associates and in different combinations, and every quotation contributes something to the stability or enlargement of the language.

When words are used equivocally, I receive them in either sense; when they are metaphorical, I adopt them in their primitive acceptation.

I have sometimes, though rarely, yielded to the temptation of exhibiting a genealogy of sentiments, by shewing how one authour copied the thoughts and diction of another: such quotations are indeed little more than repetitions, which might justly be censured, did they not gratify the mind, by affording a kind of intellectual history.

The various syntactical structures occurring in the examples have been carefully noted; the licence or negligence with which many words have been hitherto used, has made our stile capricious and indeterminate; when the different combinations of the same word are exhibited together, the preference is readily given to propriety, and I have often endeavoured to direct the choice.

Thus have I laboured to settle the orthography, display the analogy, regulate the structures, and ascertain the signification of English words, to perform all the parts of a faithful lexicographer: but I have not always executed my own scheme, or satisfied my own expectations. The work, whatever proofs of diligence and attention it may exhibit, is yet capable of many improvements: the orthography which I recommend is still controvertible, the etymology which I adopt is uncertain, and perhaps frequently erroneous; the explanations are sometimes too much contracted, and sometimes too much diffused, the significations are distinguished rather with subtilty than skill, and the attention is harrassed with unnecessary minuteness.

The examples are too often injudiciously truncated, and perhaps sometimes, I hope very rarely, alleged in a mistaken sense; for in making this collection I trusted more to memory, than, in a state of disquiet and embarrassment, memory can contain, and purposed to supply at the review what was left incomplete in the first transcription.

Many terms appropriated to particular occupations, though necessary and significant, are undoubtedly omitted; and of the words most studiously considered and exemplified, many senses have escaped observation.

Yet these failures, however frequent, may admit extenuation and apology. To have attempted much is always laudable, even when the enterprize is above the strength that undertakes it: To rest below his own aim is incident to every one whose fancy is active, and whose views are comprehensive; nor is any man satisfied with himself because he has done much, but because he can conceive little. When first I engaged in this work, I resolved to leave neither words nor things unexamined, and pleased myself with a prospect of the hours which I should revel away in feasts of literature, the obscure recesses of northern learning, which I should enter and ransack, the treasures with which I expected every search into those neglected mines to reward my labour, and the triumph with which I should display my acquisitions to mankind. When I had thus enquired into the original of words, I resolved to show likewise my attention to things; to pierce deep into every science, to enquire the nature of every substance of which I inserted the name, to limit every idea by a definition strictly logical, and exhibit every production of art or nature in an accurate description, that my book might be in place of all other dictionaries whether appellative or technical. But these were the dreams of a poet doomed at last to wake a lexicographer. I soon found that it is too late to look for instruments, when the work calls for execution, and that whatever abilities I had brought to my task, with those I must finally perform it. To deliberate whenever I doubted, to enquire whenever I was ignorant, would have protracted the undertaking without end, and, perhaps, without much improvement; for I did not find by my first experiments, that what I had not of my own was easily to be obtained: I saw that one enquiry only gave occasion to another, that book referred to book, that to search was not always to find, and to find was not always to be informed; and that thus to persue perfection, was, like the first inhabitants of Arcadia, to chace the sun, which, when they had reached the hill where he seemed to rest, was still beheld at the same distance from them.

I then contracted my design, determining to confide in myself, and no longer to solicit auxiliaries, which produced more incumbrance than assistance: by this I obtained at least one advantage, that I set limits to my work, which would in time be finished, though not completed.

Despondency has never so far prevailed as to depress me to negligence; some faults will at last appear to be the effects of anxious diligence and persevering activity. The nice and subtle ramifications of meaning were not easily avoided by a mind intent upon accuracy, and convinced of the necessity of disentangling combinations, and separating similitudes. Many of the distinctions which to common readers appear useless and idle, will be found real and important by men versed in the school philosophy, without which no dictionary ever shall be accurately compiled, or skilfully examined.

Some senses however there are, which, though not the same, are yet so nearly allied, that they are often confounded. Most men think indistinctly, and therefore cannot speak with exactness; and consequently some examples might be indifferently put to either signification: this uncertainty is not to be imputed to me, who do not form, but register the language; who do not teach men how they should think, but relate how they have hitherto expressed their thoughts.

The imperfect sense of some examples I lamented, but could not remedy, and hope they will be compensated by innumerable passages selected with propriety, and preserved with exactness; some shining with sparks of imagination, and some replete with treasures of wisdom.

The orthography and etymology, though imperfect, are not imperfect for want of care, but because care will not always be successful, and recollection or information come too late for use.

That many terms of art and manufacture are omitted, must be frankly acknowledged; but for this defect I may boldly allege that it was unavoidable: I could not visit caverns to learn the miner's language, nor take a voyage to perfect my skill in the dialect of navigation, nor visit the warehouses of merchants, and shops of artificers, to gain the names of wares, tools and operations, of which no mention is found in books; what favourable accident, or easy enquiry brought within my reach, has not been neglected; but it had been a hopeless labour to glean up words, by courting living information, and contesting with the sullenness of one, and the roughness of another.

To furnish the academicians della Crusca * with words of this kind, a series of comedies called *la Fiera*, or *the Fair*, was professedly written by Buonaroti; but I had no such assistant, and therefore was content to want what they must have wanted likewise, had they not luckily been so supplied.

Nor are all words which are not found in the vocabulary, to be lamented as omissions. Of the laborious and mercantile part of the people, the diction is in a great measure casual and mutable; many of their terms are formed for some temporary or local convenience, and though current at certain times and places, are in others utterly unknown. This fugitive cant, which is always in a state of increase or decay, cannot be regarded as any part of the durable materials of a language, and therefore must be suffered to perish with other things unworthy of preservation.

Care will sometimes betray to the appearance of negligence. He that is catching opportunities which seldom occur, will suffer those to pass by unregarded, which he expects hourly to return; he that is searching for rare and remote things, will neglect those that are obvious and familiar: thus many of the most common and cursory words have been inserted with little illustration, because in gathering the authorities, I forebore to copy those which I thought likely to occur whenever they were wanted. It is remarkable that, in reviewing my collection, I found the word *sea* unexemplified.

Thus it happens, that in things difficult there is danger from ignorance, and in things easy from confidence; the mind, afraid of greatness, and disdainful of littleness, hastily withdraws herself from painful searches, and passes with scornful rapidity over tasks not adequate to her powers, sometimes too secure for caution, and again too anxious for vigorous effort;

* The Accademia della Crusca was founded in 1582 to purify and standardize the Italian language. Its *Vocabulario* was published in 1612.

sometimes idle in a plain path, and sometimes distracted in labyrinths, and dissipated by different intentions.

A large work is difficult because it is large, even though all its parts might singly be performed with facility; where there are many things to be done, each must be allowed its share of time and labour, in the proportion only which it bears to the whole; nor can it be expected, that the stones which form the dome of a temple, should be squared and polished like the diamond of a ring.

Of the event of this work, for which, having laboured it with so much application, I cannot but have some degree of parental fondness, it is natural to form conjectures. Those who have been persuaded to think well of my design, require that it should fix our language, and put a stop to those alterations which time and chance have hitherto been suffered to make in it without opposition. With this consequence I will confess that I flattered myself for a while; but now begin to fear that I have indulged expectation which neither reason nor experience can justify. When we see men grow old and die at a certain time one after another, from century to century, we laugh at the elixir that promises to prolong life to a thousand years; and with equal justice may the lexicographer be derided, who being able to produce no example of a nation that has preserved their words and phrases from mutability, shall imagine that his dictionary can embalm his language, and secure it from corruption and decay, that it is in his power to change sublunary nature, or clear the world at once from folly, vanity, and affectation.

With this hope, however, academies have been instituted, to guard the avenues of their languages, to retain fugitives, and repulse intruders; but their vigilance and activity have hitherto been vain; sounds are too volatile and subtile for legal restraints; to enchain syllables, and to lash the wind, are equally the undertakings of pride, unwilling to measure its desires by its strength. The French language has visibly changed under the inspection of the academy; the stile of Amelot's translation of father Paul is observed by Le Courayer to be *un peu passé;* and no Italian will maintain, that the diction of any modern writer is not perceptibly different from that of Boccace, Machiavel, or Caro.°

Total and sudden transformations of a language seldom happen; conquests and migrations are now very rare: but there are other causes of change, which, though slow in their operation, and invisible in their progress, are perhaps as much superiour to human resistance, as the revolutions of the sky, or intumescence of the tide. Commerce, however necessary, however lucrative, as it depraves the manners, corrupts the language; they that have frequent intercourse with strangers, to whom they endeavour to accommodate themselves, must in time learn a mingled dialect, like the jargon which serves the traffickers on the Mediterranean and Indian coasts. This will not always be confined to the exchange, the warehouse, or the port, but will be communicated by degrees to other ranks of the people, and be at last incorporated with the current speech.

There are likewise internal causes equally forcible. The language most likely to continue long without alteration, would be that of a nation raised a little, and but a little, above barbarity, secluded from strangers, and totally employed in procuring the conveniencies of life; either without books, or, like some of the Mahometan countries, with very few: men thus busied and unlearned, having only such words as common use requires, would perhaps long continue to express the same notions by the same signs. But no such constancy can be expected in a people polished by arts, and classed by subordination, where one part of the community is sustained and accommodated by the labour of the other. Those who have much leisure to think, will always be enlarging the stock of ideas, and every increase of knowledge, whether real or fancied, will produce new words, or combinations of words. When the mind is unchained from necessity, it will range after convenience;

° Le Courayer made a French translation of Father Paolo Sarpi's *History of the Council of Trent* in 1736; Amelot had made an earlier one in 1683. The first edition of the dictionary of the French Academy appeared in 1694. Boccaccio (d. 1375), Machiavelli (d. 1527), and the poet Annibale Caro (d. 1566) were too early to benefit from the dictionary published by the Accademia della Crusca in 1612.

when it is left at large in the fields of speculation, it will shift opinions; as any custom is disused, the words that expressed it must perish with it; as any opinion grows popular, it will innovate speech in the same proportion as it alters practice.

As by the cultivation of various sciences, a language is amplified, it will be more furnished with words deflected from their original sense; the geometrician will talk of a courtier's zenith, or the excentrick virtue of a wild hero, and the physician of sanguine expectations and phlegmatick delays. Copiousness of speech will give opportunities to capricious choice, by which some words will be preferred, and others degraded; vicissitudes of fashion will enforce the use of new, or extend the signification of known terms. The tropes of poetry will make hourly encroachments, and the metaphorical will become the current sense: pronunciation will be varied by levity or ignorance, and the pen must at length comply with the tongue; illiterate writers will at one time or other, by publick infatuation, rise into renown, who, not knowing the original import of words, will use them with colloquial licentiousness, confound distinction, and forget propriety. As politeness increases, some expressions will be considered as too gross and vulgar for the delicate, others as too formal and ceremonious for the gay and airy; new phrases are therefore adopted, which must, for the same reasons, be in time dismissed. Swift, in his petty treatise on the English language, allows that new words must sometimes be introduced, but proposes that none should be suffered to become obsolete. But what makes a word obsolete, more than general agreement to forbear it? and how shall it be continued, when it conveys an offensive idea, or recalled again into the mouths of mankind, when it has once by disuse become unfamiliar, and by unfamiliarity unpleasing.

There is another cause of alteration more prevalent than any other, which yet in the present state of the world cannot be obviated. A mixture of two languages will produce a third distinct from both, and they will always be mixed, where the chief part of education, and the most conspicuous accomplishment, is skill in ancient or in foreign tongues. He that has long cultivated another language, will find its words and combinations croud upon his memory; and haste and negligence, refinement and affectation, will obtrude borrowed terms and exotick expressions.

The great pest of speech is frequency of translation. No book was ever turned from one language into another, without imparting something of its native idiom; this is the most mischievous and comprehensive innovation; single words may enter by thousands, and the fabrick of the tongue continue the same, but new phraseology changes much at once; it alters not the single stones of the building, but the order of the columns. If an academy should be established for the cultivation of our stile, which I, who can never wish to see dependance multiplied, hope the spirit of English liberty will hinder or destroy, let them, instead of compiling grammars and dictionaries, endeavour, with all their influence, to stop the licence of translatours, whose idleness and ignorance, if it be suffered to proceed, will reduce us to babble a dialect of France.

If the changes that we fear be thus irresistible, what remains but to acquiesce with silence, as in the other insurmountable distresses of humanity? it remains that we retard what we cannot repel, that we palliate what we cannot cure. Life may be lengthened by care, though death cannot be ultimately defeated: tongues, like governments, have a natural tendency to degeneration; we have long preserved our constitution, let us make some struggles for our language.

In hope of giving longevity to that which its own nature forbids to be immortal, I have devoted this book, the labour of years, to the honour of my country, that we may no longer yield the palm of philology to the nations of the continent. The chief glory of every people arises from its authours: whether I shall add any thing by my own writings to the reputation of English literature, must be left to time: much of my life has been lost under the pressures of disease; much has been trifled away; and much has always been spent in provision for the day that was passing over me; but I shall not think my employment useless or ignoble, if by my assistance foreign nations, and distant ages, gain access to the propagators of knowledge, and understand the teachers of truth; if my labours afford light to the repositories of science, and add celebrity to Bacon, to Hooker, to Milton, and to Boyle.

When I am animated by this wish, I look with pleasure on my book, however defective, and deliver it to the world with the spirit of a man that has endeavoured well. That it will immediately become popular I have not promised to myself: a few wild blunders, and risible absurdities, from which no work of such multiplicity was ever free, may for a time furnish folly with laughter, and harden ignorance in contempt; but useful diligence will at last prevail, and there never can be wanting some who distinguish desert; who will consider that no dictionary of a living tongue ever can be perfect, since while it is hastening to publication, some words are budding, and some falling away; that a whole life cannot be spent upon syntax and etymology, and that even a whole life would not be sufficient; that he, whose design includes whatever language can express, must often speak of what he does not understand; that a writer will sometimes be hurried by eagerness to the end, and sometimes faint with weariness under a task, which Scaliger compares to the labours of the anvil and the mine; that what is obvious is not always known, and what is known is not always present; that sudden fits of inadvertency will surprize vigilance, slight avocations will seduce attention, and casual eclipses of the mind will darken learning; and that the writer shall often in vain trace his memory at the moment of need, for that which yesterday he knew with intuitive readiness, and which will come uncalled into his thoughts tomorrow.

In this work, when it shall be found that much is omitted, let it not be forgotten that much likewise is performed; and though no book was ever spared out of tenderness to the authour, and the world is little solicitous to know whence proceeded the faults of that which it condemns; yet it may gratify curiosity to inform it, that the *English Dictionary* was written with little assistance of the learned, and without any patronage of the great; not in the soft obscurities of retirement, or under the shelter of academick bowers, but amidst inconvenience and distraction, in sickness and in sorrow: and it may repress the triumph of malignant criticism to observe, that if our language is not here fully displayed, I have only failed in an attempt which no human powers have hitherto completed. If the lexicons of ancient tongues, now immutably fixed, and comprised in a few volumes, be yet, after the toil of successive ages, inadequate and delusive; if the aggregated knowledge, and cooperating diligence of the Italian academicians, did not secure them from the censure of Beni, if the embodied cricks of France, when fifty years had been spent upon their work, were obliged to change its oeconomy, and give their second edition another form, I may surely be contented without the praise of perfection, which, if I could obtain, in this gloom of solitude, what would it avail me? I have protracted my work till most of those whom I wished to please, have sunk into the grave, and success and miscarriage are empty sounds: I therefore dismiss it with frigid tranquillity, having little to fear or hope from censure or from praise.

Johnson's Dictionary

A MODERN SELECTION

A

a′bbey-lubber. A slothful loiterer in a religious house, under pretence of retirement and austerity.

> This is no Father Dominic, no huge overgrown *abbey-lubber;* this is but a diminutive sucking friar.
> Dryden, *Spanish Friar.*

abeceda′rian. He that teaches or learns the alphabet, or first rudiments of literature.

a′bject. A man without hope; a man whose miseries are irretrievable.

> But in mine adversity they rejoiced, and gathered themselves together; yea, the *abjects* gathered themselves together against me, and I knew it not; they did tear me, and ceased not.   *Psalm* xxxv, 15.

to abla′ctate. To wean from the breast.

to a′blegate. To send abroad upon some employment; also to send a person out of the way that one is weary of.

ablu′tion. (3) The cup given, without consecration, to the laity in the popish churches.

to abo′de. To foretoken or foreshow; to be a prognostic, to be ominous. It is taken, with its derivatives, in the sense either of good or ill.

---

ablution. (3) I.e., the third definition of this word.

> Every man,
> After the hideous storm that follow'd, was
> A thing inspir'd; and, not consulting, broke
> Into a general prophecy, that this tempest,
> Dashing the garment of this peace, *aboded*
> The sudden breach of it.   Shakespeare's *Henry VIII*.

abo'dement. A secret anticipation of something future; an impression upon the mind of some event to come; prognostication; omen.

abo'minable. (3) In low and ludicrous language, it is a word of loose and indeterminate censure.

> They say you are a melancholy fellow.—I am so; I do love it better than laughing.—Those that are in extremity of either, are *abominable* fellows, and betray themselves to every modern censure, worse than drunkards. Shakespeare's *As You Like It*.

abo'rtive. That which is born before the due time.

> Take the fine skin of an *abortive*, and, with starch thin laid on, prepare your ground or tablet.
> Peacham, *On Drawing*.

above-board. In open sight; without artifice or trick. A figurative expression, borrowed from gamesters, who, when they put their hands under the table, are changing their cards. It is used only in familiar language.

> It is the part also of an honest man to deal *above-board*, and without tricks.   L'Estrange.

abracada'bra. A superstitious charm against agues.

Abraham's balm. The name of an herb.

to absco'nd. To hide one's self; to retire from the public view: generally used of persons in debt, or criminals eluding the law.

absente'e. He that is absent from his station or employment, or country. A word used commonly with regard to Irishmen living out of their country.

a'bsonous. Absurd, contrary to reason.

to absu'me. To bring to an end by a gradual waste; to eat up.

abu'se. (3) Seducement.

Abraham's balm. An example of a definition which does not define.

Was it not enough for him to have deceived me, and
through the deceit abused me, and, after the *abuse*, forsaken me, but that he must now, of all the company,
and before all the company, lay want of beauty to my
charge.   Sidney, b. ii.

abu′sive. (3) Deceitful; a sense little used, yet not improper.

aca′cia. (1) A drug brought from Egypt, which, being supposed the inspissated juice of a tree, is imitated by the juice
of sloes, boiled to the same consistence.

Dictionaire de Commerce. Savary. Trevoux.

a′ccidence. The little book containing the first rudiments of
grammar, and explaining the properties of the eight parts
of speech.

I do confess I do want eloquence,
And never yet did learn mine *accidence*.
Taylor the Water-poet.

to acco′st. To speak to first; to address; to salute.

You mistake, knight: *accost* her, front her, board her,
woo her, assail her.   Shakespeare's *Twelfth Night*.

to accro′ach. To draw to one as with a hook; to gripe, to draw
away by degrees what is another's.

accuba′tion. The antient posture of leaning at meals.

It will appear, that *accubation*, or lying down at meals,
was a gesture used by very many nations.
Browne's *Vulgar Errours*, b. v.

a′ce. (2) A small quantity.

I'll not wag an *ace* farther: the whole world shall not
bribe me to it.   Dryden's *Spanish Friar*.

a′cme. The height of any thing; more especially used to denote
the height of a distemper, which is divided into four periods.
1. The *arche*, the beginning or first attack. 2. *Anabasis*, the
growth. 3. *Acme*, the height. And, 4. *Paracme*, which is the
declension of the distemper.   Quincy.

aco′usticks. (2) Medicines to help the hearing.   Quincy.

acqu′ittance. (2) A writing testifying the receipt of a debt.

They had got a worse trick than that; the same man
bought and sold to himself, paid the money, and gave
the *acquittance*.   Arbuthnot's *History of John Bull*.

acroama'tical. Of or pertaining to deep learning; the opposite of exoterical.

acro'ss. Athwart, laid over something so as to cross it.

> There is a set of artisans, who, by the help of several poles, which they lay *across* each others shoulders, build themselves up into a kind of pyramid; so that you see a pile of men in the air of four or five rows rising one above another. Addison, *On Italy*.

a'ction-taking. Accustomed to resent by means of law; litigious.

to a'ctivate. To make active. This word is perhaps used only by the author alleged.

> As snow and ice, especially being holpen, and their cold *activated* by nitre or salt, will turn water into ice, and that in a few hours; so it may be, it will turn wood or stiff clay into stone, in longer time.
> Bacon's *Natural History*, No. 83.

a'ctuary. The register who compiles the minutes of the proceedings of a court; a term of the civil law.

a'damant. (3) Adamant is taken for the loadstone.

> You draw me, you hard-hearted *adamant!*
> But yet you draw not iron; for my heart
> Is true as steel.
> Shakespeare's *Midsummer Night's Dream*.

to adco'rporate. To unite one body with another; more usually wrote *accorporate;* which see.

a'dder. A serpent, a viper, a poisonous reptile; perhaps of any species. In common language, *adders* and *snakes* are not the same.

a'ddice. (For which we corruptly speak and write *adz*, from Saxon an axe.)

a'ddle. Originally applied to eggs, and signifying such as produce nothing, but grow rotten under the hen; thence transferred to brains that produce nothing.

> After much solitariness, fasting, or long sickness, their brains were *addle*, and their bellies as empty of meat as their heads of wit. Burton, *On Melancholy*.

---

adcorporate. Johnson forgot to put in *accorporate*.

addre′ss. (5) Manner of directing a letter; a sense chiefly mercantile.

adhe′sion. (1) The act or state of sticking to something. *Adhesion* is generally used in the natural, and *adherence* in the metaphorical sense; as, *the adhesion of iron to the magnet;* and *adherence of a client to his patron.*

a′djugate. To yoke to; to join to another by a yoke.

admoni′tioner. A liberal dispenser of admonition; a general adviser. A ludicrous term.

to admo′ve. To bring one thing to another.

If, unto the powder of loadstone or iron, we *admove* the north-pole of the loadstone, the powders, or small divisions, will erect and conform themselves thereto. Browne's *Vulgar Errours,* b. ii.

admurmura′tion. The act of murmuring, or whispering to another.

ado′. (3) It has a light and ludicrous sense, implying more tumult and shew of business, than the affair is worth; in this sense it is generally used.

Come, come, says Puss, without any more *ado,* 'tis time for me to go to breakfast; for cats don't live upon dialogues. L'Estrange, *Fables,* ii.

adsciti′tious. That which is taken in to complete something else, though originally extrinsick; supplemental; additional.

adstri′ction. The act of binding together; and applied, generally, to medicaments and applications, which have the power of making the part contract.

adu′lt. A person above the age of infancy, or grown to some degree of strength; sometimes full grown: a word used chiefly by medicinal writers.

to adu′lter. To commit adultery with another: a word not classical.

His chaste wife
He *adulters* still: his thoughts lye with a whore.
Ben. Jonson.

adu′lterate. (1) Tainted with the guilt of adultery.
—That incestuous, that *adulterate* beast. Shakespeare, *Hamlet.*

adu'lterine. A child born of an adulteress: a term of canon law.

to adu'mbrate. To shadow out; to give a slight likeness; to exhibit a faint resemblance, like that which shadows afford of the bodies which they represent.

adu'ncity. Crookedness; flexure inwards; hookedness.

> There can be no question, but the *aduncity* of the pounces, and beaks of the hawks, is the cause of the great and habitual immorality of those animals.
> Arbuthnot and Pope's *Martinus Scriblerus.*

adu'st. (1) Burnt up; hot as with fire, scorched.

adva'ntage. (6) Overplus; something more than the mere lawful gain.

> You said, you neither lend nor borrow
> Upon *advantage.* Shakespeare, *Merchant of Venice.*

adve'nture. (1) An accident; a chance; a hazard; an event of which we have no direction.

advi'ce. (4) Intelligence; as, the merchants received *advice* of their loss. This sense is somewhat low, and chiefly commercial.

advo'utry. Adultery.

adz. See addice.

Aegypti'acum. An ointment consisting only of honey, verdigrease and vinegar. Quincy.

Ae'thiops-mineral. A medicine so called, from its dark colour, prepared of quicksilver and sulphur, ground together in a marble mortar to a black powder. Such as have used it most, think its virtues not very great. Quincy.

affabula'tion. The moral of a fable.

affe'ction. (1) The state of being affected by any cause, or agent. This general sense is little in use.

> Some men there are love not a gaping pig;
> Some that are mad if they behold a cat;
> And others, when the bag-pipe sings i' th' nose,
> Cannot contain their urine, for *affection.* Shakespeare, *Merchant of Venice.*

(8) Lively representation in painting.

> *Affection* is the lively representment of any passion whatsoever, as if the figures stood not upon a cloth or

board, but as if they were acting upon a stage. Wotton's
Architecture.

affi'ance. (1) A marriage-contract.

(3) Trust in the divine promises and protection. To this
sense it is now almost confined.

affilia'tion. Adoption; the act of taking a son. Chambers.

affla'tus. Communication of the power of prophecy.

a'ffluence. (1) The act of flowing to any place; concourse. It
is almost always used figuratively.

> I shall not relate the *affluence* of young nobles from
> hence into Spain, after the voice of our prince being
> there had been noised. Wotton.

to affro'nt. (1) To meet face to face; to encounter. This seems
the genuine and original sense of the word, which was
formerly indifferent to good or ill.

> We have closely sent for Hamlet hither,
> That he, as 'twere by accident, may here
> *Affront* Ophelia. Shakespeare's *Hamlet.*

affro'nt. (3) Open opposition; encounter: a sense not frequent,
though regularly deducible from the derivation.

a'fterclap. Unexpected events happening after an affair is supposed to be at an end.

a'ftergame. The scheme which may be laid, or the expedients
which are practised after the original design has miscarried; methods taken after the first turn of affairs.

> This earl, like certain vegetables, did bud and open
> slowly; nature sometimes delighting to play an *after-
> game,* as well as fortune, which had both their turns and
> tides in course. Wotton.

a'ggregate. The complex or collective result of the conjunc-
tion or acervation of many particulars.

agi'llochum. Aloes-wood.

> A tree in the East-Indies, brought to us in small bits, of
> a very fragrant scent. It is hot, drying, and accounted a
> strengthener of the nerves in general. The best is of a
> blackish purple colour, and so light as to swim upon
> water. Quincy.

to agni'ze. To acknowledge; to own; to avow. This word is
now obsolete.

ago′g. (1) In a state of desire; in a state of imagination; heated with the notion of some enjoyment; longing.

agoni′stes. A prize-fighter; one that contends at any public solemnity for a prize. Milton has so stiled his tragedy, because Sampson was called out to divert the Philistines with feats of strength.

ago′uty. An animal of the Antilles, of the bigness of a rabbet, with bright red hair, and a little tail without hair. He has but two teeth in each jaw, holds his meat in his forepaws like a squirrel, and has a very remarkable cry. When he is angry, his hair stands on end, and he strikes the earth with his hindfeet, and, when chased, he flies to a hollow tree, whence he is expelled by smoke. Trevoux.

agra′mmatist. An illiterate man.

to agu′ise. To dress; to adorn; to deck: a word now not in use.

to ail. (4) It is remarkable, that this word is never used but with some indefinite term, or the word *nothing;* as, *What ails* him? *What* does he *ail? He ails something:* he *ails nothing. Something ails* him; *nothing ails* him. Thus we never say, a fever *ails* him, or he *ails* a fever, or use definite terms with this verb.

aim. (5) Conjecture; guess.

> There is a history in all mens lives,
> Figuring the nature of the times deceas'd;
> The which observ'd, a man may prophesy,
> With a near *aim,* of the main chance of things,
> As yet not come to life, which, in their seeds
> And weak beginnings, lie intreasur'd. Shakespeare,
> *Henry IV.*

air. (1) The element encompassing the terraqueous globe. If I were to tell what I mean by the word *air,* I may say, it is that fine matter which we breathe in and breathe out continually; or it is that thin fluid body, in which the birds fly, a little above the earth; or it is that invisible matter, which fills all places near the earth, or which immediately encompasses the globe of earth and water. Watts's *Logick.*

(7) Vent; utterance; emission into the air.

(8) Publication; exposure to the publick view and knowledge.

> I am sorry to find it has taken *air*, that I have some hand
> in these papers. Pope's *Letters*.

(9) Intelligence; information.

(15) (In horsemanship.) *Airs* denote the artificial or practised motions of a managed horse. Chambers.

to air. (4) To air liquors; to warm them by the fire: a term used in conversation.

(5) To make nests. In this sense, it is derived from *aery*, a nest. It is now out of use.

air-drawn. Drawn or painted in air.

> This is the very painting of your fear,
> This is the *air-drawn* dagger, which, you said,
> Led you to Duncan. Shakespeare, *Macbeth*.

a'irling. A young, light, thoughtless, gay person.

> Some more there be, slight *airlings*, will be won
> With dogs, and horses, and perhaps a whore.
> Ben. Jonson, *Catiline*.

a'iry. Fluttering; loose; as if to catch the air; full of levity.

> By this name of ladies, he means all young persons,
> slender, finely shaped, *airy*, and delicate: such as are
> nymphs and Naiads. Dryden's *Dufresnoy*.

aisle. (Thus the word is written by Addison, but perhaps improperly; since it seems deducible only from either *aile*, a wing, or *allée*, a path; and is therefore to be written *aile*.) The walks in a church, or wings of a quire.

> The abbey is by no means so magnificent as one would
> expect from its endowments. The church is one huge
> nef, with a double *aisle* to it; and, at each end, is a
> large quire. Addison.

to ake. (2) It is frequently applied, in an improper sense, to the heart; as, *the heart akes;* to imply grief or fear. Shakespeare has used it, still more licentiously, of the soul.

> My soul *akes*
> To know when two authorities are up,
> Neither supreme, how soon confusion
> May enter. Shakespeare, *Coriolanus*.

ala′criously. (From *alacrious,* supposed to be formed from *alacris;* but of *alacrious* I have found no example.) Cheerfully; without dejection.

> Epaminondas *alacriously* expired, in confidence that he left behind him a perpetual memory of the victories he had atchieved for his country. *Government of the Tongue,* sect. 4.

ala′crity. Cheerfulness, expressed by some outward token; sprightliness; gayety; liveliness; cheerful willingness.

alamo′de. According to the fashion: a low word. It is used likewise by shopkeepers for a kind of thin silken manufacture.

a′lchymy. (1) The more sublime and occult part of chymistry, which proposes, for its object, the transmutation of metals, and other important operations.

(2) A kind of mixed metal used for spoons, and kitchen utensils.

a′lcohol. An Arabick term used by chymists for a high rectified dephlegmated spirit of wine, or for any thing reduced into an impalpable powder. Quincy.

alco′ve. A recess, or part of a chamber, separated by an estrade, or partition of a column, and other correspondent ornaments; in which is placed a bed of state, and sometimes seats to entertain company. Trevoux.

alderli′evest. Most beloved; which has held the longest possession of the heart.

a′lderman. (2) In the following passage it is, I think, improperly used.

> But if the trumpet's clangour you abhor,
> And dare not be an *alderman* of war,
> Take to a shop, behind a counter lie.
> Dryden, *Juvenal's Satires.*

ale. (2) A merry meeting used in country places.

> And all the neighbourhood, from old records
> Of antick proverbs drawn from Whitson lords,
> And their authorities at wakes and *ales,*
> With country precedents, and old wives tales,
> We bring you now. Ben. Jonson.

a′leconner. An officer in the city of London, whose business is to inspect the measures of publick houses. Four of them are chosen or rechosen annually by the common-hall of the city; and whatever might be their use formerly, their places are now regarded only as sine-cures for decayed citizens.

ale′ctryomancy, or ale′ctoromancy. Divination by a cock.

a′lehouse. A house where ale is publickly sold; a tipling-house. It is distinguished from a tavern, where they sell wine.

> One would think it should be no easy matter to bring any man of sense in love with an *alehouse;* indeed of so much sense, as seeing and smelling amounts to; there being such strong encounters of both, as would quickly send him packing, did not the love of good fellowship reconcile to these nusances. South.

a′leknight. A pot-companion; a tippler: a word now out of use.

aleta′ster. An officer appointed in every courtleet, and sworn to look to the assize and the goodness of bread and ale, or beer, within the precincts of that lordship. Cowell.

alexa′ndrine. A kind of verse borrowed from the French, first used in a poem called *Alexander*. They consist, among the French, of twelve and thirteen syllables, in alternate couplets; and, among us, of twelve.

alexipha′rmick. That which drives away poison; antidotal; that which opposes infection.

a′lgates. On any terms; every way: now obsolete.

a′lias. A Latin word, signifying otherwise; often used in the trials of criminals, whose danger has obliged them to change their names; as, Simpson *alias* Smith, *alias* Baker; that is, *otherwise* Smith, *otherwise* Baker.

a′lkahest. A word used first by Paracelsus, and adopted by his followers, to signify an universal dissolvent, or liquour, which has the power of resolving all things into their first principles.

a′lkali. (The word *alkali* comes from an herb, called by the Egyptians *kali;* by us glasswort.) This herb they burnt to ashes, boiled them in water, and, after having evaporated the water, there remained at the bottom a white salt; this they called *sal kali,* or *alkali.* It is corrosive, producing putrefaction in animal substances, to which it is applied. Arbuthnot, *On Aliments.*

Any substance, which, when mingled with acid, produces effervescence and fermentation.

alke′rmes. In medicine, a term borrowed from the Arabs, denoting a celebrated remedy, of the form and consistence of a confection; whereof the *kermes* berries are the basis. The other ingredients are pippin-cyder, rose-water, sugar, ambergrease, musk, cinnamon, aloes-wood, pearls, and leaf-gold: but the sweets are usually omitted. The *confectio alkermes* is chiefly made at Montpelier, which supplies most part of Europe therewith. The grain, which gives it the denomination, is nowhere found so plentifully as there. Chambers.

all fours. A low game at cards, played by two; so named from the four particulars by which it is reckoned, and which, joined in the hand of either of the parties, are said to make *all fours.*

to alla′y. (2) To join any thing to another, so as to abate its predominant qualities.

alla′y. (1) The metal of a baser kind mixed in coins, to harden them, that they may wear less. Gold is allayed with silver and copper, two carats to a pound Troy; silver with copper only, of which eighteen pennyweight is mixed with a pound. Cowell thinks the allay is added, to countervail the charge of coining; which might have been done only by making the coin less.

allega′tion. (3) An excuse; a plea.

a′llegory. A figurative discourse, in which something other is intended, than is contained in the words literally taken; as, *wealth is the daughter of diligence, and the parent of authority.*

alliga′tor. The crocodile. This name is chiefly used for the crocodile of America, between which, and that of Africa, naturalists have laid down this difference, that one moves the upper, and the other the lower jaw; but this is now known to be chimerical, the lower jaw being equally moved by both.

to allo'o. To set on; to incite a dog, by crying *alloo.*

allo'wance. (6) Established character; reputation.

> His bark is stoutly timber'd, and his pilot
> Of very expert and approved *allowance;*
> Therefore my hopes, not surfeited to death,
> Stand in bold awe. Shakespeare, *Othello.*

allu'minor. One who colours or paints upon paper or parchment; because he gives graces, light and ornament, to the letters or figures coloured. Cowell.

allu'vion. (2) The thing carried by water to something else.

a'lmanack. A calendar; a book in which the revolutions of the seasons, with the return of feasts and fasts, is noted for the ensuing year.

> Beware the woman too, and shun her sight,
> Who in these studies does herself delight;
> By whom a greasy *almanack* is born,
> With often handling like chast amber worn.
> Dryden, *Juvenal.*

a'lmonds of the throat, or tonsils, called improperly *almonds of the ears;* are two round glands placed on the sides of the basis of the tongue, under the common membrane of the fauces; each of them has a large oval sinus, which opens into the fauces, and in it are a great number of lesser ones, which discharge themselves through the great sinus of a mucous and slippery matter into the fauces, larynx, and oesophagus, for the moistening and lubricating those parts. When the oesophagus muscle acts, it compresses the *almonds,* and they frequently are the occasion of a sore throat. Quincy.

a'lnight. There is a service which they call *alnight,* which is a great cake of wax, with the wick in the midst; whereby it cometh to pass, that the wick fetcheth the nourishment farther off. Bacon's *Natural History,* No. 372.

alo'ne. *adv.* (1) This word is seldom used but with the word *let,* if even then it be an adverb, and implies sometimes an ironical prohibition, to help a man who is able to manage the affair himself.

> *Let* you *alone,* cunning artificer;

> See how his gorget peers above his gown,
> To tell the people in what danger he was.
> Ben. Jonson, *Catiline.*

alo′of. (5) It is applied to things not properly belonging to
each other.

> Love's not love,
> When it is mingled with regards that stand
> *Aloof* from th' entire point. Shakespeare's *King Lear.*

to a′lter. (1) To change; to make otherwise than it is. *To alter,*
seems more properly to imply a change made only in some
part of a thing; as, to *alter* a writing, may be, to blot or
interpolate it; to *change* it, may be, to substitute another in
its place.

alte′rn. Acting by turns, in succession each to the other.

alti′loquence. High speech; pompous language.

alti′volant. High flying.

a′maranth. (2) In poetry, it is sometimes an imaginary flower,
supposed, according to its name, never to fade.

ama′ritude. Bitterness.

> What *amaritude* or acrimony is deprehended in choler,
> it acquires from a commixture of melancholy, or external
> malign bodies. Harvey, *On Consumptions.*

to ama′te. (2) To terrify; to strike with horrour. In this sense,
it is derived from the old French, *matter,* to crush or subdue.

amato′rculist. A little insignificant lover; a pretender to affection.

ama′zement. (2) Extreme dejection.

a′mazon. The Amazons were a race of women famous for
valour, who inhabited Caucasus; they are so called from
their cutting off their breasts, to use their weapons better.
A warlike woman; a virago.

amba′ges. A circuit of words; a circumlocutory form of speech;
a multiplicity of words; an indirect manner of expression.

amba′ssadress. (2) In ludicrous language, a woman sent on a
message.

> Well, my *ambassadress* ——
> Come you to menace war, and loud defiance?

Or does the peaceful olive grace your brow? Rowe's
Fair Penitent.

a′mber. A yellow transparent substance of a gummous or
bituminous consistence, but a resinous taste, and a smell
like oil of turpentine; chiefly found in the Baltick sea, along
the coasts of Prussia. Some naturalists refer it to the vegetable, others to the mineral, and some even to the animal
kingdom. Pliny describes it as a resinous juice, oozing from
aged pines and firs, and discharged thence into the sea;
where, undergoing some alteration, it is thrown, in this
form, upon the shores of Prussia, which lie very low. He
adds, that it was hence the ancients gave it the denomination
of *succinum,* from *succus,* juice. This opinion of the ancient naturalist is confirmed by the observation of many of
the moderns, particularly Father Camelli. *Philosophical
Transactions,* No. 290. Some have imagined it a concretion
of the tears of birds; others, the urine of a beast; others, the
scum of the lake Cephifis, near the Atlantick; others, a con-
gelation formed in the Baltick, and in some fountains,
where it is found swimming like pitch. Others suppose it a
bitumen trickling into the sea from subterraneous sources;
but this opinion is also discarded, as good *amber* having
been found in digging at a considerable distance from the
sea, as that gathered on the coast. Boerhaave ranks it with
camphire, which is a concrete oil of aromatick plants,
elaborated by heat into a crystalline form. *Amber* assumes
all figures in the ground; that of a pear, an almond, a pea;
and, among others, there have been found letters very well
formed, and even Hebrew and Arabick characters. Within
some pieces of *amber* have been found leaves, and insects
included; which seems to indicate, either that the *amber*
was originally in a fluid state, or, that having been exposed to the sun, it was softened, and rendered susceptible
of the leaves and insects. *Amber,* when rubbed, draws or
attracts bodies to it; and, by friction, is brought to yield
light pretty copiously in the dark. Some distinguish *amber*
into yellow, white, brown, and black: but the two latter are
supposed to be of a different nature and denomination; the

one called *jet*, the other *ambergris*. The white is most
valued for medicinal uses, and the yellow for being
wrought into beads and toys, because of its transparency.
Trevoux. Chambers.

a'mbergris. A fragrant drug, that melts almost like wax, commonly of a greyish or ash colour, used both as a perfume
and a cordial. It is found on the sea coasts of several warm
countries, and on the western coasts of Ireland. Some
imagine it to be the excrement of a bird, which, being
melted by the heat of the sun, and washed off the shore by
the waves, is swallowed by whales, who return it back in
the condition we find it. Others conclude it to be the excrement of a cetaceous fish, because sometimes found in the
intestines of such animals. But we have no instance of any
excrement capable of melting like wax; and if it were the
excrement of a whale, it should rather be found where
these animals abound, as about Greenland. Others take
it for a kind of wax or gum, which distils from trees, and
drops into the sea, where it congeals. Many of the
orientals imagine it springs out of the sea, as naphtha does
out of some fountains. Others suppose it a sea mushroom,
torn up from the bottom by the violence of tempests. Others assert it to be a vegetable production, issuing out of the
root of a tree, whose roots always shoot toward the sea, and
discharge themselves into it. Others maintain, that *ambergris* is made from the honey-combs, which fall into the
sea from the rocks, where the bees had formed their
nests; several persons having seen pieces that were half
ambergris, and half plain honey-comb; and others have
found large pieces of *ambergris*, in which, when broke,
honey-comb, and honey too, were found in the middle.
Some affirm it to be a true animal concrete, formed in balls
in the body of the male spermaceti whale, and lodged in a
large oval bag over the testicles. But, besides that it is not
one spermaceti whale in a hundred, that is found to have
ambergris, Neumann, chemist to the king of Prussia, absolutely denies it to be an animal substance, as not yielding

in the analysis, any one animal principle. It may indeed be found in whales, but it must have been swallowed by them. He concludes it to be a bitumen issuing out of the earth into the sea; at first of a viscous consistence, but hardening, by its mixture with some liquid naphtha, into the form in which we find it. Trevoux. Chambers.

amber seed, or *musk seed,* resembles millet, is of a bitterish taste, and brought dry from Martinico and Egypt. The Egyptians use it internally as a cordial. It gives a grateful scent to the breath after eating. Chambers.

ambide′xter. (2) A man who is equally ready to act on either side, in party disputes. This sense is ludicrous.

ambi′guous. (2) Applied to persons using doubtful expressions. It is applied to expressions, or those that use them, not to a dubious, or suspended state of mind.

ambi′tude. Compass; circuit; circumference.

to a′mble. (2) To move easily, without hard shocks, or shaking.

(3) In a ludicrous sense, to move with submission, and by direction; as, a horse that *ambles,* uses a gait not natural.

> A laughing, toying, wheedling, whimpering she,
> Shall make him *amble* on a gossip's message,
> And take the distaff with a hand as patient,
> As ere did Hercules. Rowe's *Jane Shore.*

(4) To walk daintily and affectedly.

a′mbry. (A word corrupted from *almonry.*) (1) The place where the almoner lives, or where alms are distributed.

(2) The place where plate, and utensils for housekeeping, are kept; also a cupboard for keeping cold victuals: a word still used in the northern counties, and in Scotland.

ambs ace. A double ace; so called when two dice turn up the ace.

> I had rather be in this choice, than throw *ambs ace* for my life. Shakespeare's *All's well that ends well.*

a′mel. The matter with which the variegated works are overlaid, which we call *enamelled.*

a′miable. (2) Pretending love; shewing love.

ami′ss. (7) Impaired in health; as, I was somewhat *amiss* yesterday, but am well to day.

ami′ssion. Loss.

ammuni′tion bread. Bread for the supply of the armies or garrisons.

amni′colist. Inhabiting near a river.

a′morist. An inamorato; a galant; a man professing love.

amo′rt. In the state of the dead; dejected; depressed; spiritless.

> How fares my Kate? what, sweeting, all *amort?*
> Shakespeare's *Taming of the Shrew.*

amortiza′tion, amo′rtizement. The right or act of transferring lands to mortmain; that is, to some community, that never is to cease.

to amo′rtize. To alien lands or tenements to any corporation, guild or fraternity, and their successors; which cannot be done without licence of the king, and the lord of the manour. Blount.

a′mper. A tumour, with inflammation; bile: a word said, by Skinner, to be much in use in Essex; but, perhaps, not found in books.

amphibolo′gical. Doubtful.

amphi′bolous. Tossed from one to another; striking each way.

> Never was there such an *amphibolous* quarrel, both parties declaring themselves for the king, and making use of his name in all their remonstrances, to justify their actions. Howell.

amphisbae′na. A serpent supposed to have two heads.

> That the *amphisbaena,* that is, a smaller kind of serpent, which moveth forward and backward, hath two heads, or one at either extreme, was affirmed by Nicander, and others. Browne's *Vulgar Errours,* b. iii.

a′mplifier. One that enlarges any thing; one that exaggerates; one that represents any thing with a large display of the best circumstances; it being usually taken in a good sense.

to a′mplify. (2) To form large or pompous representations.

a'mulet. An appended remedy, or preservative: a thing hung about the neck, or any other part of the body, for preventing or curing of some particular diseases.

amurco'sity. The quality of lees or mother of any thing.

amu'ser. He that amuses, as with false promises. The French word is always taken in an ill sense.

an. (6) Sometimes it is a contraction of *as if*.

> My next pretty correspondent, like Shakespeare's lion in Pyramus and Thisbe, roars *an'* it were any nightingale. Addison, *Guardian*, No. 121.

a'na. Books so called from the last syllables of their titles; as, *Scaligerana, Thuaniana;* they are loose thoughts, or casual hints, dropped by eminent men, and collected by their friends.

anaca'mptick. Reflecting, or reflected: an *anacamptick* sound, an echo; an *anacamptick* hill, a hill that produces an echo.

anacatha'rtick. Any medicine that works upwards. Quincy.

ana'chorete, ana'chorite. (Sometimes viciously written *anchorite*.) A monk, who, with the leave of his superiour, leaves the convent for a more austere and solitary life.

anacla'ticks. The doctrine of refracted light; dioptricks. It has no singular.

anagoge'tical. That which contributes or relates to spiritual elevation, or religious raptures; mysterious; elevated above humanity.

anaplero'tick. That which fills up any vacuity; used of applications which promote flesh.

anastoma'tick. That which has the quality of opening the vessels, or of removing obstructions.

anati'ferous. Producing ducks.

> If there be *anatiferous* trees, whose corruption breaks forth into barnacles; yet, if they corrupt, they degenerate

---

amulet. When Johnson was thirty months old, he was taken to London to be "touched" by Queen Anne for scrofula, which the Stuart monarchs supposedly were able to cure. He was presented with an amulet, which he wore, but neither the Queen nor the amulet cured him.

anachorete. By *viciously* Johnson means only *corruptly*.

into maggots, which produce not them again.
Browne's *Vulgar Errours.*

ana'tocism. The accumulation of interest upon interest; the addition of the interest due for money lent, to the original sum. A species of usury generally forbidden.

ana'tomy. (3) The act of dividing any thing, whether corporeal or intellectual.

> When a moneyed man hath divided his chests, he seemeth to himself richer than he was; therefore, a way to amplify any thing, is to break it, and to make *anatomy* of it in several parts. Bacon's *Essays.*

(4) The body stripped of its integuments; a skeleton.

(5) By way of irony or ridicule, a thin meagre person.

to a'nchor. (2) To stop at; to rest on.

> My tongue should to my ears not name my boys,
> 'Till that my nails were *anchor'd* in thine eyes.
> Shakespeare, *Richard III.*

a'nchor. Shakespeare seems to have used this word for *anchoret,* or an abstemious recluse person.

> To desperation turn my trust and hope!
> An *anchor's* cheer in prison be my scope! Shakespeare, *Hamlet.*

a'nchor-hold. The hold or fastness of the anchor; and, figuratively, security.

a'nchorage. (1) The hold of the anchor.

ancho'vy. A little sea-fish, much used by way of sauce, or seasoning. Scaliger describes the *anchovy* as of the herring kind, about the length of a finger, having a pointed snout, a wide mouth, no teeth, but gums as rough as a saw. Others make it a sort of sardine, or pilchard; but others, with better reason, hold it a peculiar species, very different from either. It is caught in the months of May, June, and July, on the coasts of Catalonia, Provence, &c. when it constantly repairs up the Straits of Gibraltar into the Mediterranean. The fishing is chiefly in the night time; when a light

---

anatiferous. The quotation alludes to the old belief that barnacles developed on trees and dropped into water to form ducks.

being put on the stern of their little fishing vessels, the *anchovies* flock round, and are caught in nets. When the fishery is over, they cut off the heads, take out the galls and guts, then lay them in barrels, and salt them. Savary.

a'ncient. The bearer of a flag, as was *Ancient Pistol;* whence in present use, ensign.

a'ncientry. The honour of ancient lineage; the dignity of birth.

There is nothing in the between, but getting wenches with child, wronging the *ancientry,* stealing, fighting. Shakespeare, *Winter's Tale.*

and. (1) The particle by which sentences or terms are joined, which it is not easy to explain by any synonimous word.

Sure his honesty
Got him small gains, but shameless flattery
And filthy beverage, *and* unseemly thift,
And borrow base, *and* some good lady's gift. Spenser.

(2) *And* sometimes signifies *though,* and seems a contraction of *and if.*

It is the nature of extreme self-lovers, as they will set an house on fire, *and* it were but to roast their eggs. Bacon.

andro'gynal. Having two sexes; hermaphroditical.

a'necdote. Something yet unpublished; secret history.

ane'nt. A word used in the Scotch dialect.

(1) Concerning; about; as, *he said nothing* anent *this particular.*

(2) Over against; opposite to; as, *he lives* anent *the market-house.*

anfra'ctuose, anfra'ctuous. Winding; mazy; full of turnings and winding passages.

a'ngel. (5) A piece of money anciently coined and impressed with an angel, in memory of an observation of Pope Gregory, that the pagan *Angli,* or English, were so beautiful, that, if they were christians, they would be *Angeli,* or *angels.* The coin was rated at ten shillings.

Cousin, away for England; haste before,
And, ere our coming, see thou shake the bags

Of hoarding abbots; their imprison'd *angels*
Set thou at liberty. Shakespeare's *King John*.

a'ngel shot. Chain shot, being a cannon bullet cut in two, and the halves being joined together by a chain.

a'ngelot. A musical instrument, somewhat resembling a lute.

a'ngerly. In an angry manner; like one offended.

Why, how now, Hecat, you look *angerly*. Shakespeare, *Macbeth*.

a'ngle-rod. The stick to which the line and hook are hung.

He makes a May-fly to a miracle, and furnishes the whole country with *angle-rods*. Addison, *Spectator*, No. 108.

anhela'tion. The act of panting; the state of being out of breath.

a'niented. Frustrated; brought to nothing.

ani'ghts. In the night time.

to animadve'rt. (2) To inflict punishments.

a'nimal. (1) A living creature corporeal, distinct, on the one side, from pure spirit, on the other, from mere matter.

to a'nimate. (3) To encourage; to incite.

The more to *animate* the people, he stood on high, from whence he might be best heard, and cried unto them with a loud voice. Knolles's *History of the Turks*.

a'nise. A species of apium or parsley, with large sweet scented seeds. This plant is not worth propagating in England for use, because the seeds can be had much better and cheaper from Italy. Miller.

a'nnats. (1) First fruits; because the rate of first fruits paid of spiritual livings, is after one year's profit. Cowell.

to anne'al. (1) To heat glass, that the colours laid on it may pierce through.

to anni'hilate. (3) To annul; to destroy the agency of any thing.

There is no reason, that any one commonwealth should *annihilate* that whereupon the whole world has agreed. Hooker.

anno'isance. It hath a double signification, being as well for any hurt done either to a publick place, as highway, bridge, or common river, or to a private, by laying any thing that may breed infection, by encroaching, or such like means; as also, for the writ that is brought upon this transgression. Blount.

a'nnolis. An American animal, like a lizard.

to annu'l. (2) To reduce to nothing; to obliterate.

ano'maly. Irregularity; deviation from the common rule.

ano'n. (2) Sometimes; now and then; at other times. In this sense is used *ever and anon*.

ano'nymous. Wanting a name.

> They would forthwith publish slanders unpunished, the authors being *anonymous,* the immediate publishers thereof sculking. *Notes on the Dunciad.*

anore'xy. Inappetency, or loathing of food. Quincy.

ano'thergaines. (See *anotherguess.*) Of another kind. This word I have found only in Sidney.

> If my father had not plaid the hasty fool, I might have had *anothergaines* husband than Dametas. Sidney.

ano'therguess. (This word, which though rarely used in writing, is somewhat frequent in colloquial language, I conceive to be corrupted from *another guise;* that is, of a different *guise*, or manner, or form.) Of a different kind.

> Oh Hocus! where art thou? It used to go in *anotherguess* manner in thy time. Arbuthnot's *History of John Bull.*

to a'nswer. (7) To be equivalent to; to stand for something else.

> A feast is made for laughter, and wine maketh merry: but money *answereth* all things. *Ecclesiastes*, x. 19.

(10) To stand as opposite or correlative to something else.

(11) To bear proportion to.

(14) To succeed, to produce the wished event.

> Jason followed her counsel, whereto, when the event had *answered,* he again demanded the fleece.
> Raleigh's *History of the World.*

(16) To be over-against any thing.

> Fire *answers* fire, and, by their paly beams,
> Each battle sees the other's umber'd face. Shakespeare, *Henry V.*

---

anomaly. "Deviation from the common rule; irregularity." *Webster's New Collegiate Dictionary*, 1961.

a'nswer-jobber. He that makes a trade of writing answers.

> What disgusts me from having any thing to do with *answer-jobbers*, is, that they have no conscience. Swift.

ant. An emmet; a pismire. A small insect that lives in great numbers together in hillocks.

ant-bear. An animal that feeds on ants.

an't. A contraction for *and it*, or rather *and if it*; as, *an't please you*; that is, *and if it please you.*

anta'lgick. That which softens pain; anodyne.

antaphrodi'tick. That which is efficacious against the venereal disease.

a'ntelope. A goat with curled or wreathed horns.

anteme'tick. That which has the power of calming the stomach; of preventing or stopping vomiting.

a'ntepast. A foretaste; something taken before the proper time.

> Were we to expect our bliss only in the satiating our appetites, it might be reasonable, by frequent *antepasts*, to excite our gust for that profuse perpetual meal. *Decay of Piety.*

antesto'mach. A cavity which leads into the stomach.

> In birds there is no mastication or comminution of the meat in the mouth; but it is immediately swallowed into a kind of *antestomach*, which I have observed in piscivorous birds. Ray.

antho'logy. (1) A collection of flowers.

anthropo'logy. The doctrine of anatomy; the doctrine of the form and structure of the body of man.

anthropo'phagi. Man-eaters; cannibals; those that live upon human flesh.

anthropophagi'nian. A ludicrous word, formed by Shakespeare from *anthropophagi*, for the sake of a formidable sound.

> Go, knock, and call; he'll speak like an *anthropophaginian* unto thee: knock, I say. Shakespeare, *Merry Wives of Windsor.*

anticipa'tion. (3) Opinion implanted before the reasons of that opinion can be known.

> What nation is there, that, without any teaching, have

not a kind of *anticipation*, or preconceived notion of a
Deity? Derham's *Physico-Theology*.

a′ntick. Odd; ridiculously wild; buffoon in gesticulation.

The prize was to be conferred on the whistler, that could
go through his tune without laughing, though provoked
by the *antick* postures of a merry Andrew, who was to
play tricks. Addison, *Spectator,* No. 179.

a′ntick. (1) He that plays anticks; he that uses odd gesticulation: a buffoon.

(2) Odd appearance.

For ev'n at first reflection she espies

Such toys, such *anticks,* and such vanities,

As she retires and shrinks for shame and fear.

Sir J. Davies.

anticli′max. A sentence in which the last part is lower than the
first.

antidysente′rick. Good against the bloody flux.

anti′logy. A contradiction between any words and passages in
an authour.

a′ntimony. (The stibium of the ancients, by the Greeks called
στίμμι. The reason of its modern denomination is referred to
Basil Valentine, a German monk; who, as the tradition relates, having thrown some of it to the hogs, observed, that,
after it had purged them heartily, they immediately fat-
tened; and therefore, he imagined, his fellow monks would
be the better for a like dose. The experiment, however, succeeded so ill, that they all died of it; and the medicine was
thenceforward called *antimoine; antimonk.*)

Antimony is a mineral substance, of a metalline nature,
having all the seeming characters of a real metal, except
malleability; and may be called a semimetal, being a fossile
glebe of some undetermined metal, combined with a
sulphurous and stony substance.

a′ntinomy. A contradiction between two laws, or two articles
of the same law.

antiperi′stasis. The opposition of a contrary quality, by which
the quality it opposes, becomes heightened or intended; or

the action, by which a body attacked by another, collects itself, and becomes stronger by such opposition: or an intention of the activity of one quality caused by the opposition of another. Thus quicklime is set on fire by the affusion of cold water; so water becomes warmer in winter than in summer; and thunder and lightening are excited in the middle region of the air, which is continually cold, and all by *antiperistasis*. This is an exploded principle in the Peripatetick philosophy.

antipestile′ntial. Efficacious against the infection of the plague.

anti′que. (4) Odd; wild; antick.

> And sooner may a gulling weather-spy
> By drawing forth heav'n's scheme, tell certainly
> What fashion'd hats or ruffs, or suits next year,
> Our giddy-headed *antique* youth will wear. Donne.

anti′quity. (4) Old age: a ludicrous sense.

> Is not your voice broken? your wind short? your chin double? your wit single? and every part about you blasted with *antiquity*? and will you yet call yourself young? Shakespeare's *Henry IV*.

a′ntler. Properly the first branches of a stag's horns; but, popularly and generally, any of his branches.

a′ntre. A cavern; a cave; a den.

> With all my travels history:
> Wherein of *antres* vast, and desarts idle,
> It was my hent to speak. Shakespeare, *Othello*.

ape. (1) A kind of monkey remarkable for imitating what he sees.

ape′ak, or ape′ek. In a posture to pierce the ground.

ape′ritive. That which has the quality of opening the excrementious passages of the body.

a′phony. A loss of speech. Quincy.

aphrodisi′acal, aphrodisi′ack. Relating to the venereal disease.

api′ces of a flower. Little knobs that grow on the tops of the stamina, in the middle of a flower. They are commonly of a dark purplish colour. By the microscope they have

---

antre. *Hent* is the reading of the quarto of *Othello*, but Johnson forgot to record the word when he came to "h," where he gives only *hint*.

been discovered to be a sort of *capsulae seminales,* or seed vessels, containing in them small globular, and often oval particles, of various colours, and exquisitely formed. Quincy.

a'pish. (2) Foppish; affected.

(3) Silly; trifling; insignificant.

apo'calypse. Revelation; discovery: a word used only of the sacred writings.

apo'crypha. Books whose authours are not known. It is used for the books appended to the sacred writings, which, being of doubtful authours, are less regarded.

apo'cryphal. (3) It is sometimes used for an account of uncertain credit.

a'pologue. Fable; story contrived to teach some moral truth.

> An *apologue* of Aesop is beyond a syllogism, and proverbs more powerful than demonstration. Browne's *Vulgar Errours.*

a'pophthegm. A remarkable saying; a valuable maxim uttered on some sudden occasion.

a'poplexy. A sudden deprivation of all internal and external sensation, and of all motion, unless of the heart and thorax. The cause is generally a repletion, and indicates evacuation, joined with stimuli. Quincy.

apo'state. One that has forsaken his profession; generally applied to one that has left his religion.

appa'lement. Depression; discouragement; impression of fear.

appara'tus. Things provided as means to any certain end, as the tools of a trade; the furniture of a house; ammunition for war; equipage; show.

appari'tion. (5) Astronomically, the visibility of some luminary, opposed to *occultation.*

> A month of *apparition* is the space wherein the moon appeareth, deducting three days wherein it commonly disappeareth; and this containeth but twenty-six days and twelve hours. Browne's *Vulgar Errours,* b. iv, c. 12.

to appa'y. To satisfy; to content: whence *well appayed, is pleased; ill appayed, is uneasy.* It is now obsolete.

> Ay, Willy, when the heart is ill assay'd,

How can bagpipe or joints be well *appaid*. Spenser's
Pastorals.

to appe′al. (4) To charge with a crime; to accuse.

to appe′ar. (1) To be in sight; to be visible; sometimes with
the particle *in*.

And half her knee, and half her breast *appear*,
By art, like negligence, disclos'd and bare. Prior.

appe′llant. (1) A challenger; one that summons another to
answer either in the lists or in a court of justice.

These shifts refuted, answer thy *appellant*,
Though by his blindness maim'd for high attempts,
Who now defies thee thrice to single fight. Milton's
Samson Agonistes.

appe′llate. The person appealed against.

appe′ndage. Something added to another thing, without being
necessary to its essence, as a portico to the house.

a′ppetence, a′ppetency. Carnal desire; sensual desire.

Bred only and completed to the taste
Of lustful *appetence;* to sing, to dance,
To dress, to troule the tongue, and roll the eye. Milton's
Paradise Lost, b. xi, l. 619.

applica′tion. (7) The condition of being used as means to an
end.

This principle acts with the greatest force in the worst
application; and the familiarity of wicked men more
successfully debauches, than that of good men reforms.
Rogers.

to appl′y. (9) To ply; to busy; to keep at work: an antiquated
sense.

Far away they spy'd
A varlet running towards hastily,
Whose flying feet so fast their way *apply'd*,
That round about a cloud of dust did fly.
Fairy Queen, b. ii.

appo′intment. (4) Equipment; furniture.

They have put forth the haven: further on,
Where their *appointment* we may best discover,

And look on their endeavour. Shakespeare, *Antony and Cleopatra.*

(5) An allowance paid to any man, commonly used of allowances to publick officers.

apprehe'nsive. (1) Quick to understand.

And gives encouragement to those who teach such *apprehensive* scholars. Holder's *Elements of Speech.*

appre'ntice. One that is bound by covenant, to serve another man of trade, for a certain term of years, upon condition, that the artificer, or tradesman, shall, in the mean time, endeavour to instruct him in his art or mystery. Cowell.

appro'of. Approbation; commendation: a word rightly derived, but old.

O most perilous mouths,
That bear in them one and the self-same tongue
Either of condemnation or *approof!*
Shakespeare, *Measure for Measure.*

appropria'tion. (2) The claim of any thing as peculiar.

He doth nothing but talk of his horse, and make a great *appropriation* to his good parts, that he can shoe him himself. Shakespeare, *Merchant of Venice.*

appro'val. Approbation: a word not much used.

There is a censor of justice and manners, without whose *approval* no capital sentences are to be executed. Temple

to appro've. (3) To prove; to show; to justify.

In religion,
What damned errour, but some sober brow
Will bless it, and *approve* it with a text. Shakespeare, *Merchant of Venice.*

(4) To experience.

Oh, 'tis the curse in love, and still *approv'd,*
When women cannot love, where they're belov'd.
Shakespeare, *Two Gentlemen of Verona.*

to a'pricate. To bask in the sun.

to apt. (2) To fit; to qualify.

The king is melancholy,
Apted for any ill impressions. Denham's *Sophy.*

a'ptly. (3) Readily; acutely; as, he learned his business very *aptly.*

aqua fortis. A corrosive liquor made by distilling purified nitre with calcined vitriol, or rectified oil of vitriol in a strong heat: the liquor, which rises in fumes red as blood, being collected, is the spirit of nitre or *aqua fortis;* which serves as a menstruum for dissolving of silver, and all other metals, except gold. But if sea salt, or sal ammoniack, be added to *aqua fortis,* it commences *aqua regia,* and will then dissolve no metal but gold. *Aqua fortis* is commonly held to have been invented about the year 1300; though others will have it to have been known in the time of Moses. It is serviceable to refiners, in separating silver from gold and copper; to the workers in mosaick, for staining and colouring their woods; to dyers, in their colours, particularly scarlet; and to other artists, for colouring bone and ivory. With *aqua fortis* bookbinders marble the covers of books, and diamond cutters separate diamonds from metalline powders. It is also used in etching copper or brass plates. Chambers.

aqua mirabilis. The wonderful water, is prepared of cloves, galangals, cubebs, mace, cardomums, nutmegs, ginger, and spirit of wine, digested twenty four hours, then distilled. It is a good and agreeable cordial.

aqua-vitae. It is commonly understood of what is otherwise called brandy, or spirit of wine, either simple or prepared with aromaticks. But some appropriate the term brandy to what is procured from wine, or the grape; *aqua-vitae,* to that drawn after the same manner from malt. Chambers.

> I will rather trust a Fleming with my butter, parson Hugh the Welchman with my cheese, an Irishman with my *aqua vitae* bottle, or a thief to walk with my ambling gelding, than my wife with herself.
> Shakespeare, *Merry Wives of Windsor.*

a'rbitrable. Arbitrary; depending upon the will.

a'rbitrary. (1) Despotick; absolute; bound by no law; following the will without restraint. It is applied both to persons and things.

> In vain the Tyrian queen resigns her life
> For the chaste glory of a virtuous wife,
> If lying bards may false amours rehearse,
> And blast her name with *arbitrary* verse. Walsh.

arbitra′tor. (3) He that has the power of acting by his own choice without limit or controul.

arbi′trement. (1) Decision; determination.

> Aid was granted, and the quarrel brought to the *arbitrement* of the sword. Hayward.

(2) Compromise.

> Lukewarm persons think they may accommodate points of religion by middle ways, and witty reconcilements; as if they would make an *arbitrement* between God and man. Bacon's *Essays*.

arbo′reous. (2) A term in botany, to distinguish such funguses or mosses as grow upon trees, from those that grow on the ground. Quincy.

a′rbuscle. Any little shrub.

a′rbute. *Arbute,* or strawberry tree, grows common in Ireland. It is difficult to be raised from the seeds, but may be propagated by layers. It grows to a goodly tree, endures our climate, unless the weather be very severe, and makes beautiful hedges. Mortimer's *Art of Husbandry*.

arc. (2) An arch.

> Load some vain church with old theatrick state,
> Turn *arcs* of triumph to a garden gate;
> Reverse your ornaments, and hang them all
> On some patch'd dog-hole ek'd with ends of wall. Pope.

archaio′logy. A discourse on antiquity.

a′rchives. The places where records or ancient writings are kept. It is perhaps sometimes used for the writings themselves.

a′rduous. (1) Lofty; hard to climb.

> High on Parnassus' top her sons she show'd,
> And pointed out those *arduous* paths they trod. Pope.

to are′ad, or are′ed. To advise; to direct.

> But mark what I *aread* thee now: avant,
> Fly thither whence thou fled'st! If from this hour

[63]

Within these hallow'd limits thou appear,
Back to th' infernal pit I drag thee chain'd. *Paradise
Lost.*

arefa'ction. The state of growing dry; the act of drying.

arena'tion. Is used by some physicians for a sort of dry bath,
when the patient sits with his feet upon hot sand.

a'rgosy. (Derived by Pope from *Argo,* the name of Jason's
ship.) A large vessel for merchandise; a carrack.

to a'rgue. (3) To prove, as an argument.

So many laws *argue* so many sins
Among them: how can God with such reside? *Paradise
Lost.*

(4) To charge with, as a crime; with *of.*

a'rgute. (1) Subtile; witty; sharp.

(2) Shrill.

arieta'tion. (1) The act of butting like a ram.

ariola'tion, or hariola'tion. Soothsaying; vaticination.

aristo'cracy. That form of government which places the supreme power in the nobles, without a king, and exclusively
of the people.

The *aristocracy* of Venice hath admitted so many abuses
through the degeneracy of the nobles, that the period
of its duration seems to approach. Swift.

ari'thmancy. A foretelling future events by numbers.

to arm. (3) To furnish; to fit up; as, to *arm* a loadstone, is to
case it with iron.

arma'da. An armament for sea; a fleet of war. It is often erroneously spelt *armado.*

armadi'llo. A four-footed animal of Brasil, as big as a cat,
with a snout like a hog, a tail like a lizard, and feet like
a hedge-hog. He is armed all over with hard scales like
armour, whence he takes his name, and retires under them
like the tortoise. He lives in holes, or in the water, being
of the amphibious kind. His scales are of a bony or car-
tilaginous substance; but they are easily pierced. This animal hides himself a third part of the year under ground.
He feeds upon roots, sugar-canes, fruits, and poultry. When
he is caught, he draws up his feet and head to his belly,
and rolls himself up in a ball, which the strongest hand

cannot open; and he must be brought near the fire before
he will shew his nose. His flesh is white, fat, tender, and
more delicate than that of a sucking pig. Trevoux.

a′rmature. Armour; something to defend the body from hurt.

a′rmgaunt. Slender as the arm.

> So he nodded,
> And soberly did mount an *armgaunt* steed.
> Shakespeare, *Antony and Cleopatra.*

arm-hole. The cavity under the shoulder.

> Tickling is most in the soles of the feet, and under the
> *arm-holes*, and on the sides. The cause is the thinness
> of the skin in those parts, joined with the rareness of
> being touched there. Bacon's *Natural History*, No. 766.

armi′potent. Powerful in arms; mighty in war.

> Beneath the low'ring brow, and on a bent,
> The temple stood of Mars *armipotent*. Dryden's *Fables.*

a′rmistice. A short truce; a cessation of arms for a short time.

a′rmpit. The hollow place under the shoulder.

> Others hold their plate under the left *arm-pit,* the best
> situation for keeping it warm. Swift's *Directions to the
> Footman.*

a′rmy. (1) A collection of armed men, obliged to obey one
man. Locke.

> The meanest soldier, that has fought often in an *army,*
> has a truer knowledge of war, than he that has writ
> whole volumes, but never was in any battle. South.

aroma′tical. Spicy; fragrant; high scented.

> All things that are hot and *aromatical* do preserve liq-
> uors or powders. Bacon's *Natural History*, No. 346.

aro′ynt. (A word of uncertain etymology, but very ancient
use.) Be gone; away: a word of expulsion, or avoiding.

> Saint Withold footed thrice the wold,
> He met the night-mare, and her name told,
> Bid her alight, and her troth plight,
> And *aroynt* thee, witch, *aroynt* thee right. Shakespeare,
> *King Lear.*

a′rquebuse. A hand gun. It seems to have anciently meant
much the same as our carabine, or fusee.

a′rrach, o′rrach, or o′rrage. One of the quickest plants both in coming up and running to seed. Its leaves are very good in pottage. It should be used as soon as it peeps out, because it decays quickly. It thrives very well in all sorts of ground. Mortimer's *Art of Husbandry.*

arra'ck, or ara'ck. A spirituous liquor imported from the East Indies, used by way of dram and in punch. The word *arack* is an Indian name for strong waters of all kinds; for they call our spirits and brandy English *arack.* But what we understand by the name *arack,* is really no other than a spirit procured by distillation from a vegetable juice called toddy, which flows by incision out of the cocoa-nut tree. There are divers kinds of it; single, double, and treble distilled. The double distilled is commonly sent abroad, and is preferred to all other *aracks* of India. Chambers.

a'rrant. (A word of uncertain etymology, but probably from *errant,* which being at first applied to its proper signification to vagabonds, as an *errant* or *arrant rogue,* that is, a *rambling rogue,* lost, in time, its original signification, and being by its use understood to imply something bad, was applied at large to any thing that was mentioned with hatred or contempt.) Bad in a high degree.

> And let him every deity adore,
> If his new bride prove not an *arrant* whore. Dryden,
> *Juvenal.*

a'rrantly. Corruptly; shamefully.

> Funeral tears are as *arrantly* hired out as mourning clokes. L'Estrange.

to arre'st. (3) To seize; to lay hands on.

> Age itself, which, of all things in the world, will not be baffled or denied, shall begin to *arrest,* seize, and remind us of our mortality. South.

arri'vance. Company coming.

to arri've. (1) To come to any place by water.

> At length *arriving* on the banks of Nile,
> Wearied with length of ways, and worn with toil,
> She laid her down. Dryden.

(6) To happen; with *to* before the person. This sense seems not proper.

[66]

> Happy! *to* whom this glorious death *arrives*,
> More to be valued than a thousand lives. Waller.

to arro'de. To gnaw or nibble.

a'rrogance, a'rrogancy. The act or quality of taking much upon one's self; that species of pride which consists in exorbitant claims.

> Stanley, notwithstanding she's your wife,
> And loves not me; be you, good lord, assur'd,
> I hate not you for her proud *arrogance*. Shakespeare, *Richard III*.

a'rrow. The pointed weapon which is shot from a bow. Darts are thrown by the hand, but in poetry they are confounded.

> Here were boys so desperately resolved, as to pull *arrows* out of their flesh, and deliver them to be shot again by the archers on their side. Sir J. Hayward.

arse. The buttocks, or hind part of an animal.

to hang an arse. A vulgar phrase, signifying to be tardy, sluggish, or dilatory.

> For Hudibras wore but one spur,
> As wisely knowing, could he stir
> To active trot one side of 's horse,
> The other would not *hang an arse. Hudibras*, canto i.

arse foot. A kind of water fowl, called also a *didapper*.

to arti'culate. (2) To draw up in articles.

(3) To make terms. These two latter significations are unusual.

arti'ficer. (2) A forger; a contriver.

artisa'n. (2) Manufacturer; low tradesman.

as. (4) In the state of another.

> Madam, were I *as* you, I'd take her counsel;
> I'd speak my own distress. A. Philips, *Distrest Mother*.

a'safoetida, a'ssafoetida. A gum or resin brought from the East Indies, of a sharp taste, and a strong offensive smell; which is said to distil, during the heat of summer, from a little shrub, frequent in Media, Persia, Assyria, and Arabia. It is at first white, bordering on yellow, then on red, and, lastly, violet; and melts under the fingers like wax. It is of known efficacy in some uterine disorders; but the rankness of its smell occasions it to be seldom used but by farriers; yet, in the East Indies, it makes an ingredient in their ragouts. Chambers.

asbe′stos. A sort of native fossile stone, which may be split into threads and filaments, from one inch to ten inches in length, very fine, brittle, yet somewhat tractable, silky, and of a greyish colour, not unlike talc of Venice. It is almost insipid to the taste, indissoluble in water, and endued with the wonderful property of remaining unconsumed in the fire, which only whitens it. But, notwithstanding the common opinion, in two trials before the Royal Society, a piece of cloth made of this stone was found to lose a dram of its weight each time. Paper as well as cloth has been made of this stone; and Pliny says he had seen napkins of it, which, being taken foul from the table, were thrown into the fire, and better scowered than if they had been washed in water. This stone is found in many places of Asia and Europe; particularly in the island of Anglesey in Wales, and in Aberdeenshire in Scotland. Chambers.

asce′nsion. (2) The thing rising, or mounting.

> Men err in the theory of inebriation, conceiving the brain doth only suffer from vaporous *ascensions* from the stomach. Browne's *Vulgar Errours.*

to ascerta′in. (2) To make confident; to take away doubt; often with *of.*

> This makes us act with a repose of mind and wonderful tranquillity, because it *ascertains* us *of* the goodness of our work. Dryden's *Dufresnoy.*

asce′tick. He that retires to devotion and mortification; a hermit.

> He that preaches to man, should understand what is in man; and that skill can scarce be attained by an *ascetick* in his solitudes. Atterbury's *Sermons.*

asciti′tious. Supplemental; additional; not inherent; not original.

> Homer has been reckoned an *ascititious* name, from some accident of his life. Pope's *Essay on Homer.*

a′sinine. Belonging to an ass.

You shall have more ado to drive our dullest youth,
our stocks and stubs, from such nurture, than we have
now to hale our choicest and hopefullest wits to that
asinine feast of sow thistles and brambles. Milton, *On
Education.*

to ask. (5) To require, as physically necessary.

a′sker. A water newt.

aske′w. Aside; with contempt; contemptuously; disdainfully.

> For when ye mildly look with lovely hue,
>> Then is my soul with life and love inspir'd:
> But when ye lowre, or look on me *askew,*
>> Then do I die. Spenser, *Sonnet* vii.

asp, a′spick. A kind of serpent, whose poison is so dangerous
and quick in its operation, that it kills without a possibility
of applying any remedy. It is said to be very small, and
peculiar to Egypt and Lybia. Those that are bitten by it,
die within three hours; and the manner of their dying being by sleep and lethargy, without any pain, Cleopatra
chose it, as the easiest way of dispatching herself. Calmet.

to aspe′ct. To behold.

> Happy in their mistake, those people whom
> The northern pole *aspects;* whom fear of death
> (The greatest of all human fears) ne'er moves. Temple.

asper. Rough; rugged. This word I have found only in the following passage.

> All base notes, or very treble notes, give an *asper* sound;
> for that the base striketh more air than it can well
> strike equally. Bacon.

to a′sperate. To roughen; to make rough or uneven.

aspe′rity. (3) Roughness, or ruggedness of temper; morose-
ness; sourness; crabbedness.

> Avoid all unseemliness and *asperity* of carriage; do
> nothing that may argue a peevish or froward spirit.
> Rogers.

to aspe′rse. To bespatter with censure or calumny.

> Curb that impetuous tongue, nor rashly vain,
> And singly mad, *asperse* the sov'reign reign. Pope's
> *Iliad.*

aspha'ltos. A solid, brittle, black, bituminous, inflammable substance, resembling pitch, and chiefly found swimming on
the surface of the *Lacus Asphaltites,* or Dead sea, where
anciently stood the cities of Sodom and Gomorrah. It is
cast up from time to time, in the nature of liquid pitch,
from the earth at the bottom of this sea; and, being thrown
upon the water, swims like other fat bodies, and condenses
gradually by the heat of the sun, and the salt that is in it.
It burns with great vehemence. The Arabs use it for
pitching their ships; and much of it was employed in the
embalming of the ancients.

aspha'ltum. A bituminous stone found near the ancient Babylon, and lately in the province of Neufchâtel; which,
mixed with other matters, makes an excellent cement, in-
corruptible by air, and impenetrable by water; supposed
to be the mortar so much celebrated among the ancients,
with which the walls of Babylon were laid. Chambers.

ass. (1) An animal of burden, remarkable for sluggishness,
patience, hardiness, coarseness of food, and long life.

>You have among you many a purchas'd slave,
>Which, like your *asses,* and your dogs and mules,
>You use in abject and in slavish part,
>Because you bought them. Shakespeare, *Merchant of
>Venice.*

(2) A stupid, heavy, dull fellow; a dolt.

>That such a crafty mother
>Should yield the world to this ass!—a woman that
>Bears all down with her brain; and her son
>Cannot take two from twenty for his heart,
>And leave eighteen. Shakespeare, *Cymbeline.*

assapa'nick. A little animal of Virginia, which is said to fly
by stretching out its shoulders and its skin, and is called
in English the flying squirrel. Trevoux.

assa'rt. An offence committed in the forest, by plucking up
those woods by the roots, that are thickets or coverts of
the forest, and by making them as plain as arable land.
Cowell.

[70]

to assa'ssinate. (2) To way-lay; to take by treachery. This meaning is perhaps peculiar to Milton.

> Such usage as your honourable lords
> Afford me, *assassinated* and betray'd,
> Who durst not, with your whole united pow'rs,
> In fight withstand one single and unarm'd. *Samson Agonistes.*

assa'tion. Roasting.

> The egg expiring less in the elixation or boiling; whereas, in the *assation* or roasting, it will sometimes abate a drachm. Browne's *Vulgar Errours,* b. iii.

assa'y. (4) Attack; trouble.

> She heard with patience all unto the end,
> And strove to master sorrowful *assay. Fairy Queen,* b. i.

to assa'y. (2) To apply to, as the touchstone in *assaying* metals.

> Whom thus afflicted, when sad Eve beheld,
> Desolate where she sat, approaching nigh,
> Soft words to his fierce passion she *assay'd. Paradise Lost,* b. x.

asse'ssor. (2) He that sits by another as next in dignity.

a'sshead. One slow of apprehension; a blockhead.

> Will you help an *asshead,* and a coxcomb, and a knave, a thin-faced knave, a gull. Shakespeare, *Hamlet.*

assie'nto. (In Spanish a contract or bargain.) A contract or convention between the king of Spain and other powers, for furnishing the Spanish dominions in America with negro slaves. This contract was transferred from the French to the English South-Sea company, by the treaty of 1713, for thirty years; who were likewise permitted to send a register ship, of 500 tuns, yearly to the Spanish settlements, with European goods. Chambers.

to assi'milate. (1) To convert to the same nature with another thing.

> Birds *assimilate* less, and excern more, than beasts; for their excrements are ever liquid, and their flesh generally more dry. Bacon's *Natural History.*

(2) To bring to a likeness, or resemblance.

assi′stant. (2) Sometimes it is only a softer word for an attendant.

> The pale *assistants* on each other star'd,
> With gaping mouths for issuing words prepar'd. Dryden.

assi′ze. (7) Measure; rate: for which we now use *size*.

> On high hill's top I saw a stately frame,
> An hundred cubits high by just *assize*,
> With hundred pillars. Spenser, *Vision of Bellay*.

a′ssonant. Sounding in a manner resembling another sound.

to asso′rt. To range in classes, as one thing suits with another.

to asso′t. To infatuate; to besot: a word out of use.

> But whence they sprung, or how they were begot,
> Uneath is to assure, uneath to weene
> That monstrous errour which doth some *assot*.
> *Fairy Queen.*

to assu′bjugate. To submit to.

assu′etude. Accustomance; custom.

> We see that *assuetude* of things hurtful, doth make
> them lose the force to hurt. Bacon's *Natural History*,
> No. 67.

assu′ming. Arrogant; haughty.

to assu′re. (5) To affiance; to betroth.

assu′red. (3) Immodest; viciously confident.

a′sterisk. A mark in printing or writing, in form of a little
star; as °.

a′sterism. (2) An asterisk, or mark. This is a very improper
use.

a′sthma. A frequent, difficult, and short respiration, joined with
a hissing sound and a cough, especially in the night-time,
and when the body is in a prone posture; because then the
contents of the lower belly bear so against the diaphragm,
as to lessen the capacity of the breast, whereby the lungs
have less room to move. Quincy.

astra′ddle. With one's legs across any thing.

astri′ction. The act or power of contracting the parts of the
body by applications.

> Such lenitive substances are proper for dry atrabilarian

constitutions, who are subject to *astriction* of the belly and the piles. Arbuthnot, *On Diet.*

astri′ctive. Stiptick; of a binding quality.

astri′de. With the legs open.

> To lay their native arms aside,
> Their modesty, and ride *astride. Hudibras.*

to astri′nge. To press by contraction; to make the parts draw together.

> Tears are caused by a contraction of the spirits of the brain; which contraction, by consequence, *astringeth* the moisture of the brain, and thereby sendeth tears into the eyes. Bacon.

astri′ngency. The power of contracting the parts of the body; opposed to the power of *relaxation.*

> Acid, acrid, austere, and bitter substances, by their *astringency,* create horrour, that is, stimulate the fibres. Arbuthnot.

astro′logy. The practice of foretelling things by the knowledge of the stars; an art now generally exploded, as without reason.

> I know it hath been the opinion of the learned, who think of the art of *astrology,* that the stars do not force the actions or wills of men. Swift.

astro-theology. Divinity founded on the observation of the celestial bodies.

at. (5) *At* before a person, is seldom used otherwise than ludicrously; as, he longed to be *at* him, that is, to attack him.

a′tabal. A kind of tabour used by the Moors.

a′theous. Atheistick; godless.

> Thy Father, who is holy, wise, and pure,
> Suffers the hypocrite, or *atheous* priest,
> To tread his sacred courts. *Paradise Regained,* b. i.

athle′tick. (2) Strong of body; vigorous; lusty; robust.

> Science distinguishes a man of honour from one of those *athletick* brutes, whom undeservedly we call heroes. Dryden.

[73]

athwa′rt. (2) Wrong.

> The baby beats the nurse, and quite *athwart*
> Goes all decorum. Shakespeare, *Measure for Measure.*

a′tlas. (4) A rich kind of silk or stuff made for women's cloaths.

a′tmosphere. The exteriour part of this our habitable world is the air, or *atmosphere;* a light, thin, fluid, or springy body, that encompasses the solid earth on all sides. Locke.

a′tom. (1) Such a small particle as cannot be physically divided: and these are the first rudiments, or the component parts of all bodies. Quincy.

a′tomy. An obsolete word for *atom.*

> Drawn with a team of little *atomies,*
> Athwart men's noses, as they be asleep. Shakespeare, *Romeo and Juliet.*

to a′tone. (From *at one,* as the etymologists remark, *to be at one,* is the same as *to be in concord.* This derivation is much confirmed by the following passage.) (1) To agree; to accord.

> He and Ausidus can no more *atone,*
> Than violentest contrariety. Shakespeare, *Coriolanus.*

atrabila′rian. Melancholy; replete with black choler.

> The *atrabilarian* constitution, or a black, viscous, pitchy consistence of the fluids, makes all secretions difficult and sparing. Arbuthnot, *On Diet.*

a′trophy. Want of nourishment; a disease in which what is taken at the mouth cannot contribute to the support of the body.

to atta′int. (2) To taint; to corrupt.

atta′int. (1) Any thing injurious, as illness, weariness. This sense is now obsolete.

(2) Stain; spot; taint.

atta′inture. Reproach; imputation.

> Hume's knavery will be the duchess's wreck,
> And her *attainture* will be Humphry's fall.
> Shakespeare's *Henry VI.*

to atte′mper. (1) To mingle; to weaken by the mixture of something else; to dilute.

[74]

(4) To fit to something else.

to atte'nd. (2) To stay; to delay.

> Plant anemonies after the first rains, if you will have flowers very forward; but it is surer to *attend* till October, or the month after. Evelyn's *Kalendar.*

atte'ndance. (5) Expectation; a sense now out of use.

> That which causeth bitterness in death, is the languishing *attendance* and expectation thereof ere it come. Hooker, b. i.

a'tter. Corrupt matter. A word much used in Lincolnshire. Skinner.

atti're. (2) In hunting. The horns of a buck or stag.

atto'rney. (2) It was anciently used for those who did any business for another; now only in law.

> Why should calamity be full of words?—
> —Windy *attorneys* to their client woes,
> Airy succeeders of intestate joys.
> Shakespeare, *Richard III.*

attra'ct. Attraction; the power of drawing.

> Feel darts and charms, *attracts* and flames,
> And woe and contract in their names. *Hudibras.*

attra'ctical. Having the power to draw to it.

> Some stones are endued with an electrical or *attractical* virtue. Ray, *On the Creation.*

attra'ctive. That which draws or incites allurement; except that *attractive* is of a good or indifferent sense, and *allurement* generally bad.

a'ttribute. (4) Reputation; honour.

attri'te. Ground; worn by rubbing.

attri'tion. (2) (With divines.) Grief for sin, arising only from the fear of punishment; the lowest degree of repentance.

a'udit. A final account.

> He took my father grossly, full of bread,
> With all his crimes broad blown, and flush as May;
> And how his *audit* stands, who knows save heav'n?
> *Hamlet.*

a'uditress. The woman that hears; a she hearer.

> Yet went she not, as not with such discourse

Delighted, or not capable her ear
Of what was high: such pleasure she reserv'd,
Adam relating, she sole *auditress*. Milton, *Paradise Lost*, b. viii.

a'uger. A carpenter's tool to bore holes with.

The *auger* hath a handle and bit; its office is to make great round holes. When you use it, the stuff you work upon is commonly laid low under you, that you may the easier use your strength; for in twisting the bit about by the force of both your hands, on each end of the handle one, it cuts great chips out of the stuff. Moxon's *Mechanical Exercises*.

auld. A word now obsolete; but still used in the Scotch dialect.

to auma'il. (From *maille*, Fr. the mesh of a net; whence a coat of *amail*, a coat with network of iron.) To variegate; to figure.

auri'cular. (2) Secret; told in the ear; as *auricular* confession.

ausculta'tion. A hearkening or listening to.

a'uspice. (2) Protection; favour shewn by prosperous men.

auste're. (2) Sower of taste; harsh.

Austere wines, diluted with water, cool more than water alone, and at the same time do not relax. Arbuthnot, *On Aliments*.

to a'ustralize. To tend towards the south.

autho'rity. (4) Support; justification; countenance.

Do'st thou expect th' *authority* of their voices,
Whose silent wills condemn thee? Ben. Jonson, *Catiline*.

auto'maton. A machine that hath the power of motion within itself, and which stands in need of no foreign assistance. Quincy.

a'utopsy. Ocular demonstration; seeing a thing one's self. Quincy.

to ava'il. (2) To promote; to prosper; to assist.

Meantime he voyag'd to explore the will
Of Jove on high Dodona's holy hill,
What means might best his safe return *avail*.
Pope's *Odyssey*.

ava'il. Profit; advantage; benefit.

> I charge thee,
> As heav'n shall work in me for thine *avail*,
> To tell me truly. Shakespeare, *All's well that ends well.*

ava'ilable. (1) Profitable; advantageous.

(2) Powerful; in force.

to ava'le. To let fall; to depress; to make abject; to sink: a word out of use.

ava'st. Enough; cease. A word used among seamen.

ava'unt. A word of abhorrence, by which any one is driven away.

> After this process
> To give her the *avaunt!* it is a pity
> Would move a monster. Shakespeare, *Henry VIII.*

to ave'l. To pull away.

> The beaver in chase makes some divulsion of parts, yet are not these parts *avelled* to be termed testicles. Browne's *Vulgar Errours.*

a've Mary. A form of worship repeated by the Romanists in honour of the Virgin Mary.

a'verage. (2) In navigation, a certain contribution that merchants and others proportionably make towards the losses of such as have their goods cast overboard for the safety of the ship; or of the goods and lives of those in the ship, in a tempest; and this contribution seems to be so called, because it is so proportioned, after the rate of every man's *average* or goods carried. Cowell.

(3) A small duty which merchants, who send goods in another man's ship, pay to the master thereof for his care of them, over and above the freight. Chambers.

ave'rment. (1) Establishment of any thing by evidence.

(2) An offer of the defendant to justify an exception, and the act as well as the offer. Blount.

to averru'ncate. To root up; to tear up by the roots.

aversa'tion. (1) Hatred; abhorrence; turning away with detestation.

> Hatred is the passion of defiance, and there is a kind of *aversation* and hostility included in its essence. South.

ave'rse. (1) Malign; not favourable.

to a′vocate. To call off from business; to call away.

avoca′tion. (1) The act of calling aside.

> The bustle of business, the *avocations* of our senses, and the din of a clamorous world, are impediments. Glanvill's *Scepsis.*

(2) The business that calls; or the call that summons away.

> By the secular cares and *avocations* which accompany marriage, the clergy have been furnished with skill in common life. Atterbury.

to avo′id. (3) To evacuate; to quit.

> He desired to speak with some few of us; whereupon six of us only stayed, and the rest *avoided* the room. Bacon's *New Atlantis.*

avola′tion. The act of flying away; flight; escape.

avo′wtry. (See *advowtry.*) Adultery.

avu′lsion. The act of pulling one thing from another.

> Spare not the little offsprings, if they grow
> Redundant; but the thronging clusters thin
> By kind *avulsion.* Philips.

awa′re. Vigilant; in a state of alarm; attentive.

> Ere I was *aware*, I had left myself nothing but the name of a king. Sidney.

awa′y. (6) It is often used with a verb; as, to *drink away* an estate; to *idle away* a manor; that is, to drink or idle till an estate or manor is gone.

(8) Perhaps the phrase, *he cannot away with*, may mean *he cannot travel with; he cannot bear the company.*

a′wful. (1) That which strikes with awe, or fills with reverence.

to awha′pe. (This word I have met with only in Spenser, nor can I discover whence it is derived; but imagine, that the Teutonick language had anciently *wapen*, to strike, or some such word, from which *weapons*, or offensive arms, took their denomination.)

> Ah! my dear gossip, answer'd then the ape,
> Deeply do your sad words my wits *awhape*,
> Both for because your grief doth great appear,
> And eke because myself am touched near. *Hubberd's Tale.*

awk. (A barbarous contraction of the word *awkward.*) Odd; out of order.

> We have heard as arrant jangling in the pulpits, as the steeples; and professors ringing as *awk* as the bells to give notice of the conflagration. L'Estrange.

awry'. (4) Not equally between two points.

> Not tyrants fierce that unrepenting die,
> Not Cynthia when her manteau's pinn'd *awry,*
> Ere felt such rage. Pope's *Rape of the Lock.*

a'xle, a'xle-tree. The pin which passes through the midst of the wheel, on which the circumvolutions of the wheel are performed.

> The fly sate upon the *axle-tree* of the chariot-wheel, and said, what a dust do I raise? Bacon's *Essays.*

B

ba′bery. Finery to please a babe or child.

ba′bish. Childish.

> If he be bashful, and will soon blush, they call him a *babish* and ill brought up thing. Ascham's *Schoolmaster*.

babo′on. (*babouin*, Fr. It is supposed by Skinner to be the augmentation of *babe*, and to import a *great babe*.) A monkey of the largest kind.

> You had looked through the grate like a geminy of *baboons*. Shakespeare, *Merry Wives of Windsor*.

ba′by. (2) A small image in imitation of a child, which girls play with.

> Since no image can represent the great Creator, never think to honour him by your foolish puppets, and *babies* of dirt and clay. Stillingfleet's *Defence of Discourse concerning Idolatry in the Church of Rome*.

ba′cchus bole. A flower not tall, but very full and broad-leaved; of a sad light purple, and a proper white; having the three outmost leaves edged with a crimson colour, bluish bottom, and dark purple. Mortimer.

bacci′ferous. Berry-bearing.

back. (1) The hinder part of the body, from the neck to the thighs.

(2) The outer part of the hand when it is shut; opposed to the *palm*.

(3) The outward part of the body; that which requires cloaths; opposed to the *belly*.

> Those who, by their ancestors, have been set free from a constant drudgery to their *backs* and their bellies, should bestow some time on their heads. Locke.

to back. (1) To mount on the back of a horse.

(2) To break a horse; to train him to bear upon his back.

ba′ckbiter. A privy calumniator; a censurer of the absent.

ba′ckfriend. A friend backwards; that is, an enemy in secret.

> Set the restless importunities of talebearers and *back-friends* against fair words and professions. L'Estrange.

ba′ckside. (2) The hind part of an animal.

> A poor ant carries a grain of corn, climbing up a wall with her head downwards and her *backside* upwards. Addison.

ba′ckward, ba′ckwards. (10) Perversely; from the wrong end.

> I never yet saw man,
> But she would spell him *backward;* if fair-fac'd,
> She'd swear the gentleman should be her sister;
> If black, why, nature, drawing of an antick,
> Made a foul blot; if tall, a launce ill-headed.
> Shakespeare, *Much ado about Nothing.*

ba′con. (1) The flesh of a hog salted and dried.

(2) To save the *bacon*, is a phrase for preserving one's self from being hurt; borrowed from the care of housewives in the country, where they have seldom any other provision in the house than dried bacon, to secure it from the marching soldiers.

> What frightens you thus? my good son! says the priest;
> You murder'd, are sorry, and have been confest.
> O father! my sorrow will scarce save my *bacon;*
> For 'twas not that I murder'd, but that I was taken.
> Prior.

bad. (5) Sick.

ba′dger. (1) An animal that earths in the ground, used to be hunted.

---

bacon. (2) The first edition reads *unhurt;* corrected in the fourth edition, 1773.

(2) One that buys corn and victuals in one place, and carries it unto another. Cowell.

ba′dger legged. Having legs of an unequal length, as the badger is supposed to have.

>His body crooked all over, big-bellied, *badger legged*, and his complexion swarthy. L'Estrange.

ba′ffle. A defeat.

bag. (2) That part of animals in which some particular juices are contained, as the poison of vipers.

to bag. To swell like a full bag.

>Two kids that in the valley stray'd,
>
>I found by chance, and to my fold convey'd:
>
>They drain two *bagging* udders every day. Dryden's *Virgil*.

ba′gnio. A house for bathing, sweating, and otherwise cleansing the body.

to bait. (1) To stop at any place for refreshment; perhaps this word is more properly *bate;* to *abate* speed.

>In all our journey from London to his house, we did not so much as *bait* at a whig inn. Addison, *Spectator*, No. 126.

(2) To clap the wings; to make an offer of flying; to flutter.

bait. (3) A refreshment on a journey.

baize. A kind of coarse open cloth stuff, having a long nap; sometimes frized on one side, and sometimes not frized, according to the uses it is intended for. This stuff is without wale, being wrought on a loom with two treddles, like flannel. Chambers.

balco′ny. A frame of iron, wood, or stone, before the window of a room.

>When dirty waters from *balconies* drop,
>
>And dext'rous damsels twirl the sprinkling mop. Gay.

ba′lderdash. Any thing jumbled together without judgment; rude mixture; a confused discourse.

to ba′lderdash. To mix or adulterate any liquor.

ba′ldness. (3) Meanness of writing; inelegance.

ba′ldrick. (1) A girdle. By some dictionaries it is explained a *bracelet;* but I have not found it in that sense.

bale. Misery; calamity.

balk. A ridge of land left unploughed between the furrows, or at the end of the field.

to balk. (3) To omit, or refuse any thing.

ba'lkers. (In fishery.) Men who stand on a cliff, or high place on the shore, and give a sign to the men in the fishing-boats, which way the passage or shole of herrings is. Cowell.

ball. (7) The parchment spread over a hollow piece of wood, stuffed with hair or wool, which the printers dip in ink, to spread it on the letters.

ba'llad. A song.

> *Ballad* once signified a solemn and sacred song, as well as trivial, when Solomon's Song was called the *ballad of ballads;* but now it is applied to nothing but trifling verse. Watts.

ba'lliards. A play at which a ball is driven by the end of a stick; now corruptly called *billiards.*

ballo'n, ballo'on. (3) In fireworks; a ball of pasteboard, stuffed with combustible matter, which, when fired, mounts to a considerable height in the air, and then bursts into bright sparks of fire, resembling stars.

balm. (1) The sap or juice of a shrub, remarkably odoriferous.

ba'lneary. A bathing-room.

ba'lustrade. An assemblage of one or more rows of little turned pillars, called balusters, fixed upon a terras, or the top of a building, for separating one part from another.

to bambo'ozle. (A cant word not used in pure or in grave writings.) To deceive; to impose upon; to confound.

> After Nick had *bamboozled* about the money, John called for counters. Arbuthnot's *John Bull.*

bambo'ozler. A tricking fellow; a cheat.

to ban. To curse; to execrate.

ba'ndog. (From *ban* or *band*, and *dog*. The original of this word is very doubtful. Caius, *de canibus Britannicis*, derives it from *band*, that is, *a dog chained up.* Skinner inclines to deduce it from *bana*, a *murderer.* May it not come from *ban* a *curse*, as we say a *curst cur;* or rather from *baund*, swelled or large, a Danish word; from whence, in

some counties, they call a great nut a *ban-nut.*) A kind
of large dog.

> Or privy, or pert, if any bin,
> We have great *bandogs* will tear their skin. Spenser,
> *Pastorals.*

ba′ndoleers. Small wooden cases covered with leather, each
of them containing powder that is a sufficient charge for
a musket.

ba′ndy. A club turned round at bottom for striking a ball at
play.

ba′ndyleg. A crooked leg.

> He tells aloud your greatest failing,
> Nor makes a scruple to expose
> Your *bandyleg*, or crooked nose. Swift.

bane. (1) Poison.

to bane. To poison.

> What if my house be troubled with a rat,
> And I be pleas'd to give ten thousand ducats
> To have it ban'd. Shakespeare, *Merchant of Venice.*

ba′neful. (2) Destructive.

> The nightly wolf is *baneful* to the fold,
> Storms to the wheat, to buds the bitter cold. Dryden's
> *Virgil.*

bang. A blow; a thump; a stroke: a low word.

> I am a bachelor.—That's to say, they are fools that
> marry; you'll bear me a *bang* for that. Shakespeare,
> *Julius Caesar.*

ba′nkrupt. A man in debt beyond the power of payment.

ba′nnock. A kind of oaten or pease meal cake, mixed with
water, and baked upon an iron plate over the fire; used
in the northern counties, and in Scotland.

ba′nstickle. A small fish, called also a stickleback.

to ba′nter. (A barbarous word, without etymology, unless it
be derived from *badiner,* Fr.) To play upon; to rally; to
turn to ridicule; to ridicule.

> Could Alcinous' guests withold
> From scorn or rage? Shall we, cries one, permit
> His leud romances, and his *bant'ring* wit? Tate's
> *Juvenal.*

ba′ntling. (If it has any etymology, it is perhaps corrupted from the old word *bairn, bairnling,* a little child.) A little child: a low word.

> If the object of their love
> Chance by Lucina's aid to prove,
> They seldom let the *bantling* roar,
> In basket, at a neighbour's door. Prior.

barb. (1) Any thing that grows in the place of the beard. The barbel, so called by reason of his *barb* or wattels at his mouth, under his chaps. Walton's *Angler.*

to barb. (1) To shave; to dress out the beard.

> Shave the head, and tie the beard, and say it was the desire of the penitent to be so *barbed* before his death. Shakespeare, *Measure for Measure.*

to ba′rbecue. A term used in the West-Indies for dressing a hog whole; which, being split to the backbone, is laid flat upon a large gridiron, raised about two foot above a charcoal fire, with which it is surrounded.

> Oldfield, with more than harpy throat endu'd,
> Cries, send me, gods, a whole hog *barbecu'd.* Pope.

barber-monger. A word of reproach in Shakespeare, which seems to signify a fop; a man decked out by his barber.

> Draw, you rogue; for though it be night, the moon shines; I'll make a sop of the moonshine of you; you whoreson, cullionly, *barber-monger,* draw. Shakespeare, *King Lear.*

ba′rebone. Lean, so that the bones appear.

ba′regnawn. Eaten bare.

> Know my name is lost;
> By treason's tooth *baregnawn* and cankerbit.
> Shakespeare, *King Lear.*

ba′rgain. (4) An unexpected reply, tending to obscenity.

> No maid at court is less asham'd,
> Howe'er for selling *bargains* fam'd. Swift.

(5) An event; an upshot: a low sense.

> I am sorry for thy misfortune; however we must make the best of a bad *bargain;* thou art in jeopardy, that is certain. Arbuthnot's *History of John Bull.*

ba′rleybrake. A kind of rural play.

barley broth. A low word, sometimes used for strong beer.

barm. Yeast; the ferment put into drink to make it work, and into bread, to lighten and swell it.

ba′rnacle. (1) A bird like a goose, fabulously supposed to grow on trees.

ba′rrack. (1) Little cabins made by the Spanish fishermen on the sea shore; or little lodges for soldiers in a camp.

ba′rrator. A wrangler, and encourager of law suits.

> Will it not reflect as much on thy character, Nic, to turn *barrator* in thy old days, a stirrer up of quarrels amongst thy neighbours. Arbuthnot's *History of John Bull.*

ba′rratry. The practice or crime of a barrator; foul practice in law.

ba′rrel-bellied. Having a large belly.

> Dauntless at empty noises; lofty neck'd,
> Sharp headed, *barrel-belly'd,* broadly back'd. Dryden, *Virgil.*

ba′rrow. A hog; whence *barrow* grease, or hog's lard.

base-born. Born out of wedlock.

base. (5) Stockings, or perhaps the armour for the legs, from *bas,* Fr.

> Nor shall it e'er be said that wight,
> With gauntlet blue and *bases* white,
> And round blunt truncheon by his side,
> So great a man at arms defy'd. *Hudibras.*

(8) An old rustick play; written by Skinner, *bays.*

ba′seness. (3) Bastardy.

> Why brand they us
> With base? with *baseness?* bastardy? Shakespeare, *King Lear.*

to bash. To be ashamed; to be confounded with shame.

ba′shful. (2) Sheepish; vitiously modest.

> He looked with an almost *bashful* kind of modesty, as if he feared the eyes of man. Sidney.

ba′shfulness. (2) Vitious or rustick shame.

ba′sil. (1) The angle to which the edge of a joiner's tool is ground away.

(2) The skin of a sheep tanned.

basi'lica. The middle vein of the arm so called, by way of pre-eminence. It is likewise attributed to many medicines for the same reason. Quincy.

ba'silisk. (1) A kind of serpent, called also a cockatrice, which is said to drive away all others by his hissing, and to kill by looking.

> Make me not sighted like the *basilisk;*
> I've look'd on thousands who have sped the better
> By my regard, but kill'd none so. Shakespeare, *Winter's Tale.*

to bask. To warm by laying out in the heat; used almost always of animals.

> And stretched out all the chimney's length,
> *Basks* at the fire his hairy strength. Milton.

ba'sket. A vessel made of twigs, rushes, or splinters, or some other slender body interwoven.

ba'sket-woman. A woman that plies at markets with a basket, ready to carry home any thing that is bought.

to ba'stard. To convict of being a bastard; to stigmatize with bastardy.

> She lived to see her brother beheaded, and her two sons deposed from the crown, *bastarded* in their blood, and cruelly murdered. Bacon's *Henry VII.*

to baste. (1) To beat with a stick.

bastina'de, bastina'do. (1) The act of beating with a cudgel; the blow given with a cudgel.

bat. An animal having the body of a mouse and the wings of a bird; not with feathers, but with a sort of skin which is extended. It lays no eggs, but brings forth its young alive, and suckles them. It never grows tame, feeds upon flies, insects, and fatty substances, such as candles, oil, and cheese; and appears only in the summer evenings, when the weather is fine. Calmet.

> Some animals are placed in the middle betwixt two kinds, as *bats*, which have something of birds and beasts. Locke.

bat-fowling. A particular manner of birdcatching in the night time, while they are at roost upon perches, trees, or hedges. They light torches or straw, and then beat the bushes; upon which the birds flying to the flames, are caught either with nets, or otherwise.

bate. Strife; contention; as a *make-bate.*

ba'teful. Contentious.

bath. (2) A state in which great outward heat is applied to the body, for the mitigation of pain, or any other purpose.

> In the height of this *bath,* when I was more than half stewed in grease like a Dutch dish, to be thrown into the Thames. Shakespeare's *Merry Wives of Windsor.*

ba'ting, or aba'ting. Except.

> If we consider children, we have little reason to think, that they bring many ideas with them, *bating,* perhaps, some faint ideas of hunger and thirst. Locke.

ba'tlet. A square piece of wood, with a handle, used in beating linen when taken out of the buck.

ba'ttaillous. Having the appearance of a battle; warlike; with military appearance.

batta'lia. The order of battle.

to ba'tten. (2) To fertilize.

to ba'tter. (3) Applied to persons: to wear out with service.

> As the same dame, experienc'd in her trade,
>
> By names of toasts retails each *batter'd* jade. Pope.

ba'ubee. A word used in Scotland, and the northern counties, for a halfpenny.

ba'varoy. A kind of cloke, or surtout.

ba'vin. A stick like those bound up in faggots; a piece of waste wood.

ba'wbling. Trifling; contemptible: a word not now in use, except in conversation.

ba'wcock. A familiar word, which seems to signify the same as *fine fellow.*

> Why, how now, my *bawcock?* how dost thou, chuck? Shakespeare, *Twelfth Night.*

bawd. A procurer, or procuress; one that introduces men and women to each other, for the promotion of debauchery.

to bawd. To procure; to provide gallants with strumpets.

>And in four months a batter'd harridan;
>Now nothing's left, but wither'd, pale, and shrunk,
>To *bawd* for others, and go shares with punk. Swift.

ba'wdiness. Obsceneness.

ba'wdrick. (See *baldrick.*) A belt.

ba'wdry. (2) Obscenity; unchaste language.

>I have no salt: no *bawdry* he doth mean:
>For witty, in his language, is obscene. B. Jonson.

ba'wdy. Obscene; unchaste; generally applied to language.

ba'wdy-house. A house where traffick is made by wickedness and debauchery.

>Has the pope lately shut up the *bawdy-houses,* or does he continue to lay a tax upon sin? Dennis.

to bawl. (1) To hoot; to cry with great vehemence, whether for joy or pain. A word always used in contempt.

>So on the tuneful Margarita's tongue
>The list'ning nymphs, and ravish'd heroes hung;
>But citts and fops the heav'n born musick blame,
>And *bawl,* and hiss, and damn her into fame.
>Smith, *On J. Philips.*

bde'llium. An aromatick gum brought from the Levant, used as a medicine and a perfume. *Bdellium* is mentioned both by the ancient naturalists and in scripture; but it is doubtful whether any of these be the same with the modern kind. Chambers.

bead. (1) Small globes or balls of glass or pearl, or other substance, strung upon a thread, and used by the Romanists to count their prayers; from whence the phrase to *tell beads,* or to be at one's *beads,* is to be at prayer.

be'agle. A small hound with which hares are hunted.

beal. A whelk or pimple.

to beal. To ripen; to gather matter, or come to a head, as a sore does.

beam. (4) The horn of a stag.

to bear. (1) This is a word used with such latitude, that it is not easily explained.

>We say to *bear* a burden, to *bear* sorrow or reproach, to

bear a name, to *bear* a grudge, to *bear* fruit, or to *bear* children. The word *bear* is used in very different senses. Watts's *Logick*.

(25) To supply.

What have you under your arm? Somewhat, that will *bear* your charges in your pilgrimage? Dryden's *Spanish Friar*.

(36) *To bear in hand.* To amuse with false pretences; to deceive.

bear. (1) A rough savage animal.

bear-fly. An insect.

bear-garden. A word used in familiar or low phrase for *rude* or *turbulent;* as, a *bear-garden* fellow; that is, a man rude enough to be a proper frequenter of the bear-garden. *Bear-garden sport,* is used for gross inelegant entertainment.

to beard. (1) To take or pluck by the beard, in contempt or anger.

be'arded. (3) Barbed or jagged.

be'arherd. A man that tends bears.

be'arward. A keeper of bears.

The bear is led after one manner, the multitude after another; the *bearward* leads but one brute, and the mountebank leads a thousand. L'Estrange.

beast. (3) A brutal savage man, a man acting in any manner unworthy of a reasonable creature.

to beat. (21) *To beat the hoof.* To walk; to go on foot.

be'ater. (2) A person much given to blows.

The best schoolmaster of our time, was the greatest *beater*. Ascham's *Schoolmaster*.

beatifica'tion. A term in the Romish church, distinguished from canonization. *Beatification* is an acknowledgment made by the pope, that the person beatified is in heaven, and therefore may be reverenced as blessed; but is not a concession of the honours due to saints, which are conferred by canonization.

beau. (*beau,* Fr. It is sounded like *bo,* and has often the French plural *beaux.*) A man of dress; a man whose great care is to deck his person.

be'aver. (1) An animal, otherwise named the *castor*, amphibious, and remarkable for his art in building his habitation;
of which many wonderful accounts are delivered by travel-
lers. His skin is very valuable on account of the fur.

> The *beaver* being hunted, biteth off his stones, know-
> ing that for them only his life is sought. Hakewell, *On
> Providence.*

to beau'tify. To grow beautiful; to advance in beauty.

to beau'ty. To adorn; to beautify; to embellish.

> The harlot's cheek, *beautied* with plast'ring art,
> Is not more ugly to the thing that helps it,
> Than is my deed to your most painted word.
> Shakespeare, *Hamlet.*

beauty-spot. A spot placed to direct the eye to something else,
or to heighten some beauty; a foil; a patch.

> The filthiness of swine makes them the *beauty-spot* of
> the animal creation. Grew's *Cosmologia Sacra*, b. iii,
> c. 2, sect. 49.

becafi'co. A bird like a nightingale, feeding on figs and grapes;
a fig-pecker. Pineda.

to becha'nce. To befal; to happen to: a word proper, but now
in little use.

> My sons, God knows what has bechanced them.
> Shakespeare, *Henry VI*, p. ii.

to beck. To make a sign with the head.

to becli'p. To embrace.

to beco'me. (3) In the following passage, the phrase, *where
is he become*, is used for *what is become of him*.

> I cannot joy, until I be resolved
> *Where* our right valiant father *is become.* Shakespeare,
> *Henry VI.*

beco'ming. Behaviour: a word not now in use.

> Sir, forgive me,
> Since my *becomings* kill me, when they do not
> Eye well to you. Shakespeare, *Antony and Cleopatra.*

beco'mingness. Decency; elegant congruity; propriety.

bed. (3) Marriage.

to bed. (2) To be placed in bed.

(5) To lay in a place of rest, or security.

to beda′bble. To wet; to besprinkle. It is generally applied to persons, in a sense including inconvenience.

to beda′ggle. To bemire; to soil cloaths, by letting them reach the dirt in walking.

to beda′sh. To bemire by throwing dirt; to bespatter; to wet with throwing water.

to beda′wb. To dawb over; to besmear; to soil, with spreading any viscous body over it.

> A piteous coarse, a bloody piteous coarse,
> Pale, pale as ashes, all *bedawb'd* in blood,
> All in gore blood. Shakespeare, *Romeo and Juliet.*

be′dehouse. An hospital or almshouse, where the poor people prayed for their founders and benefactors.

to bedi′ght. To adorn; to dress; to set off.

to bedi′zen. To dress out.

be′dlam. (2) A madman; a lunatick.

be′dmaker. A person in the universities, whose office it is to make the beds, and clean the chambers.

be′dpresser. A heavy lazy fellow.

> This sanguine coward, this *bedpresser*, this horseback-breaker, this huge hill of flesh. Shakespeare, *Henry IV,* p. i.

to bedra′ggle. To soil the cloaths, by suffering them, in walking, to reach the dirt.

be′drite. The privilege of the marriage bed.

bedswe′rver. One that is false to the bed; one that ranges or swerves from one bed to another.

> She's a *bedswerver*, even as bad as those,
> That vulgars give bold'st titles to. Shakespeare, *Winter's Tale.*

to bedu′ng. To cover, or manure with dung.

to bedu′st. To sprinkle with dust.

bee. (1) The animal that makes honey, remarkable for its industry and art.

(2) An industrious and careful person. This signification is only used in familiar language.

be′emol. This word I have found only in the example, and know nothing of the etymology, unless it be a corruption of *by-module,* from *by* and *modulus,* a note; that is, a note out of the regular order.

There be intervenient in the rise of eight, in tones, two *beemols,* or half notes; so as, if you divide the tones equally, the eight is but seven whole and equal notes. Bacon's *Natural History.*

be′etle. (1) An insect distinguished by having hard cases or sheaths, under which he folds his wings.

(2) A heavy mallet, or wooden hammer, with which wedges are driven.

to be′etle. To jut out; to hang over.

Or where the hawk,
High in the *beetling* cliff, his airy builds. Thomson's *Spring.*

beetlebro′wed. Having prominent brows.

beetlehe′aded. Loggerheaded; wooden headed; having a head stupid, like the head of a wooden beetle.

A whoreson, *beetleheaded,* flap-ear'd knave.
Shakespeare, *Taming of the Shrew.*

to befo′ol. To infatuate; to fool; to deprive of understanding; to lead into errour.

befo′rehand. (3) In a state of accumulation, or so as that more has been received than expended.

Stranger's house is at this time rich, and much *beforehand;* for it hath laid up revenue these thirty-seven years. Bacon.

be′ggar. (2) One who supplicates for any thing; a petitioner; for which, *beggar* is a harsh and contemptuous term.

What subjects will precarious kings regard?
A *beggar* speaks too softly to be heard. Dryden, *Conquest of Granada.*

to be′ggar. (3) To exhaust.

For her person,
It *beggar'd* all description; she did lie
In her pavilion, cloth of gold, of tissue,
O'er-picturing Venus. Shakespeare, *Antony and Cleopatra.*

to begna'w. To bite; to eat away; to corrode; to nibble.

His horse is stark spoiled with the staggers, *begnawn* with the bots, waid in the back, and shoulder shotten. Shakespeare, *Taming of the Shrew.*

to begre'ase. To soil or dawb with unctuous or fat matter.

be'hemoth. *Behemoth,* in Hebrew, signifies beasts in general, particularly the larger kind, fit for service. But Job speaks of an animal, which he calls *behemoth,* and describes its particular properties at large, in chap. xl. 15. Bochart has taken much care to make it appear to be the *hippopotamus,* or river-horse. Sanctius thinks it is an ox. The Fathers suppose the devil to be meant by it. But we agree with the generality of interpreters, in their opinion, that it is the elephant. Calmet.

to behi'ght. (1) To promise.

(3) Perhaps to call; to name; *hight* being often put, in old authors, for *named,* or *was named.*

to beho'ove. To be fit; to be meet; either with respect to duty, necessity, or convenience. It is used only impersonally with *it.*

beho'oveful. Useful; profitable; advantageous. This word is somewhat antiquated.

to beho'wl. (1) To howl at.

(2) Perhaps, to howl over, or lament clamorously.

to bela'bour. To beat; to thump; a word in low speech.

He sees virago Nell *belabour,*

With his own staff, his peaceful neighbour. Swift.

to bela'ce. (Sea term.) To fasten; as to *belace* a rope.

bela'ted. Benighted; out of doors late at night.

Fairy elves,

Whose midnight revels, by a forest side,

Or fountain, some *belated* peasant sees,

Or dreams he sees. Milton's *Paradise Lost,* b. i, l. 781.

to belch. To throw out from the stomach; to eject from any hollow place. It is a word implying coarseness; hatefulness; or horrour.

When I an am'rous kiss design'd,

I *belch'd* an hurricane of wind. Swift.

belch. (1) The act of eructation.

    (2) A cant term for malt liquour.

    A sudden reformation would follow, among all sorts of people; porters would no longer be drunk with *belch.* Dennis.

belda'm. (1) An old woman; generally a term of contempt, marking the last degree of old age, with all its faults and miseries.

belga'rd. A soft glance; a kind regard: an old word, now wholly disused.

beli'ke. (2) It is sometimes used in a sense of irony; as, *we are to suppose.*

bell. (4) *To bear the bell.* To be the first, from the wether, that carries a *bell* among the sheep, or the first horse of a drove that has *bells* on his collar.

be'llibone. A woman excelling both in beauty and goodness. A word now out of use.

    Pan may be proud, that ever he begot
        Such a *bellibone,*
    And Syrinx rejoice, that ever was her lot
        To bear such a one. Spenser's *Pastorals.*

be'lling. A hunting term, spoken of a roe, when she makes a noise in rutting time.

to be'llow. (3) To vociferate; to clamour. In this sense, it is a word of contempt.

    The dull fat captain, with a hound's deep throat,
    Would *bellow* out a laugh in a base note.
    Dryden, *Persius,* Sat. v.

be'lluine. Beastly; belonging to a beast; savage; brutal.

be'lly. (1) That part of the human body which reaches from the breast to the thighs, containing the bowels.

          The body's members
    Rebell'd against the *belly;* thus accus'd it;—
    That only like a gulf it did remain,
    Still cupboarding the viand, never bearing
    Like labour with the rest. Shakespeare, *Coriolanus.*

(3) The womb; in this sense, it is commonly used ludicrously or familiarly.

The secret is grown too big for the pretence, like Mrs.
Primly's big *belly*. Congreve's *Way of the World*.

be'llybound. Diseased, so as to be costive, and shrunk in the
belly.

be'llygod. A glutton; one who makes a god of his belly.

What infinite waste they made this way, the only story
of Apicius, a famous *bellygod*, may suffice to shew.
Hakewell, *On Providence*.

be'lly-timber. Food; materials to support the belly.

be'lomancy. *Belomancy*, or divination by arrows, hath been in
request with Scythians, Alans, Germans, with the Africans
and Turks of Algier. Browne's *Vulgar Errours*, b. v., c. 22.

to belo'wt. To treat with opprobrious language; to call names.

Sieur Gaulard, when he heard a gentleman report, that,
at a supper, they had not only good cheer, but also
savoury epigrams, and fine anagrams, returning home,
rated and *belowted* his cook, as an ignorant scullion, that
never dressed him either epigrams or anagrams.
Camden's *Remains*.

belswa'gger. A cant word for a whoremaster.

You are a charitable *belswagger;* my wife cried out fire,
and you called out for engines. Dryden's *Spanish Friar*.

to bema'd. To make mad; to turn the brain.

to bemo'nster. To make monstrous.

bench. (1) A seat, distinguished from a *stool* by its greater
length.

to bend. (4) To put any thing in order for use; a metaphor
taken from bending the bow.

As a fowler was *bending* his net, a blackbird asked him
what he was doing. L'Estrange, *Fables*, xcvi.

be'nedict. Having mild and salubrious qualities: an old physical term.

bene'mpt. Appointed; marked out; an obsolete word.

Much greater gifts for guerdon thou shalt gain,
Than kid or cosset, which I thee *benempt;*
Then up, I say. Spenser's *Pastorals*.

to bepi'ss. To wet with urine.

One caused, at a feast, a bagpipe to be played, which

made the knight *bepiss* himself, to the great diversion of all then present, as well as confusion of himself. Derham's *Physico-Theology*.

to beshre'w. (1) To wish a curse to.

(2) To happen ill to.

to beslu'bber. To dawb; to smear.

be'som. An instrument to sweep with.

Bacon commended an old man that sold *besoms*: a proud young fellow came to him for a *besom* upon trust; the old man said, borrow of thy back and belly, they will never ask thee again; I shall dun thee every day. Bacon's *Apophthegms*.

to bespa'wl. To dawb with spittle.

to bespe'ak. (5) To betoken; to shew.

When the abbot of St. Martin was born, he had so little of the figure of a man, that it *bespoke* him rather a monster. Locke.

to bespe'w. To dawb with spew or vomit.

to bespu'tter. To sputter over something; to dawb any thing by sputtering, or throwing out spittle upon it.

to besti'ck. To stick over with any thing; to mark any thing by infixing points or spots here and there.

to bethu'mp. To beat; to lay blows upon: a ludicrous word.

I was never so *bethumpt* with words,
Since first I call'd my brother's father dad. Shakespeare, *King John*.

to betra'y. (2) To discover that which has been entrusted to secrecy.

(3) To make known something that were better concealed.
Be swift to hear, but be cautious of your tongue, lest you *betray* your ignorance. Watts's *Improvement of the Mind*.

be'tty. (Probably a cant word, without etymology.) An instrument to break open doors.

Record the stratagems, the arduous exploits, and the nocturnal scalades of needy heroes, describing the powerful *betty,* or the artful picklock. Arbuthnot's *History of John Bull*.

be'verage. (3) A treat upon wearing a new suit of cloaths.

(4) A treat at first coming into a prison, called also *garnish*.

to bewa're. (2) It is observable, that it is only used in such forms of speech as admit the word *be:* thus we say, *he may beware, let him beware, he will beware;* but not, *he did beware,* or *he has been ware.*

be'zoar. A medicinal stone, formerly in high esteem as an antidote, and brought from the East Indies, where it is said to be found in the dung of an animal of the goat kind, called *pazan;* the stone being formed in its belly, and growing to the size of an acorn, and sometimes to that of a pigeon's egg. Were the real virtues of this stone answerable to its reputed ones, it were doubtless a panacea. Indeed its rarity, and the peculiar manner of its formation, which is now supposed to be fabulous, have perhaps contributed as much to its reputation as its intrinsick worth. At present, it begins to be discarded in the practice of medicine, as of no efficacy at all. There are also some occidental *bezoars* brought from Peru, which are reckoned inferiour to the oriental. The name of this stone is also applied to several chymical compositions, designed for antidotes, or counter-poisons; as mineral, solar, and jovial *bezoars.* Savary. Chambers.

bib. A small piece of linen put upon the breasts of children, over their cloaths.

to bib. To tipple; to sip; to drink frequently.

> To appease a froward child, they gave him drink as often as he cried; so that he was constantly *bibbing,* and drank more in twenty four hours than I did. Locke.

biblio'grapher. A writer of books; a transcriber.

bici'pital, bici'pitous. (1) Having two heads.

bi'dale. An invitation of friends to drink at a poor man's house, and there to contribute charity.

bide'ntal. Having two teeth.

> Ill management of forks is not to be helped, when they are only *bidental.* Swift.

bi'estings. The first milk given by a cow after calving, which is very thick.

bifa'rious. Twofold; what may be understood two ways.

bi'lingsgate. (A cant word, borrowed from *Bilingsgate* in London, a place where there is always a croud of low people, and frequent brawls and foul language.) Ribaldry; foul language.

> There stript, fair rhet'rick languish'd on the ground,
> And shameful *bilingsgate* her robes adorn. *Dunciad*, b. iv.

to bill. To publish by an advertisement: a cant word.

> His masterpiece was a composition that he *billed* about under the name of a sovereign antidote. L'Estrange.

bird. A general term for the feathered kind; a fowl. In common talk, *fowl* is used for the larger, and *bird* for the smaller kind of feathered animals.

birthstra'ngled. Strangled or suffocated in being born.

> Finger of *birthstrangl'd* babe,
> Ditch deliver'd by a drab. Shakespeare, *Macbeth.*

bi'shop. A cant word for a mixture of wine, oranges, and sugar.

bi'sson. Blind.

bisu'lcous. Clovenfooted.

bit. (1) As much meat as is put into the mouth at once.

bitch. (2) A name of reproach for a woman.

> John had not run a madding so long, had it not been for an extravagant *bitch* of a wife. Arbuthnot's *History of John Bull.*

to bite. (6) To cheat; to trick; to defraud: a low phrase.

> Asleep and naked as an Indian lay,
> An honest factor stole a gem away:
> He pledg'd it to the knight; the knight had wit,
> So kept the diamond, and the rogue was *bit.* Pope.

bi'ttern. A bird with long legs, and a long bill, which feeds upon fish; remarkable for the noise which he makes, usually called *bumping.*

bitu'men. A fat unctuous matter dug out of the earth, or scummed off lakes, as the asphaltis in Judaea, of various kinds; some so hard as to be used for coals; others so glutinous as to serve for mortar. Savary.

to blab. (1) To tell what ought to be kept secret; it usually implies rather thoughtlessness than treachery; but may be used in either sense.

to bla′bber. To whistle to a horse.

black-guard. A cant word amongst the vulgar; by which is implied a dirty fellow; of the meanest kind.

blade. (2) A brisk man, either fierce or gay, called so in contempt. So we say *mettle* for *courage.*

> Then turning about to the hangman, he said,
> Dispatch me, I pri′thee, this troublesome *blade.* Prior.

to blanch. To evade; to shift; to speak soft.

blank. (3) A paper from which the writing is effaced.

> She has left him
> The *blank* of what he was;
> I tell thee, eunuch, she has quite unmann′d him. Dryden.

(6) Aim; shot.

bla′tant. Bellowing as a calf.

to bleed. (2) To die a violent death.

> The lamb thy riot dooms to *bleed* today;
> Had he thy reason, would he skip and play? Pope.

to blench. To hinder; to obstruct.

to blend. (2) To confound.

(3) To pollute; to spoil; to corrupt. This signification was anciently much in use, but is now wholly obsolete.

to bless. (4) It seems, in one place of Spenser, to signify the same as *to wave; to brandish; to flourish.*

bli′ndworm. A small viper, the least of our English serpents, but venemous.

to blink. (2) To see obscurely.

> What′s here! The portrait of a *blinking* idiot.
> Shakespeare, *Merchant of Venice.*

bli′nkard. (2) Something twinkling.

to bli′ssom. To caterwaul; to be lustful.

to bloat. To swell, or make turgid with wind.

> The strutting petticoat smooths all distinctions, levels the mother with the daughter. I cannot but be troubled to see so many well-shaped innocent virgins *bloated* up, and waddling up and down like bigbellied women. Addison, *Spectator.*

blo′blipped, blo′bberlipped. Having swelled or thick lips.

blo′ckhead. A stupid fellow; a dolt; a man without parts.

> A *blockhead* rubs his thoughtless skull,
> And thanks his stars he was not born a fool. Pope.

blood. (1) The red liquour that circulates in the bodies of animals.

(9) *For blood.* Though his blood or life was at stake: a low phrase.

to blood. (4) To heat; to exasperate.

blood-boltered. Blood-sprinkled.

blo′odsucker. (2) A cruel man; a murderer.

> The nobility cried out upon him, that he was a *bloodsucker*, a murderer, and a parricide. Hayward.

blore. Act of blowing; blast.

to blote. To smoke, or dry by the smoke; as *bloted* herrings, or red herrings.

blow. (4) The act of a fly, by which she lodges eggs in flesh.

> I much fear, lest with the *blows* of flies,
> His brass inflicted wounds are fill'd. Chapman's *Iliads*.

to blow. (12) *To blow upon.* To make stale.

> He will whisper an intrigue that is not yet *blown upon* by common fame. Addison, *Spectator*, No. 105.

blowze. A ruddy fat-faced wench.

blo′wzy. Sun burnt; high coloured.

bluff. Big; surly; blustering.

blush. (3) Sudden appearance; a signification that seems barbarous, yet used by good writers.

> All purely identical propositions, obviously and at first *blush*, appear to contain no certain instruction in them. Locke.

bo. A word of terrour; from *Bo,* an old northern captain, of such fame, that his name was used to terrify the enemy. Temple.

board. (1) A piece of wood of more length and breadth than thickness.

boa′tion. Roar; noise; loud sound.

to bob. (2) To beat; to drub; to bang.

> Those bastard Britons, whom our fathers
> Have in their own land beaten, *bobb'd,* and thump'd.
> Shakespeare, *Richard III*.

(3) To cheat; to gain by fraud.

> Here we have been worrying one another, who should have the booty, till this cursed fox has *bobbed* us both on't. L'Estrange.

bo'casine. A sort of linen cloth; a fine buckram.

to bodge. (A word in Shakespeare, which is perhaps corrupted from *boggle*.) To boggle; to stop; to fail.

bo'dice. Stays; a waistcoat quilted with whalebone, worn by women.

bog-trotter. One that lives in a boggy country.

bohe'a. (An Indian word.) A species of tea, of higher colour, and more astringent taste, than green tea.

bo'ldface. Impudence; sauciness; a term of reproach and reprehension.

> How now, *boldface!* cries an old trot; sirrah, we eat our own hens, I'd have you to know; and what you eat, you steal. L'Estrange.

bole. (2) A kind of earth.

> *Bole Armeniack* is an astringent earth, which takes its name from Armenia, the country from which we have it. Woodward.

to bo'lster. (4) To support; to hold up; to maintain. This is now an expression somewhat coarse and obsolete.

> It was the way of many to *bolster* up their crazy, doating consciences with confidences. South.

bo'mbast. (This word seems to be derived from Bombastius, one of the names of Paracelsus; a man remarkable for sounding professions, and unintelligible language.) Fustian; big words, without meaning.

bombila'tion. Sound; noise; report.

bomby'cinous. Silken; made of silk.

bona roba. A whore.

bone. (3) *To be upon the bones.* To attack.

> Puss had a month's mind *to be upon the bones* of him, but was not willing to pick a quarrel. L'Estrange.

(4) *To make no bones.* To make no scruple; a metaphor taken from a dog, who readily swallows meat that has no bones.

bo'ngrace. A forehead-cloth, or covering for the forehead. Skinner.

bo'nny. (2) Gay; merry; frolicksome; cheerful; blithe.

(3) It seems to be generally used in conversation for *plump*.

bo'oby. (A word of no certain etymology; Henshaw thinks it a corruption of *bull-beef* ridiculously; Skinner imagines it to be derived from *bobo,* foolish, Span. Junius finds *bowbard* to be an old Scottish word for a *coward,* a *contemptible fellow;* from which he naturally deduces *booby;* but the original of *bowbard* is not known.) A dull, heavy, stupid fellow; a lubber.

> Young master next must rise to fill him wine,
> And starve himself to see the *booby* dine. King.

bo'okful. Full of notions gleaned from books; crouded with un-digested knowledge.

> The *bookful* blockhead, ignorantly read,
> With loads of learned lumber in his head,
> With his own tongue still edifies his ears,
> And always list'ning to himself appears. Pope's *Essay on Criticism.*

bo'okish. Given to books; acquainted only with books. It is generally used contemptuously.

bookle'arned. Versed in books, or literature: a term implying some slight contempt.

boose. A stall for a cow or an ox.

bope'ep. To look out, and draw back as if frighted, or with the purpose to fright some other.

bora'chio. A drunkard.

> How you stink of wine! D'ye think my niece will ever endure such a *borachio!* you're an absolute *borachio.* Congreve's *Way of the World.*

bo'rough. (1) It signified anciently a surety, or a man bound for others.

bo'rrel. A mean fellow.

botch. (3) An adscititious, adventitious part clumsily added.

> If both those words are not notorious *botches,* I am much deceived; though the French translator thinks otherways. Dryden's Dedication, *Aeneid.*

bo′tcher. A mender of old cloaths; the same to a taylor as a cobler to a shoemaker.

bo′ttom. (10) A chance; an adventure; or security.

> We are embarked with them on the same *bottom,* and must be partakers of their happiness or misery.
> *Spectator,* No. 273.

to bo′ttom. (2) To wind upon something; to twist thread round something.

bought. (1) A twist; a link; a knot.

to bounce. (3) To boast; to bully: a sense used only in familiar speech.

bounce. (2) A sudden crack or noise.

> Two hazel-nuts I threw into the flame,
> And to each nut I gave a sweetheart's name;
> This with the loudest *bounce* me sore amaz'd,
> That in a flame of brightest colour blaz'd. Gay.

to bouse. To drink lavishly; to tope.

bo′usy. Drunken.

bo′utefeu. An incendiary; one who kindles feuds and discontents.

bo′utisale. (I suppose from *bouty,* or *booty,* and *sale.*) A sale at a cheap rate; as booty or plunder is commonly sold.

to bo′wssen. (Probably of the same original with *bouse,* but found in no other passage.) To drench; to soak.

> The water fell into a close walled plot; upon this wall was the frantick person set, and from thence tumbled headlong into the pond; where a strong fellow tossed him up and down, until the patient, by foregoing his strength, had somewhat forgot his fury: but if there appeared small amendment, he was *bowssened* again and again, while there remained in him any hope of life, for recovery. Carew's *Survey of Cornwal.*

to boy. To act apishly, or like a boy.

> Anthony
> Shall be brought drunken forth, and I shall see
> Some squeaking Cleopatra *boy* my greatness,
> I' th' posture of a whore. Shakespeare, *Antony and Cleopatra.*

bra′bble. A clamorous contest; a squabble; a broil.

brad. A sort of nail to floor rooms with. They are about the size of a tenpenny nail, but have not their heads made with a shoulder over their shank, as other nails, but are made pretty thick towards the upper end, that the very top may be driven into, and buried in the board they nail down; so that the tops of these *brads* will not catch the thrums of the mops, when the floor is washing. Moxon's *Mechanical Exercises*.

bra′gly. Finely; so as it may be bragged.

braid. An old word, which seems to signify *deceitful*.

> Since Frenchmen are so *braid*,
> Marry 'em that will. I'll live and die a maid.
> Shakespeare, *All's well that ends well.*

brait. A term used by jewellers for a rough diamond.

bra′nchless. (2) Without any valuable product; naked.

bra′ngle. Squabble; wrangle.

brast. Burst; broken.

bra′vo. A man who murders for hire.

> No *bravoes* here profess the bloody trade,
> Nor is the church the murd′rer's refuge made.
> Gay's *Trivia.*

to brawl. (1) To quarrel noisily and indecently.

> In council she gives licence to her tongue
> Loquacious, *brawling*, ever in the wrong.
> Dryden's *Fables.*

to bray. To pound; or grind small.

to braze. (2) To harden to impudence.

> I have so often blushed to acknowledge him, that now
> I am *brazed* to it. Shakespeare, *King Lear.*

bread-chipper. One that chips bread; a baker's servant.

breadth. The measure of any plain superficies from side to side.

to break. (30) *To break a jest*. To utter a jest unexpected.

(38) *To break wind*. To give vent to wind in the body.

break. (3) A line drawn, noting that the sense is suspended.

bre′akpromise. One that makes a practice of breaking his promise.

bre′akvow. He that practices the breach of vows.

breast. (2) The dugs or teats of women which contain the milk.

breath. (1) The air drawn in and ejected out of the body by living animals.

breech. (1) The lower part of the body; the back part.

> When the king's pardon was offered by a herauld, a lewd boy turned towards him his naked *breech,* and used words suitable to that gesture. Hayward.

bre'eches. (2) To wear the *breeches,* is, to usurp the authority of the husband.

bre'edbate. One that breeds quarrels; an incendiary.

bre'eder. (3) A female that is prolifick.

> Get thee to a nunnery; why wouldst thou be a *breeder* of sinners? Shakespeare, *Hamlet.*

breese. A stinging fly; the gadfly.

breme. Cruel; sharp; severe.

bre'viary. (1) An abridgment; an epitome; a compendium.

> Cresconius, an African bishop, has given us an abridgment, or *breviary* thereof. Ayliffe's *Parergon.*

bre'wage. Mixture of various things.

> Go, brew me a pottle of sack finely.
> —With eggs, Sir?—
> —Simple of itself: I'll no pullet-sperm in my *brewage.*
> Shakespeare, *Merry Wives of Windsor.*

bre'wis. A piece of bread soaked in boiling fat pottage, made of salted meat.

to bribe. To gain by bribes; to give bribes, rewards, or hire, to bad purposes. It is seldom, and not properly, used in a good sense.

bri'destake. It seems to be a post set in the ground, to dance round, like a maypole.

bright. (4) Witty; acute; subtle; as a *bright* genius.

bri'nded. Streaked; tabby; marked with branches.

> Thrice the *brinded* cat hath mew'd.
> Shakespeare, *Macbeth.*

brit. The name of a fish.

brize. The gadfly.

to bro'aden. To grow broad. I know not whether this word occurs, but in the following passage.

> Low walks the sun, and *broadens* by degrees,
> Just o'er the verge of day. Thomson's *Summer*, l. 1605.

bro'cage. (1) The gain gotten by promoting bargains.

(2) The hire given for any unlawful office.

(3) The trade of dealing in old things.

brock. A badger.

brogue. (2) A cant word for a corrupt dialect, or manner of pronunciation.

bro'ken meat. Fragments; meat that has been cut.

bro'ker. (2) One who deals in old houshold goods.

(3) A pimp; a match-maker.

bro'wsick. Dejected; hanging the head.

bro'wnbill. The ancient weapon of the English foot; why it is called *brown*, I have not discovered; but we now say *brown musket* from it.

bru'mal. Belonging to the winter.

bru'shwood. (From *brush* and *wood*. I know not whether it may not be corrupted from *browsewood*.) Rough, low, close, shrubby thickets; small wood fit for fire.

to bru'tify. To make a man a brute.

> O thou salacious woman! am I then *brutified?* Ay; feel it here; I sprout, I bud, I blossom, I am ripe horn mad. Congreve's *Old Batchelor*.

bub. (A cant word.) Strong malt liquour.

bu'bble. (1) A small bladder of water; a film of water filled with wind.

to bu'bble. To cheat: a cant word.

> He tells me, with great passion, that she has *bubbled* him out of his youth; and that she has drilled him on to five and fifty. Addison, *Spectator*, No. 89.

bu'bby. A woman's breast.

> Foh! say they, to see a handsome, brisk, genteel, young fellow, so much governed by a doating old woman; why don't you go and suck the *bubby?* Arbuthnot's *John Bull*.

bucani'ers. A cant word for the privateers, or pirates, of America.

buck. (1) The liquour in which cloaths are washed.

[107]

to buck. To wash clothes.

> Here is a basket; he may creep in here, and throw foul
> linen upon him, as if it were going to *bucking*.
> Shakespeare.

bu'ckle. (2) The state of the hair crisped and curled, by being
kept long in the same state.

to budge. To stir; to move off the place: a low word.

budge. Surly; stiff; formal.

> O foolishness of men! that lend their ears
> To those *budge* doctors of the stoicks. Milton

bu'dget. (1) A bag, such as may be easily carried.

buff. (1) A sort of leather prepared from the skin of the buffalo;
used for waist belts, pouches, &c.

bu'ffalo. A kind of wild ox.

bu'ffleheaded. A man with a large head, like a buffalo; dull;
stupid; foolish.

bug. A stinking insect bred in old household stuff. In the following passage, wings are erroneously ascribed to it.

> Yet let me flap this *bug* with gilded wings,
> This painted child of dirt, which stinks and stings. Pope.

bug, bu'gbear. A frightful object; a walking spectre, imagined
to be seen; generally now used for a false terrour to frighten
babes.

bu'gle. A sort of wild ox. Phillips's *World of Words.*

to bulge. (1) To take in water; to founder.

bull. (1) The male of black cattle; the male to a cow.

bull-beggar. (This word probably came from the insolence of
those who begged, or raised money by the pope's bull.)
Something terrible; something to fright children with.

bull-dog. A dog of a particular form, remarkable for his courage. He is used in baiting the bull; and this species is so
peculiar to Britain, that they are said to degenerate when
they are carried to other countries.

bulli'tion. The act or state of boiling.

bu'lly. (Skinner derives this word from *burly*, as a corruption
in the pronunciation; which is very probably right: or from

---

bug. In Great Britain, *bug* regularly means bedbug.

bulky, or *bull-eyed;* which are less probable. May it not come from *bull,* the pope's letter, implying the insolence of those who came invested with authority from the papal court?) A noisy, blustering, quarrelling fellow: it is generally taken for a man that has only the appearance of courage.

> A scolding hero is, at the worst, a more tolerable character than a *bully* in petticoats. Addison's *Freeholder,* No. 38.

bum. (1) The buttocks; the part on which we sit.

bumba'iliff. A bailiff of the meanest kind; one that is employed in arrests.

bu'mbast. (Falsely written for *bombast;* the etymology of which I am now very doubtful of; *bombast* and *bombasine* being mentioned, with great probability, by Junius, as coming from *boom,* a tree, and *sein,* silk; the silk or cotton of a tree.) (1) A cloth made by sewing one stuff upon another; patchwork.

to bump. To make a loud noise, or bomb. It is applied, I think, only to the bittern.

> Then to the water's brink she laid her head,
>
> And as a bittour *bumps* within a reed,
>
> To thee alone, O lake, she said— Dryden.

bu'mpkin. (This word is of uncertain etymology; Henshaw derives it from *pumpkin,* a kind of worthless gourd, or melon. This seems harsh. *Bump* is used amongst us for a knob, or lump; may not *bumpkin* be much the same with *clodpate, loggerhead, block,* and *blockhead.*) An awkward heavy rustick; a country lout.

bunchba'cked. Having bunches on the back.

bu'nter. A cant word for a woman who picks up rags about the street; and used, by way of contempt, for any low vulgar woman.

bu'rbot. A fish full of prickles.

bu'rden. (3) A birth: now obsolete.

bu'rdenous. (2) Useless.

to bu'rnish. To grow; to spread out.

bu'rnisher. (2) The tool with which bookbinders give a gloss to the leaves of books; it is commonly a dog's tooth set in a stick.

bu′rrock. A small wear or dam, where wheels are laid in a river for catching of fish. Phillips's *World of Words.*

burt. A flat fish of the turbot kind.

bush. (2) A bough of a tree fixed up at a door, to shew that liquours are sold there.

bu′siless. At leisure; without business; unemployed.

busk. A piece of steel or whalebone, worn by women to strengthen their stays.

but. (13) That. This seems no proper sense in this place.

> It is not therefore impossible, *but* I may alter the complexion of my play, to restore myself into the good graces of my fair criticks. Dryden's *Aurengzebe,* Preface.

bu′tter. (1) An unctuous substance made by agitating the cream of milk, till the oil separates from the whey.

bu′tterfly. A beautiful insect, so named because it first appears at the beginning of the season for butter.

bu′ttertooth. The great broad foreteeth.

bu′ttock. The rump; the part near the tail.

bu′tton. The sea urchin, which is a kind of crabfish that has prickles instead of feet. Ainsworth.

bu′xom. (1) Obedient; obsequious.

> He did tread down, and disgrace all the English; and set up and countenance the Irish; thinking thereby to make them more tractable and *buxom* to his government. Spenser's *Ireland.*

(3) Wanton; jolly.

bu′zzard. (1) A degenerate or mean species of hawk.

by-name. A nickname; name of reproach, or accidental appellation.

C

to ca**′**bbage. (A cant word among taylors.) To steal in cutting clothes.

> Your taylor, instead of shreads, *cabbages* whole yards of cloth. Arbuthnot's *History of John Bull.*

cade. Tame; soft; delicate; as a *cade* lamb, a lamb bred at home.

to cade. To breed up in softness.

ca**′**dger. A huckster; one who brings butter, eggs, and poultry, from the country to market.

ca**′**itiff. (*Cattivo*, Ital. a slave; whence it came to signify a bad man, with some implication of meanness; as *knave* in English, and *fur* in Latin; so certainly does slavery destroy virtue. . . . A slave and a scoundrel are signified by the same words in many languages.) A mean villain; a despicable knave.

to cajo**′**le. To flatter; to sooth; to coax: a low word.

ca**′**lenture. A distemper peculiar to sailors, in hot climates; wherein they imagine the sea to be green fields, and will throw themselves into it, if not restrained. Quincy.

ca**′**lid. Hot; burning; fervent.

caliga**′**tion. Darkness; cloudiness.

ca**′**llat, ca**′**llet. A trull.

> He call'd her whore; a beggar, in his drink,
> Could not have laid such terms upon his *callet.*
> Shakespeare.

ca**′**llipers. (Of this word I know not the etymology, nor does any thing more probable occur, than that, perhaps, the word is corrupted from *clippers,* instruments with which any thing is *clipped,* inclosed or embraced.) Compasses with bowed shanks.

ca′llow. Unfledged; naked; without feathers.

ca′mel. An animal very common in Arabia, Judea, and the neighbouring countries. One sort is large, and full of flesh, and fit to carry burdens of a thousand pounds weight, having one bunch upon its back. Another have two bunches upon their backs, like a natural saddle, and are fit either for burdens, or men to ride on. A third kind is leaner, and of a smaller size, called dromedaries, because of their swiftness; which are generally used for riding by men of quality.

came′lopard. An Abyssinian animal, taller than an elephant, but not so thick. He is so named, because he has a neck and head like a camel; he is spotted like a pard, but his spots are white upon a red ground. The Italians call him *giaraffa.* Trevoux.

ca′merade. One that lodges in the same chamber; a bosom companion. By corruption we now use *comrade.*

camo′ys. Flat; level; depressed. It is only used of the nose.

> Many Spaniards, of the race of Barbary Moors, though after frequent commixture, have not worn out the *camoys* nose unto this day. Browne's *Vulgar Errours,* b. vi, c. 10.

camp-fight. An old word for *combat.*

to cana′ry. A cant word, which seems to signify to frolick.

cana′ry bird. An excellent singing bird, of a green colour, formerly bred in the Canaries, and nowhere else, but now bred in several parts of Europe, particularly Germany.

candlewa′ster. That which consumes candles; a spendthrift.

to ca′ndy. (2) To form into congelations.

> Will the cold brook,
>
> *Candied* with ice, cawdle thy morning toast,
>
> To cure thy o'er-night's surfeit? Shakespeare, *Timon.*

cani′ne. (2) *Canine* hunger, in medicine, is an appetite which cannot be satisfied.

ca′nkerbit. Bitten with an envenomed tooth.

cant. (1) A corrupt dialect used by beggars and vagabonds.
(2) A particular form of speaking peculiar to some certain
class or body of men.

> I write not always in the proper terms of navigation,
> land service, or in the *cant* of any profession. Dryden.

(3) A whining pretension to goodness, in formal and affected terms.

(4) Barbarous jargon.

(5) Auction.

ca'nter. A term of reproach for hypocrites, who talk formally
of religion, without obeying it.

ca'perer. A dancer; in contempt.

to cark. To be careful; to be solicitous; to be anxious. It is now
very little used, and always in an ill sense.

ca'rpet. (4) *Carpet* is used, proverbially, for a state of ease and
luxury; as, a *carpet* knight, a knight that has never known
the field, and has recommended himself only at table.

(5) To be on the *carpet*, is the subject of consideration; an
affair in hand.

ca'rrion. (2) A name of reproach for a worthless woman.

> Shall we send that foolish *carrion*, Mrs. Quickly, to him,
> and excuse his throwing into the water. Shakespeare,
> *Merry Wives of Windsor.*

to ca'rry. (1) A hare is said, by hunters, to *carry*, when she runs
on rotten ground, or on frost, and it sticks to her feet.

to cart. To expose in a cart by way of punishment.

> No woman led a better life:
> She to intrigues was e'en hard-hearted;
> She chuckl'd when a bawd was *carted;*
> And thought the nation ne'er would thrive,
> Till all the whores were burnt alive. Prior.

case. (4) In ludicrous language, condition with regard to leanness, or health.

> For if the sire be faint, or out of *case*,
> He will be copy'd in his famish'd race. Dryden's *Virgil.*

ca'ssiowary. A large bird of prey in the East Indies.

to cast. (12) To condemn in a trial.

(44) *To cast up.* To vomit.

Thy foolish errour find;

Cast up the poison that infects thy mind. Dryden.

castiga'tion. (3) Emendation.

Their *castigations* were accompanied with encouragements; which care was taken, to keep me from looking upon as mere compliments. Boyle's *Seraphick Love.*

castle soap. (I suppose corrupted from *Castile soap.*) A kind of soap.

ca'stling. An abortive.

Ca'stor and Pollux. A firy meteor, which, at sea, appears sometimes sticking to a part of the ship, in form of one, two, or even three or four balls. When one is seen alone, it is more properly called Helena, which portends the severest part of the storm to be yet behind; two are denominated *Castor* and *Pollux,* and sometimes Tyndarides, which portend a cessation of the storm. Chambers.

to ca'strate. (2) To take away the obscene parts of a writing.

cat. A domestick animal that catches mice, commonly reckoned by naturalists the lowest order of the leonine species.

cat in the pan. (Imagined by some to be rightly written *catipan,* as coming from *catipani,* revolted governours. An unknown correspondent imagines, very naturally, that it is corrupted from *Cate in the pan.*)

There is a cunning which we, in England, call the turning of the *cat in the pan;* which is, when that which a man says to another, he lays it as if another had said it to him. Bacon.

catamo'untain. A fierce animal, resembling a cat.

cata'strophe. (1) The change or revolution, which produces the conclusion or final event of a dramatick piece.

ca'tcal. A squeaking instrument, used in the playhouse to condemn plays.

ca'ter-cousin. A corruption of *quatre-cousin,* from the ridiculousness of calling cousin or relation to so remote a degree.

caterpi'llar. A worm which, when it gets wings, is sustained by leaves and fruits.

cates. Viands; food; dish of meat; generally employed to signify nice and luxurious food.

With costly *cates* she stain'd her frugal board,
Then with ill-gotten wealth she bought a lord.
Arbuthnot.

ca′tling. (1) A dismembring knife, used by surgeons.

(2) It seems to be used by Shakespeare for catgut; the materials of fiddle strings.

(3) The down or moss growing about walnut trees, resembling the hair of a cat. Harris.

ca′tsup. A kind of pickle, made from mushrooms.

ca′udle. A mixture of wine and other ingredients, given to women in childbed, and sick persons.

cauf. A chest with holes on the top, to keep fish alive in the water. Phillips's *World of Words*.

caul. (1) The net in which women inclose their hair; the hinder part of a woman's cap.

(3) The omentum; the integument in which the guts are inclosed.

ca′utelous. (1) Cautious; wary; provident.

(2) Wily; cunning; treacherous.

cell. (5) Little bags or bladders, where fluids, or matter of different sorts are lodged; common both to animals and plants. Quincy.

ce′nto. A composition formed by joining scrapes from other authours.

If any man think the poem a *cento*, our poet will but have done the same in jest which Boileau did in earnest. Advertisement to Pope's *Dunciad*.

cera′stes. A serpent having horns, or supposed to have them.

cess. (1) A levy made upon the inhabitants of a place, rated according to their property.

cha′fer. An insect; a sort of yellow beetle.

cha′ffinch. A bird so called, because it delights in chaff, and is by some much admired for its song. Phillips's *World of Words*.

chagri′n. Ill humour; vexation; fretfulness; peevishness. It is pronounced *shagreen*.

cha′inpump. A pump used in large English vessels, which is double, so that one rises as the other falls. It yields a great quantity of water, works easily, and is easily mended, but takes up a great deal of room, and makes a disagreeable noise. Chambers.

chama'de. The beat of the drum which declares a surrender.

to cha'mber. (1) To be wanton; to intrigue.

chame'leon. The chameleon has four feet, and on each foot three claws. Its tail is long; with this, as well as with its feet, it fastens itself to the branches of trees. Its tail is flat, its nose long, and made in an obtuse point; its back is sharp, its skin plaited, and jagged like a saw from the neck to the last joint of the tail, and upon its head it has something like a comb; like a fish, it has no neck. Some have asserted, that it lives only upon air; but it has been observed to feed on flies, catched with its tongue, which is about ten inches long, and three thick; made of white flesh, round, but flat at the end; or hollow and open, resembling an elephant's trunk. It also shrinks, and grows longer. This animal is said to assume the colour of those things to which it is applied; but our modern observers assure us, that its natural colour, when at rest and in the shade, is a bluish grey; though some are yellow, and others green, but both of a smaller kind. When it is exposed to the sun, the grey changes into a darker grey, inclining to a dun colour, and its parts, which have least of the light upon them, are changed into spots of different colours. . . . Calmet.

cha'mois. An animal of the goat kind, whose skin is made into soft leather, called among us *shammy*.

cha'ngeling. (2) An ideot; a fool; a natural.

to chap. To break into *hiatus*, or gapings.

> Then would unbalanc'd heat licentious reign,
> Crack the dry hill, and *chap* the russet plain. Blackmore.

cha'peron. A kind of hood or cap worn by the knights of the garter in their habits.

cha'pman. A cheapner; one that offers as a purchaser.

> Their *chapmen* they betray,
> Their shops are dens, the buyer is their prey. Dryden.

chaps. (2) It is used in contempt for the mouth of a man.

char. Work done by the day; a single job or task.

to cha'tter. (1) To make a noise as a pie, or other unharmonious bird.

> There was a crow sat *chattering* upon the back of a sheep; Well, sirrah, says the sheep, you durst not have done this to a dog. L'Estrange.

cha'wdron. Entrails.

to che'apen. (1) To attempt to purchase; to bid for any thing; to ask the price of any commodity.

> To shops in crouds the daggled females fly,
> Pretend to *cheapen* goods, but nothing buy. Swift.

che'ektooth. The hinder tooth or tusk.

chica'ne. (1) The art of protracting a contest by petty objection and artifice.

> His attornies have hardly one trick left; they are at an end of all their *chicane*. Arbuthnot's *History of John Bull.*

chi'cken. (3) A term for a young girl.

> Then, Chloe, still go on to prate
> Of thirty-six and thirty-eight;
> Pursue your trade of scandal-picking,
> Your hints, that Stella is no *chicken*. Swift.

chi'mneysweeper. (2) It is used proverbially for one of a mean and vile occupation.

> Golden lads and girls, all must
> As *chimneysweepers,* come to dust. Shakespeare, *Cymbeline.*

chiro'grapher. He that exercises or professes the act or business of writing.

chiro'graphist. This word is used in the following passage, I think improperly, for one that tells fortunes, by examining the hand: the true word is *chirosophist*, or *chiromancer*.

> Let the phisiognomists examine his features; let the *chirographists* behold his palm; but, above all, let us consult for the calculation of his nativity. Arbuthnot and Pope's *Martinus Scriblerus.*

chiru'rgeon. One that cures ailments, not by internal medicines, but outward applications. It is now generally pronounced, and by many written, *surgeon*.

chit. (1) A child; a baby. Generally used of young persons in contempt.

chi'tchat. Prattle; idle prate; idle talk. A word only used in ludicrous conversation.

> I am a member of a female society, who call ourselves the *chitchat* club. *Spectator*, No. 560.

chi'tterlings. The guts; the bowels. Skinner.

chi'valry. (4) An adventure; an exploit.

chi'ves. (1) The threads or filaments rising in flowers, with seeds at the end.

chloro'sis. The green-sickness.

choke. The filamentous or capillary part of an artichoke. A cant word.

choke-pear. (2) Any aspersion or sarcasm, by which another is put to silence. A low term.

> Pardon me for going so low as to talk of giving *choke-pears. Clarissa.*

a cho'ker. (3) Any thing that cannot be answered.

to chop. (3) To bandy; to altercate; to return one thing or word for another.

> You'll never leave off your *chopping* of logick, 'till your skin is turned over your ears for prating. L'Estrange's *Fables*.

chop-house. A mean house of entertainment, where provision ready dressed is sold.

> I lost my place at the *chop-house,* where every man eats in publick a mess of broth, or chop of meat, in silence. *Spectator.*

cho'pping. An epithet frequently applied to infants, by way of ludicrous commendation: imagined by Skinner to signify *lusty,* from *cas,* Sax. by others to mean a child that would bring money at a market. Perhaps a greedy, hungry child, likely to live.

> Both Jack Freeman and Ned Wild,
> Would own the fair and *chopping* child. Fenton.

choro'grapher. He that describes particular regions or countries.

chough. A bird which frequents the rocks by the sea side, like a jackdaw, but bigger. Hanmer.

to chouse. (1) To cheat; to trick; to impose upon.

a chouse. (1) A bubble; a tool; a man fit to be cheated.

> A sottish *chouse,*
> Who, when a thief has robb'd his house,
> Applies himself to cunning men. *Hudibras,* part iii,
> cant. 3.

(2) A trick or sham.

to cho'wter. To grumble or mutter like a froward child. Phillips.

chro'nogram. An inscription including the date of any action. Of this kind the following is an example:

> Gloria lausque *D*eo, sae*CL*or*VM* in saec*V*la sunt.

to chu'ckle. (2) To cocker; to fondle.

> Your confessor, that parcel of holy guts and garbidge; he must *chuckle* you, and moan you. Dryden's *Spanish Fryar.*

chuff. A coarse, fat-headed, blunt clown.

> Hang ye, gorbellied knaves, are you undone? No, ye fat *chuffs,* I would your store were here. Shakespeare, *Henry IV.*

church-ale. A wake, or feast, commemoratory of the dedication of the church.

chu'rlish. (1) Rude; brutal; harsh; austere; sour; merciless; unkind; uncivil.

> A lion in love with a lass, desired her father's consent. The answer was *churlish* enough, He'd never marry his daughter to a brute. L'Estrange's *Fables.*

(2) Selfish; avaritious.

> This sullen *churlish* thief,
> Had all his mind plac'd upon Mully's beef. King's *Mully of Mountown.*

churme. A confused sound; a noise.

chyle. The white juice formed in the stomach by digestion of the aliment, and afterwards changed into blood.

to ci'curate. To tame; to reclaim from wildness; to make tame and tractable.

ci'derkin. A low word used for the liquor made of the murk or gross matter of apples, after the cider is pressed out, and a convenient quantity of boiled water added to it; the whole infusing for about forty-eight hours. Phillips's *World of Words.*

ci'meter. A sort of sword used by the Turks; short; heavy; and recurvated, or bent backward. This word is sometimes erroneously spelt *scimitar,* and *scymeter.*

ci'rcular. (3) Vulgar; mean; circumforaneous.

circumfora'neous. Wandering from house to house. As a *circumforaneous* fidler; one that plays at doors.

to circumve'nt. To deceive; to cheat; to impose upon; to delude.

cit. An inhabitant of a city, in an ill sense. A pert low townsman; a pragmatical trader.

cite'ss. A city woman. A word peculiar to Dryden.

> Cits and *citesses* raise a joyful strain;
> 'Tis a good omen to begin a reign. Dryden, *Albion and Alba.*

clack. (1) Any thing that makes a lasting and importunate noise; generally used, in contempt, for the tongue.

to clamm. To clog with any glutinous matter.

> A swarm of wasps got into a honey-pot, and there they cloyed and *clammed* themselves, 'till there was no getting out again. L'Estrange, *Fables,* cxxvi.

cla'ncular. Clandestine; secret; private; concealed; obscure; hidden.

to clap. (5) To infect with a venereal poison.

> If the patient hath been formerly *clapt,* it will be the more difficult to cure him the second time, and worse the third. Wiseman's *Surgery.*

to clappercla'w. To tongue-beat; to scold.

to cla'tter. (2) To dispute, jar, or clamour. Martin. A low word.

to claw. (6) To claw off, or away. To scold; to rail at.

cla'wback. A flatterer; a sycophant; a wheedler. The pope's *clawbacks.* Jewel.

clees. The two parts of the foot of beasts which are cloven-footed. Skinner. It is a country word, and probably corrupted from *claws.*

cle'ver. (3) Well-shaped; handsome.

She called him gundy-guts, and he called her lousy Peg,
tho' the girl was a tight *clever* wench as any was.
Arbuthnot.

(4) This is a low word, scarcely ever used but in burlesque
or conversation; and applied to any thing a man likes, without a settled meaning.

cli'cker. A low word for the servant of a salesman, who stands
at the door to invite customers.

cliente'le. The condition or office of a client. A word scarcely
used.

cli'mate. (1) A space upon the surface of the earth, measured
from the equator to the polar circles; in each of which
spaces the longest day is half an hour longer than in that
nearer to the equator. From the polar circles to the poles
climates are measured by the increase of a month.

(2) In the common and popular sense, a region, or tract of
land, differing from another by the temperature of the air.

cli'max. Gradation; ascent: a figure in rhetorick, by which the
sentence rises gradually; as Cicero says to Catiline, Thou
do'st nothing, movest nothing, thinkest nothing; but I hear
it, I see it, and perfectly understand it.

clinch. (1) A word used in a double meaning; a pun; an
ambiguity; a duplicity of meaning, with an identity of expression.

to cling. (2) To dry up; to consume; to waste; to pine away.

to clip. (1) To embrace, by throwing the arms round; to hug;
to enfold in the arms.

Here I *clip*

The anvil of my sword, and do contest

Hotly, and nobly, with thy love. Shakespeare, *Corio-
lanus*.

clo'akbag. A portmanteau; a bag in which cloaths are carried.

Why do'st thou converse with that trunk of humours,
that stuffed *cloakbag* of guts. Shakespeare, *Henry IV*,
p. i.

clo'dpate. A stupid fellow; a dolt; a thickscull.

close. (5) Viscous; glutinous; not volatile.

This oil, which nourishes the lamp, is supposed of so

close and tenacious a substance, that it may slowly evaporate. Wilkins.

close-bodied. Made to fit the body exactly.

> If any clergy shall appear in any *close-bodied* coat, they shall be suspended. Ayliffe's *Parergon*.

to cloy. (2) It seems to have, in the following passage, another sense: perhaps to strike the beak together.

> His royal bird
> Prunes the immortal wing, and *cloys* his beak,
> As when his god is pleas'd. Shakespeare, *Cymbeline*.

clung. Wasted with leanness; shrunk up with cold.

clu'ster. (3) A body of people collected: used in contempt.

a clu'tter. A noise; a bustle; a busy tumult; a hurry; a clamour. A low word.

to coagme'nt. To congregate or heap together. I have only found the participle in use.

> Had the world been *coagmented* from that supposed fortuitous jumble, this hypothesis had been tolerable. Glanvill, *Scepsis Scientifica*, c. 20.

to coa'rct. (1) To straighten; to confine into a narrow compass. (2) To contract power.

to coax. To wheedle; to flatter; to humour. A low word.

> I *coax!* I wheedle! I'm above it. Farquhar's *Recruiting Officer*.

cock. (12) The style or gnomon of a dial. Chambers.

a co'ckatrice. A serpent supposed to rise from a cock's egg.

to co'cker. To cade; to fondle; to indulge.

co'ckle. A small testaceous fish.

co'ckney. (1) A native of London, by way of contempt.

> So the *cockney* did to the eels, when she put them i' th' pasty alive. Shakespeare, *King Lear*.

(2) Any effeminate, ignorant, low, mean, despicable citizen.

co'ckshut. The close of the evening, at which time poultry go to roost.

co'cksure. Confidently certain; without fear or diffidence. A word of contempt.

cod. Any case or husk in which seeds are lodged.

coeta′neous. (1) Of the same age with another. Sometimes with *to*.

co′ffin. (2) A mould of paste for a pye.

(3) A paper case, in form of a cone, used by grocers.

to cog. (1) To flatter; to wheedle; to sooth by adulatory speeches.

(2) To obtrude by falsehood.

Fustian tragedies, or insipid comedies, have, by concerted applauses, been *cogged* upon the town for masterpieces. Dennis.

co′istril. A coward cock; a runaway.

co′llege. (4) A college in foreign universities is a lecture read in publick.

to collo′gue. To wheedle; to flatter; to please with kind words. A low word.

co′llop. (3) In burlesque language, a child.

to co′lour. To blush. A low word, only used in conversation.

to colt. To frisk; to be licentious; to run at large without rule; to riot; to frolick.

co′lubrine. (1) Relating to a serpent.

(2) Cunning; crafty.

co′medy. A dramatick representation of the lighter faults of mankind.

co′mmoner. (6) A prostitute.

Behold this ring,
Whose high respect, and rich validity,
Did lack a parallel: yet, for all that,
He gave it to a *commoner* o' the camp. Shakespeare.

to commu′te. (1) To exchange; to put one thing in the place of another; to give or receive one thing for another.

(2) To buy off, or ransom one obligation by another.

Some *commute* swearing for whoring; as if forbearance of the one were a dispensation for the other. L'Estrange.

compa′nion. (3) A familiar term of contempt; a fellow.

I scorn you, scurvy *companion!* What? you poor, base, rascally, cheating, lack-linnen mate: away, you mouldy rogue, away. Shakespeare's *Henry IV*, p. ii.

co'mpany. (10) To keep company. To frequent houses of entertainment.

(11) sometimes in an ill sense.

> Why should he call her whore? Who *keeps* her *company?* Shakespeare's *Othello.*

co'mpliment. An act, or expression of civility, usually understood to include some hypocrisy, and to mean less than it declares.

to compri'nt. The word properly signifies to print together; but it is commonly taken, in law, for the deceitful printing of another's copy or book, to the prejudice of the rightful proprietor. Phillips's *World of Words.*

compu'nction. (1) The power of pricking; stimulation; irritation.

(2) The state of being pricked by the conscience; repentance; contrition.

con. A cant word for one who is on the negative side of a question; as the *pros* and *cons.*

to con. (2) To study; to commit to memory; to fix in the mind. It is a word now little in use, except in ludicrous language.

> Here are your parts; and I am to intreat you to *con* them by to-morrow night. Shakespeare, *Midsummer Night's Dream.*

to conce'it. To conceive; to imagine; to think; to believe.

> He *conceits* himself to be struck at, when he is not so much as thought of. L'Estrange.

conce'itless. Stupid; without thought; dull of apprehension.

conce'ption. (6) Conceit; sentiment; pointed thought.

> He is too flatulent sometimes, and sometimes too dry; many times unequal, and almost always forced; and, besides, is full of *conceptions,* points of epigram, and witticisms; all which are not only below the dignity of heroic verse, but contrary to its nature. Dryden's *Juvenal,* Dedication.

conclu'sion. (6) In Shakespeare it seems to signify silence; confinement of the thoughts.

> Your wife Octavia, with her modest eyes
> And still *conclusion,* shall acquire no honour,

Demuring upon me. Shakespeare's *Antony and Cleopatra*.

to conco′ct. (1) To digest by the stomach, so as to turn food to nutriment.

(2) To purify or sublime by heat; or heighten to perfection.

concu′ssion. The act of shaking; agitation; tremefaction.

to co′ndite. To pickle; to preserve by salts or aromaticks.

to condu′ce. To conduct; to accompany in order to shew the way. In this sense I have only found it in the following passage.

He was sent to *conduce* hither the princess Henrietta-Maria. Wotton.

to confe′r. (1) To compare; to examine by comparison with other things of the same kind.

Pliny *conferring* his authors, and comparing their works together, found those that went before transcribed by those that followed. Browne's *Vulgar Errours*, b. i, c. 6.

co′nfident. (5) Bold to a vice; elated with false opinion of his own excellencies; impudent.

confi′ner. (1) A borderer; one that lives upon confines; one that inhabits the extreme parts of a country.

(2) A near neighbour.

confla′tion. (1) The act of blowing many instruments together.

The sweetest and best harmony is, when every part or instrument is not heard by itself, but a *conflation* of them all. Bacon's *Natural History*, No. 225.

confo′unded. Hateful; detestable; enormous; odious: a low cant word.

Sir, I have heard another story,
He was a most *confounded* Tory;
And grew, or he is much bely'd,
Extremely dull before he dy'd. Swift.

to conjo′bble. To concert; to settle; to discuss. A low cant word.

What would a body think of a minister that should *conjobble* matters of state with tumblers, and confer politicks with tinkers? L'Estrange.

conni′vance. (1) The act of winking: not in use.

(2) Voluntary blindness; pretended ignorance; forbearance.

> It is better to mitigate usury by declaration, than to suffer it to rage by *connivance*. Bacon, *Essay 42.*

connoisse'ur. A judge; a critick: it is often used of a pretended critick.

co'nscript. A term used in speaking of the Roman senators, who were called *Patres conscripti*, from their names being written in the register of the senate.

co'nsectary. Consequent; consequential; following by consequence.

consecu'tion. (1) Train of consequences; chain of deductions; concatenation of propositions.

conse'nsion. Agreement; accord.

conse'nt. (3) Coherence with; relation to; correspondence.

> Demons found
> In fire, air, flood, or under ground,
> Whose power hath a true *consent*
> With planet or with element. Milton.

conse'rvative. Having the power of opposing diminution or injury.

conse'rve. (1) A sweetmeat made of the inspissated juices of fruit, boiled with sugar 'till they will harden and candy.

> The more cost they were at, and the more sweets they bestowed upon them, the more their *conserves* stunk. Dennis.

to consi'der. (5) To requite; to reward one for his trouble.

> Take away with thee the very services thou hast done, which, if I have not enough *considered*, to be more thankful to thee shall be my study. Shakespeare's *Winter's Tale.*

consi'stence, consi'stency. (5) A state of rest, in which things capable of growth or decrease continue for some time at a stand, without either; as the growth, *consistence*, and return of a tree. Chambers.

co'nsistory. (4) Place of residence.

conso'ciate. An accomplice; a confederate; a partner.

consopia'tion. The act of laying to sleep.

co'nsort. (2) An assembly; a divan; a consultation.

> In one *consort* there sat
> Cruel revenge, and rancorous despite,
> Disloyal treason, and heart-burning hate. *Fairy Queen*,
> b. ii.

(3) A number of instruments playing together; a symphony. This is probably a mistake for *concert*.

conspectu'ity. Sight; view; sense of seeing. This word is, I believe, peculiar to Shakespeare, and perhaps corrupt.

> What harm can your bisson *conspectuities* glean out of this character? Shakespeare's *Coriolanus*.

conspurca'tion. The act of defiling; defilement; pollution.

co'nstable. (2) To over-run the constable. To spend more than what a man knows himself to be worth: a low phrase.

to conste'llate. To join lustre; to shine with one general light.

to co'nstipate. (1) To croud together into a narrow room; to thicken; to condense.

> It may, by amassing, cooling, and *constipating* of waters, turn them into rain. Ray, *On the Creation*.

to constra'in. (4) To violate; to ravish.

> Her spotless chastity,
> Inhuman traitors, you *constrain'd* and forc'd.
> Shakespeare, *Titus Andronicus*.

to co'nstuprate. To violate; to debauch; to defile.

co'nsult. (3) A council; a number of persons assembled in deliberation.

> A *consult* of coquets below
> Was call'd, to rig him out a beau. Swift.

consumma'tion. (3) Death; end of life.

conta'gion. (1) The emission from body to body by which diseases are communicated.

> If we two be one, and thou play false,
> I do digest the poison of thy flesh,
> Being strumpeted by thy *contagion*. Shakespeare,
> *Comedy of Errours*.

to conta'in. To live in continence.

> I felt the ardour of my passion increase, 'till I could no longer *contain*. Arbuthnot and Pope.

co′ntinent. (3) Continuous; connected.

> The North-east part of Asia is, if not *continent* with the West side of America, yet certainly it is the least disjoined by sea of all that coast of Asia. Brerewood, *On Languages.*

to co′ntrary. To oppose; to thwart; to contradict.

> When I came to court I was advised not to *contrary* the king. Latimer.

to contri′state. To sadden; to make sorrowful; to make melancholy.

contri′te. (1) Bruised; much worn.

> (2) Worn with sorrow; harrassed with the sense of guilt; penitent. In the books of divines *contrite* is sorrowful for sin, from the love of God and desire of pleasing him; and *attrite* is sorrowful for sin, from the fear of punishment.

contri′tion. (1) The act of grinding; or rubbing to powder.

> (2) Penitence; sorrow for sin: in the strict sense, the sorrow which arises from the desire to please God, distinguished from *attrition*, or imperfect repentance produced by dread of hell.

contro′l. (1) A register or account kept by another officer, that each may be examined by the other.

conu′ndrum. A low jest; a quibble; a mean conceit: a cant word.

> Mean time he smoaks, and laughs at merry tale,
> Or pun ambiguous, or *conundrum* quaint. Philips.

to conve′nt. To call before a judge or judicature.

> They sent forth their precepts to attach men, and *convent* them before themselves at private houses. Bacon's *Henry VII.*

conve′ntual. A monk; a nun;. one that lives in a convent.

conversa′tion. (3) Commerce; intercourse; familiarity.

> His apparent, open guilt;
> I mean his *conversation* with Shore's wife. Shakespeare, *Richard III.*

to conve′rse. (5) To have commerce with a different sex.

> Being asked by some of her sex, in how long a time a woman might be allowed to pray to the gods, after having *conversed* with a man? If it were a husband, says she, the next day; if a stranger, never. *Guardian*, No. 165.

conve′rsion. (4) The interchange of terms in an argument; as, *no virtue is vice; no vice is virtue.* Chambers.

to conve′y. ·(3) To remove secretly.

> There was one *conveyed* out of my house yesterday in this basket. Shakespeare's *Merry Wives of Windsor.*

conve′yance. (1) The act of removing any thing.

> Tell her, thou mad′st away her uncle Clarence,
> Her uncle Rivers; ay, and for her sake,
> Mad′st quick *conveyance* with her good aunt Ann.
> Shakespeare, *Richard III.*

(8) Secret management; juggling artifice; private removal; secret substitution of one thing for another.

> Can they not juggle, and with slight
> *Conveyance* play with wrong and right. *Hudibras,* p. ii, c. 2.

conve′yancer. A lawyer who draws writings by which property is transferred.

to convi′nce. (2) To convict; to prove guilty of.

> O seek not to *convince* me of a crime,
> Which I can ne′er repent, nor can you pardon. Dryden.

to convi′ve. To entertain; to feast. A word, I believe, not elsewhere used.

> First, all you peers of Greece, go to my tent,
> There in the full *convive* you. Shakespeare, *Troilus and Cressida.*

co′nvoluted. (Of the verb I have found no example.) Twisted; rolled upon itself.

co′ny. A rabit; an animal that burroughs in the ground.

to co′nycatch. To catch a cony, is, in the old cant of thieves, to cheat; to bite; to trick.

coop. (1) A barrel; a vessel for the preservation of liquids.

cop. The head; the top of any thing; any thing rising to a head. As a *cop*, vulgarly *cock* of hay; a *cob-castle,* properly *cop-castle,* a small castle or house on a hill. A *cob* of cherrystones for *cop,* a pile of stones one laid upon another; a tuft on the head of birds.

to cope. (2) To reward; to give in return.

> I and my friend
> Have, by your wisdom, been this day acquitted

Of grievous penalties; in lieu whereof,
Three thousand ducats, due unto the Jew,
We freely *cope* your courteous pains withal.
Shakespeare.

co'pesmate. Companion; friend. An old word.

Ne ever staid in place, ne spake to wight,
'Till that the fox his *copesmate* he had found. *Hubberd's Tale*.

co'pped. Rising to a top or head.

It was broad in its basis, and rose *copped* like a sugar-loaf. Wiseman's *Surgery*.

co'ppel. (This word is variously spelt; as *copel, cupel, cuple,* and *cuppel;* but I cannot find its etymology.) An instrument used in chymistry in the form of a dish, made of ashes, well washed, to cleanse them from all their salt; or of bones thoroughly calcined. Its use is to try and purify gold and silver, which is done by mingling lead with the metal, and exposing it in the *coppel* to a violent fire a long while. The impurities of the metal will then be carried off in dross, which is called the litharge of gold and silver. The refiners call the *coppel* a test. Harris.

copper-nose. A red nose.

He having colour enough, and the other higher, is too flaming a praise for a good complexion: I had as lieve Helen's golden tongue had commended Troilus for a *copper-nose*. Shakespeare's *Troilus and Cressida*.

co'pperworm. (1) A little worm in ships.

(2) A moth that fretteth garments.

(3) A worm breeding in one's hand. Ainsworth.

copple-stones are lumps and fragments of stone or marble, broke from the adjacent cliffs, rounded by being bowled and tumbled to and again by the action of the water. Woodward.

to coque't. To entertain with compliments and amorous tattle; to treat with an appearance of amorous tenderness.

You are *coquetting* a maid of honour, my lord looking on to see how the gamesters play, and I railing at you both. Swift.

co′ral. (2) The piece of coral which children have about their necks, imagined to assist them in breeding teeth.

co′rban. An alms-basket; a receptacle of charity; a gift; an alms.

co′rinth. A small fruit commonly called currant.

corking-pin. A pin of the largest size.

> When you put a clean pillow-case on your lady's pillow, be sure to fasten it well with three *corking-pins,* that it may not fall off in the night. Swift's *Directions to the Chambermaid.*

co′rmorant. (1) A bird that preys upon fish. It is nearly of the bigness of a capon, with a wry bill and broad feet, black on his body, but greenish about his wings. He is eminently greedy and rapacious.

(2) A glutton.

corn. (1) The seeds which grow in ears, not in pods; such as are made into bread.

(4) An excrescence on the feet, hard and painful; probably so called from its form, though by some supposed to be denominated from its *corneous* or horny substance.

> Even in men, aches and hurts and *corns* do engrieve either towards rain or towards frost. Bacon's *Natural History.*

co′rnage. A tenure which obliges the landholder to give notice of an invasion by blowing a horn.

co′rncutter. A man whose profession is to extirpate corns from the foot.

> I have known a *corncutter,* who, with a right education, would have been an excellent physician. *Spectator,* No. 307.

co′rner. (2) A secret or remote place.

> It is better to dwell in a *corner* of a house-top, than with a brawling woman and in a wide house. *Proverbs,* xxv, 24.

corni′gerous. Horned; having horns.

cornu′to. A man horned; a cuckold.

> The peaking *cornuto* her husband, dwelling in a continual larum of jealousy. Shakespeare's *Merry Wives of Windsor.*

co′rollary. (1) The conclusion: a corollary seems to be a conclusion, whether following from the premises necessarily or not.

(2) Surplus.

co′rporal. (2) Material; not spiritual. In the present language, when *body* is used philosophically in opposition to spirit, the word *corporeal* is used, as a *corporeal* being; but otherwise *corporal*. *Corporeal* is having a body; *corporal* relating to the body. This distinction seems not ancient.

co′rpulence, co′rpulency. (2) Spissitude; grossness of matter.

to corra′de. To rub off; to wear away by frequent rubbing; to scrape together.

corre′ctioner. One that has been in the house of correction; a jayl-bird. This seems to be the meaning in Shakespeare.

> I will have you soundly swinged for this, you blue-bottle rogue! you filthy famished *correctioner*. Shakespeare, *Henry IV*.

corre′ption. Objurgation; chiding; reprehension; reproof.

corri′gible. (2) He who is a proper object of punishment; punishable.

cosci′nomancy. The art of divination by means of a sieve. A very ancient practice mentioned by Theocritus, and still used in some parts of England, to find out persons unknown. Chambers.

co′shering. *Cosherings* were visitations and progresses made by the lord and his followers among his tenants; wherein he did eat them (as the English proverb is) out of house and home. Davies.

co′sier. A botcher. Hanmer.

co′sset. A lamb brought up without the dam.

co′stard. (1) A head.

> Take him over the *costard* with the belt of thy sword.
> Shakespeare's *Richard III*.

co′strel. A bottle. Skinner.

to cote. This word, which I have found only in Chapman, seems to signify the same as *To leave behind*, *To over pass*.

> Words her worth had prov'd with deeds,
> Had more ground been allow'd the race, and *coted* far
> his steeds. Chapman's *Iliads*.

co′tquean. A man who busies himself with women's affairs.

> A stateswoman is as ridiculous a creature as a *cotquean:* each of the sexes should keep within its particular bounds. Addison's *Freeholder,* No. 38.

to co′tton. (2) To cement; to unite with: a cant word.

> A quarrel between you will end in one of you being turned off, in which case it will not be easy to *cotton* with another. Swift's *Directions to the Cook.*

to couch. (3) To lye down in secret, or in ambush.

> The earl of Angus *couched* in a furrow, and was passed over for dead, until a horse was brought for his escape. Hayward.

cough. A convulsion of the lungs, vellicated by some sharp serosity. It is pronounced *coff.*

co′unter. (1) A false piece of money used as a means of reckoning.

(2) Money in contempt.

counterbu′ff. A blow in a contrary direction; a stroke that produces a recoil.

co′untercaster. A word of contempt for an arithmetician; a book-keeper; a caster of accounts; a reckoner.

countercha′rm. That by which a charm is dissolved; that which has the power of destroying the effects of a charm.

to counterdr′aw. With painters, to copy a design or painting by means of a fine linen cloth, an oiled paper, or other transparent matter, whereon the strokes appearing through are traced with a pencil. Chambers.

counterfe′sance. The act of counterfeiting; forgery.

counterma′rk. (1) A second or third mark put on a bale of goods belonging to several merchants, that it may not be opened but in the presence of them all.

(2) The mark of the goldsmiths company, to shew the metal is standard, added to that of the artificer.

(3) An artificial cavity made in the teeth of horses, that have outgrown their natural mark, to disguise their age.

(4) A mark added to a medal a long time after it is struck, by which the curious know the several changes in value which they have undergone. Chambers.

to counterro′l. (This is now generally written as it is spoken,

control.) To preserve the power of detecting frauds by a
counter account.

co'uple. (1) A chain or tye that holds dogs together.

> It is in some sort with friends as it is with dogs in *cou-
> ples;* they should be of the same size and humour.
> L'Estrange's *Fables.*

couple-beggar. One that makes it his business to marry beggars
to each other.

to courb. To bend; to bow; to stoop in supplication.

course. (21) Empty form.

> Men talk as if they believed in God, but they live as if
> they thought there was none; their vows and promises
> are no more than words of *course.* L'Estrange, *Fable* 47.

co'urser. (1) A swift horse; a war horse: a word not used in
prose.

court-dresser. One that dresses the court, or persons of rank;
a flatterer.

cover-shame. Some appearance used to conceal infamy.

co'vin, co'vine. A deceitful agreement between two or more,
to the hurt of another. Cowell.

cow. The female of the bull; the horned animal with cloven
feet, kept for her milk and calves.

co'ward. (1) A poltron; a wretch whose predominant passion
is fear.

> There was a soldier that vaunted, before Julius Caesar,
> of the hurts he had received in his face. Caesar knowing
> him to be but a *coward,* told him, You were best take
> heed, next time you run away, how you look back. Bacon,
> *Apophthegms,* 188.

cowl. (2) A vessel in which water is carried on a pole between
two.

cowl-staff. The staff on which a vessel is supported between
two men.

> Mounting him upon a *cowl-staff,*
> Which (tossing him something high)
> He apprehended to be Pegasus. Suckling.

co'xcomb. (1) The top of the head.

> As the cockney did to the eels, when she put them i' the

pasty alive; she rapt them o' th' *coxcombs* with a stick, and cried down, wantons, down. Shakespeare's *King Lear*.

(2) The comb resembling that of a cock, which licensed fools wore formerly in their caps.

coxco'mical. Foppish; conceited: a low word unworthy of use.

Because, as he was a very natural writer, and they were without prejudice, without prepossession, without affectation, and without the influence of *coxcomical*, senseless cabal, they were at liberty to receive the impressions which things naturally made on their minds. Dennis.

coy. (1) Modest; decent.

(2) Reserved; not accessible; not easily condescending to familiarity.

At this season every smile of the sun, like the smile of a *coy* lady, is as dear as it is uncommon. Pope.

coz. A cant or familiar word, contracted from *cousin*.

to co'zen. To cheat; to trick; to defraud.

co'zenage. Fraud; deceit; artifice; fallacy; trick; cheat.

Strange *coz'nage!* none would live past years again,
Yet all hope pleasure in what yet remain;
And from the dregs of life, think to receive
What the first sprightly running could not give. Dryden, *Aurengzebe*.

crab. It is used by way of contempt for any sour or degenerate fruit; as, *a* crab *cherry, a* crab *plum.*

cra'ber. The poor fish have enemies enough, beside such unnatural fishermen; as otters, the cormorant, and the *craber*, which some call the water-rat. Walton's *Angler*.

crack. (7) A man crazed.

I have invented projects for raising millions, without burthening the subject; but cannot get the parliament to listen to me, who look upon me as a *crack* and a projector. Addison, *Spectator*.

(8) A whore; in low language.

(10) A boaster. This is only in low phrase.

to crack. (4) To boast: with *of*.

> To look like her, are chimney-sweepers black.
> And since her time are colliers counted bright.
> And Ethiops *of* their sweet complexion *crack*.
> Dark needs no candles now, for dark is light.
> Shakespeare.

crack-hemp. A wretch fated to the gallows; a crack-rope. *Furcifer.*＊

crack-rope. A fellow that deserves hanging.

cra′cker. (1) A noisy boasting fellow.

crag. (3) The neck.

> They looken bigge, as bulls that been bate,
> And bearen the *cragg* so stiff and so state. Spenser's *Pastorals.*

(4) The small end of a neck of mutton: a low word.

to cram. To eat beyond satiety.

> The godly dame, who fleshly failings damns,
> Scolds with her maid, or with her chaplain *crams.* Pope's Epilogue to *Jane Shore.*

cra′mbo. (A cant word, probably without etymology.) A play at which one gives a word, to which another finds a rhyme; a rhyme.

> So Maevius, when he drain'd his skull
> To celebrate some suburb trull,
> His similes in order set,
> And ev'ry *crambo* he could get. Swift.

cramp. Difficult; knotty: a low term.

crane. (3) A siphon; a crooked pipe for drawing liquors out of a cask.

crank. (2) Any bending or winding passage.

(3) Any conceit formed by twisting or changing, in any manner, the form or meaning of a word.

to cra′nkle. To break into unequal surfaces; to break into angles.

cra′pulous. Drunken; intemperate; sick with intemperance.

cra′ven. (1) A cock conquered and dispirited.

cra′ver. A weak-hearted spiritless fellow. It is used in *Clarissa.*

to craunch. To crush in the mouth. The word is used by Swift.

cra′yon. (1) A kind of pencil; a roll of paste to draw lines with.

＊ Latin for *rascal.*

to craze. (1) To break; to crush; to weaken.

(2) To powder.

cream. (1) The unctuous or oily part of milk, which, when it is cold, floats on the top, and is changed by the agitation of the churn into butter; the flower of milk.

to cream. (2) To take the flower and quintessence of any thing: so used somewhere by Swift.

cream-faced. Pale; coward-looking.

> Thou *cream-fac'd* lown,
>
> Where got'st thou that goose-look. Shakespeare's *Macbeth*.

cre'ature. (5) A word of contempt for a human being.

> He would into the stews,
>
> And from the common *creatures* pluck a glove,
>
> And wear it as a favour. Shakespeare's *Richard III*.

to creep. (1) To move with the belly to the ground without legs; as a worm.

(3) To move forward without bounds or leaps; as insects.

(6) To move timorously without soaring, or venturing into dangers.

> Paradise Lost is admirable; but am I therefore bound to maintain, that there are no flats amongst his elevations, when it is evident he *creeps* along sometimes for above an hundred lines together? Dryden.

cre'eper. (1) A plant that supports itself by means of some stronger body.

(2) An iron used to slide along the grate in kitchens.

(3) A kind of patten or clog worn by women.

cree'phole. (1) A hole into which any animal may creep to escape danger.

(2) A subterfuge; an excuse.

cre'scent. Increasing; growing; in a state of increase.

cre'sset. A great light set upon a beacon, lighthouse, or watch-tower. Hanmer. They still raise armies in Scotland by carrying about the fire-cross.

crest-fallen. Dejected; sunk; dispirited; cowed; heartless; spiritless.

---

to cream. In Swift's *Tale of a Tub*, b. 9, cited by *O.E.D.* Like most scholars, Johnson sometimes lost his references.

They prolate their words in a whining kind of querulous tone, as if they were still complaining and *crest-fallen*. Howell.

crew. (3) It is now generally used in a bad sense.

The last was he, whose thunder slew
The Titan race, a rebel *crew*. Addison.

to crib. To shut up in a narrow habitation; to confine; to cage.

crick. (2) A painful stiffness in the neck.

cri'minous. Wicked; iniquitous; enormously guilty.

The punishment that belongs to that great and *criminous* guilt, is the forfeiture of his right and claim to all mercies, which are made over to him by Christ. Hammond, *On Fundamentals*.

crimp. (1) Friable; brittle; easily crumbled; easily reduced to powder.

(2) Not consistent; not forcible: a low cant word.

The evidence is *crimp;* the witnesses swear backwards and forwards, and contradict themselves; and his tenants stick by him. Arbuthnot's *History of John Bull*.

to cri'mple. To contract; to corrugate; to cause to shrink or contract.

cri'ncum. (A cant word.) A cramp; a contraction; whimsy.

For jealousy is but a kind
Of clap and *crincum* of the mind. *Hudibras*, p. iii, cant. I.

crisp. (1) Curled.

Bulls are more *crisp* on the forehead than cows. Bacon.

(2) Indented; winding.

cri'sping-pin. A curling-iron.

to croak. (3) It may be used in contempt for any disagreeable or offensive murmur.

Their understandings are but little instructed, when all their whole time and pains is laid out to still the *croaking* of their own bellies. Locke.

cro'codile. An amphibious voracious animal, in shape resembling a lizard, and found in Egypt and the Indies. It is covered with very hard scales, which cannot, without great difficulty, be pierced; except under the belly, where the skin is tender. It has a wide throat, with several rows of teeth, sharp and separated, which enter one another.

Though its four legs are very short, it runs with great swiftness; but does not easily turn itself. It is long lived, and is said to grow continually to its death; but this is not probable. Some are fifteen or eighteen cubits long. Its sight is very piercing upon the ground, but in the water it sees but dimly; and it is said to spend the four winter months under water. When its bowels are taken out, or it is wounded, it smells very agreeably. *Crocodiles* lay their eggs, resembling goose-eggs, sometimes amounting to sixty, on the sand near the waterside, covering them with the sand, that the heat of the sun may contribute to hatch them. The ichneumon, or Indian rat, which is as large as a tame cat, is said to break the *crocodile's* eggs whenever it finds them; and also, that it gets into the very belly of this creature, while it is asleep with its throat open, gnaws its entrails, and kills it. Calmet.

cro′ises. (1) Pilgrims who carry a cross.

(2) Soldiers who fight against infidels under the banner of the cross.

crone. (1) An old ewe.

(2) In contempt, an old woman.

> The *crone* being in bed with him on the wedding night, and finding his aversion, endeavours to win his affection by reason. Dryden's *Fables*, Preface.

cro′okbacked. Having bent shoulders.

> A dwarf as well may for a giant pass,
> As negroe for a swan; a *crookback'd* lass
> Be call'd Europa. Dryden's *Juvenal*, Sat. 8.

cro′psick. Sick with repletion; sick with excess and debauchery.

a cro′ssbite. A deception; a cheat.

> The fox, that trusted to his address and manage, without so much as dreaming of a *cross-bite* from so silly an animal, fell himself into the pit that he had digged for another. L'Estrange.

crow. (1) A large black bird that feeds upon the carcasses of beasts.

(2) To pluck a crow, is to be industrious or contentious about that which is of no value.

cro′wder. A fiddler.

Chevy-chase sung by a blind *crowder*. Sidney.

cro′wkeeper. A scarecrow. The following passage is controverted.

> That fellow handles his bow like a *crowkeeper*.
> Shakespeare.

.cru′cial. Transverse; intersecting one another.

to cru′ciate. To torture; to torment; to excruciate.

cru′el. (1) Pleased with hurting others; inhuman; hardhearted; without pity; without compassion; savage; barbarous; unrelenting.

to cruise. To rove over the sea in search of opportunities to plunder; to wander on the sea without any certain course.

cub. (2) The young of a whale, perhaps of any viviparous fish.
(3) In reproach or contempt, a young boy or girl.

> O most comical sight! a country squire, with the equipage of a wife and two daughters, came to Mr. Snipwel's shop last night; but, such two unlicked *cubs!* Congreve.

to cub. To bring forth: used of beasts, or of a woman in contempt.

> *Cub'd* in a cabbin, on a mattress laid,
> On a brown George with lousy swabbers fed;
> Dead wine, that stinks of the borrachio, sup
> From a foul jack, or greasy mapple cup. Dryden's
> *Persius, Satires.*

cu′beb. A small dried fruit resembling pepper, but somewhat longer, of a greyish-brown colour on the surface, and composed of a corrugated or wrinkled external bark, covering a single and thin friable shell or capsule, containing a single seed of a roundish figure, blackish on the surface, and white within. It has an aromatick, but not very strong smell, and is acrid and pungent to the taste, but less so than pepper. *Cubebs* are brought into Europe from the island of Java; but the plant, which produces them, is wholly unknown to us. They are warm and carminative; and the Indians steep them in wine, and esteem them provocatives to venery. Hill.

cu′ckingstool. An engine invented for the punishment of scolds and unquiet women, which, in ancient times, was called tumbrel. Cowell.

to cu′ckold. (1) To corrupt a man's wife; to bring upon a man the reproach of having an adulterous wife; to rob a man of his wife's fidelity.

> If thou canst *cuckold* him, thou do'st thyself a pleasure, and me a sport. Shakespeare's *Othello.*

cu′ckoldly. Having the qualities of a cuckold; poor; mean; cowardly; sneaking.

> Poor *cuckoldly* knave, I know him not: yet I wrong him to call him poor; they say the jealous knave hath masses of money. Shakespeare's *Merry Wives of Windsor.*

cu′ckoo. (1) A bird which appears in the spring; and is said to suck the eggs of other birds, and lay her own to be hatched in their place; from which practice, it was usual to alarm a husband at the approach of an adulterer by calling *cuckoo,* which, by mistake, was in time applied to the husband. This bird is remarkable for the uniformity of his note, from which his name in most tongues seems to have been formed.

cu′dden, cu′ddy. (Without etymology.) A clown; a stupid rustick; a low dolt: a low bad word.

to cu′ddle. (A low word, I believe, without etymology.) To lye close; to squat.

cue. (5) Humour; temper of mind: a low word.

to cuff. (2) To strike with talons.

(3) To strike with wings. This seems improper.

> Hov'ring about the coasts they make their moan,
> And *cuff* the cliffs with pinions not their own. Dryden, *Aeneid.*

cu′llion. A scoundrel; a mean wretch.

cu′lly. A man deceived or imposed upon; as, by sharpers or a strumpet.

> Yet the rich *cullies* may their boasting spare:
> They purchase but sophisticated ware. Dryden.

cu′lprit. (About this word there is great dispute. It is used by the judge at criminal trials, who, when the prisoner declares himself not guilty, and puts himself upon his trial, answers; *Culprit, God send thee a good deliverance.* It is likely that it is a corruption of *Qu'il paroit, May it so appear,* the wish of the judge being that the prisoner may be found innocent.) A man arraigned before his judge.

to cu′lture. To cultivate; to manure; to till. It is used by Thomson, but without authority.

cu′nningman. A man who pretends to tell fortunes, or teach how to recover stolen goods.

cup. (5) Cup and Can. Familiar companions. The *can* is the large vessel, out of which the *cup* is filled, and to which it is a constant associate.

> You boasting tell us where you din'd,
> And how his lordship was so kind;
> Swear he's a most facetious man;
> That you and he are *cup and can:*
> You travel with a heavy load,
> And quite mistake preferment's road. Swift.

cupi′dity. Concupiscence; unlawful or unreasonable longing.

cur. (2) A term of reproach for a man.

> This knight had occasion to inquire the way to St. Anne's-lane; upon which the person, whom he spoke to, called him a young popish *cur*, and asked him, who made Anne a saint. Addison's *Spectator*, No. 125.

curio′sity. (2) Nicety; delicacy.

> When thou wast in thy gilt, and thy perfume, they mockt thee for too much *curiosity;* in thy rags thou knowest none, but art despised for the contrary.
> Shakespeare's *Timon of Athens*.

curmu′dgeon. (It is a vitious manner of pronouncing *coeur mechant*, Fr. an unknown correspondent.) An avaritious churlish fellow; a miser; a niggard; a churl; a griper.

cu′rrentness. (3) Easiness of pronunciation.

cu′rrish. Having the qualities of a degenerate dog; brutal; sour; quarrelsome; malignant; churlish; uncivil; untractable; impracticable.

> She says your dog was a cur; and tells you, *currish* thanks is good enough for such a present. Shakespeare, *Two Gentlemen of Verona*.

cu′rship. Dogship; meanness; scoundrelship.

cu′rsorary. Cursory; hasty; careless. A word, I believe, only found in the following line.

> I have but with a *cursorary* eye

O'erglanc'd the articles. Shakespeare's *Henry V*.

curst. Froward; peevish; malignant; mischievous; malicious; snarling.

to cu′rtail. (*curto*, Latin. It was anciently written *curtal*, which perhaps is more proper; but dogs that had their tails cut, being called *curtal* dogs, the word was vulgarly conceived to mean originally *to cut the tail*, and was in time written according to that notion.) (1) To cut off; to cut short; to shorten.

cu′stard. A kind of sweetmeat made by boiling eggs with milk and sugar, 'till the whole thickens into a mass. It is a food much used in city feasts.

>He cram'd them 'till their guts did ake,
>With cawdle, *custard*, and plumb cake. *Hudibras*, cant. ii.

cu′stomer. (2) A common woman. This sense is now obsolete.

>I marry her!—What, a *customer*? Pr'ythee, bear some charity to my wit; do not think it so unwholsome. Shakespeare, *Othello*.

cu′tpurse. One who steals by the method of cutting purses: a common practice when men wore their purses at their girdles, as was once the custom. A thief; a robber.

cu′ttle. A foul mouthed fellow; a fellow who blackens the character of others. Hanmer.

>Away, you cutpurse rascal; you filthy bung, away: by this wine I'll thrust my knife in your mouldy chaps, if you play the saucy *cuttle* with me. Shakespeare's *Henry IV*, p. ii.

cy′nick. A philosopher of the snarling or currish sort; a follower of Diogenes; a rude man; a snarler; a misanthrope.

cy′prus. (I suppose from the place where it was made; or corruptly from *cypress*, as being used in mourning.) A thin transparent black stuff.

D

a dab. (3) Something moist or slimy thrown upon one.

(4) (In low language.) An artist; a man expert at something. This is not used in writing.

dae'dal. (1) Various; variegated.

(2) Skilful: this is not the true meaning, nor should be imitated.

> Nor hath
> The *daedal* hand of nature only pour'd
> Her gifts of outward grace. Philips.

to daft. To toss aside; to put away with contempt; to throw away slightly.

dag. (1) A dagger.

(2) A handgun; a pistol: so called from serving the purposes of a dagger, being carried secretly, and doing mischief suddenly.

da'inty. (5) Nice; affectedly fine: in contempt.

> Your *dainty* speakers have the curse,
> To plead bad causes down to worse. Prior.

dam. (2) A human mother: in contempt or detestation.

> This brat is none of mine;
> It is the issue of Polixena:
> Hence with it, and, together with the *dam*,
> Commit them to the fire. Shakespeare's *Winter's Tale*.

[144]

da'mnably. (2) It is indecently used in a ludicrous sense; odiously; hatefully.

to da'mnify. (1) To endamage; to injure; to cause loss to any.

He, who has suffered the damage, has a right to demand in his own name, and he alone can remit satisfaction: the *damnified* person has the power of appropriating the goods or service of the offender, by right of self-preservation. Locke.

(2) To hurt; to impair.

dan. The old term of honour for men; as we now say *master*.

Dick, if this story pleaseth thee,
Pray thank *dan* Pope, who told it me. Prior's *Alma*.

da'ndiprat. A little fellow; an urchin: a word used sometimes in fondness, sometimes in contempt.

da'pper. Little and active; lively without bulk. It is usually spoken in contempt.

A pert *dapper* spark of a magpye, fancied the birds would never be governed 'till himself should sit at the helm. L'Estrange.

da'rkling. (A participle, as it seems, from *darkle*, which yet I have never found.) Being in the dark; being without light: a word merely poetical.

to da'rrain. (This word is by Junius referred to *dare:* it seems to me more probably deducible from *arranger la battaille*.)

(1) To prepare for battle; to range troops for battle.

da'ubry. An old word for any thing artful.

She works by charms, by spells, and such *daubry* as this is beyond our element. Shakespeare's *Merry Wives of Windsor*.

da'ybed. A bed used for idleness and luxury in the daytime.

to daze. To overpower with light; to strike with too strong lustre; to hinder the act of seeing by too much light suddenly introduced.

death's-door. A near approach to death; the gates of death. . . . It is now a low phrase.

There was a poor young woman that had brought herself even to *death's-door* with grief for her sick husband. L'Estrange.

[145]

de'btor. (3) One side of an account book.

> When I look upon the *debtor* side, I find such innumerable articles, that I want arithmetick to cast them up; but when I look upon the creditor side, I find little more than blank paper. Addison's *Spectator*, No. 549.

decu'mbence, decu'mbency. The act of lying down; the posture of lying down.

to decu'ssate. To intersect at acute angles.

dedica'tion. (2) A servile address to a patron.

dedica'tor. One who inscribes his work to a patron with compliment and servility.

> Leave dang'rous truths to unsuccessful satyrs,
> And flattery to fulsome *dedicators*. Pope's *Essay on Criticism*.

dee'mster. A judge: a word yet in use in Jersey and the Isle of Man.

deep-mouthed. Having a hoarse and loud voice.

deer. That class of animals which is hunted for venison, containing many subordinate species.

defa'ilance. Failure; miscarriage: a word not in use.

defe'ature. Change of feature; alteration of countenance.

to de'fecate. (1) To purge liquors from lees or foulness; to purify; to cleanse.

(2) To purify from any extraneous or noxious mixture; to clear; to brighten.

to defe'nd. (4) To prohibit; to forbid.

> Where can you say, in any manner, age,
> That ever God *defended* marriage? Chaucer.

deflagrabi'lity. Combustibility; the quality of taking fire, and burning totally away.

deflora'tion. (2) A selection of that which is most valuable.

> The laws of Normandy are, in a great measure, the *defloration* of the English laws, and a transcript of them. Hale.

---

dedication. Johnson wrote only two dedications for his own books, his first, and, significantly, the *Plan of a Dictionary*, to Lord Chesterfield. But after he had written this definition, he wrote about twenty dedications for other people, none "servile."

deflu'ous. (1) That flows down.

(2) That falls off.

defoeda'tion. The act of making filthy; pollution.

defo'rmity. (2) Ridiculousness; the quality of something worthy to be laughed at.

> In comedy there is somewhat more of the worse likeness to be taken, because it is often to produce laughter, which is occasioned by the sight of some *deformity*. Dryden, Preface, *Dufresnoy*.

deft. Obsolete. (1) Neat; handsome; spruce.

(2) Proper; fitting.

(3) Ready; dexterous.

degluti'tion. The act or power of swallowing.

to deho'rt. To dissuade; to advise to the contrary.

to de'ify. (2) To praise excessively; to extol one as if he were a god.

> He did again so extol and *deify* the pope, as made all that he had said in praise of his master and mistress seem temperate and passable. Bacon's *Henry VII*.

dela'tor. An accuser; an informer.

> No sooner was that small colony, wherewith the depopulated earth was to be replanted, come forth of the ark, but we meet with Cham, a *delator* to his own father, inviting his brethren to that execrable spectacle of their parent's nakedness. *Government of the Tongue*, s. 2.

to de'legate. (1) To send away.

to deli'neate. (1) To draw the first draught of a thing; to design.

deli'rament. A doting or foolish idle story.

deli'very. (5) Use of the limbs; activity.

> The earl was the taller, and much the stronger; but the duke had the neater limbs, and freer *delivery*. Wotton.

dell. (1) A pit; a valley; a hole in the ground; any cavity in the earth. Obsolete.

> I know each lane, and every alley green,
> Dingle, or bushy *dell* of this wild wood. Milton, *Paradise Lost*.

de'lve. A ditch, a pitfal; a den; a cave.

deme′rsed. Plunged; drowned.

demi-devil. Partaking of infernal nature; half a devil.

demi-man. Half a man. A term of reproach.

>We must adventure this battle, lest we perish by the complaints of this barking *demi-man*. Knolles's *History of the Turks*.

demu′re. (2) Grave; affectedly modest: it is now generally taken in a sense of contempt.

>So cat, transform'd, sat gravely and *demure*,
>'Till mouse appear'd, and thought himself secure.
>Dryden.

den. (1) A cavern or hollow running horizontally, or with a small obliquity, under ground; distinct from a hole, which runs down perpendicularly.

deniza′tion. The act of infranchising, or making free.

dense. Close; compact; approaching to solidity; having small interstices between the constituent particles.

deoscula′tion. The act of kissing.

depo′sitory. The place where any thing is lodged. *Depositary* is properly used of persons, and *depository* of places; but in the following example they are confounded.

>The Jews themselves are the *depositories* of all the prophecies which tend to their own confusion. Addison.

to de′precate. (1) To implore mercy of.

>(2) To avert; to remove; to turn away.

>(3) To beg off; to pray deliverance from.

to de′prehend. (1) To catch one; to take unawares; to take in the fact.

>(2) To discover; to find out a thing; to come to the knowledge or understanding of.

to depri′ve. (3) To release; to free from.

de′relicts. Such goods are as wilfully thrown away, or relinquished by the owner.

to deri′ve. (1) To turn the course of any thing; letting out; communicating.

>Company lessens the shame of vice by sharing it, and abates the torrent of a common odium by *deriving* it into many channels. South's *Sermons*.

(5) To spread; to diffuse gradually from one place to another.

> The streams of the publick justice were *derived* into every part of the kingdom. Davies, *On Ireland*.

dern. (1) Sad; solitary.

(2) Barbarous; cruel. Obsolete.

to de'secrate. To divert from the purpose to which any thing is consecrated.

dese'rver. A man who merits rewards. It is used, I think, only in a good sense.

desi'diose. Idle; lazy; heavy.

de'sperate. (5) It is sometimes used in a sense nearly ludicrous, and only marks any bad quality predominating in a high degree.

> Concluding all mere *desp'rate* sots and fools,
> That durst depart from Aristotle's rules. Pope's *Essay on Criticism*.

de'sperately (2) In a great degree; violently: this sense is ludicrous.

> She fell *desperately* in love with him, and took a voyage into Sicily in pursuit of him, he having withdrawn thither on purpose to avoid her. Addison's *Spectator*, No. 223.

despi'te. (1) Malice; anger; malignity; maliciousness; spleen; hatred.

to despo'nsate. To betroth; to affiance; to unite by reciprocal promises of marriage.

de'spot. An absolute prince; one that governs with unlimited authority. This word is not in use, except as applied to some Dacian prince; as, the *despot* of Servia.

to dete'rmine. (9) To put an end to; to destroy.

> Now where is he, that will not stay so long
> 'Till sickness hath *determin'd* me? Shakespeare's *Henry IV*.

deterra'tion. Discovery of any thing by removal of the earth that hides it; the act of unburying.

to deto'rt. To wrest from the original import, meaning, or design.

to detru′de. To thrust down; to force into a lower place.

deuce. (1) Two: a word used in games.

(2) The devil. See *deuse.*

deuse. (More properly than *deuce*, Junius, from *Dusius*, the name of a certain species of evil spirits.) The devil: a ludicrous word.

'Twas the prettiest prologue, as he wrote it;

Well, the *deuce* take me if I ha'n't forgot it. Congreve.

to deve′lop. To disengage from something that enfolds and conceals; to disentangle; to clear from its covering.

Take him to *develop*, if you can,

And hew the block off, and get out the man. *Dunciad.*

de′vil. (3) A ludicrous term for mischief.

A war of profit mitigates the evil;

But to be tax'd, and beaten, is the *devil*. Granville.

(5) A kind of ludicrous negative in an adverbial sense.

The devil was well, the *devil* a monk was he. A proverb.

to devo′te. (2) To addict; to give up to ill.

(3) To curse; to execrate; to doom to destruction.

Let her, like me, of ev'ry joy forlorn,

Devote the hour when such a wretch was born:

Like me to deserts and to darkness run. Rowe's *Jane Shore*.

devote′e. One erroneously or superstitiously religious; a bigot.

devo′tionalist. A man zealous without knowledge; superstitiously devout.

to dew. (2) It is not used properly of an action of terrour.

In Gallick blood again

He *dews* his reeking sword, and strows the ground

With headless ranks. Philips.

de′wworm. A worm found in dew.

diabe′tes. A morbid copiousness of urine; a fatal colliquation by the urinary passages.

di′aper. (1) Linen cloth woven in flowers, and other figures.

(2) A napkin; a towel.

di′ckens. A kind of adverbial exclamation, importing, as it seems, much the same with the *devil;* but I know not whence derived.

to di'dder. To quake with cold; to shiver. A provincial word. Skinner.

to diffi'de. To distrust; to have no confidence in.

to dige'st. (1) To distribute into various classes or repositories; to range or dispose methodically.

(4) To range methodically in the mind; to apply knowledge by meditation to its proper use.

(7) To receive and enjoy.

> Cornwal and Albany,
> With my two daughters dowers, *digest* the third. Shakespeare.

to dight. To dress; to deck; to bedeck; to embellish; to adorn.

di'git. (1) The measure of length containing three fourths of an inch.

digladia'tion. A combat with swords; any quarrel or contest.

to dila'niate. To tear; to rend in pieces.

dile'ction. The act of loving; kindness.

to dilu'cidate. To make clear or plain; to explain; to free from obscurity.

dimi'nishingly. In a manner tending to vilify, or lessen.

> I never heard him censure, or so much as speak *diminishingly* of any one that was absent. Locke.

to ding. To bluster; to bounce; to huff. A low word.

to dip. (4) To engage as a pledge; generally used for the first mortgage.

diplo'ma. A letter or writing conferring some privilege, so called because they used formerly to be written on waxed tables, and folded together.

di'psas. A serpent, whose bite produces the sensation of unquenchable thirst.

dire'ctory. The book which the factious preachers published in the rebellion for the direction of their sect in acts of worship.

dire'ption. The act of plundering.

to dirt. To foul; to bemire; to make filthy; to bedawb; to soil; to pollute; to nasty.

> Ill company is like a dog, who *dirts* those most whom he loves best. Swift's *Thoughts on Various Subjects.*

disadve'nturous. Unhappy; unprosperous.

to disannu'l. (*dis* and *annul*. This word is formed contrary to
analogy by those who not knowing the meaning of the word
annul, intended to form a negative sense by the needless
use of the negative particle. It ought therefore to be rejected
as ungrammatical and barbarous.) To annul; to deprive of
authority; to vacate; to make null; to make void; to nullify.

di'sard. A prattler; a boasting talker. This word is inserted both
by Skinner and Junius; but I do not remember it.

to disarra'y. To undress any one; to divest of cloaths.

to disa'ster. (1) To blast by the stroke of an unfavourable star.
> Ah, chaste bed of mine, said she, which never hereto-
> fore couldst accuse me of one defiled thought, how canst
> thou now receive that *disastered* changling? Sidney, b. ii.

discalcea'tion. The act of pulling off the shoes.

to disca'ndy. To dissolve; to melt. Hanmer.

disca'rnate. Stripped of flesh.

to disca'se. To strip; to undress.

to disce'rp. To tear in pieces; to break; to destroy by separation
of its parts. .

disciplina'rian. (2) A follower of the presbyterian sect, so called
from their perpetual clamour about discipline.

to disclo'se. (2) To hatch; to open.
> It is reported by the ancients, that the ostrich layeth her
> eggs under sand, where the heat of the sun *discloseth*
> them. Bacon.

to disco'mfit. To defeat; to conquer; to vanquish; to overpower;
to subdue; to beat; to overthrow.

disconve'nience. Incongruity; disagreement; opposition of nature.

discou'rager. One that impresses diffidence and terror.
> Most men in years, as they are generally *discouragers* of
> youth, are like old trees, which being past bearing
> themselves, will suffer no young plants to flourish be-
> neath them. Pope.

discou'rse. (1) The act of the understanding, by which it passes
from premises to consequences.

---

disannul. The ungrammatical barbarians quoted by Johnson are Hooker,
Bacon, Herbert, and Sandys.

discre'te. (1) Distinct; disjoined; not continuous.

(2) Disjunctive; as, *I resign my life, but not my honour,* is a *discrete* proposition.

discu'mbency. The act of leaning at meat, after the ancient manner.

dise'dged. Blunted; obtunded; dulled.

to disembo'gue. To pour out at the mouth of a river; to vent.

to disgo'rge. (1) To discharge by the mouth; to spew out; to vomit.

> So, so, thou common dog, did'st thou *disgorge*
> Thy glutton bosom of the royal Richard?
> And now thou wouldst eat thy dead vomit up,
> And howl'st to find it. Shakespeare's *Henry IV,* p. ii.

to disgui'se. (4) To deform by liquor: a low term.

> I have just left the right worshipful, and his myrmidons, about a sneaker of five gallons: the whole magistracy was pretty well *disguised* before I gave them the slip. *Spectator.*

dish-washer. The name of a bird.

to disha'bit. (This word I have found only in Shakespeare.) To throw out of place; to drive from their habitation.

> But for our approach those sleeping stones,
> By the compulsion of their ordinance
> By this time from their fixed beds of lime
> Had been *dishabited,* and wide havock made.
> Shakespeare, *King Lear.*

disho'nest. (2) Disgraced; dishonoured.

(3) Disgraceful; ignominious. These two senses are scarcely English, being borrowed from the Latin idiom.

to dispa'rage. (1) To match unequally; to injure by union with something inferiour in excellence.

(5) To marry any one to another of inferiour condition.

displa'cency. (1) Incivility; disobligation.

(2) Disgust; any thing unpleasing.

to displa'y. (3) To carve; to cut up.

(4) To talk without restraint.

to disse'ver. (*dis* and *sever.* In this word the particle *dis* makes no change in the signification, and therefore the word,

though supported by great authorities, ought to be ejected
from our language.) To part in two; to break; to divide; to
sunder; to separate; to disunite.

to dissu′nder. (*dis* and *sunder*. This is a barbarous word. See
dissever.) To sunder; to separate.

disti′ller. (2) One who makes and sells pernicious and inflam-
matory spirits.

to distra′ct. (1) To pull different ways at once.

(2) To separate; to divide.

distre′ss. (1) The act of making a legal seizure.

(2) A compulsion in real actions, by which a man is assured to appear in court, or to pay a debt or duty which he
refused. *Cowell.*

(3) The thing seized by law.

ditch. (2) Any long narrow receptacle of water: used sometimes of a small river in contempt.

(4) Ditch is used, in composition, of any thing worthless, or
thrown away into ditches.

> Poor Tom, when the foul fiend rages, eats cowdung for
> sallets, swallows the old rat, and the *ditch*-dog.
> Shakespeare.

to di′zen. (This word seems corrupted from *dight.*) To dress;
to deck; to rig out. A low word.

do′dkin. A doitkin or little doit; a contemptuous name for a
low coin.

> I would not buy them for a *dodkin.* Lily's *Grammar
> construed.*

dog. (1) A domestick animal remarkably various in his species; comprising the mastiff, the spaniel, the buldog, the
greyhound, the hound, the terrier, the cur, with many
others. The larger sort are used as a guard; the less for sports.

(6) *Dog* is a particle added to any thing to mark meanness,
or degeneracy, or worthlessness; as *dog* rose.

dog-trick. An ill turn; surly or brutal treatment.

do′gbolt. Of this word I know not the meaning, unless it be,
that when meal or flower is sifted or bolted to a certain
degree, the coarser part is called *dogbolt*, or flower for *dogs.*

do'gcheap. Cheap as dogs meat; cheap as the offal bought for dogs.

> Good store of harlots, say you, and *dogcheap?* Dryden.

do'gfly. A voracious biting fly.

do'gged. Sullen; sour; morose; ill-humoured; gloomy.

do'ggish. Currish; brutal.

doghe'arted. Cruel; pitiless; malicious.

do'ghole. A vile hole; a mean habitation.

> France is a *doghole*, and it no more merits the tread of a man's foot: to the wars. Shakespeare, *All's well that ends well.*

do'gsleep. Pretended sleep.

do'gsmeat. Refuse; vile stuff; offal like the flesh sold to feed dogs.

> His reverence bought of me the flower of all the market; these are but dogsmeat to 'em. Dryden.

do'ily. A species of woollen stuff, so called, I suppose, from the name of the first maker.

doit. A small piece of money.

do'rmitory. (2) A burial place.

do'rmouse. A small animal which passes a large part of the winter in sleep.

dose. (3) It is often used of the utmost quantity of strong liquor that a man can swallow. He has his *dose*, that is, he can carry off no more.

double-dealer. A deceitful, subtle, insidious fellow; one who acts two parts at the same time; one who says one thing and thinks another.

double-minded. Deceitful; insidious.

double-tongued. Deceitful; giving contrary accounts of the same thing.

do'uble. (2) Strong beer; beer of twice the common strength.

> Here's a pot of good *double*, neighbour: drink, and fear not your man. Shakespeare's *Henry VI.*

dough. (2) My cake is dough. My affair has miscarried; my undertaking has never come to maturity.

> *My cake is dough,* but I'll in among the rest;

Out of hope of all, but my share of the feast. Shakespeare.

doughba'ked. Unfinished; not hardened to perfection; soft.

For when, through tasteless flat humility,

In *doughbak'd* men some harmlessness we see,

'Tis but his phlegm that's virtuous, and not he. Donne.

do'ughty. (2) It is now seldom used but ironically, or in burlesque.

If this *doughty* historian hath any honour or conscience
left, he ought to beg pardon. Stillingfleet's *Defence of
Discourse concerning Idolatry in the Church of Rome.*

do'wdy. An aukward, ill-dressed, inelegant woman.

Laura, to his lady, was but a kitchen wench; Dido, a
dowdy; Cleopatra, a gipsy; Helen and Hero, slidings
and harlots. Shakespeare's *Romeo and Juliet.*

down. (2) Any thing that sooths or mollifies.

Thou bosom softness! *down* of all my cares!

I could recline my thoughts upon this breast

To a forgetfulness of all my griefs,

And yet be happy. Southerne's *Oroonoko.*

do'wngyred. Let down in circular wrinkles.

Lord Hamlet, with his stockings loose,

Ungarter'd, and *downgyred* to his ancles. Shakespeare,
Hamlet.

do'wnlying. About to be in travail of childbirth.

dracu'nculus. A worm bred in the hot countries, which grows
to many yards length between the skin and flesh.

draff. Any thing thrown away; sweepings; refuse; lees; dregs.

dra'gon. (2) A fierce violent man or woman.

dra'gonfly. A fierce stinging fly.

to drago'on. To persecute by abandoning a place to the rage
of soldiers.

to dram. In low language, to drink drams; to drink distilled
spirits.

dra'ma. A poem accommodated to action; a poem in which
the action is not related, but represented; and in which
therefore such rules are to be observed as make the representation probable.

to drape. (1) To make cloth.

(2) To jeer, or sátyrize. It is used in this sense by the innovator Temple, whom nobody has imitated.

draugh. (Corruptly written for *draff*.) Refuse; swill. See *draff*.

draughthouse. A house in which filth is deposited.

to draw. (33) To wrest; to distort.

I wish that both you and others would cease from *drawing* the Scriptures to your fantasies and affections. Whitgift.

(36) To eviscerate; to embowel.

In private *draw* your poultry, clean your tripe,
And from your eels their slimy substance wipe. King's *Art of Cookery*.

drawba′ck. Money paid back for ready payment, or any other reason.

In poundage and *drawbacks* I lose half my rent;
Whatever they give me, I must be content. Swift.

dra′wer. (4) A box in a case, out of which it is drawn at pleasure.

to drawl. To utter any thing in a slow driveling way.

dra′zel. A low, mean, worthless wretch.

As the devil uses witches,
To be their cully for a space,
That, when the time's expir'd, the *drazels*
For ever may become his vassals. *Hudibras*, p. iii, cant. I.

drench. (1) A draught; a swill: by way of abhorrence or contempt.

drent. Probably corrupted from *drenched*, to make a proverbial rhyme, *brent* or *burnt*.

What flames, quoth he, when I the present see,
In danger rather to be *drent* than brent? *Fairy Queen*, b. ii.

to drib. To crop; to cut off; to defalcate. A cant word.

Merchants gains come short of half the mart;

---

drape. (2) Sir William Temple, Swift's cousin and early patron, was a Whig.

For he who drives their bargains, *dribs* a part. Dryden, *Juvenal.*

to drill. (4) To delay; to put off: in low phrase.

She has bubbled him out of his youth; she *drilled* him on to five and fifty, and she will drop him in his old age. Addison.

(5) To draw from step to step. A low phrase.

When by such insinuations they have once got within him, and are able to *drill* him on from one lewdness to another, by the same arts they corrupt and squeeze him. South's *Sermons.*

(6) To drain; to draw slowly. This sense wants better authority.

Drill'd through the sandy stratum every way,
The waters with the sandy stratum rise. Thomson's *Autumn.*

drill. (1) An instrument with which holes are bored. It is pressed hard against the thing bored, and turned round with a bow and string.

(2) An ape; a baboon.

Shall the difference of hair be a mark of a different internal specifick constitution between a changeling and a *drill,* when they agree in shape and want of reason? Locke.

(3) A small dribbling brook. This I have found no where else, and suspect it should be *rill.*

Springs through the pleasant meadows pour their *drills,*
Which snake-like glide between the bordering hills. Sandys.

dri'nkmoney. Money given to buy liquor.

Peg's servants were always asking for *drinkmoney.* Arbuthnot.

dri'pple. This word is used somewhere by Fairfax for weak, or rare; *dripple shot.*

to dri'vel. (1) To slaver; to let the spittle fall in drops, like a child, an ideot, or a dotard.

(2) To be weak or foolish; to dote.

I hate to see a brave bold fellow sotted,
Made sour and senseless, turn'd to whey by love;
A *driveling* hero, fit for a romance. Dryden's *Spanish Fryar.*

droil. A drone; a sluggard.

to drop. (7) To quit a master.

I have beat the hoof 'till I have worn out these shoes in your service, and not one penny left me to buy more; so that you must even excuse me, if I *drop* you here. L'Estrange.

dro'tchel. An idle wench; a sluggard. In Scottish it is still used.

to dru'mble. To drone; to be sluggish. Hanmer.

dry'nurse. (2) One who takes care of another: with some contempt of the person taken care of.

Mistress Quickly is in the manner of his nurse, or his *drynurse,* or his cook, or his laundry, his washer, and his wringer. Shakespeare's *Merry Wives of Windsor.*

duck. (1) A water fowl, both wild and tame.

to duck. (3) To bow low; to cringe. In Scottish *duyk,* or *juyk,* to make obeisance, is still used.

du'dgeon. (1) A small dagger.

(2) Malice; sullenness; malignity; ill will.

The cuckow took this a little in *dudgeon.* L'Estrange.

dug. (1) A pap; a nipple; a teat: spoken of beasts, or in malice or contempt of human beings.

(2) It seems to have been used formerly of the breast without reproach.

As mild and gentle as the cradle-babe,
Dying with mother's *dug* between its lips. Shakespeare, *Henry VI.*

to du'lcorate. To sweeten; to make less acrimonious.

The ancients, for the *dulcorating* of fruit, do commend swine's dung above all other dung. Bacon's *Natural History.*

dull. (8) Not exhilarating; not delightful; as, *to make dictionaries is* dull *work.*

dump. (1) Sorrow; melancholy; sadness.

Sing no more ditties, sing no mo

Of *dumps* so dull and heavy;
  The frauds of men were ever so,
Since Summer first was leafy. Shakespeare, *Much Ado about Nothing*.

(2) Absence of mind; reverie.

dung. The excrement of animals used to fatten ground.

du'nghil. (2) Any mean or vile abode.

(3) Any situation of meanness.

(4) A term of reproach for a man meanly born.

Out, *dunghil!* dar'st thou brave a nobleman? Shakespeare.

to du'plicate. (2) To fold together.

to dure. To last; to continue; to endure.

E

ea′gle. (1) A bird of prey, which, as it is reported, renews its age when it grows old. But some think that this recovery of youth happens no otherwise in the eagle than in other birds, by casting their feathers every year in the moulting season, and having others in their room. It is also said not to drink at all, like other birds with sharp claws. It is given out, that when an eagle sees its young so well grown as to venture upon flying, it hovers over their nest, flutters with its wings, and excites them to imitate it, and take their flight; and when it sees them weary, or fearful, it takes and carries them upon its back. Eagles are said to be extremely sharp-sighted, and, when they take flight, spring perpendicularly upward, with their eyes steadily fixed upon the sun, mounting 'till, by their distance, they disappear. Calmet.

ea′glestone. The *eaglestone* contains, in a cavity within it, a small loose stone, which rattles when it is shaken; and every fossil, with a nucleus in it, has obtained the name. The sort of analogy that was supposed to be between a stone, thus containing another within it, or, as the fanciful writers express it, pregnant with another, and a woman big with child, led people to imagine that it must have great virtues and effects in accelerating or retarding delivery; so that, if tied to the arm of a woman with child, it prevents abortion;

and if to the leg, it promotes delivery. It is pretended, that the eagles seek for these stones to lay in their nests, and that they cannot hatch their young without. On such idle and imaginary virtues was raised all the credit which this famous fossil possessed for many ages. Hill's *Materia Medica.*

eame. Uncle: a word still used in the wilder parts of Staffordshire.

ea′rwig. A sheath-winged insect, imagined to creep into the ear.

to ea′vesdrop. To catch what comes from the eaves; in common phrase, to listen under windows.

ebri′ety. Drunkenness; intoxication by strong liquors.

> Bitter almonds, as an antidote against *ebriety*, hath commonly failed. Browne's *Vulgar Errours,* b. ii, c. 6.

eccopro′ticks. Such medicines as gently purge the belly, so as to bring away no more than the natural excrements lodged in the intestines.

e′cho. (1) Echo was supposed to have been once a nymph, who pined into a sound for love of Narcissus.

eda′cious. Eating; voracious; devouring; predatory; ravenous; rapacious; greedy.

to e′dder. To bind or interweave a fence.

to edge. (4) To exasperate; to embitter.

> He was indigent and low in money, which perhaps might have a little *edged* his desperation. Wotton's *Life of Duke of Buckingham.*

to edify′. (1) To build.

> Men have *edify'd*
> A lofty temple, and perfum'd an altar to thy name. Chapman.

eel. A serpentine slimy fish, that lurks in mud.

effe′rvescence. The act of growing hot; production of heat by intestine motion.

effe′te. (1) Barren; disabled from generation.

> It is probable that females have in them the seeds of all the young they will afterwards bring forth, which, all

---

eame. Johnson was born in the Athens of Staffordshire, Lichfield.

spent and exhausted, the animal becomes barren and *effete*. Ray.

(2) Worn out with age.

to effi'giate. To form in semblance; to image.

ege'stion. The act of throwing out the digested food at the natural vents.

egg. (1) That which is laid by feathered animals, from which their young is produced.

egre'gious. (1) Eminent; remarkable; extraordinary.

(2) Eminently bad; remarkably vicious. This is the usual sense.

> Ah me, most credulous fool!
> *Egregious* murtherer! Shakespeare's *Cymbeline.*

e'gret. A fowl of the heron kind, with red legs. Bailey.

eigh. An expression of sudden delight.

ei'sel. Vinegar; verjuice; any acid.

> Woo't drink up *eisel,* eat a crocodile?
> I'll do't. Shakespeare's *Hamlet.*

ele'ctre. (1) Amber; which, having the quality when warmed by friction of attracting bodies, gave to one species of attraction the name of *electricity,* and to the bodies that so attract the epithet *electrick.*

ele'ctrical, ele'ctrick. (1) Attractive without magnetism; attractive by a peculiar property, supposed once to belong chiefly to amber.

> By *electrick* bodies do I conceive not such only as take up light bodies, in which number the ancients only placed jett and amber; but such as, conveniently placed, attract all bodies palpable. Browne's *Vulgar Errours,* b. ii, c. 4.

> An *electrick* body can by friction emit an exhalation so subtile, and yet so potent, as by its emission to cause no sensible diminution of the weight of the *electrick* body, and to be expanded through a sphere, whose diameter is above two feet, and yet to be able to carry up lead, copper, or leaf-gold, at the distance of above a foot from the *electrick* body. Newton.

(2) Produced by an electrick body.

If that attraction were not rather *electrical* than mag-
netical, it was wonderous what Helmont delivereth concerning a glass, wherein the magistery of loadstone
was prepared, which retained an attractive quality.
Browne's *Vulgar Errours.*

If a piece of white paper, or a white cloath, or the
end of one's finger, be held at about a quarter of an
inch from the glass, the *electrick* vapour, excited by
friction, will, by dashing against the white paper, cloth,
or finger, be put into such an agitation as to emit light.
Newton's *Opticks.*

electri'city. A property in some bodies, whereby, when rubbed
so as to grow warm, they draw little bits of paper, or such
like substances, to them. Quincy.

Such was the account given a few years ago of electricity; but the industry of the present age, first excited by the
experiments of Gray, has discovered in electricity a multitude of philosophical wonders. Bodies electrified by a
sphere of glass, turned nimbly round, not only emit flame,
but may be fitted with such a quantity of the electrical
vapour, as, if discharged at once upon a human body, would
endanger life. The force of this vapour has hitherto appeared instantaneous, persons at both ends of a long chain
seeming to be struck at once. The philosophers are now
endeavouring to intercept the strokes of lightning.

e'lephant. The largest of all quadrupeds, of whose sagacity,
faithfulness, prudence, and even understanding, many
surprising relations are given. This animal is not carnivo-
rous, but feeds on hay, herbs, and all sorts of pulse; and
it is said to be extremely long lifed. It is naturally very
gentle; but when enraged, no creature is more terrible. He
is supplied with a trunk, or long hollow cartilage, like a
large trumpet, which hangs between his teeth, and serves
him for hands: by one blow with his trunk he will kill a
camel or a horse, and will raise a prodigious weight with it.
His teeth are the ivory so well known in Europe, some of
which have been seen as large as a man's thigh, and a
fathom in length. Wild elephants are taken with the help

of a female ready for the male: she is confined to a narrow place, round which pits are dug; and these being covered with a little earth scattered over hurdles, the male elephants easily fall into the snare. In copulation the female receives the male lying upon her back; and such is his pudicity, that he never covers the female so long as any one appears in sight. Calmet.

elephanti′asis. A species of leprosy, so called from covering the skin with incrustations like those on the hide of an elephant.

to elf. To entangle hair in so intricate a manner, that it is not to be unravelled. This the vulgar have supposed to be the work of fairies in the night; and all hair so matted together, hath had the name of *elflocks*. Hanmer.

elops. A fish; reckoned however by Milton among the serpents.

to emba′se. (1) To vitiate; to depauperate; to lower; to deprave; to impair.

(2) To degrade; to vilify.

e′mbolism. (1) Intercalation; insertion of days or years to produce regularity and equation of time.

(2) The time inserted; intercalatory time.

to embro′thel. To inclose in a brothel.

> Men, which chuse
> Law practice for mere gain, boldly repute,
> Worse than *embrothel'd* strumpets prostitute. Donne.

eme′rgence, eme′rgency. (4) Pressing necessity. A sense not proper.

> In any case of *emergency*, he would employ the whole wealth of his empire, which he had thus amassed together in his subterraneous exchequer. Addison's *Freeholder*.

empa′sm. A powder to correct the bad scent of the body.

e′mpiric. A trier or experimenter; such persons as have no true education in, or knowledge of physical practice, but venture upon hearsay and observation only. Quincy.

> Such an aversion and contempt for all manner of innovators, as physicians are apt to have for *empiricks*, or lawyers for pettifoggers. Swift.

e'mption. The act of purchasing; a purchase.

encyclope'dia, encyclope'dy. The circle of sciences; the round of learning.

> Every science borrows from all the rest, and we cannot attain any single one without the *encyclopaedy.*
> Glanvill, *Scepsis Scientifica*, c. 25.

to endo'rse. (2) To cover on the back.

> Chariots, or elephants *endors'd* with tow'rs
> Of archers. Milton's *Paradise Regained*, b. iii, l. 329.

engro'sser. He that purchases large quantities of any commodity, in order to sell it at a high price.

enoda'tion. (1) The act of untying a knot.

(2) Solution of a difficulty.

enthu'siasm. (1) A vain belief of private revelation; a vain confidence of divine favour or communication.

> *Enthusiasm* is founded neither on reason nor divine revelation, but rises from the conceits of a warmed or overweening brain. Locke.

(2) Heat of imagination; violence of passion; confidence of opinion.

(3) Elevation of fancy; exaltation of ideas.

enthu'siast. (1) One who vainly imagines a private revelation; one who has a vain confidence of his intercourse with God.

enti're. (7) Honest; firmly adherent; faithful.

> No man had ever a heart more *entire* to the king, the church, or his country; but he never studied the easiest ways to those ends. Clarendon.

to entre'at. (4) To entertain; to amuse.

to enve'lop. (3) To line; to cover on the inside.

> His iron coat, all over grown with rust,
> Was underneath *enveloped* with gold,
> Darkned with filthy dust. *Fairy Queen.*

e'nvy. (3) Malice; malignity.

> Madam, this is a meer distraction;
> You turn the good we offer into *envy.* Shakespeare, *Henry VIII.*

(4) Publick odium; ill repute.

> Edward Plantagenet should be, in the most publick and

notorious manner, shewed unto the people; to discharge
the king of the *envy* of that opinion and bruit, how he
had been put to death privily. Bacon's *Henry VII.*

to enwo′mb. (1) To make pregnant.

(2) To bury; to hide as in a womb.

ephe′mera. (1) A fever that terminates in one day.

(2) An insect that lives only one day.

ephe′meris. (1) A journal; an account of daily transactions.

(2) An account of the daily motions and situations of the
planets.

ephe′merist. One who consults the planets; one who studies or
practises astrology.

ephemeron-worm. A sort of worm that lives but a day.

e′pic. Narrative; comprising narrations, not acted, but re-
hearsed. It is usually supposed to be heroick, or to contain
one great action atchieved by a hero.

epide′rmis. The scarf-skin of a man's body.

epigra′m. A short poem terminating in a point.

epi′stle. A letter. This word is seldom used but in poetry, or on
occasions of dignity and solemnity.

When loose *epistles* violate chaste eyes,

She half consents, who silently denies. Dryden.

epi′stler. A scribbler of letters.

e′pithet. (1) An adjective denoting any quality good or bad:
as, the *verdant* grove, the *craggy* mountain's *lofty* head.

(2) It is used by some writers improperly for *title, name.*
The *epithet* of shades belonged more properly to the
darkness than the refreshment. *Decay of Piety.*

(3) It is used improperly for *phrase, expression.*

epula′tion. Banquet; feast.

erra′nt. (2) Vile; abandoned; completely bad. See *arrant.*

espa′lier. Trees planted and cut so as to join.

e′ssay. (2) A loose sally of the mind; an irregular indigested
piece; not a regular and orderly composition.

e′strich. (Commonly written *ostrich.*) The largest of birds.

estua′tion. The state of boiling; reciprocation of rise and fall;
agitation; commotion.

e′surine. Corroding; eating.

to etch. (3) (This word is evidently mistaken by Ray for *edge*.) To move forwards towards one side.

> When we lie long awake in the night, we are not able to rest one quarter of an hour without shifting of sides, or at least *etching* this way and that way, more or less. Ray.

etch. A country word, of which I know not the meaning.

> Where you find dunging of land makes it rank, lay dung upon the *etch*, and sow it with barley. Mortimer's *Husbandry*.

e'ther. (1) An element more fine and subtle than air; air refined or sublimed.

(2) The matter of the highest regions above.

> There fields of light and liquid *ether* flow,
> Purg'd from the pond'rous dregs of earth below. Dryden.

e'thnick. Heathen; pagan; not Jewish; not Christian.

to eva'cate. To empty out; to throw out.

to eva'cuate. (4) To make void; to evacate; to nullify; to annul.

> The defect, though it would not *evacuate* a marriage, after cohabitation and actual consummation; yet it was enough to make void a contract. Bacon's *Henry VII*.

evacua'tion. (2) Abolition; nullification.

> Popery hath not been able to re-establish itself in any place, after provision made against it by utter *evacuation* of all Romish ceremonies. Hooker, b. iv, s. 9.

evaga'tion. The act of wandering; excursion; ramble; deviation.

eva'nid. Faint; weak; evanescent.

to eva'porate. (2) To give vent to; to let out in ebullition or sallies.

> My lord of Essex *evaporated* his thoughts in a sonnet to be sung before the queen. Wotton.

to eve'nterate. To rip up; to open by ripping the belly.

> In a bear, which the hunters *eventerated*, or opened, I beheld the young ones with all their parts distinct. Browne.

---

etch. "An aftergrowth of grass after mowing; . . . stubble" *O.E.D.*, under *eddish*.

to eve′ntilate. (1) To winnow; to sift out.

(2) To examine; to discuss.

e′ver. (7) A word of enforcement, or aggravation. *As soon as ever he had done it;* that is, immediately after he had done it. In this sense it is scarcely used but in familiar language.

e′vesdropper. Some mean fellow that skulks about a house in the night.

evi′ction. (2) Proof; evidence; certain testimony.

> A plurality of voices carries the question, in all our debates, but rather as an expedient for peace than an *eviction* of the right. L'Estrange's *Fables.*

e′vil. (5) Malady; disease: as, the *king's evil.*

> At his touch,
> Such sanctity hath heaven given his hand,
> They presently amend.
> —What's the disease he means?
> —'Tis call'd the *evil.* Shakespeare's *Macbeth.*

e′vitable. Avoidable; that may be escaped or shunned.

exaggera′tion. (1) The act of heaping together; an heap; an accumulation.

> Some towns, that were anciently havens and ports, are now, by *exaggeration* of sand between those towns and the sea, converted into firm land. Hale's *Origin of Mankind.*

to exa′gitate. (1) To shake; to put in motion.

(2) To reproach; to pursue with invectives. This sense is now disused, being purely Latin.

exa′nguious. Having no blood; formed with animal juices, not sanguineous.

exa′nimous. Lifeless; dead; killed.

to exantla′te. (1) To draw out.

(2) To exhaust; to waste away.

to exau′ctorate. (1) To dismiss from service.

(2) To deprive of a benefice.

to e′xcavate. To hollow; to cut into hollows.

exce′pting. Without inclusion of; with exception of. **An improper word.**

---

evil. The king's evil, or scrofula, from which Johnson suffered.

> People come into the world in Turkey the same way
> they do here; and yet, *excepting* the royal family, they
> get but little by it. Collier, *On Duelling*.

exci′se. A hateful tax levied upon commodities, and adjudged
not by the common judges of property, but wretches hired
by those to whom excise is paid.

> *Excise*,
> With hundred rows of teeth, the shark exceeds,
> And on all trades like Cassawar she feeds. Marvell.

to exco′ct. To boil up; to make by boiling.

to exco′riate. To flay; to strip off the skin.

excoria′tion. (2) Plunder; spoil; the act of stripping of possessions.

> It hath marvellously enhanced the revenues of the
> crown to many millions more than it was, though with
> a pitiful *excoriation* of the poorer sort. Howell's *Vocal
> Forrest*.

exe′quies. Funeral rites; the ceremony of burial; the proces-
sion of burial. For this word *obsequies* is often used, but
not so properly.

exe′sion. The act of eating through.

> Theophrastus denieth the *exesion* or forcing of vipers
> through the belly of the dam. Browne's *Vulgar Errours*,
> b. iii.

exhibi′tion. (2) Allowance; salary; pension.

> He is now neglected, and driven to live in exile upon
> a small *exhibition*. Swift.

exo′rbitant. (1) Going out of the prescribed track; deviating
from the course appointed or rule established.

(2) Anomalous; not comprehended in a settled rule or
method.

expia′tion. (3) Practices by which the threats of ominous
prodigies were averted.

> Upon the birth of such monsters the Grecians and Ro-
> mans did use divers sorts of *expiations*, and to go about

---

excise. Johnson's father had had trouble with the commissioners of
excise, in the conduct of his business as a bookseller and maker of
parchment.

their principal cities with many solemn ceremonies and sacrifices. Hayward.

e′xpletive. Something used only to take up room; something of which the use is only to prevent a vacancy.

> Oft the ear the open vowels tire,
> While *expletives* their feeble aid do join. Pope's *Essay on Criticism.*

to explo′de. (1) To drive out disgracefully with some noise of contempt; to treat with open contempt; to treat not only with neglect, but open disdain or scorn.

> Thus was th' applause they meant,
> Turn'd to *exploding* hiss, triumph to shame,
> Cast on themselves from their own mouths. Milton, *Paradise Lost.*

(2) To drive out with noise and violence.

explo′der. An hisser; one who drives out any person or thing with open contempt.

to explo′it. To perform; to atchieve.

to expo′se. (8) To censure; to treat with dispraise. A colloquial abuse of the word.

> A little wit is equally capable of *exposing* a beauty, and of aggravating a fault. Addison's *Spectator*, No. 29.

to expo′und. (2) To examine; to lay open: a Latinism.

> He *expounded* both his pockets,
> And found a watch with rings and lockets. *Hudibras.*

to exprobra′te. To charge upon with reproach; to impute openly with blame; to upbraid.

to expro′priate. To make no longer our own; to hold no longer as a property. Not in use.

expu′nction. Abolition; the act of expunging, blotting, or effacing.

expu′rgatory. Employed in purging away what is noxious: as, the *expurgatory* index of the Romanists directs the abolition or expunction of passages admitted by any authors contrary to popery.

exte′ndlessness. Unlimited extension. In this sense it is once found; but, I think, with little propriety.

> Certain *moleculae seminales* must keep the world from

an infinitude, and *extendlessness* of excursions every
moment into new figures and animals. Hale's *Origin of
Mankind*.

to extru'ct. To build; to raise; to form into a structure.

to extru'de. To thrust off; to drive off; to push out with violence.

eye. (14) A small shade of colour.

Red with an *eye* of blue, makes a purple. Boyle, *On
Colours*.

eyese'rvant. A servant that works only while watched.

eyese'rvice. Service performed only under inspection.

F

fa′bulous. Feigned; full of fables, or invented tales.

to face. (1) To carry a false appearance; to play the hypocrite.

> Thou needs must learn to laugh, to lye,
>
> To *face*, to forge, to scoff, to company. *Hubberd's Tale*.

facepai′nter. A drawer of portraits; a painter who draws from the life.

fa′ction. (2) Tumult; discord; dissension.

to fa′ddle. To trifle; to toy; to play.

to fadge. (1) To suit; to fit; to have one part consistent with another.

> How will this *fadge?* my master loves her dearly,
>
> And I, poor monster, fond as much on him;
>
> And she, mistaken, seems to dote on me. Shakespeare.

(2) To agree; not to quarrel; to live in amity.

> When they thriv'd they never *fadg'd*,
>
> But only by the ears engag'd;
>
> Like dogs that snarl about a bone,
>
> And play together when they've none. *Hudibras*, p. iii.

(3) To succeed; to hit.

(4) This is a mean word not now used, unless perhaps in ludicrous and low compositions.

fai′ry. (1) A kind of fabled beings supposed to appear in a diminutive human form, and to dance in the meadows, and reward cleanliness in houses; an elf; a fay.

fai'thbreach. Breach of fidelity; disloyalty; perfidy.

to fall. (36) To be born; to be yeaned.

> Lambs must have care taken of them at their first *falling*, else, while they are weak, the crows and magpies will be apt to pick out their eyes. Mortimer's *Husbandry*.

to fa'lsify. (4) To pierce; to run through.

> His crest is rash'd away, his ample shield
> Is *falsify'd*, and round with jav'lins fill'd. Dryden's *Aeneid*.

Of this word Mr. Dryden writes thus. My friends quarrelled at the word *falsified*, as an innovation in our language. The fact is confessed; for I remember not to have read it in any English author; though perhaps it may be found in Spenser's *Fairy Queen*. But suppose it be not there: why am I forbidden to borrow from the Italian, a polished language, the word which is wanting in my native tongue? Horace has given us a rule for coining words, *si graeco fonte cadant*, especially when other words are joined with them which explain the sense. I use the word *falsify*, in this place, to mean that the shield of Turnus was not of proof against the spears and javelins of the Trojans, which had pierced it through and through in many places. The words which accompany this new one, makes my meaning plain:

> *Ma si l'Usbergo d'Ambi era perfetto,*
> *Che mai poter* falsarlo *in nessum canto*. Ariosto, cant. xxvi.

Falsor cannot otherwise be turned than by *falsified;* for his shield was *falsed*, is not English. I might indeed have contented myself with saying his shield was pierced, and bored, and stuck with javelins. Dryden.

> Dryden, with all this effort, was not able to naturalise the new signification, which I have never seen copied, except once by some obscure nameless writer, and which indeed deserves not to be received.

to fa'lter. To sift; to cleanse. This word seems to be merely rustick or provincial.

> Barley for malt must be bold, dry, sweet, and clean *faltered* from foulness, seeds and oats. Mortimer's *Husbandry*.

to familiari'ze. (1) To make familiar; to make easy by habitude.

(2) To bring down from a state of distant superiority.

> The genius smiled upon me with a look of compassion and affability that *familiarized* him to my imagination, and at once dispelled all fear and apprehensions. Addison's *Spectator*.

fan. (1) An instrument used by ladies to move the air and cool themselves.

fancymo'nger. One who deals in tricks of imagination.

fang. (1) The long tusks of a boar or other animal; any thing like 'em.

(2) The nails; the talons.

(3) Any shoot or other thing by which hold is taken.

fa'ngle. Silly attempt; trifling scheme. It is never used, or rarely, but in contempt with the epithet *new;* as, *new fangles, new fangleness*.

fa'ngled. This word seems to signify gaudy; ridiculously shewy; vainly decorated. This is still retained in Scotland: as, he's new *fangled*, or whimsical, and very fond of novelty.

fap. Fuddled; drunk. It seems to have been a cant word in the time of Shakespeare.

> The gentleman had drunk himself out of his five senses; and being *fap*, sir, was, as they say, cashiered. Shakespeare.

far-fe'tch. A deep stratagem. A ludicrous word.

> But Jesuits have deeper reaches,
> In all their politick *farfetches;*
> And from their Coptick priest, Kircherus,
> Found out this mystick way to jeer us. *Hudibras*, p. iii.

far. The offspring of a sow; young pigs.

Sows, ready to farrow this time of the year,
Are for to be made of and counted full dear;
For now is the loss cf the *far* of the sow
More great than the loss of two calves of the cow.
Tusser.

farce. A dramatick representation written without regularity, and stuffed with wild and ludicrous conceits.

fa'rdel. A bundle; a little pack.

fart. Wind from behind.

Love is the *fart*
Of every heart;
It pains a man when 'tis kept close;
And others doth offend, when 'tis let loose. Suckling.

to fart. To break wind behind.

As when we a gun discharge,
Although the bore be ne'er so large,
Before the flame from muzzle burst,
Just at the breech it flashes first;
So from my lord his passion broke,
He *farted* first, and then he spoke. Swift.

to fa'scinate. To bewitch; to enchant; to influence in some wicked and secret manner.

fa'shion. (8) Rank; condition above the vulgar. It is used in a sense below that of quality.

It is strange that men of *fashion*, and gentlemen, should so grosly belie their own knowledge. Raleigh.

fa'sthanded. Avaricious; close-handed; closefisted; covetous.

fasti'dious. Disdainful; squeamish; delicate to a vice; insolently nice.

fati'dical. Prophetick; having the power to foretell future events.

to fa'tigate. To weary; to fatigue; to tire; to exhaust with labour; to oppress with lassitude.

fa'usen. A sort of large eel.

fa'utress. A woman that favours, or shows countenance.

fa'vourite. (2) One chosen as a companion by his superiour; a mean wretch whose whole business is by any means to please.

The great man down, you mark, his *fav'rite* flies;
The poor advanc'd, makes friends of enemies. Shakespeare, *Hamlet*.

fe'aberry. A gooseberry.

to feague. To whip; to chastise; to beat. In Scottish *feake*, to flutter; to be idly or officiously busy.

fe'astrite. Custom observed in entertainments.

feat. (1) Ready; skilful; ingenious.

   (2) It is now only used in irony and contempt.
   That *feat* man at controversy. Stillingfleet.

   (3) Nice; neat.

fe'ather. (3) An ornament; an empty title.

to fe'ather. (3) To tread as a cock.
   Dame Partlet was the sovereign of his heart;
   Ardent in love, outrageous in his play,
   He *feather'd* her a hundred times a day. Dryden.

fe'atly. Neatly; nimbly; dexterously.
   There haply by the ruddy damsel seen,
   Or shepherd-boy, they *featly* foot the green. Tickell.

fe'dary. This word, peculiar to Shakespeare, may signify either a confederate; a partner; or a dependant.
                        Damn'd paper!
   Black as the ink that's on thee, senseless bauble!
   Art thou a *fedary* for this act, and lookest
   So virgin-like without? Shakespeare's *Cymbeline*.

to feli'citate. (1) To make happy.
   What a glorious entertainment and pleasure would fill and *felicitate* his spirit, if he could grasp all in a single survey. Watts.

fenera'tion. Usury; the gain of interest; the practice of increasing money by lending.
   The hare figured not only pusilanimity and timidity from its temper, but *feneration* and usury from its fecundity and superfetation. Browne's *Vulgar Errours*, b. iii, c. 17.

fe'rret. (1) A kind of rat with red eyes and a long snout, used to catch rabbits.
   With what an eager earnestness she looked, having

threatning not only in her *ferret* eyes, but while she spoke her nose seemed to threaten her chin. Sidney, b. ii.

(2) A kind of narrow ribband.

fe′rreter. One that hunts another in his privacies.

to fe′rry. (*Faran*, to pass, Saxon; *fahr*, German, a passage. Skinner imagines that this whole family of words may be deduced from the Latin *veho*. I do not love Latin originals; but if such must be sought, may not these words be more naturally derived from *ferri*, to be carried?) To carry over in a boat.

fe′rula. (*Ferule*, Fr. from *ferula*, giant fennel, Lat.) An instrument of correction with which young scholars are beaten on the hand: so named because anciently the stalks of fennel were used for this purpose.

fescue. A small wire by which those who teach to read point out the letters.

fe′stucine. Straw-colour between green and yellow.

to fet. To fetch; to go and bring.

> Get home with thy fewel, made ready to *fet*,
> The sooner the easier carriage to get. Tusser, *Husbandry*.

to fetch. (8) To perform with suddenness or violence.

> The fox *fetched* a hundred and a hundred leaps at a delicious cluster of grapes. L'Estrange.

(9) To reach; to arrive at; to come to.

> The hare laid himself down, and took a nap; for, says he, I can *fetch* up the tortoise when I please. L'Estrange.

fe′uterer. A dogkeeper: perhaps the cleaner of the kennel.

fe′ver. A disease in which the body is violently heated, and the pulse quickened, or in which heat and cold prevail by turns. It is sometimes continual, sometimes intermittent.

to fey. To cleanse a ditch of mud.

> Such muddy deep ditches and pits in the field,
> That all a dry summer no water will yield,
> By *feying* and casting that mud upon heaps,
> Commodities many the husbandman reaps. Tusser, *Husbandry*.

fib. (A cant word among children.) A lye; a falsehood.

fi'co. An act of contempt done with the fingers, expressing a *fig for you.*

to fi'ddle. (2) To trifle; to shift the hands often, and do nothing, like a fellow that plays upon a fiddle.

> Good cooks cannot abide what they justly call *fiddling*
> work, where abundance of time is spent, and little
> done. Swift.

to fidge, to fi'dget. (A cant word.) To move nimbly and irregularly. It implies in Scotland agitation.

to fig. (See *fico.*) (1) To insult with fico's or contemptuous
motions of the fingers.

> (2) To put something useless into one's head. Low cant.
> Away to the sow she goes, and *figs* her in the crown
> with another story. L'Estrange.

fi'gpecker. A bird.

figure-flinger. A pretender to astrology and prediction.

> Quacks, *figure-flingers*, pettifoggers, and republican
> plotters cannot well live without it. Collier, *Of Con-
> fidence.*

to filch. To steal; to take by theft; to pilfer; to pillage; to
rob; to take by robbery. It is usually spoken of petty
thefts.

> Who steals my purse, steals trash; 'tis something,
> nothing;
> 'Twas mine, 'tis his, and has been slave to thousands;
> But he that *filches* from me my good name,
> Robs me of that which not enriches him,
> And makes me poor indeed. Shakespeare's *Othello.*

to file. (3) To foul; to sully; to pollute. This sense is retained
in Scotland.

> His weeds, divinely fashioned,
> All *fil'd* and mangl'd. Chapman's *Iliads*, b. xviii.

to fi'llip. (A word, says Skinner, formed from the sound. This
resemblance I am not able to discover, and therefore am
inclined to imagine it corrupted from *fill up*, by some combination of ideas which cannot be recovered.) To strike
with the nail of the finger by a sudden spring or motion.

We see, that if you *fillip* a lutestring, it sheweth double or treble. Bacon's *Natural History*, No. 183.

fi′llip. A jerk of the finger let go from the thumb.

to fi′lter. (1) To defecate by drawing off liquor by depending threads.

fi′lter. (1) A twist of thread, of which one end is dipped in the liquor to be defecated, and the other hangs below the bottom of the vessel, so that the liquor drips from it.

fi′mble hemp. The season of pulling of it is first about Lambas, when good part of it will be ripe; that is, the light summer hemp, that bears no seed, which is called *fimble hemp*. Mortimer, *Husbandry*.

fin. The wing of a fish; the limb by which he balances his body, and moves in the water.

fin-foo′ted. Palmipedous; having feet with membranes between the toes.

fi′nancier. One who collects or farms the publick revenue.

finch. A small bird of which we have three kinds, the goldfinch, chaffinch, and bulfinch.

to find. (15) To supply; to furnish: as, he *finds* me in money and in victuals.

findfa′ult. A censurer; a caviller.

fi′ndy. Plump; weighty; firm; solid. Thus the proverb,

> A cold May and a windy,
> Makes the barn fat and *findy*.

means that it stores the barn with plump and firm grain. Junius.

finefi′ngered. Nice; artful; exquisite.

fine′sse. Artifice; stratagem: an unnecessary word which is creeping into the language.

fi′nger. (1) The flexible member of the hand by which men catch and hold.

fi′nglefangle. A trifle: a burlesque word.

fi′nical. Nice; foppish; pretending to superfluous elegance.

> A whorson, glassgazing, superserviceable, *finical* rogue. Shakespeare's *King Lear*.

fi′pple. A stopper.

fi′recross. A token in Scotland for the nation to take arms: the ends thereof burnt black, and in some parts smeared with blood. It is carried like lightning from one place to another. Upon refusal to send it forward, or to rise, the last person who has it shoots the other dead.

fi'redrake. A fiery serpent: I suppose the prester.

fi'reman. (2) A man of violent passions.

> I had last night the fate to drink a bottle with two of these *firemen. Tatler,* No. 61.

to firk. To whip; to beat; to correct; to chastise.

> Besides, it is not only foppish,
> But vile, idolatrous and popish,
> For one man out of his own skin
> To *firk* and whip another's sin. *Hudibras,* p. ii, can. 2.

fish. An animal that inhabits the water.

to fi'shify. To turn to fish: a cant word.

> Here comes Romeo
> —Without his roe, like a dried herring:
> O flesh, flesh, how art thou *fishified!* Shakespeare, *Romeo and Juliet.*

fi'shmeal. Diet of fish; abstemious diet.

fit. (1) A paroxysm or exacerbation of any intermittent distemper.

(5) It is used, without an epithet of discrimination, for the hysterical disorders of women, and the convulsions of children; and by the vulgar for the epilepsy.

fi'tchat, fi'tchew. A stinking little beast, that robs the henroost and warren. Skinner calls him the *stinking ferret;* but he is much larger, at least as some provinces distinguish them, in which the polecat is termed a *fitchat,* and the *stinking ferret* a stoat.

fitz. A son. Only used in law and genealogy: as *Fitzherbert,* the son of Herbert; *Fitzthomas,* the son of Thomas; *Fitzroy,* the son of the king. It is commonly used of illegitimate children.

---

firedrake. Johnson forgot to include *prester* in the *Dictionary.* The *O.E.D.* defines it as "a fiery (or scorching) whirlwind, also a kind of venomous serpent."

fixa'tion. (1) Stability; firmness; steadiness.

(2) Residence in a certain place.

(3) Confinement; forbearance of excursion.

fi'zgig. A kind of dart or harpoon with which seamen strike fish.

fla'bby. Soft; not firm; easily shaking or yielding to the touch.

> Pulls out the rags contriv'd to prop
> Her *flabby* dugs, and down they drop. Swift.

fla'ggy. (1) Weak; lax; limber; not stiff; not tense.

(2) Weak in taste; insipid.

fla'grant. (1) Ardent; burning; eager.

(2) Glowing; flushed.

(3) Red; imprinted red.

> Their common loves, a lewd abandon'd pack,
> The beadle's lash still *flagrant* on their back. Prior.

flam. (A cant word of no certain etymology.) A falsehood; a lye; an illusory pretext.

to flam. To deceive with a lye. Merely cant.

> God is not to be *flammed* off with lyes, who knows exactly what thou can'st do, and what not. South's *Sermons.*

to flap. (1) To beat with a flap, as flies are beaten.

> Yet let me *flap* this bug with gilded wings,
> This painted child of dirt, that stinks and stings. Pope.

fla'pdragon. (From a dragon supposed to breathe fire.) (1) A play in which they catch raisins out of burning brandy, and, extinguishing them by closing the mouth, eat them.

(2) The thing eaten at flapdragon.

to fla'pdragon. To swallow; to devour. Low cant.

to flash. To strike up large bodies of water from the surface.

> If the sea-water be *flashed* with a stick or oar, the same casteth a shining colour, and the drops resemble sparkles of fire. Carew's *Survey of Cornwal.*

fla'sher. A man of more appearance of wit than reality.

fla'shy. (2) Insipid; without force or spirit.

> Distilled books are, like common distilled waters, *flashy* things. Bacon, *Essay* 51.

to fla'tter. (1) To sooth with praises; to please with blandish-

ments; to gratify with servile obsequiousness; to gain by
false compliments.

(2) To praise falsely.

(3) To please; to sooth. This sense is purely Gallick.

fla′tulent. (2) Empty; vain; big without substance or reality;
puffy.

> How many of these *flatulent* writers have sunk in their
> reputation, after seven or eight editions of their works.
> Dryden.

to flaunt. (1) To make a fluttering show in apparel.

> You sot, you loiter about alehouses, or *flaunt* about the
> streets in your new-gilt chariot, never minding me nor
> your numerous family. Arbuthnot's *History of John Bull.*

(2) To be hung with something loose and flying. This seems
not to be proper.

> Fortune in men has some small diff'rence made;
> One *flaunts* in rags, one flutters in brocade. Pope's *Essays.*

flaw. (3) A sudden gust; a violent blast.

> Oh, that that earth, which kept the world in awe,
> Should patch a wall, t' expel the winter's *flaw.* Shakespeare, *Hamlet.*

(4) A tumult; a tempestuous uproar.

(5) A sudden commotion of mind.

fle′abitten. (2) Mean; worthless.

> *Fleabitten* synod, an assembly brew'd
> Of clerks and elders ana, like the rude
> Chaos of presbyt'ry, where laymen guide,
> With the tame woolpack clergy by their side. Cleveland.

to fleer. (1) To mock; to gibe; to jest with insolence and contempt.

> Do I, like the female tribe,
> Think it well to *fleer* and gibe? Swift.

(2) To leer; to grin with an air of civility.

> How popular and courteous; how they grin and *fleer*
> upon every man they meet! Burton, *On Melancholy.*

fleet. A creek; an inlet of water. A provincial word, from which
the Fleet-prison and Fleet-street are named.

to fleet. (3) (In the country.) To skim milk; to take off the cream: whence the word *fleeting* dish.

flee'tingdish. A skimming bowl.

to flesh. (1) To initiate: from the sportsman's practise of feeding his hawks and dogs with the first game that they take, or training them to pursuit by giving them the *flesh* of animals.

(2) To harden; to establish in any practice, as dogs by often feeding on any thing.

> The women ran all away, saving only one, who was so *fleshed* in malice, that neither during nor after the fight she gave any truce to her cruelty. Sidney, b. ii.

(3) To glut; to satiate.

> He hath perverted a young gentlewoman, and this night he *fleshes* his will in the spoil of her honour. Shakespeare.

fle'shmonger. One who deals in flesh; a pimp.

> Was the duke a *fleshmonger*, a fool, and a coward, as you then reported him? Shakespeare's *Measure for Measure*.

fle'shquake. A tremor of the body; a word formed by Jonson in imitation of earthquake.

flewed. Chapped; mouthed.

fli'msy. (2) Mean; spiritless; without force.

fling. (2) A gibe; a sneer; a contemptuous remark.

> No little scribbler is of wit so bare,
> But has his *fling* at the poor wedded pair. Addison.

flipp. (A cant word.) A liquor much used in ships, made by mixing beer with spirits and sugar.

> The tarpawlin and swabber is lolling at Madagascar, with some drunken sunburnt whore, over a can of *flip*. Dennis.

flippa'nt. (A word of no great authority, probably derived from *flip-flap*.) (1) Nimble; moveable. It is used only of the act of speech.

(2) Pert; talkative.

to flirt. (1) To jeer; to gibe at one.

(2) To run about perpetually; to be unsteady and fluttering.

flirt. (1) A quick elastick motion.

flirta′tion. A quick sprightly motion. A cant word among women.

to flit. (2) To remove; to migrate. In Scotland it is still used for removing from one place to another at quarter-day, or the usual term.

flix. Down; fur; soft hair.

> With his loll'd tongue he faintly licks his prey;
> His warm breath blows her *flix* up as she lies:
> She trembling creeps upon the ground away,
> And looks back to him with beseeching eyes. Dryden.

flo′rid. (1) Productive of flowers; covered with flowers.

to flounce. (1) To move with violence in the water or mire; to struggle or dash in the water.

(2) To move with weight and tumult.

(3) To move with passionate agitation.

flo′under. The name of a small flat fish.

> Like the *flounder*, out of the frying-pan into the fire.
> Camden.

flue. (A word of which I know not the etymology, unless it be derived from *flew* of *fly*.) (2) Soft down or fur, such as may fly in the wind.

flush. (2) Affluent; abounding. A cant word.

> Lord Strut was not very *flush* in ready, either to go to law or clear old debts; neither could he find good bail. Arbuthnot.

to flu′ster. To make hot and rosy with drinking; to make half drunk.

fob. A small pocket.

> Orphans around his bed the lawyer sees,
> And takes the plaintiff's and defendant's fees;
> His fellow pick-purse, watching for a job,
> Fancies his fingers in the cully's *fob*. Swift.

to fob. (1) To cheat; to trick; to defraud.

(2) To fob off. To shift off; to put aside with an artifice; to delude by a trick.

foh. An interjection of abhorrence: as if one should at sight of any thing hated cry out *a foh!*

to foist. To insert by forgery.

fo′istiness. Fustiness; mouldiness.

fo′lio. A large book, of which the pages are formed by a sheet of paper once doubled.

folk. (4) It is now used only in familiar or burlesque language.

> He walk'd, and wore a threadbare cloak;
> He din'd and supp'd at charge of other *folk*. Swift.

fond. (*Fonn*, Scottish. A word of which I have found no satisfactory etymology. To *fonne* is in Chaucer to doat, to be foolish.) (1) Foolish; silly; indiscreet; imprudent; injudicious.

(2) Trifling; valued by folly.

fo′ndling. A person or thing much fondled or caressed; something regarded with great affection.

foo′dy. Eatable; fit for food.

foo′tlicker. A slave; an humble fawner; one who licks the foot.

fo′pdoodle. A fool; an insignificant wretch.

fo′ppling. A petty fop; an under-rate coxcomb.

> Thy works in Chloe's toilet gain a part,
> And, with his tailor, share the *foppling's* heart. Tickell.

fora′minous. Full of holes; perforated in many places; porous.

fo′rcipated. Formed like a pair of pincers to open and inclose.

> The locusts have antennae, or long horns before, with a long falcation or *forcipated* tail behind. Browne's *Vulgar Errours*.

to foredo′. (1) To ruin; to destroy. A word obsolete. Opposed to making happy.

> This doth betoken,
> The corse they follow did with desperate hand
> *Foredo* its own life. Shakespeare's *Hamlet*.

(2) To overdo; to weary; to harrass.

fo′rehead. (2) Impudence; confidence; assurance; audaciousness; audacity.

> I would fain know to what branch of the legislature they can have the *forehead* to apply. Swift's *Presbyterian Plea*.

to foresla′ck. To neglect by idleness.

> It is a great pity that so good an opportunity was omitted, and so happy an occasion *foreslacked*, that might

have been the eternal good of the land. Spenser's *State of Ireland*.

fo'reswat, fo'reswart. Spent with heat.

fo'retop. That part of a woman's headdress that is forward, or the top of a periwig.

fork. (1) An instrument divided at the end into two or more points or prongs, used on many occasions.

> I dine with *forks* that have but two prongs. Swift.

forlo'rn. (1) A lost, solitary, forsaken man.

> Henry
> Is of a king become a banish'd man,
> And forc'd to live in Scotland a *forlorn*. Shakespeare, *Henry VI*.

(2) Forlorn hope. The soldiers who are sent first to the attack, and are therefore doomed to perish.

to fo'rlye. To lye across.

> Knit with a golden baldric, which *forlay*
> Athwart her snowy breast, and did divide
> Her dainty paps, which, like young fruit in May,
> Now little 'gan to swell; and being ty'd,
> Through her thin weed, their places only signify'd.
> *Fairy Queen*.

form. (11) The seat or bed of a hare.

> Have you observ'd a sitting hare,
> List'ning, and fearful of the storm
> Of horns and hounds, clap back her ear,
> Afraid to keep or leave her *form*. Prior.

to fo'rnicate. To commit lewdness.

> It is a new way to *fornicate* at a distance. Browne's *Vulgar Errours*.

fo'rtunebook. A book consulted to know fortune or future events.

fo'rtuneteller. One who cheats common people by pretending to the knowledge of futurity.

fo'utra. A fig; a scoff; an act of contempt.

fowl. A winged animal; a bird. It is colloquially used of edible birds, but in books of all the feathered tribes.

fox. (1) A wild animal of the canine kind, with sharp ears and a bushy tail, remarkable for his cunning, living in holes, and preying upon fowls or small animals.

(2) By way of reproach, applied to a knave or cunning fellow.

fo′xcase. A fox's skin.

> One had better be laughed at for taking a *foxcase* for a fox, than be destroyed by taking a live fox for a case. L'Estrange.

to fract. To break; to violate; to infringe. Found perhaps only in the following passage.

> His days and times are past,
> And my reliance on his *fracted* dates
> Has smit my credit. Shakespeare's *Timon*.

fra′gmentary. Composed of fragments. A word not elegant, nor in use.

frail. (1) A basket made of rushes.

(2) A rush for weaving baskets.

fra′ischeur. Freshness; coolness. A word foolishly innovated by Dryden.

> Hither in summer-ev'nings you repair,
> To taste the *fraischeur* of the purer air. Dryden.

fra′mpold. Peevish; boisterous; rugged; crossgrained.

> Her husband! Alas, the sweet woman leads an ill life with him: she leads a very *frampold* life with him. Shakespeare.

fra′nion. A paramour; a boon companion.

frank. (1) A place to feed hogs in; a sty: so called from liberality of food.

to frank. (1) To shut up in a frank or sty. Hanmer.

(2) To feed high; to fat; to cram. Junius and Ainsworth.

fra′nklin. A steward; a bailiff of land. It signifies originally a little gentleman, and is not improperly Englished a gentleman servant.

freethi′nker. A libertine; a contemner of religion.

> Atheist is an old-fashion'd word: I'm a *freethinker*, child. Addison's *Drummer*.

to fre′nchify. To infect with the manner of France; to make a coxcomb.

fresh. (10) Fasting: opposed to eating or drinking. A low word.

freshwa'ter. Raw; unskilled; unacquainted. A low term borrowed from the sailors, who stigmatize those who come first to sea as *freshwater* men or novices.

fret. (1) A frith, or strait of the sea, where the water by confinement is always rough.

(2) Any agitation of liquors by fermentation, confinement, or other cause.

fri'bbler. A trifler.

A *fribbler* is one who professes rapture for the woman, and dreads her consent. *Spectator*, No. 288.

fricasse'e. A dish made by cutting chickens or other small things in pieces, and dressing them with strong sauce.

Oh, how would Homer praise their dancing dogs,
Their stinking cheese, and *fricacy* of frogs!
He'd raise no fables, sing no flagrant lye,
Of boys with custard choak'd at Newberry. King.

fri'ghtful. (2) A cant word among women for any thing unpleasing.

fri'ghtfully. (2) Disagreeably; not beautifully. A woman's word.

Then to her glass; and Betty, pray,
Don't I look *frightfully* to-day? Swift.

fri'pperer. One who deals in old things vamped up.

fri'ppery. (1) The place where old cloaths are sold.

(2) Old cloaths; cast dresses; tattered rags.

fri'sky. Gay; airy. A low word.

fri'tinancy. The scream of an insect, as the cricket or cicada.

fri'tter. (2) A fragment; a small piece.

Sense and putter! have I lived to stand in the taunt of one that makes *fritters* of English! Shakespeare, *Merry Wives of Windsor*.

(3) A cheesecake; a wigg. Ainsworth.

frog. (1) A small animal with four feet, living both by land and water, and placed by naturalists among mixed animals, as partaking of beast and fish. There is likewise a small green frog that perches on trees, said to be venomous.

fro'ntbox. The box in the playhouse from which there is a direct view to the stage.

to frounce. To frizzle or curl the hair about the face. This word was at first probably used in contempt.

fro'uzy. (A cant word.) Dim; foetid; musty.

> Petticoats in *frouzy* heaps. Swift.

fro'ward. Peevish; ungovernable; angry; perverse: the contrary to *toward*.

to frump. To mock; to browbeat. Skinner. Ainsworth.

to frush. To break, bruise, or crush. Hanmer.

fry. (2) Any swarm of animals; or young people in contempt.

> The young *fry* must be held at a distance, and kept under the discipline of contempt. Collier, *On Pride*.

to fub. To put off; to delay by false pretences; to cheat. It is generally written *fob*. See *fob*.

fub. A plump chubby boy.

fugh. An expression of abhorrence.

> A very filthy fellow: how odiously he smells of his country garlick! *fugh*, how he stinks of Spain! Dryden, *Don Sebastian*.

fu'lham. A cant word for false dice. Hanmer.

> Let vultures gripe thy guts, for gourd and *fulham's* hold,
> And high and low beguile the rich and poor. Shakespeare.

fu'limart. A kind of stinking ferret.

> The fichat, the *fulimart*, and the ferret, live upon the face, and within the bowels of the earth.
> Walton's *Angler*.

fu'lsome. (2) Of a rank odious smell.

> (3) Tending to obscenity.

> A certain epigram, which is ascribed to the emperor, is more *fulsome* than any passage I have met with in our poet. Dryden.

fume'tte. A word introduced by cooks, and the pupils of cooks, for the stink of meat.

> A haunch of ven'son made her sweat,
> Unless it had the right *fumette*. Swift.

fun. (A low cant word.) Sport; high merriment; frolicksome delight.

fu'ndament. The back part of the body.

funk. A stink. A low word.

fur. (3) Any moisture exhaled to such a degree as that the remainder sticks on the part.

> Methinks I am not right in ev'ry part;
> I feel a kind of trembling at my heart:
> My pulse unequal, and my breath is strong;
> Besides a filthy *fur* upon my tongue. Dryden's *Persius*, Sat. 3.

to fu'rnace. To throw out as sparks from a furnace. A bad word.

> He *furnaces*
> The thick sighs from him. Shakespeare's *Cymbeline.*

fu'rtive. Stolen; gotten by theft.

fuss. (A low cant word.) A tumult; a bustle.

fu'stian. (1) A kind of cloth made of linen and cotton, and perhaps now of cotton only.

(2) A high swelling kind of writing made up of heterogeneous parts, or of words and ideas ill associated; bombast.

> I am much deceived if this be not abominable *fustian;* that is, thoughts and words ill sorted, and without the least relation to each other. Dryden's *Spanish Fryar*, Dedication.

fu'stilarian. A low fellow; a stinkard; a scoundrel. A word used by Shakespeare only.

> Away, you scullion, you rampallian, you *fustilarian:* I'll tickle your catastrophe. Shakespeare's *Henry IV*, p. ii.

fu'sty. Ill smelling; mouldy.

fu'tile. (1) Talkative; loquacious.

fy. A word of blame and disapprobation.

> Nay, *fy*, what mean you in this open place?
> Unhand me, or, I swear, I'll scratch your face:
> Let go, for shame; you make me mad for spite:
> My mouth's my own; and if you kiss, I'll bite. Dryden.

G

---

ga'bardine. A coarse frock; any mean dress.

ga'bel. An excise; a tax.

gai'ngiving. The same as misgiving; a giving against: as gainsaying, which is still in use, is saying against, or contradicting.

ga'llant. (2) A whoremaster, who caresses women to debauch them.

ga'llantry. (4) Courtship; refined address to women.

(5) Vicious love; lewdness; debauchery.

It looks like a sort of compounding between virtue and vice, as if a woman were allowed to be vicious provided she be not a profligate; as if there were a certain point where *gallantry* ends, and infamy begins. Swift.

ga'llery. (2) The seats in the playhouse above the pit, in which the meaner people sit.

gallimau'fry. (1) A hoch-poch, or hash of several sorts of broken meat; a medley. Hanmer.

(2) Any inconsistent or ridiculous medley.

(3) It is used by Shakespeare ludicrously of a woman.
Sir John affects thy wife.
—Why, sir, my wife is not young.
—He wooes both high and low, both rich and poor;
He loves thy *gallimaufry*, friend. Shakespeare.

ga'mbler. (A cant word, I suppose, for *game* or *gamester*.) A knave whose practice it is to invite the unwary to game and cheat them.

gang. A number herding together; a troop; a company; a tribe; a herd. It is seldom used but in contempt or abhorrence.

gaol. A prison; a place of confinement. It is always pronounced and too often written *jail*, and sometimes *goal*.

to gar. To cause; to make. It is still in use in Scotland.

> Tell 'me, good Hobbinol, what *gars* thee greet?
>
> What! hath some wolf thy tender lambs ytorn?
>
> Or is thy bagpipe broke, that sounds so sweet?
>
> Or art thou of thy loved lass forlorne. Spenser's *Pastorals.*

ga'rbage. (1) The bowels; the offal; that part of the inwards which is separated and thrown away.

> When you receive condign punishment, you run to your confessor, that parcel of guts and *garbage.* Dryden, *Spanish Fryar.*

to ga'rble. To sift; to part; to separate the good from the bad.

ga'rboil. Disorder; tumult; uproar. Hanmer.

to ga'rgle. (2) To warble; to play in the throat. An improper use.

> So charm'd you were, you ceas'd a while to doat
>
> On nonsense *gargl'd* in an eunuch's throat. Fenton.

garlickea'ter. A mean fellow.

ga'rous. Resembling pickle made of fish.

> In a civet-cat a different and offensive odour proceeds, partly from its food, that being especially fish; whereof this humour may be a *garous* excretion, and olidous separation. Browne's *Vulgar Errours,* b. iii, c. 4.

ga'rret. (2) Rotten wood.

gas. (A word invented by the chymists.) It is used by Van Helmont, and seems designed to signify, in general, a spirit not capable of being coagulated: but he uses it loosely in many senses, and very unintelligibly and inconsistently. Harris.

gash. (2) The mark of a wound. I know not if this be proper.

> I was fond of back-sword and cudgel play, and I now bear in my body many a black and blue *gash* and scar. Arbuthnot.

to gasp. (3) To long for. This sense is, I think, not proper, as nature never expresses desire by gasping.

> The Castilian and his wife had the comfort to be under the same master, who, seeing how dearly they loved one

another, and *gasped* after their liberty, demanded a
most exorbitant price for their ransom. *Spectator,* No.
198.

to gast. To make aghast; to fright; to shock; to terrify; to fear; to
affray.

to gaude. To exult; to rejoice at any thing.

ga'udy. A feast; a festival; a day of plenty.

He may surely be content with a fast to-day, that is sure
of a *gaudy* to-morrow. Cheyne.

ga'vel. A provincial word for ground.

gawk. (1) A cuckow.

(2) A foolish fellow. In both senses it is retained in Scotland.

gay. An ornament; an embellishment.

gazette'er. (1) A writer of news.

(2) It was lately a term of the utmost infamy, being usually
applied to wretches who were hired to vindicate the court.

ge'ason. Wonderful.

It to Leeches seemed strange and *geason. Hubberd's
Tale.*

to geck. To cheat; to trick.

gem. (2) The first bud.

The orchard loves to wave
With winter winds, before the *gems* exert
Their feeble heads. Philips.

gemina'tion. Repetition; reduplication.

ge'nerous. (1) Not of mean birth; of good extraction.

gene'va. We used to keep a distilled spirituous water of juniper
in the shops; but the making of it became the business of the
distiller, who sold it under the name of *geneva.* At present
only a better kind is distilled from the juniper-berry: what
is commonly sold is made with no better an ingredient than
oil of turpentine, put into the still, with a little common salt,
and the coarsest spirit they have, which is drawn off much
below proof strength, and is consequently a liquor that one
would wonder any people could accustom themselves to
drink with pleasure. Hill's *Materia Medica.*

ge'nial. (1) That which contributes to propagation.

Creator Venus, *genial* pow'r of love,
The bliss of men below and gods above! Dryden's
Fables.

genicula'tion. Knottiness; the quality in plants of having knots
or joints.

ge'ntile. (1) One of an uncovenanted nation; one who knows
not the true God.

(2) A person of rank. Obsolete.

ge'ntilism. Heathenism; paganism.

gentili'tious. (1) Endemial; peculiar to a nation.

That an unsavory odour is *gentilitious,* or national unto
the Jews, reason or sense will not induce. Browne's *Vulgar Errours.*

(2) Hereditary; entailed on a family.

genti'lity. (4) Paganism; heathenism.

ge'ntle. (2) A particular kind of worm.

ge'omancer. A fortuneteller; a caster of figures; a cheat who
pretends to foretell futurity by other means than the astrologer.

Fortunetellers, jugglers, *geomancers,* and the incantatory impostors, though commonly men of inferior rank,
daily delude the vulgar. Browne's *Vulgar Errours,* b. i.

george. (1) A figure of St. George on horseback worn by the
knights of the garter.

(2) A brown loaf. Of this sense I know not the original.

ge'rmin. A shooting or sprouting seed.

gi'bbe. Any old worn-out animal.

gi'bcat. An old worn-out cat.

gi'blets. The parts of a goose which are cut off before it is
roasted.

to gi'ggle. To laugh idly; to titter; to grin with merry levity. It
is retained in Scotland.

gill. (3) The flesh under the chin.

(5) The appellation of a woman in ludicrous language.

I can, for I will,
Here at Burley o' th' Hill,
Give you all your fill,
Each Jack with his *Gill.* Ben. Jonson's *Gypsies.*

(6) The name of a plant; ground-ivy.

(7) Malt liquor medicated with ground-ivy.

gi′llhouse. A house where gill is sold.

gilt. Golden show; gold laid on the surface of any matter. Now obsolete.

gim. (An old word.) Neat; spruce; well dressed.

gi′mcrack. (Supposed by Skinner to be ludicrously formed from *gin*, derived from *engine*.) A slight or trivial mechanism.

gi′mmal. Some little quaint devices or pieces of machinery. Hanmer.

gi′mmer. Movement; machinery.

gin. (4) (Contracted from *geneva*, which see.) The spirit drawn by distillation from juniper berries.

to gip. To take out the guts of herrings. Bailey.

to gird. To break a scornful jest; to gibe; to sneer.

> Men of all sorts take a pride to *gird* at me: the brain of this foolish compounded clay, man, is not able to invent any thing that tends to laughter more than I invent, or is invented on me: I am not only witty in myself, but the cause that wit is in other men. Shakespeare's *Henry IV*, p. ii.

to girn. Seems to be a corruption of *grin*. It is still used in Scotland, and is applied to a crabbed, captious, or peevish person.

to girt. To gird; to encompass; to encircle. Not proper.

> In the dread ocean, undulating wide
> Beneath the radiant line, that *girts* the globe,
> The circling Typhon whirl'd from point to point.
> Thomson.

to give. (1) To rush; to fall on; to give the assault. A phrase merely French, and not worthy of adoption.

> Your orders come too late, the fight's begun;
> The enemy *gives* on with fury led. Dryden, *Indian Emperour*.

(9) to give out. To cease; to yield.

> Madam, I always believ'd you so stout,
> That for twenty denials you would not *give out*. Swift.

gi′zzard. (2) It is proverbially used for apprehension or conception of mind: as, he *frets his gizzard,* he harrasses his imagination.

to glance. (5) To censure by oblique hints.

It was objected against him that he had written verses, wherein he *glanced* at a certain reverend doctor, famous for dulness. Swift.

to glass. (1) To see as in a glass; to represent as in a glass or mirrour.

Methinks I am partaker of thy passion,

And in thy case do *glass* mine own debility. Sidney, b. ii.

to glaver. To flatter; to wheedle. A low word.

Kingdoms have their distempers, intermissions, and paroxysms, as well as natural bodies; and a *glavering* council is as dangerous on the one hand as a wheedling priest, or a flattering physician is on the other. L'Estrange's *Fables.*

gle′by. Turfy; perhaps in the following passage fat or fruitful, if it has indeed any meaning.

Pernicious flatt'ry! thy malignant seeds

In an ill hour, and by a fatal hand

Sadly diffus'd o'er virtue's *gleby* land,

With rising pride amidst the corn appear,

And choke the hopes and harvest of the year. Prior.

glee. Joy; merriment; gayety. It anciently signified musick played at feasts. It is not now used, except in ludicrous writing, or with some mixture of irony and contempt.

gleek. Musick; or musician.

to gleek. (1) To sneer; to gibe; to droll upon.

(2) In Scotland it is still retained, and signifies to fool or spend time idly, with something of mimickry or drollery.

to gleen. To shine with heat or polish. I know not the original notion of this word: it may be of the same race with *glow* or with *gleam.*

glib. They have another custom from the Scythians, the wearing of mantles and long *glibs;* which is a thick curled bush of hair hanging down over their eyes, and monstrously disguising them. Spenser, *On Ireland.*

to glib. To castrate.

to gloar. (1) To squint; to look askew. Skinner.

(2) In Scotland, to stare: as, *what a* gloar and *quean.*

to gloat. To cast side glances as a timorous lover.

glo′bard. A glow-worm.

to glose. To flatter; to collogue. Hanmer. See to *gloze.*

to glout. (A low word of which I find no etymology.) To pout; to look sullen. It is still used in Scotland.

glo′wworm. A small creeping insect with a luminous tail.

to gloze. (1) To flatter; to wheedle; to insinuate; to fawn.

(2) To comment. This should be *gloss.*

gloze. (1) Flattery; insinuation.

(2) Specious show; gloss.

to glut. (1) To swallow; to devour.

> 'Till cram'd and gorg'd, nigh burst
> With suck'd and *glutted* offal. Milton's *Paradise Lost,*
> b. x.

gna′tsnapper. A bird so called, because he lives by catching gnats.

go to. Come, come, take the right course. A scornful exhortation.

> My favour is not bought with words like these:
> *Go to;* you'll teach your tongue another tale. Rowe.

goat. A ruminant animal that seems a middle species between deer and sheep.

goa′tmilker. A kind of owl so called from sucking goats. Bailey.

gob. A small quantity. A low word.

> Do'st think I have so little wit as to part with such a *gob* of money? L'Estrange.

go′bbet. A mouthful; as much as can be swallowed at once.

to go′bbet. To swallow at a mouthful. A low word.

go′dwit. A bird of particular delicacy.

go′ldfinch. A singing bird, so named from his golden colour. This is called in Staffordshire a *proud taylor.*

go′ldfinder. One who finds gold. A term ludicrously applied to those that empty jakes.

goll. Hands; paws; claws. Used in contempt, and obsolete.

goo′dy. A low term of civility used to mean persons.

Plain *goody* would no longer down;
'Twas madam in her grogram gown. Swift.

goose. (1) A large waterfowl proverbially noted, I know not why, for foolishness.

go'rbelly. A big paunch; a swelling belly. A term of reproach for a fat man.

gord. An instrument of gaming, as appears from Beaumont and Fletcher.

Thy dry bones can reach at nothing now, but *gords* and ninepins. Beaumont and Fletcher.

go'sling. (2) A cat's tail on nut-trees and pines.

to go'spel. To fill with sentiments of religion. This word in Shakespeare, in whom alone I have found it, is used, though so venerable in itself, with some degree of irony: I suppose from the gospellers, who had long been held in contempt.

Are you so *gospell'd*
To pray for this good man, and for his issue,
Whose heavy hand hath bow'd you to the grave? Shakespeare.

go'speller. A name of the followers of Wicklif, who first attempted a reformation from popery, given them by the Papists in reproach, from their professing to follow and preach only the gospel.

go'ssip. (1) One who answers for the child in baptism.

(2) A tippling companion.

(3) One who runs about tattling like women at a lying-in.

gove. A mow.

to gove. To mow; to put in a gove, goff, or mow. An old word.

to gra'bble. To grope; to feel eagerly with the hands.

My blood chills about my heart at the thought of these rogues, with their bloody hands *grabbling* in my guts, and pulling out my very entrails. Arbuthnot's *History of John Bull.*

gra'dient. Walking; moving by steps.

grail. Small particles of any kind.

grain. (11) Died or stained substance.

---

to gove. Johnson does not define *goff*; it is an alternative form of *gove*.

How the red roses flush up in her cheeks,
And the pure snow with goodly vermil stain,
Like crimson dy'd in *grain*. Spenser's *Prothalamion*.
(13) The heart; the bottom.

The one being tractable and mild, the other stiff and impatient of a superior, they lived but in cunning concord, as brothers *glued* together, but not united in *grain*. Hayward.

gra'mmar. (1) The science of speaking correctly; the art which teaches the relations of words to each other.

We make a countryman dumb, whom we will not allow to speak but by the rules of *grammar*. Dyrden's *Dufresnoy*.

gra'mmar school. A school in which the learned languages are grammatically taught.

Thou hast most traitorously corrupted the youth of the realm in erecting a *grammar school*. Shakespeare's *Henry VI*.

grammatica'ster. A mean verbal pedant; a low grammarian.

gratifica'tion. (3) Reward; recompence. A low word.

to gra'vel. (2) To stick in the sand.

William the Conqueror, when he invaded this island, chanced at his arrival to be *gravelled*; and one of his feet stuck so fast in the sand, that he fell to the ground. Camden.

(3) To puzzle; to stop; to put to a stand; to embarrass.
I would kiss before I spoke.
—Nay, you were better speak first, and when you were *gravell'd* for lack of matter you might take occasion to kiss. Shakespeare.

gra'vy. The serous juice that runs from flesh not much dried by the fire.

They usually boil and roast their meat until it falls almost off from the bones; but we love it half raw, with the blood trickling down from it, delicately terming it the *gravy*, which in truth looks more like an ichorous or raw bloody matter. Harvey, *On Consumptions*.

to grease. (2) To bribe; to corrupt with presents.

Envy not the store
Of the *greas'd* advocate that grinds the poor. Dryden,
Persius.

greece. A flight of steps.

greeze. (Otherwise written *greece.* See *greece,* or *grieze,* or *grice,* from *degrees.*) A flight of steps; a step.

grice. (1) A little pig. Gouldman.

(2) A step or *greeze.*

to gride. To cut; to make way by cutting. A word elegant, but not in use.

So sore
The *griding* sword, with discontinuous wound,
Pass'd through him! Milton's *Paradise Lost,* b. vi.

gri'ffin, gri'ffon. A fabled animal, said to be generated between the lion and eagle, and to have the head and paws of the lion, and the wings of the eagle.

grig. (1) It seems originally to have signified any thing below the natural size.

(2) A small eel.

(3) A merry creature.

Hard is her heart as flint or stone,
She laughs to see me pale;
And merry as a *grig* is grown,
And brisk as bottle-ale. Swift.

to gri'lly. This word signifies, as it seems, to harrass; to hurt: as we now say, *to roast a man,* for *to teaze him.*

grima'lkin. (1) Grey little woman; the name of an old cat.

to grin. (1) To set the teeth together and withdraw the lips.

grin. The act of closing the teeth and shewing them.

gro'undling. A fish which keeps at the bottom of the water: hence one of the low vulgar. Hanmer.

It offends me to the soul, to hear a robusteous perriwig-pated fellow tear a passion to tatters, to very rags, to split the ears of the *groundlings.* Shakespeare's *Hamlet.*

gro'wthead, gro'wtnol. (1) A kind of fish.

(2) An idle lazy fellow.

grub. (1) A small worm that eats holes in bodies.

(2) A short thick man; a dwarf. In contempt.

to gru′bble. To feel in the dark.

> Thou hast a colour;
> Now let me rowl and *grubble* thee:
> Blind men say white feels smooth, and black feels rough:
> Thou hast a rugged skin; I do not like thee. Dryden.

gru′bstreet. Originally the name of a street in Moorfields in London, much inhabited by writers of small histories, dictionaries, and temporary poems; whence any mean production is called grubstreet.

> Χαῖρ᾽ Ἰθάκη μετ᾽ ἄεθλα μετ᾽ ἄλγεα πικρὰ
> Ἀσπασίως τεὸν οὖδας ἱκάνομαι.

to grudge. (5) To give or have any uneasy remains. I know not whether the word in this sense be not rather *grugeons*, or remains; *grugeons* being the part of corn that remains after the fine meal has passed the sieve.

> My Dolabella,
> Hast thou not still some *grudgings* of thy fever? Dryden.

grum. Sour; surly; severe. A low word.

to grutch. (Corrupted for the sake of rhyme from *grudge*.) To envy; to repine; to be discontented.

> But what we're born for we must bear,
> Our frail condition it is such,
> That what to all may happen here,
> If't chance to me, I must not *grutch*. Ben. Jonson.

gry. Any thing of little value: as, the paring of the nails.

gu′dgeon. (1) A small fish found in brooks and rivers, easily caught, and therefore made a proverbial name for a man easily cheated.

(2) Something to be caught to a man's own disadvantage; a bait; an allurement: *gudgeons* being commonly used as baits for pike.

to gu′ggle. To sound as water running with intermissions out of a narrow mouthed vessel.

---

grubstreet. Johnson never lived in Grub Street, but he salutes that home of poor writers like himself with the quotation: "Hail, Ithaca! After toil and bitter woe, I am glad to reach your soil" (*Greek Anthology*, ix, 458).

guine′adropper. One who cheats by dropping guineas.

gui′neapig. A small animal with a pig's snout.

gulch, gu′lchin. A little glutton. Skinner.

gull. (2) A cheat; a fraud; a trick.

    (3) A stupid animal; one easily cheated.

> Why have you suffer'd me to be imprison'd,
> Kept in a dark house, visited by the priest,
> And made the most notorious geck and *gull*
> That e'er invention plaid on. Shakespeare, *Twelfth Night*.

gu′llcatcher. A cheat; a man of trick; one who catches silly people.

gu′llyhole. The hole where the gutters empty themselves in the subterraneous sewer.

gulo′sity. Greediness; gluttony; voracity.

gurge. Whirlpool; gulf.

gut. (1) The long pipe reaching with many convolutions from the stomach to the vent.

> This lord wears his wit in his belly, and his *guts* in his head. Shakespeare's *Troilus and Cressida*.

to gu′ttle. To swallow.

> The fool spit in his porridge, to try if they'd hiss: they did not hiss, and so he *guttled* them up, and scalded his chops. L'Estrange.

gu′ttler. A greedy eater.

---

guineadropper. A sharper drops a counterfeit guinea, which is picked up by a partner, deceiving an innocent—one variant of the confidence game.

H

ha'bnab. At random; at the mercy of chance; without any rule or certainty of effect.

to hack. To hackney; to turn hackney or prostitute. Hanmer.

ha'ckney. (3) A hireling; a prostitute.

ha'gard. (1) Wild; untamed; irreclaimable.

(2) Lean. To this sense I have put the following passage; for so the author ought to have written.

> A *hagged* carion of a wolf, and a jolly sort of dog, with good flesh upon's back, fell into company together. L'Estrange.

(3) Ugly; rugged; deformed; wildly disordered.

ha'ggard. (1) Any thing wild or irreclaimable.

> I will be married to a wealthy widow,
> Ere three days pass, which has as long lov'd me
> As I have lov'd this proud disdainful *haggard*. Shakespeare.

(2) A species of hawk.

(3) A hag. So Garth has used it for want of understanding it.

> Beneath the gloomy covert of an yew,
> . In a dark grot, the baleful *haggard* lay,
> Breathing black vengeance, and infecting day. Garth.

ha'ggardly. Deformed; ugly.

ha'ggess. A mass of meat, generally pork chopped, and inclosed in a membrane. In Scotland it is commonly made in a sheep's maw of the entrails of the same animal, cut small, with suet and spices.

to ha'ggle. To cut; to chop; to mangle.

ha'lcyon. A bird, of which it is said that she breeds in the sea, and that there is always a calm during her incubation.

half-blooded. Mean; degenerate.

half-seas over. A proverbial expression for any one far advanced. It is commonly used of one half drunk.

halm. Straw. Pronounced *hawm*.

ha'lsening. Sounding harshly; inharmonious in the throat or tongue.

to ha'ndsel. To use or do any thing the first time.

ha'rdbound. Costive.

> Just writes to make his barrenness appear,
> And strains from *hardbound* brains eight lines a year.
> Pope.

hare. (1) A small quadruped, with long ears and short tail, that moves by leaps, remarkable for timidity, vigilance, and fecundity; the common game of hunters.

to hare. To fright; to hurry with terrour.

> To *hare* and rate them, is not to teach but vex them.
> Locke.

ha'rlot. (*herlodes*, Welsh, a girl. Others for *horelet*, a little whore. Others from the name of the mother of William the Conqueror. *Hurlet* is used in Chaucer for a low male drudge.) A whore; a strumpet.

harrida'n. A decayed strumpet.

> She just endur'd the winter she began,
> And in four months a batter'd *harridan;*
> Now nothing's left, but wither'd, pale, and shrunk,
> To bawd for others, and go shares with punk. Swift.

ha'tchet-face. An ugly face; such, I suppose, as might be hewn out of a block by a hatchet.

> An ape his own dear image will embrace;
> An ugly beau adores a *hatchet-face.* Dryden.

to ha'tter. To harass; to weary; to wear out with fatigue.

ha'ver is a common word in the northern counties for oats: as, *haver* bread for oaten bread.

to dance the hay. To dance in a ring: probably from dancing round a hay cock.

heart-breaker. A cant name for a woman's curls, supposed to break the heart of all her lovers.

> Like Sampson's *heartbreakers,* it grew
> In time to make a nation rue. *Hudibras,* p. i.

hearts-ease. A plant.

> *Hearts-ease* is a sort of violet that blows all summer, and often in winter: it sows itself. Mortimer.

he′artless. Without courage; spiritless.

he′ater. An iron made hot, and put into a box-iron, to smooth and plait linnen.

to heave. (4) To keck; to feel a tendency to vomit.

to hebe′tate. To dull; to blunt; to stupify.

> Beef may confer a robustness on the limbs of my son, but will *hebetate* and clog his intellectuals. Arbuthnot and Pope's *Martinus Scriblerus.*

he′ctor. (1) A bully; a blustering, turbulent, pervicacious, noisy fellow.

to he′ctor. To threaten; to treat with insolent authoritative terms.

hedge, prefixed to any word, notes something mean, vile, of the lowest class: perhaps from a *hedge,* or *hedge-born man,* a man without any known place of birth.

hedge-hog. (1) An animal set with prickles, like thorns in an hedge.

hedge-note. A word of contempt for low writing.

> When they began to be somewhat better bred, they left these *hedge-notes* for another sort of poem, which was also full of pleasant raillery. Dryden's *Juvenal,* Dedication.

hedge-pig. A young hedge-hog.

heigh-ho. (1) An expression of slight languour and uneasiness. (2) It is used by Dryden, contrarily to custom, as a voice of exultation.

> We'll toss off our ale 'till we cannot stand,
> And *heigh-ho* for the honour of old England. Dryden.

hell. (5) The place into which the taylor throws his shreds.

> In Covent-garden did a taylor dwell,

Who might deserve a place in his own *hell*.
King's *Cookery*.

helm. (6) In the following line it is difficult to determine whether *steersma* or *defender* is intended: I think *steersman*.

> You slander
> The *helms* o' th' state, who care for you like fathers,
> When you curse them as enemies. Shakespeare, *Coriolanus*.

hen-hearted. Dastardly; cowardly; like a hen. A low word.

to hend. (1) To seize; to lay hold on.

(2) To croud; to surround. Perhaps the following passage is corrupt, and should be read *hemmed*.

> The generous and gravest citizens
> Have *hent* the gates, and very near upon
> The duke is entering. Shakespeare, *Measure for Measure*.

he'resy. An opinion of private men different from that of the catholick and orthodox church.

he'ron. (1) A bird that feeds upon fish.

(2) It is now commonly pronounced *hern*.

he'rring. A small sea-fish.

hey. An expression of joy, or mutual exhortation; the contrary to the Latin *hei*.

he'yday. An expression of frolick and exultation, and sometimes of wonder.

he'ydegives. A wild frolick dance.

hiccius doccius. A cant word for a juggler; one that plays fast and loose.

> An old dull sot, who told the clock
> For many years at Bridewell dock,
> At Westminster and Hicks's hall,
> And *hiccius doccius* play'd in all;
> Where, in all governments and times,
> H' had been both friend and foe to crimes. *Hudibras*,
> p. iii.

higgledy-piggeldy. A cant word, corrupted from *higgle*, which denotes any confused mass, as higglers carry a huddle of provisions together.

hi′ggler. One who sells provisions by retail.

high-fli′er. One that carries his opinions to extravagance.

> She openly professeth herself to be a *high-flier;* and it is not improbable she may also be a papist at heart. Swift.

hi′lding. (1) A sorry, paltry, cowardly fellow.

(2) It is used likewise for a mean woman.

hi′nderling. A paltry, worthless, degenerate animal.

hippoce′ntaur. A fabulous monster, half horse and half man.

hi′ppogriff. A winged horse.

hippo′potamus. The river horse. An animal found in the Nile.

to hiss. To utter a noise like that of a serpent and some other animals. It is remarkable, that this word cannot be pronounced without making the noise which it signifies.

hist. An exclamation commanding silence.

to hitch. To catch; to move by jerks. I know not where it is used but in the following passage.

> Whoe′er offends, at some unlucky time
> Slides in a verse, or *hitches* in a rhyme;
> Sacred to ridicule his whole life long,
> And the sad burthen of some merry song. Pope's *Horace.*

ho′bnob. This is probably corrupted from *hab nab* by a coarse pronunciation. See *hab nab.*

hocus pocus. (The original of this word is referred by Tillotson to a form of the Romish church. Junius derives it from *hocced*, Welsh, a cheat, and *poke* or *pocus*, a bag, jugglers using a bag for conveyance. It is corrupted from some words that had once a meaning, and which perhaps cannot be discovered.) A juggle; a cheat.

hog. (3) To bring hogs to a fair market. To fail of one's design.

ho′ggerel. A two year old ewe. Ainsworth.

ho′iden. An ill-taught awkward country girl.

to ho′iden. To romp indecently.

> Some of them would get a scratch; but we always discovered, upon examining, that they had been *hoidening* with the young apprentices. Swift.

to ho′ney. To talk fondly.

> Nay, but to live
> In the rank sweat of an incestuous bed,

Stew'd in corruption, *honeying* and making love
Over the nasty sty. Shakespeare's *Hamlet*.

to ho'od-wink. (1) To blind with something· bound over the eyes.

(2) To cover; to hide.

(3) To deceive; to impose upon.

She delighted in infamy, which often she had used to her husband's shame, filling all mens ears, but his, with reproach; while he, *hood-winked* with kindness, least of all men knew who struck him. Sidney.

hop. (3) A place where meaner people dance.

ho'peful. (2) Full of hope; full of expectation of success. This sense is now almost confined to Scotland, though it is analogical, and found in good writers.

I was *hopeful* the success of your first attempts would encourage you to make trial also of more nice and difficult experiments. Boyle.

ho'pefully. (2) With hope; without despair. This sense is rare.

From your promising and generous endeavours we may *hopefully* expect a considerable enlargement of the history of nature. Glanvill, *Scepsis Scientifica*, Preface.

ho'rnet. A very large strong stinging fly, which makes its nest in hollow trees.

Silence, in times of suff'ring, is the best;
'Tis dangerous to disturb a *hornet's* nest. Dryden.

ho'rrid. (2) Shocking; offensive; unpleasing: in womens cant.

Already I your tears survey,
Already hear the *horrid* things they say. Pope.

horse. (1) A neighing quadruped, used in war, and draught and carriage.

(5) Joined to another substantive, it signifies something large or coarse: as, a *horseface,* a face of which the features are large and indelicate.

to horse. (4) To cover a mare.

If you let him out to *horse* more mares than your own, you must feed him well. Mortimer's *Husbandry*.

ho'rselaugh. A loud violent rude laugh.

ho'rseplay. Coarse, rough, rugged play.

He is too much given to *horseplay* in his raillery, and comes to battle like a dictator from the plough. Dryden, *Fables,* Preface.

hospita′lity. The practice of entertaining strangers.

ho′thouse. (1) A bagnio; a place to sweat and cup in.

Now she professes a *hothouse,* which, I think, is a very ill house too. Shakespeare, *Measure for Measure.*

(2) A brothel.

Where lately harbour'd many a famous whore,
A purging bill, now fix'd upon the door,
Tells you it is a *hothouse;* so it may,
And still be a whorehouse: th' are synonyma.
Ben. Jonson.

hotmou′thed. Headstrong; ungovernable.

ho′urglass. (2) Space of time. A manner of speaking rather affected than elegant.

We, within the *hourglass* of two months, have won one town, and overthrown great forces in the field. Bacon.

ho′usling. Provided for entertainment at first entrance into a house; housewarming.

houss. Covering of cloath originally used to keep off dirt, now added to saddles as ornamental; housings. This word, though used by Dryden, I do not remember in any other place.

Six lions hides, with thongs together fast,
His upper part defended to his waist;
And where man ended, the continu'd vest,
Spread on his back, the *houss* and trappings of a beast.
Dryden.

ho′ven. Raised; swelled; tumefied.

Tom Piper hath *hoven* and puffed up cheeks;
If cheese be so *hoven*, make Cisse to seek creeks. Tusser.

hu′bbub. A tumult; a riot.

hu′ckster, hu′cksterer. (1) One who sells goods by retail, or in small quantities; a pedlar.

(2) A trickish mean fellow.

to hu′ddle. (1) To dress up close so as not to be discovered; to mobble.

(2) To put on carelessly in a hurry.

(3) To cover up in haste.

(4) To perform in a hurry.

hue′r. One whose business is to call out to others.

huff. (2) A wretch swelled with a false opinion of his own value.

> Lewd shallow-brained *huffs* make atheism and contempt of religion the sole badge and character of wit. South.

hu′ggermugger. Secrecy; bye-place.

> There's a distinction betwixt what's done openly and barefaced, and a thing that's done in *huggermugger*, under a seal of secrecy and concealment. L'Estrange's *Fables*.

huke. A cloak.

to hull. To float; to drive to and fro upon the water without sails or rudder.

> They saw a sight full of piteous strangeness; a ship, or rather the carcase of the ship, or rather some few bones of the carcase, *hulling* there, part broken, part burned, and part drowned. Sidney.

hu′manist. A philologer; a grammarian.

hu′morist. (1) One who conducts himself by his own fancy; one who gratifies his own humour.

(2) One who has violent and peculiar passions.

hu′morous. (1) Full of grotesque or odd images.

(2) Capricious; irregular; without any rule but the present whim.

to hunch. (1) To strike or punch with the fists.

hunks. A covetous sordid wretch; a miser; a curmudgeon.

> The old *hunks* was well served, to be tricked out of a whole hog for the securing of his puddings. L'Estrange.

to hurl. (2) To utter with vehemence.

hurl. Tumult; riot; commotion.

> He in the same *hurl* murdering such as he thought would withstand his desire, was chosen king. Knolles.

to hu′rtle. To clash; to skirmish; to run against any thing; to jostle; to meet in shock and encounter. Hanmer.

hu′sband. (2) The male of animals.

(3) An oeconomist; a man that knows and practises the methods of frugality and profit. Its signification is always modified by some epithet implying good or bad.

(4) A tiller of the ground; a farmer.

hu'shmoney. A bribe to hinder information; pay to secure silence.

hu'ssy. A sorry or bad woman; a worthless wench. It is often used ludicrously in slight disapprobation.

> Get you in, *hussy*, go: now will I personate this hopeful young jade. Southerne's *Innocent Adultery*.

hu'swife. (1) A bad manager; a sorry woman. It is common to use *housewife* in a good, and *huswife* or *hussy* in a bad sense.

to huzz. To buzz; to murmur.

hy'dra. A monster with many heads slain by Hercules: whence any multiplicity of evils is termed a *hydra*.

> New rebellions raise
> Their *hydra* heads, and the false North displays
> Her broken league to imp her serpent wings. Milton.

hy'dromancy. Prediction by water.

hy'en, hye'na. An animal like a wolf, said fabulously to imitate human voices.

> A wonder more amazing would we find;
> The *hyena* shews it, of a double kind:
> Varying the sexes in alternate years,
> In one begets, and in another bears. Dryden's *Fables*.

to hyp. To make melancholy; to dispirit.

> I have been, to the last degree, *hypped* since I saw you. *Spectator*.

hypochondri'acal, hypochondri'ack. (1) Melancholy; disordered in the imagination.

(2) Producing melancholy.

I

ice. (3) To break the ice. To make the first opening to any attempt.

ichne′umon. A small animal that breaks the eggs of the crocodile.

ide′al. Mental; intellectual; not perceived by the senses.

i′diotism. (1) Peculiarity of expression; mode of expression peculiar to a language.

> Scholars sometimes in common speech, or writing, in their native language, give terminations and *idiotisms* suitable to their native language unto words newly invented. Hale.

to igno′re. Not to know; to be ignorant of. This word Boyle endeavoured to introduce; but it has not been received.

> I *ignored* not the stricter interpretation, given by modern criticks to divers texts, by me alleged. Boyle.

illa′pse. (1) Gradual immission or entrance of one thing into another.

(2) Sudden attack; casual coming.

to illa′queate. To entangle; to entrap; to ensnare.

illa′tion. Inference; conclusion drawn from premises.

to imbe′cile. (From the adjective. This word is corruptly written *embezzle*.) To weaken a stock or fortune by clandestine expences or unjust appropriations.

> Princes must in a special manner be guardians of pupils

and widows, not suffering their persons to be oppressed, or their states *imbeciled.* Taylor's *Rule of Living Holy.*

to imbo′som. (1) To hold on the bosom; to cover fondly with the folds of one's garment; to hide under any cover.

(2) To admit to the heart, or to affection.

to imbra′ngle. To intangle. A low word.

imma′nity. Barbarity; savageness.

immate′rial. (1) Incorporeal; distinct from matter; void of matter.

(2) Unimportant; without weight; impertinent; without relation. This sense has crept into the conversation and writings of barbarians; but ought to be utterly rejected.

i′mminence. Any ill impending; immediate or near danger. A word not in use.

imp. (1) A son; the offspring; progeny.

The tender *imp* was weaned from the teat. Fairfax.

to imp. To lengthen or enlarge with any thing adscititious.

New creatures rise,

A moving mass at first, and short of thighs;

'Till shooting out with legs, and *imp'd* with wings,

The grubs proceed to bees with pointed stings. Dryden.

to impe′ach. (1) To hinder; to impede. This sense is little in use.

Each door he opened without any breach;

There was no bar to stop, nor foe him to *impeach. Fairy Queen.*

impe′ccable. Exempt from possibility of sin.

to impi′gnorate. To pawn; to pledge.

impra′cticable. (2) Untractable; unmanageable.

That fierce *impracticable* nature

Is govern'd by a dainty-finger'd girl. Rowe.

to impre′gn. To fill with young; to fill with any matter or quality.

to impre′gnate. (1) To fill with young; to make prolifick.

Hermaphrodites, although they include the parts of both sexes, cannot *impregnate* themselves. Browne's *Vulgar Errours.*

impreju′dicate. Unprejudiced; not prepossessed; impartial.

to impre′ss. (3) To force into service. This is generally now
spoken and written *press*.

to improli′ficate. To impregnate; to fecundate. A word not used.

A difficulty in the doctrine of eggs is how the sperm of
the cock *improlificates*, and makes the oval conception
fruitful. Browne's *Vulgar Errours.*

to impro′ve. (2) To disprove.

Though the prophet Jeremy was unjustly accused, yet
doth not that improve any thing that I have said.
Whitgift.

ina′ne. Empty; void.

We sometimes speak of place in the great *inane*, beyond
the confines of the world. Locke.

to ina′nimate. To animate; to quicken. This word is not in use.

There's a kind of world remaining still,

Though she which did *inanimate* and fill

The world be gone; yet in this last long night

Her ghost doth walk, that is, a glimmering light. Donne.

inarti′culate. Not uttered with distinctness like that of the syllables of human speech.

to inca′rcerate. To imprison; to confine. It is used in the Scots
law to denote imprisoning or confining in a gaol; otherwise
it is seldom found.

The pestilent contagion may be propagated by those
dense bodies, that easily *incarcerate* the infected air; as
woollen cloaths. Harvey, *On Consumptions.*

to inca′rnadine. To dye red. This word I find only once.

Will all great Neptune's ocean wash this blood

Clean from my hand? No, this my hand will rather

The multitudinous sea *incarnadine*,

Making the green one red. Shakespeare's *Macbeth.*

inca′rnate. (1) Cloathed with flesh; embodied in flesh.

(2) It may be doubted whether Swift understood this word.

But he's possest,

Incarnate with a thousand imps. Swift.

inch. (1) A measure of length supposed equal to three grains
of barley laid end to end; the twelfth part of a foot.

A foot is the sixth part of the stature of man, a span one

[215]

eighth of it, and a thumb's breadth or *inch* one seventy-second. Holder, *On Time.*

i'nchipin. Some of the inside of a deer. Ainsworth.

i'nchmeal. A piece an inch long.

> All th' infections that the sun sucks up
> From bogs, fens, flats, on Prospero fall, and make him
> By *inchmeal* a disease! Shakespeare, *Tempest.*

to i'nchoate. To begin; to commence.

inco'mparably. (2) Excellently; to the highest degree. A low phrase.

> There are the heads of Antoninus Pius, the Faustina's, and Marcus Aurelius, all *incomparably* well cut.
> Addison, *On Italy.*

inco'nsequent. Without just conclusion; without regular inference.

inco'ny. (1) Unlearned; artless.

(2) In Scotland it denotes mischievously unlucky: as, he's an *incony* fellow. This seems to be the meaning in Shakespeare.

> O' my troth, most sweet jests, most *incony* vulgar wit,
> When it comes so smoothly off. Shakespeare.

to i'ncrepate. To chide; to reprehend.

to i'ncubate. To sit upon eggs.

incu'mbency. (1) The act of lying upon another.

to i'ndagate. To search; to beat out.

to inde'nt. (From the method of cutting counterparts of a contract together, that, laid on each other, they may fit, and any want of conformity may discover a fraud.) To contract; to bargain; to make a compact.

indepe'ndent. One who in religious affairs holds that every congregation is a complete church, subject to no superiour authority.

indesc'rt. Want of merit.

> Those who were once looked on as his equals, are apt to think the fame of his merit a reflection on their own *indeserts.* Addison's *Spectator.*

inde'sinently. Without cessation.

indevo′tion. Want of devotion; irreligion.

indi′ction. (1) Declaration; proclamation.

i′ndigent. (3) Void; empty.

> Such bodies have the tangible parts *indigent* of moisture. Bacon's *Natural History.*

to indi′gitate. To point out; to show.

indi′gn. (1) Unworthy; undeserving.

> (2) Bringing indignity. This is a word not in use.

indo′cil. Unteachable; incapable of being instructed.

> These certainly are the fools in the text, *indocil,* intractable fools, whose stolidity can baffle all arguments, and is proof against demonstration itself. Bentley's *Sermons.*

i′ndolence, i′ndolency. (1) Freedom from pain.

indra′ught. (1) An opening in the land into which the sea flows.

> (2) Inlet; passage inwards.

to indu′e. (1) To invest.

> (2) It seems sometimes to be, even by good writers, confounded with *endow* or *indow,* to furnish or enrich with any quality or excellence.

indu′lgence, indu′lgency. (4) Grant of the church of Rome, not defined by themselves.

> In purgatory, *indulgences,* and supererogation, the assertors seem to be unanimous in nothing but in reference to profit. *Decay of Piety.*

to infa′tuate. To strike with folly; to deprive of understanding.

infa′usting. The act of making unlucky. An odd and inelegant word.

infinite′simal. Infinitely divided.

info′rmal. Offering an information; accusing. A word not used.

to infri′nge. (1) To violate; to break laws or contracts.

> (2) To destroy; to hinder.

inganna′tion. Cheat; fraud; deception; juggle; delusion; imposture; trick; slight. A word neither used nor necessary.

i′njury. (4) Contumelious language; reproachful appellation.

> Casting off the respects fit to be continued between great kings, he fell to bitter invectives against the French

king; and, by how much he was the less able to do,
talking so much the more, spake all the *injuries* he could
devise of Charles. Bacon.

ink. The black liquor with which men write.

He that would live clear of envy must lay his finger upon
his mouth, and keep his hand out of the *ink* pot.
L'Estrange.

to inla'w. To clear of outlawry or attainder.

i'nmate. *Inmates* are those that be admitted to dwell for their
money jointly with another man, though in several rooms of
his mansion-house, passing in and out by one door. Cowell.

to inn. To house; to put under cover.

Howsoever the laws made in that parliament did
bear good fruit, yet the subsidy bare a fruit that proved
harsh and bitter: all was *inned* at last into the king's
barn. Bacon's *Henry VII.*

i'nnocent. (2) A natural; an idiot.

Innocents are excluded by natural defects. Hooker.

to i'nquinate. To pollute; to corrupt.

An old opinion it was, that the ibis feeding upon serpents, that venomous food so *inquinated* their oval conceptions, that they sometimes came forth in serpentine
shapes. Browne.

to i'nsolence. To insult; to treat with contempt. A very bad
word.

The bishops, who were first faulty, *insolenced* and as-
saulted. King Charles.

to inspi'ssate. To thicken; to make thick.

insti'ncted. Impressed as an animating power. This, neither
musical nor proper, was perhaps introduced by Bentley.

What native unextinguishable beauty must be impressed and *instincted* through the whole, which the
defedation of so many parts by a bad printer and a worse
editor could not hinder from shining forth. Bentley's
Preface to Milton.

to i'nstitute. (2) To educate; to instruct; to form by instruction.

If children were early *instituted,* knowledge would in-
sensibly insinuate itself. *Decay of Piety.*

insu'lt. (1) The act of leaping upon any thing. In this sense
it has the accent on the last syllable: the sense is rare.

The bull's *insult* at four she may sustain,
But after ten from nuptial rites refrain. Dryden's *Virgil.*

to interco'mmon. To feed at the same table.

interde'al. Traffick; intercourse.

The Gaulish speech is the very British, which is yet
retained of the Welshmen and Britons of France; though
the alteration of the trading and *interdeal* with other
nations has greatly altered the dialect. Spenser.

i'nterlude. Something plaid at the intervals of festivity; a
farce.

inte'rminable. Immense; admitting no boundary.

to inti'midate. To make fearful; to dastardize; to make cowardly.

Now guilt once harbour'd in the conscious breast,
Intimidates the brave, degrades the great. *Irene.*

into'lerant. Not enduring; not able to endure.

to into'ne. To make a slow protracted noise.

So swells each wind-pipe; ass *intones* to ass
Harmonick twang. Pope's *Dunciad,* b. ii.

intromi'ssion. (2) (In the Scottish law.) The act of intermed-
dling with another's effects: as, *he shall be brought to an
account for his* intromissions *with such an estate.*

to inu're. (2) To bring into use; to practise again.

The wanton boy was shortly well recur'd
Of that his malady;
But he soon after fresh again *inur'd*
His former cruelty. Spenser.

to inva'lidate. To weaken; to deprive of force or efficacy.

Tell a man, passionately in love, that he is jilted, bring a
score of witnesses of the falshood of his mistress, and it
is ten to one but three kind words of her's shall *invali-
date* all their testimonies. Locke.

invali'dity. (2) Want of bodily strength. This is no English
meaning.

---

to intimidate. Johnson quotes from his play oftener than from any other
of his works, perhaps because of parental affection for a failure.

He ordered, that none who could work should be idle;
and that none who could not work, by age, sickness, or
invalidity, should want. Temple.

i′nward. (1) Any thing within, generally the bowels. Seldom
has this sense a singular.

They esteem them most profitable, because of the
great quantity of fat upon their *inwards.* Mortimer's
Husbandry.

(2) Intimate; near acquaintance.

Sir, I was an *inward* of his; a sly fellow was the duke;
and I know the cause of his withdrawing. Shakespeare.

i′ronwood. A kind of wood extremely hard, and so ponderous
as to sink in water. It grows in America. *Robinson Crusoe.*

irre′gular. (3) Not being according to the laws of virtue.
A soft word for *vitious.*

itch. (1) A cutaneous disease extremely contagious, which
overspreads the body with small pustules filled with a
thin serum, and raised as microscopes have discovered by a
small animal. It is cured by sulphur.

---

ironwood. Johnson rarely quotes Defoe.

J

ja'cent. Lying at length.

jack. (1) The diminutive of *John*. Used as a general term of contempt for saucy or paltry fellows.

(2) The name of instruments which supply the place of a boy, as an instrument to pull off boots.

(3) An engine which turns the spit.

(6) A cup of waxed leather.

> Dead wine, that stinks of the borrachio, sup
> From a foul *jack*, or greasy mapple cup. Dryden's *Persius*.

jack pudding. A zani; a merry Andrew.

jackale'nt. A simple sheepish fellow.

jacka'l. A small animal supposed to start prey for the lyon.

ja'ckanapes. (1) Monkey; an ape.

(2) A coxcomb; an impertinent.

ja'cket. (2) To beat one's jacket, is to beat the man.

> She fell upon the *jacket* of the parson, who stood gaping at her. L'Estrange.

ja'cob's staff. (1) A pilgrim's staff.

(2) Staff concealing a dagger.

jade. (2) A sorry woman. A word of contempt noting sometimes age, but generally vice.

(3) A young woman: in irony and slight contempt.

You see now and then some handsome young *jades* among them: the sluts have very often white teeth and black eyes. Addison.

to jade. (2) To overbear; to crush; to degrade; to harass, as a horse that is ridden too hard.

> If we live thus tamely,
> To be thus *jaded* by a piece of scarlet,
> Farewel nobility. Shakespeare's *Henry VIII.*

jail. A gaol; a prison; a place where criminals are confined. See *gaol.* It is written either way; but commonly by latter writers *jail.*

ja'ilbird. One who has been in a jail.

jakes. A house of office.

> Some have fished the very *jakes* for papers left there by men of wit. Swift.

ja'nty. Showy; fluttering.

> This sort of woman is a *janty* slattern: she hangs on her cloaths, plays her head, and varies her posture.
> *Spectator.*

to japa'n. (2) To black shoes. A low phrase.

japa'nner. (2) A shoeblacker.

> The poor have the same itch;
> They change their weekly barber, weekly news,
> Prefer a new *japanner* to their shoes. Pope's *Horace.*

ja'rgon. Unintelligible talk; gabble; gibberish.

to jaunt. To wander here and there; to bustle about. It is now always used in contempt or levity.

to ja'vel. To bemire; to soil over with dirt through unnecessary traversing and travelling. This word is still retained in Scotland and the northern counties.

ja'vel. A wandering fellow.

je'opardy. Hazard; danger; peril. A word not now in use.

ji'ggumbob. A trinket; a knick-knack; a slight contrivance in machinery.

job. (A low word now much in use, of which I cannot tell the etymology.) (1) A low mean lucrative busy affair.

(2) Petty, piddling work; a piece of chance work.

> No cheek is known to blush, no heart to throb,

Save when they lose a question, or a *job*. Pope.

(3) A sudden stab with a sharp instrument.

jobberno'wl. Loggerhead; blockhead.

to jo'ckey. (1) To justle by riding against one.

(2) To cheat; to trick.

jo'gger. One who moves heavily and dully.

They, with their fellow *joggers* of the plough. Dryden.

to joll. To beat the head against any thing; to clash with violence.

The tortoises envied the easiness of the frogs, 'till they saw them *jolled* to pieces and devoured for want of a buckler. L'Estrange.

jo'rden. A pot.

They will allow us ne'er a *jorden,* and then we leak in your chimney; and your chamberlye breeds fleas like a loach. Shakespeare.

The copper-pot can boil milk, heat porridge, hold small-beer, or, in case of necessity, serve for a *jorden.* Swift.

jo'urney. (1) The travel of a day.

jo'wter. Plenty of fish is vented to the fish-drivers, whom we call *jowters.* Carew.

to juke. (1) To perch upon any thing: as, birds.

(2) *Juking,* in Scotland, denotes still any complaisance by bending of the head.

Two asses travelled; the one laden with oats, the other with money: the money-merchant was so proud of his trust, that he went *juking* and tossing of his head. L'Estrange.

ju'mart. Mules and *jumarts,* the one from the mixture of an ass and a mare, the other from the mixture of a bull and a mare, are frequent. Locke.

ju'ment. Beast of burthen.

Juments, as horses, oxen, and asses, have no eructation, or belching. Browne's *Vulgar Errours,* b. i.

to jump. (4) To agree; to tally; to join.

This shews how perfectly the rump

---

jorden. Loach is a fish; Johnson is quoting from *I Henry IV,* II.i.22.

And commonwealth in nature *jump:*
For as a fly that goes to bed,
Rests with his tail above his head;
So in this mungrel state of ours,
The rabble are the supreme powers. *Hudibras,* p. iii.

ju′ncate. (1) Cheesecake; a kind of sweetmeat of curds and sugar.

(2) Any delicacy.

(3) A furtive or private entertainment. It is now improperly written *junket* in this sense, which alone remains much in use. See *junket.*

to ju′nket. (1) To feast secretly; to make entertainments by stealth.

Whatever good bits you can pilfer in the day, save them to *junket* with your fellow servants at night. Swift.

just. (10) Full; of full dimensions.

There is not any one particular abovementioned, but would take up the business of a *just* volume. Hale's *Origination of Mankind.*

K

to keck. To heave the stomach; to reach at vomiting.

> The faction, is it not notorious?
> *Keck* at the memory of glorious. Swift's *Miscellanies*.

ke'cksy. Skinner seems to think *kecksy* or *kex* the same as hemlock. It is used in Staffordshire both for hemlock, and any other hollow jointed plant.

to ke'elhale. To punish in the seamens way, by dragging the criminal under water on one side of the ship and up again on the other.

to keen. To sharpen. An unauthorized word.

kell. A sort of pottage. Ainsworth. It is so called in Scotland, being a soupe made with shreded greens.

ke'nnel. (1) A cot for dogs.

> A dog sure, if he could speak, had wit enough to describe his *kennel*. Sidney.

(4) The watercourse of a street.

> He always came in so dirty, as if he had been dragged through the *kennel* at a boarding-school. Arbuthnot.

to ke'nnel. To lie; to dwell: used of beasts, and of man in contempt.

> The dog *kennelled* in a hollow tree, and the cock roosted upon the boughs. L'Estrange's *Fables*.

kern. Irish foot soldier; an Irish boor.

Out of the fry of these rake-hell horseboys, growing up
in knavery and villainy, are their *kearn* supplied.
Spenser.

ki′ckshaw. (1) Something uncommon; fantastical; something
ridiculous.

(2) A dish so changed by the cookery that it can scarcely
be known.

ki′cksy-wicksey. A made word in ridicule and disdain of a wife.
Hanmer.

ki′lderkin. A small barrel.

to ki′ndle. (2) (From *cennan*, to bring forth, Saxon.)

Are you native of this place?

—As the coney that you see dwells where she is *kindled*.
Shakespeare.

kingse′vil. A scrofulous distemper, in which the glands are
ulcerated, commonly believed to be cured by the touch of
the king.

ki′ssingcrust. Crust formed where one loaf in the oven touches
another.

kit. (1) A large bottle.

(2) A small diminutive fiddle.

(3) A small wooden vessel, in which Newcastle salmon is
sent up to town.

ki′tchenstuff. The fat of meat scummed off the pot, or
gathered out of the dripping-pan.

As a thrifty wench scrapes *kitchenstuff*,

And barreling the droppings and the snuff

Of wasting candles, which in thirty year,

Reliquely kept, perchance buys wedding cheer. Donne.

to knab. To bite. Perhaps properly to bite something brittle,
that makes a noise when it is broken; so as that *knab* and
knap may be the same.

I had much rather lie *knabbing* crusts, without fear, in
my own hole, than be mistress of the world with cares.
L'Estrange.

knack. (1) A little machine; a petty contrivance; a toy.

He expounded both his pockets,

And found a watch, with rings and lockets;

A copper-plate, with almanacks
Engrav'd upon't, with other *knacks*. *Hudibras.*

kna'cker. (1) A maker of small work.

(2) A ropemaker. Ainsworth.

to knap. To make a short sharp noise.

knight of the post. A hireling evidence.

There are *knights of the post*, and holy cheats enough, to swear the truth of the broadest contradictions, where pious frauds shall give them an extraordinary call. South's *Sermons.*

to knu'ckle. To submit: I suppose from an odd custom of striking the under side of the table with the knuckles, in confession of an argumental defeat.

knuff. A lout. An old word preserved in a rhyme of prediction.

The country *knuffs*, Hob, Dick, and Hick,
With clubs and clouted shoon,
Shall fill up Dussendale
With slaughtered bodies soon. Hayward.

L

La. See; look; behold.

> *La* you! if you speak ill of the devil,
> How he takes it at heart. Shakespeare, *Twelfth Night.*

to la'befy. To weaken; to impair.

lac. *Lac* is usually distinguished by the name of a gum, but improperly, because it is inflammable and not soluble in water. We have three sorts of it, which are all the product of the same tree. 1. The stick *lac.* 2. The seed *lac.* 3. The shell *lac.* Authors leave us uncertain whether this drug belongs to the animal or the vegetable kingdom. Hill.

lace. (6) Sugar. A cant word.

> If haply he the sect pursues,
> That read and comment upon news;
> He takes up their mysterious face,
> He drinks his coffee without *lace.* Prior.

laced mutton. An old word for a whore.

> Ay, Sir, I, a lost mutton, gave your letter to her a *lac'd mutton,* and she gave me nothing for my labour. Shakespeare.

lack. (1) Want; need; failure.

(2) *Lack,* whether noun or verb, is now almost obsolete.

la'ctary. Milky; full of juice like milk.

la'dy-bird, la'dy-cow, la'dy-fly. A small red insect vaginopennous.

Fly *lady-bird*, north, south, or east or west,
Fly where the man is found that I love best. Gay's
Pastorals.

lag. (1) The lowest class; the rump; the fag end.

The rest of your foes, O gods, the senators of Athens,
together with the common *lag* of people, what is amiss in
them, make suitable for destruction. Shakespeare,
Timon of Athens.

lambs-wool. Ale mixed with the pulp of roasted apples.

la′mentable. (3) Miserable, in a ludicrous or low sense;
pitiful; despicable.

la′minated. Plated: used of such bodies whose contexture dis-
covers such a disposition as that of plates lying over one another.

to lamm. To beat soundly with a cudgel.

lam′ping. Shining; sparkling.

la′mprey. Many fish much like the eel frequent both the sea
and fresh rivers; as, the lamprel, *lamprey,* and lamperne.
Walton.

land. (6) Urine.

Probably this was a coarse expression in the cant strain,
formerly in common use, but since laid aside and forgotten, which meant the taking away a man's life. For
land or *lant* is an old word for urine, and to stop the
common passages and functions of nature is to kill.
Hanmer.

la′ndloper. A landman; a term of reproach used by seamen of
those who pass their lives on shore.

la′ntern jaws. A term used of a thin visage, such as if a candle
were burning in the mouth might transmit the light.

lap. (1) The loose part of a garment, which may be doubled
at pleasure.

If a joint of meat falls on the ground, take it up gently,
wipe it with the *lap* of your coat, and then put it into
the dish. Swift's *Directions to a Footman.*

la′pwing. A clamorous bird with long wings.

lard. (1) The grease of swine.

(2) Bacon; the flesh of swine.

lark. A small singing bird.

lass. A girl; a maid; a young woman: used now only of mean girls.

la′sslorn. Forsaken by his mistress.

la′ted. Belated; surprised by the night.

> The west glimmers with some streaks of day:
> Now spurs the *lated* traveller apace
> To gain the timely inn. Shakespeare's *Macbeth*.

lath. A part of a county.

latiro′strous. Broad-beaked.

la′titant. Delitescent; concealed; lying hid.

> This is evident in snakes and lizzards, *latitant* many months in the year, which containing a weak heat in a copious humidity, do long subsist without nutrition. Browne.

la′titudinarian. Not restrained; not confined; thinking or acting at large.

la′trant. Barking.

to lave′er. To change the direction often in a course.

lax. A looseness; a diarrhoea.

la′ystall. An heap of dung.

la′zar. One deformed and nauseous with filthy and pestilential diseases.

lead. Guidance; first place: a low despicable word.

> Yorkshire takes the *lead* of the other countries. Herring.

to leak. (1) To let water in or out.

> They will allow us ne'er a jordan, and then we *leak* in your chimney. Shakespeare.

le′aky. (2) Loquacious; not close.

> Women are so *leaky*, that I have hardly met with one that could not hold her breath longer than she could keep a secret. L'Estrange.

to lease. To glean; to gather what the harvest men leave.

> She in harvest us'd to *lease;*
> But harvest done, to chare-work did aspire,
> Meat, drink, and two-pence, was her daily hire. Dryden.

le′asing. Lies; falshood.

> As folks, quoth Richard, prone to *leasing,*

Say things at first, because they're pleasing;
Then prove what they have once asserted,
Nor care to have their lie deserted:
Till their own dreams at length deceive them,
And oft repeating they believe them. Prior.

le′asy. Flimsy; of weak texture.

le′ather. (2) Skin; ironically.

Returning sound in limb and wind,
Except some *leather* lost behind. Swift.

to leave. To levy; to raise: a corrupt word, made, I believe,
by Spenser, for a rhyme.

> An army strong she *leav'd*,
To war on those which him had of his realm bereav'd.
Spenser's *Fairy Queen*, b. ii.

to lech. To lick over. Hanmer.

le′cher. A whoremaster.

to le′cher. To whore.

Die for adultery? no. The wren goes to't, and the small
gilded fly does *letcher* in my sight. Shakespeare, *King
Lear*.

le′cture. (2) The act or practice of reading; perusal.

to le′cture. (2) To instruct insolently and dogmatically.

lee. (2) (Sea term; supposed by Skinner from *l'eau*, French.)
It is generally that side which is opposite to the wind,
as the *lee* shore is that the wind blows on. To be under
the *lee* of the shore, is to be close under the weather
shore. A *leeward* ship is one that is not fast by a wind,
to make her way so good as she might. To lay a ship
by the *lee*, is to bring her so that all her sails may lie
against the masts and shrouds flat, and the wind to come
right on her broadside, so that she will make little
or no way. *Dictionary*.

leech. (2) A kind of small water serpent, which fastens on
animals, and sucks the blood: it is used to draw blood where
the lancet is less safe, whence perhaps the name.

---

lee. Johnson has combined four of Bailey's definitions, including a mis-
leading one, and has erroneously changed Bailey's "make her way
so well" to "so good." Johnson had not seen the ocean at this date.

I drew blood by *leeches* behind his ear. Wiseman's
Surgery.

leef. Kind; fond.

leer. (2) A laboured cast of countenance.

Damn with faint praise, concede with civil *leer.* Pope.

to leese. To lose: an old word.

le′eward. Towards the wind. See *lee.*

leg. (1) The limb by which we walk; particularly that part
between the knee and the foot.

le′gend. (1) A chronicle or register of the lives of saints.

There are in Rome two sets of antiquities, the christian
and the heathen; the former, though of a fresher date,
are so embroiled with fable and *legend,* that one receives
but little satisfaction. Addison's *Remarks on Italy.*

le′gume, legu′men. Seeds not reaped, but gathered by the
hand; as, beans: in general, all larger seeds; pulse.

le′isure. (1) Freedom from business or hurry; vacancy of mind;
power to spend time according to choice.

A gentleman fell very sick, and a friend said to him,
Send for a physician; but the sick man answered, It is no
matter; for if I die, I will die at *leisure.*
Bacon's *Apophthegms.*

le′man. A sweetheart; a gallant; or a mistress. Hanmer.

le′opard. A spotted beast of prey.

le′porine. Belonging to a hare; having the nature of a hare.

lere. A lesson; lore; doctrine. This sense is still retained in Scotland.

le′rry. A rating; a lecture. Rustick word.

le′sser. A barbarous corruption of *less,* formed by the vulgar
from the habit of terminating comparatives in *er;* afterwards adopted by poets, and then by writers of prose.

It is the *lesser* blot, modesty finds,
Women to change their shapes than men **their minds.**
Shakespeare's *Two Gentlemen of Verona.*

le′sson. (4) Tune pricked for an instrument.

Those good laws were like good *lessons* set for a flute

leeward. Wrong. Johnson gives the same definition of *windward.*

[232]

out of tune; of which *lessons* little use can be made, till
the flute be made fit to be played on. Davies, *On Ireland.*

to let. (8) To more than permit.

There's a letter for you, Sir, if your name be Horatio,
as I am *let* to know it is. Shakespeare's *Hamlet.*

let. Hindrance; obstacle; obstruction; impediment.

Solyman without *let* presented his army before the city
of Belgrade. Knolles's *History of the Turks.*

le'thargy. A morbid drowsiness; a sleep from which one cannot
be kept awake.

A *lethargy* is a lighter sort of apoplexy, and demands the
same cure and diet. Arbuthnot, *On Diet.*

leucophle'gmancy. Paleness, with viscid juices and cold sweat-
ings.

le'vce. (1) The time of rising.

to le'vel. (4) To make attempts; to aim.

Ambitious York did *level* at thy crown. Shakespeare.

le'veret. A young hare.

le'verook. This word is retained in Scotland, and denotes the
lark.

leve't. A blast on the trumpet; probably that by which the
soldiers are called in the morning.

lewd. (1) Lay; not clerical. Obsolete.

For *lewyd* men this book I writ. Bishop Grosthead.°

le'wdster. A lecher; one given to criminal pleasures.

lexico'grapher. A writer of dictionaries; a harmless drudge, that
busies himself in tracing the original, and detailing the
signification of words.

le'xicon. A dictionary; a book teaching the signification of
words.

Though a linguist should pride himself to have all the
tongues that Babel cleft the world into, yet if he had
not studied the solid things in them as well as the
words and *lexicons,* yet he were nothing so much to be
esteemed a learned man as any yeoman competently
wise in his mother dialect only. Milton.

° An old variant of *Grosseteste,* Bishop of Lincoln.

li'ard. (1) Mingled roan. Markham.

(2) *Liard* in Scotland denotes gray-haired: as, he's a *liard* old man.

li'bbard. A leopard.

li'beral. (1) Not mean; not low in birth; not low in mind.

li'bertine. (1) One unconfined; one at liberty.

libra'rian. (2) One who transcribes or copies books.

li'cense. (1) Exorbitant liberty; contempt of legal and necessary restraint.

> They baul for freedom in their senseless moods,
> And still revolt when truth would set them free;
> *Licence* they mean, when they cry liberty. Milton.

li'censer. A granter of permission; commonly a tool of power.

lich. A dead carcase; whence *lichwake,* the time or act of watching by the dead; *lichgate,* the gate through which the dead are carried to the grave; *Lichfield,* the field of the dead, a city in Staffordshire, so named from martyred christians. *Salve magna parens. Lichwake* is still retained in Scotland in the same sense.

li'chowl. A sort of owl, by the vulgar supposed to foretel death.

lick. A blow; rough usage: a low word.

> He turned upon me as round as a chafed boar and gave me a *lick* across the face. Dryden.

li'ckerish, li'ckerous. (1) Nice in the choice of food; squeamish.

(2) Eager; greedy.

> In vain he profer'd all his goods to save
> His body, destin'd to that living grave;
> The *liquorish* hag rejects the pelf with scorn,
> And nothing but the man would serve her turn. Dryden.

(3) Nice; delicate; tempting the appetite.

to lie (22) To lie at. To importune; to teaze.

(29) To lie with. To converse in bed.

> Pardon me, Bassanio,
> For by this ring she *lay with* me. Shakespeare.

---

lich. Johnson's salutation to his birthplace, his "great parent," is, as with many of his most personal remarks, "veiled in the obscurity of a learned language."

lief. Willingly.
lieve. Willingly.

> Action is death to some sort of people, and they would as *lieve* hang as work. L'Estrange.

li'feeverlasting. An herb. Ainsworth.
lifegua'rd. The guard of a king's person.
li'festring. Nerve; strings imagined to convey life.
to lift. (3) To rob; to plunder.

> So weary bees in little cells repose,
> But if night robbers *lift* the well-stor'd hive,
> An humming through their waxen city grows. Dryden.

lift. (2) (In Scottish.) The sky: for in a starry night they say, *How clear the* lift *is!*

(3) Effect; struggle. *Dead lift* is an effort to raise what with the whole force cannot be moved; and figuratively any state of impotence and inability.

(4) *Lift,* in Scotland, denotes a load or surcharge of any thing; as also, if one be disguised much with liquor, they say, *He has got a great* lift.

light. (8) Unencumbered; unembarrassed; clear of impediments.

> Unmarried men are best masters, but not best subjects; for they are *light* to run away. Bacon.

(13) Not chaste; not regular in conduct.

> Let me not be *light,*
> For a *light* wife doth make a heavy husband. Shakespeare.

li'ghtfoot. Nimble in running or dancing; active.
li'ghtly. (6) Not chastly.

> If I were *lightly* disposed, I could still perhaps have offers, that some, who hold their heads higher, would be glad to accept. Swift's *Story of an injured Lady.*

li'king. (Perhaps because plumpness is agreeable to the sight.) Plump; in a state of plumpness.
li'mature. Filings of any metal; the particles rubbed off by a file.
to limb. (1) To supply with limbs.

(2) To tear asunder; to dismember.

li'mmer. A mongrel. Ainsworth.

li'mous. Muddy; slimy.

to lin. To stop; to give over.

li'nctus. Medicine licked up by the tongue.

line. (15) A *line* is one tenth of an inch. Locke.

   (17) Lint or flax.

to line. (7) To impregnate, applied to animals generating.

      Thus from the Tyrian pastures *lin'd* with Jove

      He bore Europa, and still keeps his love. Creech.

ling. (1) Heath. This sense is retained in the northern counties;
yet Bacon seems to distinguish them.

      Heath, and *ling*, and sedges. Bacon's *Natural History*.

li'nget. A small mass of metal.

li'ngo. Language; tongue; speech. A low cant word.

      I have thoughts to learn somewhat of your *lingo*, before

      I cross the seas. Congreve's *Way of the World*.

lingua'cious. Full of tongue; loquacious; talkative.

link. (7) Perhaps in the following passage it may mean lamp-
black.

      There was no *link* to colour Peter's hat;

      And Walter's dagger was not come from sheathing.
Shakespeare.

li'nnet. A small singing bird.

li'on. The fiercest and most magnanimous of fourfooted beasts.

to lip. To kiss. Obsolete.

               Oh! 'tis the fiend's arch mock,

      To *lip* a wanton, and suppose her chaste. Shakespeare.

lipla'bour. Action of the lips without concurrence of the mind;
words without sentiments.

li'ppitude. Blearedness of eyes.

li'pwisdom. Wisdom in talk without practice.

lisne. A cavity; a hollow.

li'sted. Striped; particoloured in long streaks.

li'teral (3) Consisting of letters; as, the *literal* notation of numbers was known to Europeans before the cyphers.

li'thomancy. Prediction by stones.

to li'tter. (1) To bring forth: used of beasts, or of human
beings in abhorrence or contempt.

> Then was this iland,
> Save for the son that she did *litter* here,
> A freckled whelp, hag-born, not honour'd with
> A human shape. Shakespeare's *Tempest*.

li′velode. Maintenance; support; livelihood.

li′very. (1) The act of giving or taking possession.

li′xivium. Lye; water impregnated with salt of whatsoever kind; a liquor which has the power of extraction.

li′zard. An animal resembling a serpent, with legs added to it. There are several sorts of *lizards;* some in Arabia of a cubit long. In America they eat *lizards;* it is very probable likewise that they were eaten sometimes in Arabia and Judaea, since Moses ranks them among the unclean creatures. Calmet.

load. (3) As much drink as one can bear.

> There are those that can never sleep without their *load,* nor enjoy one easy thought, till they have laid all their cares to rest with a bottle. L'Estrange.

loaf. (1) A mass of bread as it is formed by the baker: a loaf is thicker than a cake.

lo′athingly. In a fastidious manner.

lo′athly. Hateful; abhorred; exciting hatred.

lob. (1) Any one heavy, clumsy, or sluggish.

(2) Lob's pound; a prison. Probably a prison for idlers, or sturdy beggars.

(3) A big worm.

to lob. To let fall in a slovenly or lazy manner.

lo′cket. A small lock; any catch or spring to fasten a necklace, or other ornament.

lo′ckram. A sort of coarse linen. Hanmer.

to lodge. (8) To lay flat.

> We'll make foul weather with despised tears;
> Our sighs, and they, shall *lodge* the summer corn,
> And make a dearth in this revolting land. Shakespeare.

lo′ggats. *Loggats* is the ancient name of a play or game, which is one of the unlawful games enumerated in the thirty-third statute of Henry VIII. It is the same which is now called kittlepins, in which boys often make use of bones instead of wooden pins, throwing at them with another bone instead of bowling. Hanmer.

lo'ggerhead. A dolt; a blockhead; a thickscul.

to fall to loggerheads, to go to loggerheads. To scuffle, to fight without weapons.

lo'gomachy. A contention in words; a contention about words.

to loll. (Of this word the etymology is not known. Perhaps it might be contemptuously derived from *lollard*, a name of great reproach before the reformation; of whom one tenet was, that all trades not necessary to life are unlawful.)

(1) To lean idly; to rest lazily against any thing.

lomp. A kind of roundish fish.

long. By the fault; by the failure. A word now out of use, but truly English.

> Maine, Bloys, Poictiers, and Tours are won away,
> *Long* all of Somerset, and his delay. Shakespeare, *Henry VI.*

longani'mity. Forbearance; patience of offences.

lo'ngtail. Cut and long tail: a canting term for, one or another.

> He will maintain you like a gentlewoman.
> —Aye, that I will come cut and *longtail* under the degree of a squire. Shakespeare's *Merry Wives of Windsor.*

lo'oby. A lubber; a clumsy clown.

> The vices trace
> From the father's scoundrel race.
> Who could give the looby such airs?
> Were they masons, were they butchers? Swift.

lo'ofed. Gone to a distance.

loon. (This word, which is now used only in Scotland, is the English word *lown.*) A sorry fellow; a scoundrel; a rascal.

> This young lord had an old cunning rogue, or, as the Scots call it, a false *loon* of a grandfather, that one might call a Jack of all trades. Arbuthnot's *History of John Bull.*

lo'oped. Full of holes.

to lo'osen. (5) To make not costive.

> Fear *looseneth* the belly; because the heat retiring towards the heart, the guts are relaxed in the same

manner as fear also causeth trembling. Bacon's *Natural History*, No. 41.

lop. (2) A flea.

lo'ppered. Coagulated; as, *loppered* milk. Ainsworth.

lo'rding. Lord in contempt or ridicule.

> To *lordings* proud I tune my lay,
> Who feast in bower or hall;
> Though dukes they be, to dukes I say,
> That pride will have a fall. Swift.

lore. Lost; destroyed.

lo'rel. An abandoned scoundrel. Obsolete.

to lo'ricate. To plate over.

> Nature hath *loricated*, or plaistered over, the sides of the tympanum in animals with ear-wax, to stop and entangle any insects that should attempt to creep in there. Ray.

lo'sel. A scoundrel; a sorry worthless fellow. A word now obsolete.

> A gross hag!
> And, *losel*, thou art worthy to be hang'd,
> That wilt not stay her tongue. Shakespeare, *Winter's Tale*.

louse. A small animal, of which different species live on the bodies of men, beasts, and perhaps of all living creatures.

> Not that I value the money the fourth part of the skip of a *louse*. Swift.

to louse. To clean from lice.

> You sat and *lous'd* him all the sun-shine day. Swift.

lo'usily. In a paltry, mean, and scurvy way.

lo'usy. (2) Mean; low born; bred on the dunghil.

to lout. To pay obeisance; to bend; to bow; to stoop. Obsolete. It was used in a good sense. In Scotland they say, a fellow with *lowtan* or *luttan* shoulders; that is, one who bends forwards; his shoulders or back.

lo'vemonger. One who deals in affairs of love.

> Thou art an old *lovemonger*, and speakest skilfully. Shakespeare.

lo'vetoy. Small presents given by lovers.

Has this amorous gentleman presented himself with any *lovetoys*, such as gold snuff-boxes. Arbuthnot and Pope's *Martinus Scriblerus*.

lown. A scoundrel; a rascal.

> King Stephen was a worthy peer,
> His breeches cost him but a crown,
> He thought them sixpence all too dear,
> And therefore call'd the taylor *lown*. Shakespeare.

lowtho'ughted. Having the thoughts with-held from sublime or heavenly meditations; mean of sentiment; narrow minded-ness.

lo'zenge. (2) *Lozenge* is a form of medicine made into small pieces, to be held or chewed in the mouth till melted or wasted.

lu'bber. A sturdy drone; an idle, fat, bulky losel; a booby.

> How can you name that superannuated *lubber*?
> Congreve.

lu'brick. (1) Slippery; smooth on the surface.

(2) Uncertain; unsteady.

(3) Wanton; lewd.

> Why were we hurry'd down
> This *lubrick* and adult'rate age;
> Nay, added fat pollutions of our own,
> T' encrease the steaming ordures of the stage. Dryden.

lucri'ferous. Gainful; profitable.

lucubra'tion. Study by candlelight; nocturnal study; any thing composed by night.

lu'culent. (1) Clear; transparent; lucid. This word is per-haps not used in this sense by any other writer.

> And *luculent* along
> The purer rivers flow. Thomson's *Winter*, l. 715.

luff. (In Scotland.) The palm of the hand; as, clap me arles in my *luff*.

lu'ggage. Any thing cumbrous and unweildy that is to be car-ried away; any thing of more weight than value.

lu'mber. Any thing useless or cumbersome; any thing of more bulk than value.

lunch, lu'ncheon. As much food as one's hand can hold.

When hungry thou stood'st staring, like an oaf,
I slic'd the *luncheon* from the barley loaf;
With crumbled bread I thicken'd well the mess. Gay.

to lurch. (1) To devour; to swallow greedily.

Too far off from great cities may hinder business; or too near *lurcheth* all provisions, and maketh every thing dear. Bacon's *Essays*.

(2) To defeat; to disappoint. A word now used only in burlesque. (From the game *lurch*.)

(3) To steal privily; to filch; to pilfer.

lu'rid. Gloomy; dismal.

lu'scious. (1) Sweet, so as to nauseate.

lu'sern. A lynx.

lusk. Idle; lazy; worthless.

lu'stre. (4) The space of five years.

luta'rious. Living in mud; of the colour of mud.

luxu'rious. (1) Delighting in the pleasures of the table.
(3) Lustful; libidinous.

lyca'nthropy. A kind of madness, in which men have the qualities of wild beasts.

ly'mphated. Mad.

lynx. A spotted beast, remarkable for speed and sharp sight.

M

macaro′on. (1) A coarse, rude, low fellow; whence
macaronick poetry, in which the language is purposely corrupted.

> Like a big wife, at sight of lothed meat,
> Ready to travail; so I sigh and sweat,
> To hear this *macaroon* talk on in vain. Donne.

maca′w. A bird in the West-Indies.

ma′ckerel. A sea-fish.

to mad. To make mad; to make furious; to enrage.

> This *mads* me, that perhaps ignoble hands
> Have overlaid him, for they cou'd not conquer. Dryden.

mad. An earth worm. Ainsworth.

madefa′ction. The act of making wet.

to ma′ffle. To stammer. Ainsworth.

magazi′ne. (2) Of late this word has signified a miscellaneous
pamphlet, from a periodical miscellany named the *Gentleman's Magazine,* by Edward Cave.

ma′ggot. (2) Whimsy; caprice; odd fancy.

> She pricked his *maggot,* and touched him in the tender

---

magazine. Johnson had edited the *Gentleman's Magazine* under Cave,
the founder and publisher of the first general magazine in English.
Cave had died recently, and this reference memorializes a long-time
friend.

point; then he broke out into a violent passion.
Arbuthnot.

magna'lity. A great thing; something above the common rate.
Not used.

to ma'gnify. (5) A cant word for *to have effect.*

My governess assured my father I had wanted for nothing; that I was almost eaten up with the green-sickness:
but this *magnified* but little with my father. *Spectator,*
No. 432.

ma'idenhead, ma'idenhode, ma'idenhood. (2) Newness; freshness; uncontaminated state. This is now become a low
word.

Some who attended with much expectation, at their first
appearing have stained the *maidenhead* of their credit
with some negligent performance. Wotton.

main. (5) A hand at dice.

To pass our tedious hours away,
We throw a merry *main.* Earl Dorset's *Song.*

(7) A hamper. Ainsworth.

majora'tion. Encrease; enlargement.

to make. (6) To make away with. To destroy; to kill; to
make away. This phrase is improper.

The women of Greece were seized with an unaccount-
able melancholy, which disposed several of them to
make away with themselves. Addison's *Spectator,* No.
231.

make. Companion; favourite friend.

For since the wise town,
Has let the sports down,
Of May games and morris,
The maids and their *makes,*
At dancing and wakes,
Had their napkins and posies,
And the wipers for their noses. Benj. Jonson's *Owls.*

ma'kebate. Breeder of quarrels.

mali'gnant. (1) A man of ill intention; malevolently disposed.

ma'lkin. A kind of mop made of clouts for sweeping ovens;

thence a frightful figure of clouts dressed up; thence a dirty wench. Hanmer.

> The kitchen *malkin* pins
> Her richest lockram 'bout her reechy neck,
> Clamb'ring the walls to eye him. Shakespeare, *Coriolanus*.

ma'lthorse. It seems to have been, in Shakespeare's time, a term of reproach for a dull dolt.

> Mome, *malthorse,* capon, coxcomb, idiot, patch. Shakespeare.

ma'mmet. A puppet, a figure dressed up. Hammer.

ma'nchet. A small loaf of fine bread.

to ma'ncipate. To enslave; to bind; to tie.

ma'ndrake. The flower of the *mandrake* consists of one leaf in the shape of a bell, and is divided at the top into several parts; the pointal afterwards becomes a globular soft fruit, in which are contained many kidney-shaped seeds: the roots of this plant is said to bear a resemblance to the human form. The reports of tying a dog to this plant, in order to root it up, and prevent the certain death of the person who dares to attempt such a deed, and of the groans emitted by it when the violence is offered, are equally fabulous. Miller.

ma'nifest. (2) Detected, with *of*.

> Calistho there stood *manifest of* shame,
> And turn'd a bear, the northern star became. Dryden.

ma'niple. (1) A handful.

(2) A small band of soldiers.

manque'ller. A murderer; a mankiller; a manslayer.

mansu'ete. Tame; gentle; not ferocious; not wild.

manti'ger. A large monkey or baboon.

to ma'ntle. (4) To gather any thing on the surface; to froth.

> From plate to plate your eye-balls roll,
> And the brain dances to the *mantling* bowl. Pope's *Horace*.

(5) To ferment; to be in sprightly agitation.

to manu're. (1) To cultivate by manual labour.

> They mock our scant *manuring,* and require

More hands than ours to lop their wanton growth. Milton.

mare. (2) A kind of torpor or stagnation, which seems to press the stomach with a weight; the night hag.

> Mushrooms cause the incubus, or the *mare* in the stomach. Bacon's *Natural History*, No. 546.

ma'rish. A bog; a fen; a swamp; watry ground; a marsh; a morass; a more.

ma'rjoram. A fragrant plant of many kinds; the bastard kind only grows here.

mark. (7) The evidence of a horse's age.

> At four years old cometh the *mark* of tooth in horses, which hath a hole as big as you may lay a pea within it; and weareth shorter and shorter every year, till at eight years old the tooth is smooth. Bacon's *Natural History*, No. 754.

marr'owbone. (1) Bone boiled for the marrow.

(2) In burlesque language, the knees.

> Upon this he fell down upon his *marrowbones,* and begged of Jupiter to give him a pair of horns. L'Estrange's *Fables.*

to ma'rvel. To wonder; to be astonished. Disused.

mast. (2) The fruit of the oak and beech.

> Trees that bear *mast,* and nuts, are more lasting than those that bear fruits; as oaks and beeches last longer than apples and pears. Bacon's *Natural History,* No. 583.

ma'tadore. A hand of cards so called from its efficacy against the adverse player.

to mate. (4) To subdue; to confound; to crush.

> I think you are all *mated,* or stark mad. Shakespeare.

ma'trice. (1) The womb; the cavity where the foetus is formed.

> If the time required in vivification be of any length, the spirit will exhale before the creature be mature, except it be enclosed in a place where it may have continuance of the heat, and closeness that may keep it from exhaling; and such places are the wombs and *matrices* of the females. Bacon.

ma'tron. (1) An elderly lady.

> Your wives, your daughters,
> Your *matrons* and your maids, could not fill up
> The cistern of my lust. Shakespeare's *Macbeth*.

(2) An old woman.

ma'udlin. (*Maudlin* is the corrupt appellation of *Magdelen*, who being drawn by painters with swoln eyes, and disordered look, a drunken countenance, seems to have been so named from a ludicrous resemblance to the picture of *Magdelen*.) Drunk; fuddled.

> And the kind *maudling* crowd melts in her praise.
> Southerne's *Spartan Dame*.

maund. A hand-basket.

to ma'under. To grumble; to murmur.

> He made me many visits, *maundring* as if I had done
> him a discourtesy in leaving such an opening. Wiseman's
> *Surgery*.

ma'vis. A thrush. An old word.

ma'wkish. Apt to give satiety; apt to cause loathing.

> Flow, Welsted! flow, like thine inspirer beer,
> So sweetly *mawkish,* and so smoothly dull. Pope.

ma'wmet. A puppet, anciently an idol.

ma'wmish. Foolish; idle; nauseous.

> It is one of the most nauseous, *mawmish* mortifications,
> for a man of sense to have to do with a punctual, finical
> fop. L'Estrange.

maw-worm. Ordinary gut-worms loosen, and slide off from, the intern tunick of the guts, and frequently creep into the stomach for nutriment, being attracted thither by the sweet chyle; whence they are called stomach or *maw-worms*. Harvey, *On Consumptions*.

ma'zard. A jaw. Hanmer.

> Now my lady Worm's chapless, and knockt about the
> *mazard* with a sexton's spade. Shakespeare, *Hamlet*.

ma'zer. A maple cup.

me. (2) *Me* is sometimes a kind of ludicrous expletive.

> I, having been acquainted with the smell before, knew

it was Crab, and goes *me* to the fellow that whips the dogs. Shakespeare, *Two Gentlemen of Verona*.

me′acock. An uxorious or effeminate man.

mealy-mouthed. Soft mouthed; unable to speak freely.

She was a fool to be *mealy-mouthed* where nature speaks so plain. L'Estrange.

mea′nder. Maze; labyrinth; flexuous passage; serpentine winding; winding course.

Law is a bottomless pit: John Bull was flattered by the lawyers, that his suit would not last above a year; yet ten long years did Hocus steer his cause through all the *meanders* of the law, and all the courts. Arbuthnot.

me′asure. (12) Limit; boundary. In the same sense is

Μέτρον

Τρεῖς ἐτέων δεκάδας, τριάδας δύο, μέτρον ἔθηκαν
Ἡμετέρης βιοτῆς μάντιες αἰθέριοι·
Ἀρκοῦμαι τούτοισιν·

Lord, make me to know mine end, and the *measure* of my days what it is, that I may know how frail I am. *Psalms*.

mecha′nical, mecha′nick. (1) Mean; servile; of mean occupation.

Hang him, *mechanical* salt-butter rogue; I will stare him out of his wits; I will hew him with my cudgel. Shakespeare.

meeting-house. Place where Dissenters assemble to worship.

me′grim. Disorder of the head.

There screen'd in shades from day's detested glare,
Spleen sighs for ever on her pensive bed,
Pain at her side, and *megrim* at her head. Pope.

melancho′ly. (2) A kind of madness, in which the mind is always fixed on one object.

---

measure. The Greek quotation is part of an anonymous epigram: "Three decades and twice three years did the heavenly augurs fix as the measure of my life. I am content therewith . . ." (*Greek Anthology*, VII, 157, trans. Paton). Johnson is referring to his own age when writing this, in the spring or summer of 1746.

I have neither the scholar's *melancholy*, which is emulation; nor the musician's, which is fantastical; nor the courtier's, which is proud; nor the soldier's, which is ambitious; nor the lawyer's, which is politick; nor the lady's, which is nice; nor the lover's, which is all these; but it is a *melancholy* of mine own, compounded of many simples, extracted from many objects, and, indeed, the sundry contemplation of my travels, in which my often rumination wraps me in a most humorous sadness. Shakespeare, *As you like it*.

men-ple′aser. One too careful to please others.

Servants be obedient to them that are your masters: not with eye-service, as *men-pleasers;* but as the servants of Christ, doing the will of God from the heart. *Ephesians*, vi, 6.

me′nial. (1) Belonging to the retinue, or train of servants. (2) Swift seems not to have known the meaning of this word.

The women attendants perform only the most *menial* offices. *Gulliver's Travels*.

to me′rchand. To transact by traffick.

Ferdinando *merchanded* with France for the restoring Roussiglion and Perpignan, oppignorated to them. Bacon.

me′rchant. One who trafficks to remote countries.

me′rcurial. (1) Formed under the influence of mercury; active; sprightly.

me′rcury. (3) A news-paper. Ainsworth.

(4) It is now applied, in cant phrase, to the carriers of news and pamphlets.

meretri′cious. Whorish; such as is practised by prostitutes; alluring by false show.

me′rrimake. A festival; a meeting for mirth.

merry-a′ndrew. A buffoon; a zany; a jack-pudding.

He would be a statesman because he is a buffoon; as if there went no more to the making of a counsellor than the faculties of a *merry-andrew* or tumbler. L'Estrange.

me′rrythought. A forked bone on the body of fowls; so called because boys and girls pull in play at the two sides, the longest part broken off betokening priority of marriage.

Let him not be breaking *merrythoughts* under the table with my cousin. Eachard's *Contempt of the Clergy.*

me′thodist. (1) A physician who practises by theory.

(2) One of a new kind of puritans lately arisen, so called from their profession to live by rules and in constant method.

to mew. (2) To shed the feathers. It is, I believe, used in this sense, because birds are, by close confinement, brought to shed their feathers.

mi′asm. Such particles or atoms as are supposed to arise from distempered, putrefying, or poisonous bodies, and to affect people at a distance.

mi′cher. A lazy loiterer, who skulks about in corners and by-places, and keeps out of sight; a hedge-creeper. Hanmer.

Mich or *Mick* is still retained in the cant language for an indolent, lazy fellow.

mi′ghtily. (3) In a great degree; very much. This is a sense scarcely to be admitted but in low language.

An ass and an ape conferring grievances: the ass complained *mightily* for want of horns, and the ape for want of a tail. L'Estrange's *Fables.*

mi′lklivered. Cowardly; timorous; faint-hearted.

mi′llepedes. Wood-lice, so called from their numerous feet.

mime. A buffoon who practises gesticulations, either representative of some action, or merely contrived to raise mirth.

mi′mick. (1) A ludicrous imitator; a buffoon who copies another's act or manner so as to excite laughter.

(2) A mean or servile imitator.

Of France the *mimick,* and of Spain the prey. Anon.

to mince. (1) To walk nicely by short steps; to act with appearance of scrupulousness and delicacy; to affect nicety.

A harlot form soft sliding by,
With *mincing* step, small voice, and languid eye.
Dunciad.

---

mimick. (2) Johnson quotes from his poem *London,* l. 106.

(2) To speak small and imperfectly.

> The reeve, miller, and cook, are as much distinguished from each other, as the *mincing* lady prioress and the broadspeaking wife of Bath. Dryden's *Fables*.

mi'nim. (1) A small being; a dwarf.

mi'nion. A favourite; a darling; a low dependant; one who pleases rather than benefits. A word of contempt, or of slight and familiar kindness.

> Edward sent one army into Ireland; not for conquest, but to guard the person of his *minion* Piers Gaveston. Davies.

to mi'nish. To lessen; to lop; to impair.

mi'nnock. Of this word I know not the precise meaning. It is not unlikely that *minnock* and *minx* are originally the same word.

> An ass's nole I fixed on his head;
> Anon his Thisbe must be answered,
> And forth my *minnock* comes. Shakespeare.

minx. A young, pert, wanton girl.

> Lewd *minx!*
> Come, go with me apart. Shakespeare.

mi'screant. (1) One that holds a false faith; one who believes in false gods.

(2) A vile wretch.

mi'ser. (1) A wretched person; one overwhelmed with calamity.

> Do not disdain to carry with you the woful words of a *miser* now despairing; neither be afraid to appear before her, bearing the base title of the sender. Sidney, b. ii.

(2) A wretch; a mean fellow.

mi'serable. (3) Culpably parsimonious; stingy.

mi'shmash. A low word. A mingle or hotchpotch.

miss. (1) The term of honour to a young girl.

> Where there are little masters and *misses* in a house, they are great impediments to the diversions of the servants. Swift.

(2) A strumpet; a concubine; a whore; a prostitute.

This gentle cock, for solace of his life,
Six *misses* had besides his lawful wife. Dryden.

mi′ssive. (1) A letter sent: it is retained in Scotland in that sense.

(2) A messenger.

mi′ster. What *mister*, what *kind* of.

The redcross knight toward him crossed fast,
To weet what *mister* wight was so dismay'd,
There him he finds all senseless and aghast. Spenser.

mi′ttens. (3) To handle one without mittens. To use one roughly. A low phrase. Ainsworth.

mi′zmaze. A maze; a labyrinth.

Those who are accustomed to reason have got the true key of books, and the clue to lead them through the *mizmaze* of variety of opinions and authors to truth. Locke.

mo. Further; longer.

Sing no more ditties, sing no *mo*
Of dumps so dull and heavy;
The frauds of men were ever so,
Since summer was first leafy. Shakespeare.

mo′bile. The populace; the rout; the mob.

The *mobile* are uneasy without a ruler, they are restless with one. L'Estrange's *Fables*.

mobi′lity. (2) (In cant language.) The populace.

to moble. To dress grossly or inelegantly.

But who, oh! hath seen the *mobled* queen,
Run barefoot up and down. Shakespeare, *Hamlet*.

mo′cking-stock. A but for merriment.

mode′ller. Planner; schemer; contriver.

Our great *modellers* of gardens have their magazines of plants to dispose of. *Spectator*, No. 414.

mo′dern. (2) In Shakespeare, vulgar; mean; common.

We have our philosophical persons to make *modern* and familiar things supernatural and causeless. Shakespeare.

mo′dernism. Deviation from the ancient and classical manner. A word invented by Swift.

Scribblers send us over their trash in prose and verse,

with abominable curtailings and quaint *modernisms*. Swift.

modesty-piece. A narrow lace which runs along the upper part of the stays before, being a part of the tucker, is called the *modesty-piece*. Addison's *Guardian*, No. 118.

mo'hock. The name of a cruel nation of America given to ruffians who infested, or rather were imagined to infest, the streets of London.

moi'dered. Crazed. Ainsworth.

to moil. (1) To labour in the mire.

(2) To toil; to drudge.

Oh the endless misery of the life I lead! cries the *moiling* husband; to spend all my days in ploughing. L'Estrange.

mokes of a net. The meshes. Ainsworth.

mo'ky. Dark: as, *moky* weather. Ainsworth. It seems a corruption of murky: and in some places they call it muggy, dusky.

mole. (4) A little beast that works under-ground.

molo'sses, mola'sses. Treacle; the spume or scum of the juice of the sugar-cane.

mome. A dull, stupid blockhead, a stock, a post: this owes its original to the French word *momon*, which signifies the gaming at dice in masquerade, the custom and rule of which is, that a strict silence is to be observed; whatsoever sum one stakes another covers, but not a word is to be spoken; from hence also comes our word *mum* for silence. Hanmer.

mo'neyscrivener. One who raises money for others.

mo'nsieur. A term of reproach for a Frenchman.

mo'nstrous. Exceedingly; very much. A cant term.

Add, that the rich have still a gibe in store,
And will be *monstrous* witty on the poor. Dryden's *Juvenal*.

monte'th. (From the name of the inventor.) A vessel in which glasses are washed.

New things produce new words, and thus *Monteth*
Has by one vessel sav'd his name from death. King.

month's mind. Longing desire.

moon-calf. (1) A monster; a false conception: supposed perhaps anciently to be produced by the influence of the moon.

(2) A dolt; a stupid fellow.

moon-eyed. (1) Having eyes affected by the revolutions of the moon.

(2) Dim eyed; purblind. Ainsworth.

to mop. To make wry mouths in contempt.

mo′pus. (A cant word from *mope*.) A drone; a dreamer.

to mo′ralize. (2) In Spenser it seems to mean, to furnish with manners or examples.

> Fierce warres and faithful loves shall *moralize* my song.
> *Fairy Queen*, b. i.

(3) In Prior, who imitates the foregoing line, it has a sense not easily discovered, if indeed it has any sense.

> High as their trumpets tune his lyre he strung,
> And with his prince's arms he *moraliz'd* his song. Prior.

morda′cious. Biting; apt to bite.

more. (3) Again; a second time.

> Little did I think I should ever have business of this
> kind on my hands *more*. *Tatler*, No. 83.

mo′reland. A mountainous or hilly country: a tract of Staffordshire is called the *Morlands*.

mori′sco. A dancer of the morris or moorish dance.

>   I have seen
> Him caper upright like a wild *morisco*,
> Shaking the bloody darts, as he his bells. Shakespeare,
> *Henry VI*.

mo′rkin. (Among hunters.) A wild beast, dead through sickness or mischance. Bailey.

mo′rris, mo′rris-dance. (1) A dance in which bells are gingled, or staves or swords clashed, which was learned by the Moors, and was probably a kind of Pyrrhick or military dance.

mo′rrow. (3) *To morrow* is sometimes, I think improperly, used as a noun.

> *To morrow* is the time when all is to be rectified.
> *Spectator*.

morse. A sea-horse.

It seems to have been a tusk of the *morse* or waltron, called by some the sea-horse. Woodward, *On Fossils.*

mo'rsel. (1) A piece fit for the mouth; a mouthful.

A wretch is pris'ner made,
Whose flesh torn off by lumps, the rav'nous foe
In *morsels* cut, to make it farther go. Tate's *Juvenal.*

(3) A small quantity. Not proper.

Of the *morsels* of native and pure gold, he had seen some weighed many pounds. Boyle.

mort. (1) A tune sounded at the death of the game.

(2) A great quantity. Not in elegant use.

mo'rtal. (5) Extreme; violent. A low word.

The birds were in a *mortal* apprehension of the beetles, till the sparrow reasoned them into understanding. L'Estrange.

mo'rtgage. (1) A dead pledge; a thing put into the hands of a creditor.

mo'rtpay. Dead pay; payment not made.

mo'rtuary. A gift left by a man at his death to his parish church, for the recompence of his personal tythes and offerings not duly paid in his life-time. Harris.

moth. A small winged insect that eats cloths and hangings.

mo'ther. (5) Hysterical passion; so called, as being imagined peculiar to women.

This stopping of the stomach might be the *mother;* forasmuch as many were troubled with *mother* fits, although few returned to have died of them. Graunt's *Bills.*

(8) A thick substance concreting in liquors; the lees or scum concreted.

Potted fowl, and fish come in so fast,
That ere the first is out the second stinks,
And mouldy *mother* gathers on the brinks. Dryden.

(9) A young girl. Now totally obsolete.

A sling for a *mother,* a bow for a boy,
A whip for a carter. Tusser's *Husbandry.*

mo'thery. Concreted; full of concretions; dreggy; seculent: used of liquors.

mo'tor. A mover.

mould. (1) A kind of concretion on the top or outside of things kept, motionless and damp; now discovered by microscopes to be perfect plants.

> All *moulds* are inceptions of putrefaction, as the *moulds* of pies and flesh, which *moulds* turn into worms. Bacon.

mo'uldwarp. A mole; a small animal that throws up the earth.

> With gins we betray the vermin of the earth, namely, the fichat and the *mouldwarp*. Walton's *Angler*.

to mounch, to maunch. (*Mouch*, to eat much. Ainsworth. This word is retained in Scotland, and denotes the obtunded action of toothless gums on a hard crust, or any thing eatable: it seems to be a corruption of the French word *manger*. Macbean.)

> A sailor's wife had chesnuts in her lap,
> And *mouncht*, and *mouncht*, and *mouncht*. Shakespeare, *Macbeth*.

mo'untainet. A hillock; a small mount. Elegant, but not in use.

> Her breasts sweetly rose up like two fair *mountainets* in the pleasant vale of Tempe. Sidney.

mo'untebank. (1) A doctor that mounts a bench in the market, and boasts his infallible remedies and cures.

> She, like a *mountebank*, did wound
> And stab herself with doubts profound,
> Only to shew with how small pain
> The sores of faith are cur'd again. *Hudibras*, p. i.

to mo'untebank. To cheat by false boasts or pretences.

mouse. The smallest of all beasts; a little animal haunting houses and corn fields, destroyed by cats.

> The eagle England being in prey,
> To her unguarded nest the weazel Scot
> Comes sneaking, and so sucks her princely eggs;
> Playing the *mouse* in absence of the cat. Shakespeare.

---

to mounch. Macbean, a Scot who was one of Johnson's assistants, furnished much information about Northern words.

to mouse. (2) I suppose it means, in the following passage, sly; insidious; or predatory, rapacious; interested.

> A whole assembly of *mousing* saints, under the mask of zeal and good nature, lay many kingdoms in blood. L'Estrange.

mouth. (1) The aperture in the head of any animal at which the food is received.

(4) A speaker; a rhetorician; the principal orator. In burlesque language.

> Every coffee-house has some particular statesman belonging to it, who is the *mouth* of the street where he lives. Addison.

(7) Down in the mouth. Dejected; clouded in the countenance.

mo′uth-friend. One who professes friendship without intending it.

mo′uth-honour. Civility outwardly expressed without sincerity.

mo′yle. A mule; an animal generated between the horse and the ass.

mu′chwhat. Nearly.

mu′cilage. A slimy or viscous body; a body with moisture sufficient to hold it together.

muck. (1) Dung for manure of grounds.

> The swine may see the pearl, which yet he values but with the ordinary *muck*. Glanvill's *Apology*.

(2) Any thing low, mean, and filthy.

(3) To run a muck, signifies, I know not from what derivation, to run madly and attack all that we meet.

mu′ckender. A handkerchief.

> For thy dull fancy a *muckender* is fit,
> To wipe the slabberings of thy snotty wit. Dorset.

to mu′cker. To scramble for money; to hoard up; to get or save meanly: a word used by Chaucer, and still retained in conversation.

mu′cksweat. (*Muck* and *sweat*: in this low word, *muck* signifies wet, moist.) Profuse sweat.

mu′ckworm. (1) A worm that lives in dung.

(2) A miser; a curmudgeon.

>Worms suit all conditions;
>Misers are *muckworms,* silkworms beaus,
>And death-watches physicians. Swift's *Miscellanies.*

mud. The slime and uliginous matter at the bottom of still water.

to mu'ddle. (2) To make half drunk; to cloud or stupify.

>I was for five years often drunk, always *muddled;* they carried me from tavern to tavern. Arbuthnot, *History of John Bull.*

mu'dsucker. A sea fowl.

to mue. To moult; to change feathers.

mu'ggy, mu'ggish. (A cant word.) Moist; damp; mouldy.

mu'ghouse. An alehouse; a low house of entertainment.

>Our sex has dar'd the *mughouse* chiefs to meet,
>And purchas'd fame in many a well fought street. Tickell.

mu'gient. Bellowing.

mula'tto. One begot between a white and a black, as a mule between different species of animals.

mull'grubs. Twisting of the guts. Ainsworth.

mu'llock. Rubbish. Ainsworth.

multifa'rious. Having great multiplicity; having different respects; having great diversity in itself.

>There is a *multifarious* artifice in the structure of the meanest animal. More's *Divine Dialogues.*

multi'parous. Bringing many at a birth.

>Animals feeble and timorous are generally *multiparous;* or if they bring forth but few at once, as pigeons, they compensate that by their often breeding. Ray, *On the Creation.*

mum. (Of this word I know not the original: it may be observed, that when it is pronounced it leaves the lips closed.) A word denoting prohibition to speak, or resolution not to speak; silence; hush.

>The citizens are *mum,* say not a word. Shakespeare, *Richard III.*

to mu'mble. (2) To chew; to bite softly; to eat with the lips close.

The man, who laugh'd but once to see an ass
Mumbling to make the gross-grain'd thistles pass,
Might laugh again to see a jury chaw
The prickles of unpalateable law. Dryden.

mu'mmy. (1) A dead body preserved by the Egyptian art of embalming.

We have two different substances preserved for medicinal use under the name of *mummy:* one is the dried flesh of human bodies embalmed with myrrh and spice; the other is the liquor running from such *mummies* when newly prepared, or when affected by great heat, or by damps: this is sometimes of a liquid, sometimes of a solid form, as it is preserved in vials well stopped, or suffered to dry and harden in the air: the first kind is brought to us in large pieces, of a lax and friable texture, light and spungy, of a blackish brown colour, and often black and clammy on the surface; it is of a strong but not agreeable smell: the second sort, in its liquid state, is a thick, opake, and viscous fluid, of a blackish and a strong, but not disagreeable smell: in its indurated state it is a dry, solid substance, of a fine shining black colour and close texture, easily broken, and of a good smell: this sort is extremely dear, and the first sort so cheap, that as all kinds of *mummy* are brought from Egypt we are not to imagine it to be the ancient Egyptian *mummy*. What our druggists are supplied with is the flesh of executed criminals, or of any other bodies the Jews can get, who fill them with the common bitumen so plentiful in that part of the world, and adding aloes, and some other cheap ingredients, send them to be baked in an oven till the juices are exhaled, and the embalming matter has penetrated so thoroughly that the flesh will keep. *Mummy* has been esteemed resolvent and balsamick; and besides it, the skull, and even the moss growing on the skulls of human skeletons, have been celebrated for antiepileptick virtues; the fat also of the human body has been recommended in rheumatisms, and every other part or humour have been in repute for the cure of some disease: at present we are wise enough to know, that the virtues ascribed to the parts of the human body are all either imaginary, or such as may be found in other animal substances: the *mummy* and the skull alone of all these horrid medicines retain their places in the shops. Hill's *Materia Medica*.

(2) *Mummy* is used among gardeners for a sort of wax used in the planting and grafting of trees. Chambers.

(3) To beat to a mummy. To beat soundly. Ainsworth.

to mump. (1) To nibble; to bite quick; to chew with a continued motion.

(2) To talk low and quick.

(3) (In cant language.) To go a begging. Ainsworth.

to mu'ndify. To cleanse; to make clean.

mundu'ngus. Stinking tobacco. Bailey.

mu'ngrel. Generated between different natures; base-born; degenerate.

> *Mungrel* curs bawl, snarle and snap, where the fox flies before them, and clap their tails between the legs when an adversary makes head against them. L'Estrange.

mu'shroom. (2) An upstart; a wretch risen from the dunghill; a director of a company.

> Mushrooms come up in a night, and yet they are unsown; and therefore such as are upstarts in state, they call in reproach *mushrooms*. Bacon's *Natural History*.

musk. *Musk* is a dry, light and friable substance of a dark blackish colour, with some tinge of a purplish or blood colour in it, feeling somewhat smooth or unctuous: its smell is highly perfumed, and too strong to be agreeable in any large quantity: its taste is bitterish: it is brought from the East Indies, mostly from the kingdom of Bantam,

---

mushroom. Except for the Bank of England, chartered joint stock companies before the date of the *Dictionary* were highly speculative. In 1719, after the collapse of the South Sea Company, unincorporated companies, according to the *Britannica*, were declared common nuisances, and indictable as such. There is no record of *mushroom* relating to directors of companies in the *O.E.D.* A personal reference may be suspected.

some from Tonquin and Cochin China: the animal which produces it is of a very singular kind, not agreeing with any established genus: it is of the size of a common goat but taller; its head resembles that of the greyhound, and its ears stand erect like those of the rabbit: its tail is also erect and short, its legs moderately long, and its hoofs deeply cloven: its hair is a dusky brown, variegated with a faint cast of red and white, every hair being partycoloured: the bag which contains the *musk*, is three inches long and two wide, and situated in the lower part of the creature's belly; it consists of a thin membrane covered thinly with hair, resembling a small purse, and when genuine, the scent is so strong as to offend the head greatly: toward the orifice of the bag there are several glands, which serve for the secretion of this precious perfume, for the sake of which the Indians kill the animal. Hill.

mu′ster. (3) A collection: as, a *muster* of peacocks. Ainsworth.

to mute. To dung as birds.

> I could not fright the crows,
>
> Or the least bird from *muting* on my head. Ben. Jonson.

muttonfi′st. A hand large and red.

mu′zzle. (1) The mouth of any thing; the mouth of a man in contempt.

> But ever and anon turning her *muzzle* toward me, she threw such a prospect upon me, as might well have given a surfeit to any weak lover's stomach. Sidney, b. ii.

to mu′zzle. (2) To fondle with the mouth close. A low word.

> The nurse was then *muzzling* and coaxing of the child. L'Estrange's *Fables*.

my′rmidon. Any rude ruffian; so named from the soldiers of Achilles.

myro′polist. One who sells unguents.

my′stery. (3) A trade; a calling: in this sense it should, according to Warburton, be written *mistery*, from *mestier*, French, a trade.

N

naff. A kind of tufted sea-bird.

nag. (2) A paramour; in contempt.

> Your ribauld *nag* of Egypt
> Hoists sails, and flies. Shakespeare's *Antony and Cleopatra.*

na'ptaking. Surprize; seizure on a sudden; unexpected onset, like that made on men asleep.

na'sicornous. Having the horn on the nose.

> Some unicorns are among insects; as those four kinds of *nasicornous* beetles described by Muffetus. Browne's *Vulgar Errours.*

na'turalist. A student in physicks, or natural philosophy.

na'ture. (11) Physics; the science which teaches the qualities of things.

> *Nature* and *nature's* laws lay hid in night,
> God said, let Newton be, and all was light. Pope.

naught. Bad; corrupt; worthless.

> Thy sister's *naught:* Oh Regan! she hath tied
> Sharp-tooth'd unkindness like a vulture here. Shakespeare.

nau'lage. The freight of passengers in a ship.

nau'tilus. A shell fish furnished with something analogous to oars and a sail.

> Learn of the little *nautilus* to sail,

Spread the thin oar and catch the driving gale. Pope.

na'yword. (2) A proverbial reproach; a bye word.

If I do not gull him into a *nayword,* and make him a common recreation, do not think I have wit enough to lie straight in my bed. Shakespeare's *Twelfth Night.*

neaf. A fist. It is retained in Scotland; and in the plural *neaves.*

Give me thy *neaf,* Monsieur Mustardseed. Shakespeare.

neat. (1) Black cattle; oxen. It is commonly used collectively.

Set it in rich mould, with *neats* dung and lime mingled. Mortimer's *Art of Husbandry.*

(2) A cow or ox.

ne'atherd. A cowkeeper; one who has the care of black cattle. Βουκόλος, bubulcus.

neb. (1) Nose; beak; mouth. Retained in the north.

(2) (In Scotland.) The bill of a bird. See *nib.*

ne'cessaries. Things not only convenient but needful; things not to be left out of daily use. *Quibus doleat natura negatis.*

ne'ckbeef. The coarse flesh of the *neck* of cattle, sold to the poor at a very cheap rate.

ne'ckweed. Hemp.

to neese. To sneeze; to discharge flatulencies by the nose. Retained in Scotland.

He went up and stretched himself upon him; and the child *neesed* seven times, and opened his eyes. *2 Kings,* iv, 35.

nefa'rious. Wicked; abominable.

The most *nefarious* bastards, are they whom the law stiles incestuous bastards, which are begotten between ascendants and descendants, and between collateral, as far as the divine prohibition extends. Ayliffe's *Parergon.*

neif. Fist.

Sweet knight, I kiss thy *neif.* Shakespeare, *Henry IV,* p. ii.

---

neatherd. Johnson gives the Greek and Latin equivalents for no particular reason.

necessaries. The Latin is from Horace, *Satires,* 1.1.75: "such things as, if withheld, mean pain to human nature." The reference is to Johnson's poverty.

ne′rvous. (1) Well strung; strong; vigorous.

> What *nervous* arms he boasts, how firm his tread,
> His limbs how turn'd. Pope's *Odyssey*, b. viii.

(2) Relating to the nerves; having the seat in the nerves.

(3) (In medical cant.) Having weak or diseased nerves.

ne′rvy. Strong; vigorous. Not in use.

nescience. Ignorance; the state of not knowing.

nesh. Soft; tender; easily hurt. Skinner.

nest. (3) An abode; place of residence; a receptacle. Generally in a bad sense: as, a *nest* of rogues and thieves.

(4) A warm close habitation, generally in contempt.

> Some of our ministers having livings offered unto them;
> will neither, for zeal of religion, nor winning souls to
> God, be drawn forth from their warm *nests*. Spenser.

ne′stegg. An egg left in the nest to keep the hen from forsaking it.

> Books and money laid for shew,
> Like *nesteggs*, to make clients lay. *Hudibras.*

ne′twork. Any thing reticulated or decussated, at equal distances, with interstices between the intersections.

new. This is, I think, only used in composition for *newly*, which the following examples may explain.

> Your master's lines
> Are full of *new*-found oaths; which he will break
> As easily as I do tear this paper. Shakespeare.

> Our house has sent to-day
> T'insure our *new*-built vessel, call'd a play. Dryden.

> A *new*-married man and an ass, are bride-led; an old-
> married man and a pack-horse, sadd-led. Arbuthnot and
> Pope.

> Learn all the *new*-fashion words and oaths. Swift.

newfa′ngled. Formed with vain or foolish love of novelty.

> Those charities are not *newfangled* devices of yesterday,
> but are most of them as old as the reformation.
> Atterbury.

ne′ws-monger. One that deals in news; one whose employment it is to hear and to tell news.

Many tales devis'd,
Which oft the ear of greatness needs must hear,
By smiling pick-thanks and base *news-mongers*. Shakespeare.

new-year's-gift. Present made on the first day of the year.

If I be served such a trick, I'll have my brains taken out and buttered, and give them to a dog for a *new-year's-gift*. Shakespeare's *Merry Wives of Windsor*.

ni'as. Simple, silly, and foolish.

A *nias* hawk is one taken newly from the nest, and not able to help itself; and hence nisey, a silly person. Bailey.

nib. (1) The bill or beck of a bird. See *neb*.

ni'ceness. (2) Superfluous delicacy or exactness.

Unlike the *niceness* of our modern dames,
Affected nymphs, with new affected names. Dryden.

to nick. (4) To defeat or cozen, as at dice; to disappoint by some trick or unexpected turn.

Why should he follow you?
The itch of his affection should not then
Have *nick'd* his captainship, at such a point. Shakespeare.

nickna'me. A name given in scoff or contempt; a term of derision; an opprobrious or contemptuous appellation.

So long as her tongue was at liberty, there was not a word to be got from her, but the same *nickname* in derision. L'Estrange.

to ni'ctate. To wink.

nide. A brood: as, a *nide* of pheasants.

nidget. (Corrupted from *nithing* or *niding*. The opprobrious term with which the man was anciently branded who refused to come to the royal standard in times of exigency.) A coward; a dastard.

nidifica'tion. The act of building nests.

ni'ding. *Niding*, an old English word signifying abject, baseminded, false-hearted, coward, or nidget. Carew.

nido'rous. Resembling the smell or taste of roasted fat.

Incense and *nidorous* smells, such as of sacrifices, were thought to intoxicate the brain, and to dispose men to

[264]

devotion; which they may do by a kind of contristation of the spirits, and partly also by heating and exalting them. Bacon.

nightbra'wler. One who raises disturbances in the night.

ni'ghthag. Witch supposed to wander in the night.

ni'ghtman. One who carries away ordure in the night.

ni'ghtrail. A loose cover thrown over the dress at night.

An antiquary will scorn to mention a pinner or *night-rail;* but will talk as gravely as a father of the church on the vitta and peplus. Addison, *On Ancient Medals.*

ni'ghtrule. A tumult in the night.

to nill. Not to will; to refuse; to reject.

to nim. To take. In cant, to steal.

They could not keep themselves honest of their fingers, but would be *nimming* something or other for the love of thieving. L'Estrange, *Fable* 241.

ni'mmer. A thief; a pilferer.

ni'ncompoop. (A corruption of the Latin *non compos.*) A fool; a trifler.

ni'nnyhammer. A simpleton.

Another vents her passion in scurrilous terms; an old *ninny-hammer,* a dotard, a nincompoop, is the best language she can afford me. Addison's *Guardian,* No. 109.

nit. The egg of a louse, or small animal.

ni'thing. A coward, dastard, poltroon.

ni'tid. Bright; shining; lustrous.

ni'ttily. Lousily.

One Bell was put to death at Tyburn for moving a new rebellion; he was a man *nittily* needy, and therefore adventrous. Hayward.

ni'zy. A dunce; a simpleton. A low word.

no'cent. (1) Guilty; criminal.

(2) Hurtful; mischievous.

nock. (1) A slit; a nick; a notch.

(2) The fundament. *Les fesses.*

When the date of *nock* was out,
Off dropt the sympathetick snout. *Hudibras.*

no'ddle. A head; in contempt.

Her care shall be

To comb your *noddle* with a three-legg'd stool. Shakespeare.

noi'ous. Hurtful; mischievous; troublesome; inconvenient. Obsolete.

noli'tion. Unwillingness; opposed to volition.

no'mancy. The art of divining the fates of persons by the letters that form their names.

nonce. Purpose; intent; design. Not now in use.

They used at first to fume the fish in a house built for the *nonce.* Carew.

nonju'ror. One who conceiving James II unjustly deposed, refuses to swear allegiance to those who have succeeded him.

no'nplus. Puzzle; inability to say or do more. A low word.

nonre'sident. One who neglects to live at the proper place.

As to nonresidence, there are not ten clergymen in the kingdom who can be termed *nonresidents.* Swift.

no'nsense. (1) Unmeaning or ungrammatical language.

This *nonsense* got into all the following editions by a mistake of the stage editors. Pope's *Notes on Shakespeare.*

(2) Trifles; things of no importance.

noo'dle. A fool; a simpleton.

nope. A kind of bird called a bullfinch or redtail.

nose. (4) To lead by the nose. To drag by force: as, a bear by his ring. To lead blindly.

(5) To thrust one's nose into the affairs of others. To be meddling with other people's matters; to be a busy body.

(6) To put one's nose out of joint. To put one out in the affections of another.

to nose. To look big; to bluster.

Adult'rous Anthony

Gives his potent regiment to a trull

That *noses* it against us. Shakespeare, *Antony and Cleopatra.*

no'strum. A medicine not yet made publick, but remaining in some single hand.

no'table. (2) Careful; bustling, in contempt and irony.

This absolute monarch was as *notable* a guardian of the fortunes, as of the lives of his subjects. When any man grew rich, to keep him from being dangerous to the state, he sent for all his goods. Addison's *Freeholder*, No. 10.

noto′rious. Publickly known; evident to the world; apparent; not hidden. It is commonly used of things known to their disadvantage; whence by those who do not know the true signification of the word, an atrocious crime is called a *notorious* crime, whether publick or secret.

to nott. To shear. Ainsworth.

to nou′sel. To nurse up.

Bald friars and knavish shavelings sought to *nousel* the common people in ignorance, lest being once acquainted with the truth of things, they would in time smell out the untruth of their packed pelf and masspenny religion. Spenser.

no′vel. (1) A small tale, generally of love.

nowadays. (This word, though common and used by the best writers, is perhaps barbarous.) In the present age.

nuga′city. Futility; trifling talk or behaviour.

nu′merous. (2) Harmonious; consisting of parts rightly numbered; melodious; musical.

Thy heart, no ruder than the rugged stone,
I might, like Orpheus, with my *num'rous* moan
Melt to compassion. Waller.

nu′mskulled. Dull; stupid; doltish.

Hocus has saved that clod-pated, *numskulled*, ninny-hammer of yours from ruin, and all his family. *John Bull*.

nu′nchion. A piece of victuals eaten between meals.

Laying by their swords and trunchions,
They took their breakfasts or their *nunchions*. *Hudibras*.

O

oaf. (1) A changeling; a foolish child left by the fairies.

> These, when a child haps to be got,
> Which after proves an idiot,
> When folk perceives it thriveth not,
> The fault therein to smother:
> Some silly doating brainless calf,
> That understands things by the half,
> Says that the fairy left this *oaf*,
> And took away the other. Drayton, *Nymphidia*.

(2) A dolt; a blockhead; an idiot.

oats. A grain, which in England is generally given to horses, but in Scotland supports the people.

o'belisk. (1) A magnificent high piece of solid marble, or other fine stone, having usually four faces, and lessening upwards by degrees, till it ends in a point like a pyramid. Harris.

(2) A mark of censure in the margin of a book, in the form of a dagger (†).

> He published the translation of the Septuagint, having compared it with the Hebrew, and noted by asterisks what was defective, and by *obelisks* what redundant. Grew.

oberra'tion. The act of wandering about.

obno'xious. (1) Subject.

> I propound a character of justice in a middle form, be-tween the speculative discourses of philosophers, and

the writings of lawyers, which are tied and *obnoxious* to their particular laws. Bacon's *Holy War*.

(2) Liable to punishment.

All are *obnoxious,* and this faulty land,
Like fainting Hester, does before you stand,
Watching your sceptre. Waller.

(3) Liable; exposed.

Long hostility had made their friendship weak in itself, and more *obnoxious* to jealousies and distrusts. Hayward.

obsce'ne. (2) Offensive; disgusting.

A girdle foul with grease binds his *obscene* attire. Dryden.

(3) Inauspicious; ill omined.

Care shuns thy walks, as at the chearful light
The groaning ghosts, and birds *obscene* take flight. Dryden.

obsecra'tion. Intreaty; supplication.

obse'quious. (1) Obedient; compliant; not resisting.

(2) In Shakespeare it seems to signify, funereal; such as the rites of funerals require.

Your father lost a father;
That father his; and the surviver bound
In filial obligation, for some term,
To do *obsequious* sorrow. Shakespeare, *Hamlet*.

obse'rvable. Remarkable; eminent; such as may deserve notice.

The great and more *observable* occasions of exercising our courage, occur but seldom. Rogers.

obse'rvant. (2) Obedient; respectful.

We are told how *observant* Alexander was of his master Aristotle. Digby, *On the Soul,* Dedication.

(4) Meanly dutiful; submissive.

How could the most base men attain to honour but by such an *observant* slavish course. Raleigh.

obse'ssion. (1) The act of besieging.

(2) The first attack of Satan, antecedent to possession.

obstru'ction. (4) In Shakespeare it once signifies something heaped together.

Aye but to die, and go we know not where;
To lie in cold *obstruction*, and to rot;
This sensible warm motion to become
A kneaded clod. Shakespeare's *Measure for Measure*.

obstupefa′ction. The act of inducing stupidity, or interruption of the mental powers.

to obte′nd. (1) To oppose; to hold out in opposition.
(2) To pretend; to offer as the reason of any thing.
Thou dost with lies the throne invade,
Obtending Heav'n for whate'er ills befal. Dryden.

to obte′st. To beseech; to supplicate.
Suppliants demand
A truce, with olive branches in their hand;
Obtest his clemency, and from the plain
Beg leave to draw the bodies of their slain. Dryden.

to obu′mbrate. To shade; to cloud.

obve′ntion. Something happening not constantly and regularly, but uncertainly; incidental advantage.

o′bvious. (1) Meeting any thing; opposed in front to any thing.
To the evil turn
My *obvious* breast; arming to overcome
By suffering, and earn rest from labour won. Milton.
(2) Open; exposed.

occeca′tion. The act of blinding or making blind.
Those places speak of obduration and *occecation*, so as if the blindness that is in the minds, and hardness that is in the hearts of wicked men, were from God. Sanderson.

occi′sion. The act of killing.

occu′lt. Secret; hidden; unknown; undiscoverable.
These instincts we call *occult* qualities; which is all one with saying that we do not understand how they work. L'Estrange.

octa′vo. A book is said to be in *octavo* when a sheet is folded into eight leaves.

ode. A poem written to be sung to musick; a lyrick poem; the ode is either of the greater or less kind. The less is characterised by sweetness and ease; the greater by sublimity, rapture, and quickness of transition.

o'ffal. (1) Waste meat; that which is not eaten at the table.

He let out the *offals* of his meat to interest, and kept a register of such debtors in his pocket-book. Arbuthnot.

(2) Carrion; coarse flesh.

I should have fatted all the region kites
With this slave's *offal*. Shakespeare, *Hamlet*.

to o'ffice. To perform; to discharge; to do.

I will be gone, altho'
The air of Paradise did fan the house,
And angels *offic'd* all. Shakespeare, *All's well that ends well*.

offici'nal. Used in a shop, or belonging to it: thus *officinal* plants and drugs are those used in the shops.

offi'cious. (1) Kind; doing good offices.

to offu'scate. To dim; to cloud; to darken.

o'glio. A dish made by mingling different kinds of meat; a medley; a hotchpotch.

He that keeps an open house, should consider that there are *oglio's* of guests, as well as of dishes, and that the liberty of a common table is as good as a tacit invitation to all sorts of intruders. L'Estrange.

oil. (2) Any fat, greasy, unctuous, thin matter.

to olfa'ct. To smell. A burlesque word.

There is a machiavilian plot,
Tho' every nare *olfact* it not. *Hudibras*, p. i.

o'lio. A mixture; a medly. See *oglio*.

I am in a very chaos to think I should so forget myself. But I have such an *olio* of affairs, I know not what to do. Congreve's *Way of the World*.

o'litory. Belonging to the kitchen garden.

o'mbre. A game of cards played by three.

to o'minate. To foretoken; to shew prognosticks.

o'minous. (2) Exhibiting tokens good or ill.

Though he had a good *ominous* name to have made a peace, nothing followed. Bacon's *Henry VII*.

oneirocri'tick. An interpreter of dreams.

onoma'ntical. Predicting by names.

Theodatus, when curious to know the success of his wars

against the Romans, an *onomantical* or name-wisard Jew, willed him to shut up a number of swine and give some of them Roman names, others Gothish names with several marks, and there to leave them. Camden.

onto′logy. The science of the affections of being in general; metaphysicks.

opa′que.

> They
> Shot upward still direct, whence no way round
> Shadow from body *opaque* can fall. Milton, *Paradise Lost*.

opinia′tor. One fond of his own notion; inflexible; adherent to his own opinion.

opinia′trety, opi′niatry. Obstinacy; inflexibility; determination of mind; stubbornness. This word, though it has been tried in different forms, is not yet received, nor is it wanted.

> I can pass by *opiniatry* and the busy meddling of those who thrust themselves into every thing.
> Woodward, *Letters*.

to opi′nion. To opine; to think. A word out of use, and unworthy of revival.

> It is *opinioned,* that the earth rests as the world's centre; while the heavens are the subject of the universal motions. Glanvill, *Scepsis*, c. xi.

o′pium. A juice, partly of the resinous, partly of the gummy kind. It is brought to us in flat cakes or masses, usually of a roundish figure, very heavy and of a dense texture, not perfectly dry: its colour is a dark brownish yellow; its smell is very unpleasant, of a dead faint kind; and its taste very bitter and very acrid. It is brought from Natolia, from Egypt, and from the East-Indies, where it is produced from the white garden poppy; a plant of which every part is full of a milky juice, and with which the fields of Asia-Minor are in many places sown as ours are with corn. When the heads grow to maturity, but are yet soft, green and full of juice, incisions are made in them, and from every one of these a

---

opaque. Johnson forgot to put in the definition. In the abridgment he gave it: "not transparent."

few drops flow of a milky juice, which soon hardens into a solid consistence. These drops are gathered with great care, and the finest *opium* proceeds from the first incisions. In the countries where *opium* is produced, multitudes are employed in preparing it with water, honey and spices, and working it up into cakes; but what we generally have is the mere crude juice, or at most worked up with water, or a small quantity of honey sufficient to bring it into form. The ancients were greatly divided about the virtues and use of *opium;* some calling it a poison, and others the greatest of all medicines. At present it is in high esteem, and externally applied it is emollient, relaxing and discutient, and greatly promotes suppuration. A moderate dose of *opium* taken internally, is generally under a grain, yet custom will make people bear a dram as a moderate dose; but in that case nature is vitiated. Its first effect is the making the patient cheerful, as if he had drank moderately of wine; it removes melancholy, excites boldness, and dissipates the dread of danger; and for this reason the Turks always take it when they are going to battle in a larger dose than ordinary: it afterward quiets the spirits, eases pain, and disposes to sleep. After the effect of a dose of *opium* is over, the pain generally returns in a more violent manner; the spirits, which had been elevated by it, become lower than before, and the pulse languid. An immoderate dose of *opium* brings on a sort of drunkenness, cheerfulness and loud laughter, at first, and, after many terrible symptoms, death itself. Those who have accustomed themselves to an immoderate use of *opium*, are subject to relaxations and weaknesses of all the parts of the body; they are apt to be faint, idle and thoughtless, and are generally in a stupid and uncomfortable state, except just after they have taken a fresh dose: they lose their appetite, and in fine grow old before their time. Hill.

o'ppidan. A townsman; an inhabitant of a town.

to oppi'gnerate. To pledge; to pawn.

> Ferdinando merchanded at this time with France, for the restoring Roussillion and Perpignan, *oppignorated* to them. Bacon's *Henry VII.*

to o'ppilate. To heap up obstruction.

to oppu'gn. To oppose; to attack; to resist.

opsi'mathy. Late education; late erudition.

orb. (3) Wheel; any rolling body.

> The *orbs*
> Of his fierce chariot roll'd as with the sound
> Of torrent floods. Milton's *Paradise Lost*, b. vi.

orbity. Loss, or want of parents or children.

o'rdeal. A trial by fire or water, by which the person accused appealed to heaven, by walking blindfold over hot bars of iron; or being thrown, I suppose, into the water; whence the vulgar trial of witches.

o'rdinary. (1) Established judge of ecclesiastical causes.

(4) Regular price of a meal.

> Our courteous Antony,
> Being barber'd ten times o'er, goes to the feast;
> And for his *ordinary* pays his heart
> For what his eyes eat only. Shakespeare, *Antony and Cleopatra.*

(5) A place of eating established at a certain price.

> They reckon all their errors for accomplishments; and all the odd words they have picked up in a coffee-house, or a gaming *ordinary,* are produced as flowers of style. Swift.

orga'sm. Sudden vehemence.

> By means of the curious lodgment and inosculation of the auditory nerves, the *orgasms* of the spirits should be allayed, and perturbations of the mind quieted.
> Derham's *Physico-Theology.*

o'rgies. Mad rites of Bacchus; frantick revels.

orgi'llous. Proud; haughty.

orni'thology. A discourse on birds.

orpha'notrophy. An hospital for orphans.

o'rrery. An instrument which by many complicated movements represents the revolutions of the heavenly bodies. It was first made by Mr. Rowley, a mathematician born at Litchfield, and so named from his patron the earl of Orrery: by one or other of this family almost every art has been encouraged or improved.

osci'tancy. (1) The act of yawning.

(2) Unusual sleepiness; carelessness.

o'spray. The sea-eagle, of which it is reported, that when he hovers in the air, all the fish in the water turn up their bellies, and lie still for him to seize which he pleases. Hanmer.

ossi'frage. A kind of eagle, whose flesh is forbid under the name of gryphon. The *ossifraga* or *ospray*, is thus called, because it breaks the bones of animals in order to come at the marrow. It is said to dig up bodies in church-yards, and eat what it finds in the bones, which has been the occasion that the Latins called it *avis bustaria*. Calmet.

o'stent. (1) Appearance; air; manner; mien.

>Use all th' observance of civility,
>Like one well studied in a sad *ostent*,
>To please his grandam. Shakespeare, *Merchant of Venice*.

(2) Show; token. These senses are peculiar to Shakespeare.

>Be merry, and employ your chiefest thoughts
>To courtship, and such fair *ostents* of love
>As shall conveniently become you there. Shakespeare.

(3) A portent; a prodigy; any thing ominous.

>Latinus, frighted with this dire *ostent*,
>For counsel to his father Faunus went;
>And sought the shades renown'd for prophecy,
>Which near Albunia's sulph'rous fountain lie. Dryden.

osti'ary. The opening at which a river disembogues itself.

>It is generally received, that the Nilus hath seven *ostiaries*, that is, by seven channels disburtheneth itself unto the sea. Browne's *Vulgar Errours*, b. vi.

o'strich. *Ostrich* is ranged among birds. It is very large, its wings very short, and the neck about four or five spans. The feathers of its wings are in great esteem, and are used as an ornament for hats, beds, canopies: they are stained of several colours, and made into pretty tufts. They are hunted by way of course, for they never fly; but use their wings to assist them in running more swiftly. The *ostrich* swallows bits of iron or brass, in the same manner as other birds will swallow small stones or gravel, to assist in digesting or comminuting their food. It lays its eggs upon the ground, hides them under the sand, and the sun hatches them. Calmet.

o'thergates. In another manner.

> If sir Toby had not been in drink, he would have tickled you *othergates* than he did. Shakespeare, *Twelfth Night.*

o'tter. An amphibious animal that preys upon fish.

ouch. An ornament of gold or jewels.

> *Ouches* or spangs, as they are of no great cost, so they are of most glory. Bacon, *Essay* 38.

ouch of a boar. The blow given by a boar's tusk. Ainsworth.

ought. (1) Owed; was bound to pay; have been indebted.

> This blood which men by treason sought,
> That followed, sir, which to myself I *ought*. Dryden.

ounce. A lynx; a panther.

ouphe. A fairy; a goblin.

> Nan Page and my little son, we'll dress
> Like urchins, *ouphes,* and fairies, green and white.
> Shakespeare.

ou'sel. A blackbird.

to out. To expel; to deprive.

> So many of their orders, as were *outed* from their fat possessions, would endeavour a re-entrance against those whom they account hereticks. Dryden.

o'utcry. (3) A publick sale; an auction. Ainsworth.

to outkna've. To surpass in knavery.

> The world calls it out-witting a man, when he's only *out-knaved.* L'Estrange.

outla'ndish. Not native; foreign.

> Tedious waste of time to sit and hear
> So many hollow compliments and lies,
> *Outlandish* flatteries. Milton, *Paradise Regained,* b. iv.

to ou'trage. To commit exorbitancies.

> Three or four great ones in court will *outrage* in apparel, huge hose, monstrous hats, and garish colours. Ascham.

to o′ver-cloy. To fill beyond satiety.

> A scum of Britons and base lackey peasants,
> Whom their *o′er-cloyed* country vomits forth
> To desperate adventures and destruction. Shakespeare.

to o′ver-crow. To crow as in triumph.

> A base varlet, that being but of late grown out of the
> dunghil, beginneth now to *over-crow* so high mountains,
> and make himself the great protector of all out-laws.
> Spenser.

overni′ght. Night before bed-time.

> Will confesses, that for half his life his head ached every
> morning with reading men *over-night*. Addison.

to overo′ffice. To lord by virtue of an office.

> This might be the fate of a politician which this ass *over-
> offices*. Shakespeare, *Hamlet*.

to overre′ach. (2) To deceive; to go beyond; to circumvent. A
sagacious man is said to have a long *reach*.

> John had got an impression that Lewis was so deadly
> cunning a man, that he was afraid to venture himself
> alone with him; at last he took heart of grace; let him
> come up, quoth he, it is but sticking to my point, and he
> can never *overreach* me. *History of John Bull*.

overre′acher. A cheat; a deceiver.

overse′en. Mistaken; deceived.

> They rather observed what he had done, and suffered
> for the king and for his country, without farther enquir-
> ing what he had omitted to do, or been *overseen* in do-
> ing. Clarendon.

to oversli′p. To pass undone, unnoticed, or unused; to neglect.

overso′ld. Sold at too high a price.

> Life with ease I can disclaim,
> And think it *over-sold* to purchase fame. Dryden.

to oversta′re. To stare wildly.

> Some warlike sign must be used; either a slovenly bus-
> kin, or an *overstaring* frounced head. Ascham.

overthwa′rt. (2) Crossing any thing perpendicularly.

(3) Perverse; adverse; contradictious.

to overwa'tch. To subdue with long want of rest.
> Morpheus is dispatch'd;
> Which done, the lazy monarch *overwatch'd*,
> Down from his propping elbow drops his head,
> Dissolv'd in sleep, and shrinks within his bed. Dryden.

to overwhe'lm. (2) To overlook gloomily.
> An apothecary late I noted,
> In tatter'd weeds with *overwhelming* brows,
> Culling of simples. Shakespeare, *Romeo and Juliet.*

overwrou'ght. (3) It has in Shakespeare a sense which I know not well how to reconcile to the original meaning of the word, and therefore conclude it misprinted for *overraught;* that is, *overreached* or cheated.
> By some device or other,
> The villain is *o'erwrought* of all my money:
> They say this town is full of cozenage. Shakespeare.

to owe. (5) A practice has long prevailed among writers, to use *owing*, the active participle of *owe*, in a passive sense, for *owed* or *due.* Of this impropriety Bolinbroke was aware, and, having no quick sense of the force of English words, has used *due*, in the sense of consequence or imputation, which by other writers is only used of *debt.* We say, the money is *due* to me; Bolinbroke says, the effect is *due* to the cause.

owl, o'wlet. A bird that flies about in the night and catches mice.

o'wler. One who carries contraband goods. Perhaps from the necessity of carrying on an illicit trade by night.

ox. (1) The general name for black cattle.

oye's. Is the introduction to any proclamation or advertisement given by the publick criers both in England and Scotland. It is thrice repeated.

o'ysterwench, o'ysterwoman. A woman whose business is to sell oysters. Proverbially. A low woman.
> The *oysterwomen* lock'd their fish up,
> And trudg'd away to cry no bishop. *Hudibras.*

P

pabula′tion. The act of feeding or procuring provender.

pace. (5) A measure of five feet. The quantity supposed to be measured by the foot from the place where it is taken up to that where it is set down.

to pack. (3) To sort the cards so as that the game shall be iniquitously secured. It is applied to any iniquitous procurement of collusion.

(4) To unite picked persons in some bad design.

> The expected council was dwindling into a conventicle; a *pack′d* assembly of Italian bishops, not a free convention of fathers from all quarters. Atterbury.

pad. (1) The road; a foot path.

> The squire of the *pad* and the knight of the post,
> Find their pains no more baulk′d, and their hopes no more crost. Prior.

(3) A robber that infests the roads on foot.

to pad. (1) To travel gently.

(2) To rob on foot.

(3) To beat a way smooth and level.

to pa′ddle. (1) To row; to beat water as with oars.

(3) To finger.

pa′ddock. A great frog or toad.

pa′geant. (1) A statue in a show.

pa′god. (1) An Indian idol.

They worship idols called *pagods,* after such a terrible representation as we make of devils. Stillingfleet.

pailma′il. (This is commonly written pellmell; nor do I know which of the two is right.) Violent; boisterous.

pai′nim. Pagan; infidel.

The cross hath been a very ancient bearing, even before the birth of our Saviour, among the *Painims* themselves. Peacham, *On Blazoning.*

pa′leeyed. Having eyes dimmed.

Shrines, where their vigils *paleey′d* virgins keep,
And pitying saints, whose statues learn to weep. Pope.

pa′linode, pa′linody. A recantation.

I, of thy excellence, have oft been told;
But now my ravisht eyes thy face behold:
Who therefore in this weeping *palinod*
Abhor myself, that have displeas′d my God,
In dust and ashes mourn. Sandys's *Paraphrase on Job.*

pa′lliardise. Fornication; whoring. Obsolete.

to palm. (1) To conceal in the palm of the hand, as jugglers.

(2) To impose by fraud.

Moll White has made the country ring with several imaginary exploits *palmed* upon her. Addison's *Spectator.*

(3) To handle.

Frank carves very ill, yet will *palm* all the meat. Prior.

pa′lmer. A pilgrim: they who returned from the holy land carried branches of palm.

pa′lmerworm. A worm covered with hair, supposed to be so called because he wanders over all plants.

pa′lmipede. Webfooted; having the toes joined by a membrane.

pa′lmistry. (1) The cheat of foretelling fortune by the lines of the palm.

(2) Addison uses it for the action of the hand.

Going to relieve a common beggar, he found his pocket was picked; that being a kind of *palmistry* at which this vermin are very dextrous. Addison's *Spectator.*

to pa′lpitate. To beat as the heart; to flutter; to go *pit a pat.*

to pa′lter. To shift; to dodge; to play tricks.

> Be these juggling fiends no more believ'd,
> That *palter* with us in a double sense;
> That keep the word of promise to our ear,
> And break it to our hope. Shakespeare, *Macbeth*.

to pa'mper. To glut; to fill with food; to saginate; to feed luxuriously.

pa'mphlet. A small book, properly a book sold unbound, and only stitched.

pamphletee'r. A scribbler of small books.

to pan. An old word denoting to close or join together. Ainsworth.

pana'do. Food made by boiling bread in water.

pande'mick. Incident to a whole people.

pa'nderly. Pimping; pimplike.

to pang. To torment cruelly.

> I grieve myself
> To think, when thou shalt be disedg'd by her,
> Whom now thou tir'st on, how thy memory
> Will then be *pang'd* by me. Shakespeare.

pa'ntaloon. A man's garment anciently worn, in which the breeches and stockings were all of a piece. Hanmer.

pa'nthcr. A spotted wild beast; a lynx; a pard.

pa'ntlcr. The officer in a great family, who keeps the bread. Hanmer.

pap. (1) The nipple; the dug sucked.

> In weaning young creatures, the best way is never to let them suck the *paps*. Ray, *On the Creation*.

to pa'per. To register.

> He makes up the file
> Of all the gentry: and his own letter
> Must fetch in him he *papers*. Shakespeare's *Henry VIII*.

papi'st. One that adheres to the communion of the pope and church of Rome.

papi'stry. Popery; the doctrine of the Romish church.

> A great number of parishes in England consist of rude and ignorant men, drowned in *papistry*. Whitgift.

parado'xical. (2) Inclined to new tenets, or notions contrary to received opinions.

pa'ragon. (2) Companion; fellow.

to pa'ragon. (1) To compare.

> I will give thee bloody teeth,
> If thou with Caesar *paragon* again
> My man of men. Shakespeare.

(2) To equal.

> He hath atchiev'd a maid
> That *paragons* description and wild fame;
> One that excels the quirks of blazoning pens. Shakespeare.

pa'ramour. (1) A lover or wooer.

(2) A mistress. It is obsolete in both senses, though not inelegant or unmusical.

pa'ranymph. (1) A brideman; one who leads the bride to her marriage.

(2) One who countenances or supports another.

parapherna'lia. Goods in the wife's disposal.

pa'raphrase. A loose interpretation; an explanation in many words.

pa'rasite. One that frequents rich tables, and earns his welcome by flattery.

> Diogenes, when mice came about him, as he was eating, said, I see, that even Diogenes nourisheth *parasites*. Bacon.

parasi'tical, parasi'tick. Flattering; wheedling.

pa'rbreak. Vomit.

> Her filthy *parbreak* all the place defiled has. *Fairy Queen.*

pa'rchment. Skins dressed for the writer. Among traders, the skins of sheep are called parchment, those of calves vellum.

pard, pa'rdale. The leopard; in poetry, any of the spotted beasts.

pa'rdoner. (2) Fellows that carried about the pope's indulgencies, and sold them to such as would buy them, against whom Luther incensed the people of Germany. Cowell.

parego'rick. Having the power in medicine to comfort, mollify and assuage.

parenta'tion. Something done or said in honour of the dead.

pa'rergy. Something unimportant; something done by the by.

The scripture being serious, and commonly omitting such *parergies,* it will be unreasonable to condemn all laughter. Browne's *Vulgar Errours.*

to park. To inclose as in a park.

How are we *park'd,* and bounded in a pale?
A little herd of England's tim'rous deer,
Maz'd with a yelping kennel of French curs. Shakespeare.

parle. Conversation; talk; oral treaty; oral discussion of any thing.

pa'rlous. Keen; sprightly; waggish.

> Midas durst communicate
> To none but to his wife his ears of state;
> One must be trusted, and he thought her fit,
> As passing prudent, and a *parlous* wit. Dryden.

pa'rody. A kind of writing, in which the words of an author or his thoughts are taken, and by a slight change adapted to some new purpose.

pa'rricide. (2) One who destroys or invades any to whom he owes particular reverence; as his country or patron.

pa'rrot. A particoloured bird of the species of the hooked bill, remarkable for the exact imitation of the human voice.

to partiali'ze. To make partial. A word, perhaps, peculiar to Shakespeare, and not unworthy of general use.

Such neighbour-nearness to our sacred blood
Should nothing privilege him, nor *partialize*
Th' unstooping firmness of my upright soul. Shakespeare.

parti'cular. (2) Individual; private person.

It is the greatest interest of *particulars,* to advance the good of the community. L'Estrange.

(3) Private interest.

They apply their minds even with hearty affection and zeal, at the least, unto those branches of publick prayer, wherein their own *particular* is moved. Hooker, b. 5.

(4) Private character; single self; state of an individual.

pa'rtlet. A name given to a hen; the original signification being a ruff or band, or covering for the neck. Hanmer.

party-coloured. Having diversity of colours.

party-ju′ry. A jury in some trials half foreigners and half natives.

pa′rvitude. Littleness; minuteness.

pas. Precedence; right of going foremost.

> In her poor circumstances, she still preserv'd the mien of a gentlewoman; when she came into any full assembly, she would not yield the *pas* to the best of them.
> Arbuthnot.

pash. A kiss. Hanmer.

to pash. To strike; to crush.

pa′squil, pa′squin, pa′squinade. (From *pasquino,* a statue at Rome, to which they affix any lampoon or paper of satirical observation.) A lampoon.

> The *pasquils,* lampoons, and libels, we meet with now-a-days, are a sort of playing with the four and twenty letters, without sense, truth, or wit. *Tatler,* No. 92.

to pass. (12) To put an end to.

> This night
> We'll *pass* the business privately and well. Shakespeare.

(13) To surpass; to excel.

> Martial, thou gav'st far nobler epigrams
> To thy Domitian, than I can my James;
> But in my royal subject I *pass* thee,
> Thou flattered'st thine, mine cannot flatter'd be.
> B. Jonson.

(20) To send from one place to another: as, *pass* that beggar to his own parish.

(21) To pass away. To spend; to waste.

pass. (4) An order by which vagrants or impotent persons are sent to their place of abode.

pa′steboard. Masses made anciently by pasting one paper on another: now made sometimes by macerating paper and casting it in moulds, sometimes by pounding old cordage, and casting it in forms.

pa′stern. (1) The knee of an horse.

---

pastern. (1) In fact, part of the foot of a horse. When a lady asked Johnson how he came to define the word in this way, he answered, "Ignorance, Madam, pure ignorance." But he didn't bother to correct his definition until eighteen years later.

I will not change my horse with any that treads on four
pasterns. Shakespeare's *Henry V*.

The colt that for a stallion is design'd,
Upright he walks on *pasterns* firm and straight,
His motions easy, prancing in his gait. Dryden.

(2) The legs of an human creature in contempt.

So straight she walk'd, and on her *pasterns* high:
If seeing her behind, he lik'd her pace,
Now turning short, he better lik'd her face. Dryden.

pa'storal. A poem in which any action or passion is represented
by its effects upon a country life; or according to the common practice in which speakers take upon them the character of shepherds; an idyl; a bucolick.

pat. Fit; convenient; exactly suitable either as to time or place.
This is a low word, and should not be used but in burlesque
writings.

They never saw two things so *pat*,
In all respects, as this and that. *Hudibras,* p. ii.

to patch. (2) To decorate the face with small spots of black
silk.

We begg'd her but to *patch* her face,
She never hit one proper place. Swift.

pate. The head. Now commonly used in contempt or ridicule,
but antiently in serious language.

pa'ted. Having a pate. It is used only in composition: as, long-
pated or cunning; shallow-*pated* or foolish.

pa'tly. Commodiously; fitly.

pa'triot. One whose ruling passion is the love of his country.

pa'tron. (1) One who countenances, supports or protects. Commonly a wretch who supports with insolence, and is paid
with flattery.

to pa'tronage. To patronize; to protect. A bad word.

Dar'st thou maintain the former words thou spak'st?
Yes, sir, as well as you dare *patronage*
The envious barking of your saucy tongue. Shakespeare.

---

patriot. The fourth edition adds: "It is sometimes used for a factious
disturber of the government."

pa'tten. A shoe of wood with an iron ring, worn under the common shoe by women to keep them from the dirt.

> Good housewives
> Underneath th' umbrella's oily shed,
> Safe through the wet on clinking *pattens* tread. Gay.

to pa'ttern. (1) To make in imitation of something; to copy. (2) To serve as an example to be followed. Neither sense is now much in use.

to paunch. To pierce or rip the belly; to exenterate; to take out the paunch; to eviscerate.

to paw. (2) To handle roughly.
(3) To fawn; to flatter. Ainsworth.

pa'yser. (For *poiser.*) One that weighs.

> To manage this coinage, porters bear the tin, *poizers* weigh it, a steward, comptroller and receiver keep the account. Carew.

to peach. To accuse of some crime.

> If you talk of *peaching,* I'll *peach* first, and see whose oath will be believed; I'll trounce you. Dryden.

to peak. (1) To look sickly.
(2) To make a mean figure; to sneak.

peat. A little fondling; a darling; a dear play thing. It is now commonly called *pet.*

peck. (2) Proverbially. (In low language.) A great deal.

> Her finger was so small, the ring
> Would not stay on which they did bring;
> It was too wide a *peck;*
> It look'd like the great collar just
> About our young colt's neck. Suckling.

pe'ctinated. Put one within another alternately. This seems to be the meaning.

> To sit cross leg'd or with our fingers *pectinated,* is accounted bad. Browne's *Vulgar Errours.*

pecu'liar. (3) Particular; single. To join *most* with *peculiar,* though found in Dryden, is improper.

> I neither fear, nor will provoke the war;
> My fate is Juno's most *peculiar* care. Dryden.

ped. (1) A small packsaddle. A *ped* is much shorter than a pannel, and is raised before and behind, and serves for small burdens.

(2) A basket; a hamper.

to pe'dagogue. To teach with superciliousness.

> This may confine their younger stiles,
> Whom Dryden *pedagogues* at Will's;
> But never cou'd be meant to tie
> Authentic wits, like you and I. Prior.

pe'dant. (1) A schoolmaster.

(2) A man vain of low knowledge; a man awkwardly ostentatious of his literature.

to pe'ddle. To be busy about trifles. Ainsworth. It is commonly written *piddle:* as, what *piddling* work is here.

pee'ler. (2) A robber; a plunderer.

> Yet otes with her sucking a *peeler* is found,
> Both ill to the maister and worse to some ground. Tusser.

pe'lican. There are two sorts of *pelicans;* one lives upon the water and feeds upon fish; the other keeps in deserts, and feeds upon serpents and other reptiles: the *pelican* has a peculiar tenderness for its young; it generally places its nest upon a craggy rock: the *pelican* is supposed to admit its young to suck blood from its breast. Calmet.

pe'lting. This word in Shakespeare signifies, I know not why, mean; paltry; pitiful.

> They from sheepcotes and poor *pelting* villages
> Enforce their charity. Shakespeare.

pe'nguin. (1) A bird. This bird was found with this name, as is supposed, by the first discoverers of America; and *penguin* signifying in Welsh a white head, and the head of this fowl being white, it has been imagined, that America was peopled from Wales; whence *Hudibras:*

> British Indians nam'd from *penguins.*

Grew gives another account of the name, deriving it from *pinguis*, Lat. *fat;* but is, I believe, mistaken.

> The *penguin* is so called from his extraordinary fatness: for though he be no higher than a large goose, yet he

weighs sometimes sixteen pounds: his wings are extreme short and little, altogether unuseful for flight, but by the help whereof he swims very swiftly. Grew's *Musaeum*.

pe'nnyworth. (2) Any purchase; any thing bought or sold for money.

Lucian affirms, that the souls of usurers after their death are translated into the bodies of asses, and there remain certain days for poor men to take their *pennyworths* out of their bones and sides by cudgel and spur. Peacham.

(3) Something advantageously bought; a purchase got for less than it is worth.

For fame he pray'd, but let the event declare
He had no mighty *penn'worth* of his prayer. Dryden.

(4) A small quantity.

My friendship I distribute in *pennyworths* to those about me and who displease me least. Swift.

pe'nsion. An allowance made to any one without an equivalent. In England it is generally understood to mean pay given to a state hireling for treason to his country.

pe'nsioner. (2) A slave of state hired by a stipend to obey his master.

pe'nthouse. A shed hanging out aslope from the main wall.

pe'ppercorn. Any thing of inconsiderable value.

pe'rclose. Conclusion; last part.

pe'regrine. Foreign; not native; not domestick.

to perfe'ctionate. To make perfect; to advance to perfection. This is a word proposed by Dryden, but not received nor worthy of reception.

He has founded an academy for the progress and *perfectionating* of painting. Dryden.

to pe'rflate. To blow through.

The first consideration in building of cities, is to make them open, airy and well *perflated*. Arbuthnot, *On Air*.

pe'riapt. Amulet; charm worn as preservatives against diseases or mischief. Hanmer.

---

pension. Johnson received a pension of £300 seven years after this was published.

periclita′tion. (1) The state of being in danger.

(2) Trial; experiment.

perie′rgy. Needless caution in an operation; unnecessary diligence.

pe′rilous. (2) It is used by way of emphasis, or ludicrous exaggeration of any thing bad.

> Thus was th' accomplish'd squire endu'd
> With gifts and knowledge *per'lous* shrewd. *Hudibras.*

(3) Smart; witty. In this sense it is, I think, only applied to children, and probably obtained its signification from the notion, that children eminent for wit, do not live; a witty boy was therefore a *perilous* boy, or a boy in danger. It is vulgarly *parlous.*

> 'Tis a *per'lous* boy,
> Bold, quick, ingenious, forward, capable;
> He's all the mother's from the top to toe. Shakespeare.

to pe′riod. To put an end to. A bad word.

to perk. To hold up the head with an affected briskness.

> If you think it a disgrace,
> That Edward's miss thus *perks* it in your face,
> To see a piece of failing flesh and blood,
> Let the modest matrons of the town
> Come here in crouds, and stare the strumpet down.
> Pope.

perni′cious. (2) Quick. An use which I have found only in Milton, and which, as it produces an ambiguity, ought not to be imitated.

> Part incentive reed
> Provide, *pernicious* with one touch of fire. Milton.

to perple′x. (3) To plague; to torment; to vex. A sense not proper.

> Chloe's the wonder of her sex,
> 'Tis well her heart is tender,
> How might such killing eyes *perplex*,
> With virtue to defend her. Granville.

pe′rquisite. Something gained by a place or office over and above the settled wages.

> Tell me, perfidious, was it fit

To make my cream a *perquisite*,
And steal to mend your wages. *Widow and Cat.*

to pe'rsecute. (3) To importune much: as, he *persecutes* me with daily solicitations.

to pe'rsonate. (1) To represent by a fictitious or assumed character, so as to pass for the person represented.

pe'rspicil. A glass through which things are viewed; an optick glass.

pe'rtly. (1) Briskly; smartly.

I find no other difference betwixt the common town-wits and the downright country fools, than that the first are *pertly* in the wrong, with a little more gaiety; and the last neither in the right nor the wrong. Pope.

(2) Saucily; petulantly.

When you *pertly* raise your snout,
Fleer, and gibe, and laugh, and flout;
This, among Hibernian asses,
For sheer wit, and humour passes. Swift.

perturba'tour. Raiser of commotions.

pertu'sion. (1) The act of piercing or punching.

(2) Hole made by punching or piercing.

pervica'cious. Spitefully obstinate; peevishly contumacious.

May private devotions be efficacious upon the mind of one of the most *pervicacious* young creatures! *Clarissa.*

pe'rvious. (2) Pervading; permeating. This sense is not proper.

What is this little, agile, *pervious* fire,
This flutt'ring motion which we call the mind? Prior.

pe'ssary. Is an oblong form of medicine, made to thrust up into the uterus upon some extraordinary occasions.

Of cantharides he prescribes five in a *pessary*, cutting off their heads and feet, mixt with myrrh. Arbuthnot.

pe'stilent. (3) In ludicrous language, it is used to exaggerate the meaning of another word.

One *pestilent* fine,
His beard no bigger though than thine,
Walked on before the rest. Suckling.

perquisite. The quotation is from Prior.

pestle of pork. A gammon of bacon. Ainsworth.

pet. (1) A slight passion; a slight fit of anger.

> They cause the proud their visits to delay,
> And send the godly in a *pet* to pray. Pope.

(2) A lamb taken into the house, and brought up by hand. A cade lamb. Hanmer.

pe′tar, pe′tard. A *petard* is an engine of metal, almost in the shape of an hat, about seven inches deep, and about five inches over at the mouth: when charged with fine powder well beaten, it is covered with a madrier or plank, bound down fast with ropes, running through handles, which are round the rim near the mouth of it: this *petard* is applied to gates or barriers of such places as are designed to be surprized, to blow them up: they are also used in countermines to break through into the enemies galleries.
Military Dictionary.

petre′scent. Growing stone; becoming stone.

> A cave, from whose arched roof there dropped down a *petrescent* liquor, which oftentimes before it could fall to the ground congealed. Boyle.

pettifo′gger. A petty small-rate lawyer.

petti′toes. (1) The feet of a sucking pig.

(2) Feet in contempt.

pharmaco′polist. An apothecary; one who sells medicines.

pheni′copter. A kind of bird, which is thus described by Martial:

> *Dat mihi penna rubens nomen sed lingua gulosis*
> *Nostra sapit; quid si garrula lingua foret?*

phe′nix. The bird which is supposed to exist single, and to rise again from its own ashes.

philoso′phick, philoso′phical. (3) Frugal; abstemious.

> This is what nature's wants may well suffice:
> But since among mankind so few there are,
> Who will conform to *philosophick* fare,
> I'll mingle something of our times to please. Dryden.

---

phenicopter. The quotation is Martial's epigram "Flamingoes" (13.71): "My ruddy wing gives me a name, but my tongue is a delicacy to gluttons. What if my tongue were to speak?" (Tr. Ker.)

phiz. The face, in a sense of contempt.

> His air was too proud, and his features amiss,
> As if being a traitor had alter'd his *phiz*. Stepney.

phlegm. (1) The watry humour of the body, which, when it predominates, is supposed to produce sluggishness or dulness.

(2) Water.

physio'gnomy. (1) The art of discovering the temper, and foreknowing the fortune by the features of the face.

phyti'vorous. That eats grass or any vegetable.

> Hairy animals with only two large foreteeth, are all *phytivorous*, and called the hare-kind. Ray.

picaro'on. A robber; a plunderer.

to pick. (3) To separate from any thing useless or noxious, by gleaning out either part; to clean by picking away filth.

> You are not to wash your hands, till you have *picked* your sallad. Swift.

(4) To clean, by gathering off gradually any thing adhering.

> Hope is a pleasant premeditation of enjoyment; as when a dog expects, till his master has done *picking* a bone. More.

(9) To pick a hole in one's coat. A proverbial expression for one finding fault with another.

pi'ckapack. In manner of a pack.

> In a hurry she whips up her darling under her arms, and carries the other a *pickapack* upon her shoulders. L'Estrange.

to pi'ckeer. (1) To pirate; to pillage; to rob.

(2) To make a flying skirmish. Ainsworth.

pi'ckerel-weed. A water plant, from which pikes are fabled to be generated.

> The luce or pike is the tyrant of the fresh waters; they are bred, some by generation, and some not; as of a weed called *pickerel-weed*, unless Gosner be mistaken. Walton.

pi'ckle. (3) Condition; state. A word of contempt and ridicule.

> How cam'st thou in this *pickle?* Shakespeare.

to pi′ckle. (2) To season or imbue highly with any thing bad: as, a *pickled* rogue, or one consummately villainous.

pi′ckleherring. A jack-pudding; a merry-andrew; a zany; a buffoon.

picktha′nk. An officious fellow, who does what he is not desired; a whispering parasite.

pict. A painted person.

> Your neighbours would not look on you as men,
> But think the nations all turn'd *picts* again. Lee.

picto′rial. Produced by a painter. A word not adopted by other writers, but elegant and useful.

> Sea horses are but grotesco delineations, which fill up empty spaces in maps, as many *pictorial* inventions, not any physical shapes. Browne's *Vulgar Errours*.

to pi′ddle. (1) To pick at table; to feed squeamishly, and without appetite.

> From stomach sharp, and hearty feeding,
> To *piddle* like a lady breeding. Swift's *Miscellanies*.

(2) To trifle; to attend to small parts rather than to the main. Ainsworth.

pie. (3) The old popish service book, so called, as is supposed, from the different colour of the text and rubrick.

(4) Cock and *pie* was a slight expression in Shakespeare's time, of which I know not the meaning.

> Mr. Slender, come; we stay for you.—
> —I'll eat nothing, I thank you, Sir.—
> —By cock and *pie*, you shall not chuse, Sir; come, come.
> Shakespeare, *Merry Wives of Windsor*.

pie′led. Perhaps for *peeled,* or bald; or *piled,* or having short hair.

pi′epowder court. A court held in fairs for redress of all disorders committed therein.

pi′gmy. A small nation, fabled to be devoured by the cranes; thence any thing mean or inconsiderable.

pi′gsney. A word of endearment to a girl. It is used by Butler for the eye of a woman, I believe, improperly.

pigwi′dgeon. This word is used by Drayton as the name of a fairy, and is a kind of cant word for any thing petty or small.

to pill (2) For *peel;* to strip off the bark.

> Jacob took him rods of green poplar, and *pilled* white streaks in them. *Genesis*, xxx, 37.

pi′mping. Little; petty: as, a *pimping* thing. Skinner.

pin. (8) A note; a strain. In low language.

> As the woman was upon the peevish *pin*, a poor body comes, while the froward fit was upon her, to beg. L'Estrange.

pi′neal. Resembling a pineapple. An epithet given by Des Cartes from the form, to the gland which he imagined the seat of the soul.

> Courtiers and spaniels exactly resemble one another in the *pineal* gland. Arbuthnot and Pope.

pink. (3) Any thing supremely excellent. I know not whether from the flower or the eye, or a corruption of *pinacle.*

> I am the very *pink* of courtesy. Shakespeare, *Romeo and Juliet.*

to pink. To wink with the eyes.

pi′nner. (1) The lappet of a head which flies loose.

> Her goodly countenance I've seen,
> Set off with kerchief starch'd and *pinners* clean. Gay.

pio′neer. One whose business is to level the road, throw up works, or sink mines in military operations.

pi′ping. (From *pipe.* This word is only used in low language.)

> (1) Weak; feeble; sickly: from the weak voice of the sick.
> I, in this weak *piping* time of peace,
> Have no delight to pass away the time,
> Unless to spy my shadow in the sun. Shakespeare.

(2) Hot; boiling: from the sound of any thing that boils.

piquee′rer. A robber; a plunderer. Rather *pickeerer.*

pi′rate. (2) Any robber; particularly a bookseller who seizes the copies of other men.

to pi′rate. To take by robbery.

> They publickly advertised, they would *pirate* his edition. Pope.

pish. A contemptuous exclamation. This is sometimes spoken and written *pshaw.* I know not their etymology, and imagine them formed by chance.

She frowned and cried *pish,* when I said a thing that I stole. *Spectator,* No. 268.

to piss. To make water.

One ass *pisses,* the rest *piss* for company. L'Estrange.

piss. Urine; animal water.

My spleen is at the little rogues, it would vex one more to be knock'd on the head with a *piss*-pot than a thunder bolt. Pope to Swift.

pi'ssabed. A yellow flower growing in the grass.

pi'tapat. (1) A flutter; a palpitation.

(2) A light quick step.

Now I hear the *pitapat* of a pretty foot through the dark alley: no, 'tis the son of a mare that's broken loose, and munching upon the melons. Dryden's *Don Sebastian.*

to pitch. (5) To darken.

Damon

Rose early from his bed; but soon he found
The welkin *pitch'd* with sullen cloud. Addison.

(6) To pave. Ainsworth.

pi'tcher. (2) An instrument to pierce the ground in which any thing is to be fixed.

To the hills poles must be set deep in the ground, with a square iron *pitcher* or crow. Mortimer's *Husbandry.*

pi't-man. He that in sawing timber works below in the pit.

pi't-saw. The large saw used by two men, of whom one is in the pit.

pi'tfall. A pit dug and covered, into which a passenger falls unexpectedly.

pi'zzle. The *pizzle* in animals is official to urine and generation. Browne's *Vulgar Errours,* b. iii.

placa'rd, placa'rt. An edict; a declaration; a manifesto.

to pla'cate. To appease; to reconcile. This word is used in Scotland.

pla'cit. Decree; determination.

We spend time in defence of their *placits,* which might have been employed upon the universal author. Glanvill.

---

pissabed. Dandelion.

pla′cket. A petticoat.

pla′giary. (1) A thief in literature; one who steals the thoughts or writings of another.

> The ensuing discourse, lest I chance to be traduced for a *plagiary* by him who has played the thief, was one of those that, by a worthy hand, were stolen from me. South.

(2) The crime of literary theft. Not used.

pla′guily. Vexatiously; horribly. A low word.

> You look'd scornful, and snift at the dean;
> But he durst not so much as once open his lips,
> And the doctor was *plaguily* down in the hips. Swift.

pla′guy. Vexatious; troublesome. A low word.

plaice. A flat fish.

plaid. A striped or variegated cloth; an outer loose weed worn much by the highlanders in Scotland: there is a particular kind worn too by the women; but both these modes seem now nearly extirpated among them; the one by act of parliament, and the other by adopting the English dresses of the sex.

pla′inwork. Needlework as distinguished from embroidery; the common practice of sewing or making linen garments.

pla′nched. Made of boards.

plane′tstruck. Blasted; *sidere afflatus*.

> Wonder not much if thus amaz'd I look,
> Since I saw you, I have been *planetstruck;*
> A beauty, and so rare, I did descry. Suckling.

to pla′nish. To polish; to smooth. A word used by manufacturers.

plant. (3) The sole of the foot. Ainsworth.

pla′tform. (1) The sketch of any thing horizontally delineated; the ichnography.

> When the workmen began to lay the *platform* at Chal-

---

plaid. In order to break the power of the clans after the rebellion of Bonnie Prince Charlie in 1745, the government forbade men or boys to wear the plaid under penalty of transportation. The act was repealed in 1782.

planetstruck. The Latin phrase is the equivalent of *planetstruck*.

cedon, eagles conveyed their lines to the other side of
the streight. Sandys's *Journey*.

(2) A place laid out after any model.

(3) A level place before a fortification.

(4) A scheme; a plan.

I have made a *platform* of a princely garden by precept,
partly by drawing not a model, but some general lines of
it. Bacon's *Essays*.

plau'dit, plau'dite. Applause.

She would so shamefully fail in the last act, that instead
of a *plaudite*, she would deserve to be hissed off the
stage. More.

plau'sible. Such as gains approbation; superficially pleasing or
taking; specious; popular; right in appearance.

plau'sibly. (1) With fair show; speciously.

They could talk *plausibly* about that they did not understand, but their learning lay chiefly in flourish. Collier.

(2) With applause. Not in use.

I hope they will *plausibly* receive our attempts, or can-
didly correct our misconjectures. Browne's *Vulgar Errours*.

pla'ypleasure. Idle amusement.

He taketh a kind of *playpleasure* in looking upon the
fortunes of others. Bacon's *Essays*.

plea'seman. A pickthank; an officious fellow.

to plea'sure. To please; to gratify. This word, though supported
by good authority, is, I think, inelegant.

Things, thus set in order,
Shall further thy harvest, and *pleasure* thee best. Tusser.

plebei'an. (1) Popular; consisting of mean persons.

As swine are to gardens, so are tumults to parliaments,
and *plebeian* concourses to publick counsels.
King Charles.

(3) Vulgar; low; common.

Dishonour not the vengeance I design'd.

A queen! and own a base *plebeian* mind! Dryden.

pledge. (1) Any thing put to pawn.

ple'dget. A small mass of lint.

plesh. (A word used by Spenser instead of *plash*, for the convenience of rhyme.) A puddle; a boggy marsh.

ple'thora. The state in which the vessels are fuller of humours than is agreeable to a natural state of health; arises either from a diminution of some natural evacuations, or from debauch and feeding higher or more in quantity than the ordinary powers of the viscera can digest: evacuations and exercise are its remedies.

pleu'risy. *Pleurisy* is an inflammation of the pleura, though it is hardly distinguishable from an inflammation of any other part of the breast, which are all from the same cause, a stagnated blood; and are to be remedied by evacuation, suppuration or expectoration, or all together. Quincy.

to plight. (2) To braid; to weave.

> Her head she fondly would aguise
> With gaudie girlonds, or fresh flowrets dight
> About her neck, or rings of rushes *plight*. *Fairy Queen.*

plight. (2) Good case.

(4) A fold; a pucker; a double; a purfle; a plait.

pluck. (2) The heart, liver and lights of an animal.

plum. (2) Raisin; grape dried in the sun.

(3) (In the cant of the city.) The sum of one hundred thousand pounds.

> Ask you,
> Why she and Sapho raise that monstrous sum?
> Alas! they fear a man will cost a *plum*. Pope.

(4) A kind of play, called how many *plums* for a penny. Ainsworth.

to plume. (2) To strip of feathers.

> Such animals, as feed upon flesh, devour some part of the feathers of the birds they gorge themselves with, because they will not take the pains fully to *plume* them. Ray.

(3) To strip; to pill.

> They stuck not to say, that the king cared not to *plume* the nobility and people to feather himself. Bacon.

plump. A knot; a tuft; a cluster; a number joined in one mass.

England, Scotland, Ireland lie all in a *plump* together, not accessible but by sea. Bacon.

plu'mper. Something worn in the mouth to swell out the cheeks.

She dex'trously her *plumpers* draws,

That serve to fill her hollow jaws. Swift's *Miscellanies*.

plunge. (2) Difficulty; strait; distress.

She was weary of her life, since she was brought to that *plunge;* to conceal her husband's murder, or accuse her son. Sidney, b. ii.

to poach. (2) To begin without completing: from the practice of boiling eggs slightly. Not in use.

Of later times, they have rather *poached* and offered at a number of enterprizes, than maintained any constantly. Bacon.

(3) To stab; to pierce.

poa'chy. Damp; marshy. A cant word.

What uplands you design for mowing, shut up the beginning of February; but marsh lands lay not up till April, except your marshes be very *poachy*. Mortimer's *Husbandry*.

pocket. The small bag inserted into cloaths.

to poc'kct. (2) To pocket up. A proverbial form that denotes the doing or taking any thing clandestinely.

He lays his claim

To half the profit, half the fame,

And helps to *pocket* up the game. Prior.

po'cketbook. A paper book carried in the pocket for hasty notes.

po'esy. (3) A short conceit engraved on a ring or other thing.

A paltry ring, whose *poesy* was,

For all the world like cutler's poetry

Upon a knife; love me, and leave me not. Shakespeare.

poe'taster. A vile petty poet.

Horace hath exposed those trifling *poetasters*, that spend themselves in glaring descriptions, and sewing here and there some cloth of gold on their sackcloth. Felton.

poi'gnancy. (1) The power of stimulating the palate; sharpness.

> I sat quietly down at my morsel, adding only a principle of hatred to all succeeding measures by way of sauce; and one point of conduct in the dutchess's life added much *poignancy* to it. Swift.

(2) The power of irritation; asperity.

point. (2) A string with a tag.

> King James was wont to say, that the duke of Buckingham had given him a groom of his bed-chamber, who could not truss his *points*. Clarendon.

poi'ntingstock. Something made the object of ridicule.

> I, his forlorn dutchess,
> Was made a wonder and a *pointingstock*
> To every idle rascal follower. Shakespeare, *Henry VI.*

poke. A pocket; a small bag.

> I will not buy a pig in a *poke*. Camden's *Remains*.

po'lecat. The fitchew; a stinking animal.

> Out of my door, you witch! you hag, you *polecat!* out, out, out; I'll conjure you. Shakespeare, *Merry Wives of Windsor*.

po'licy. (3) A warrant for money in the publick funds.

politica'ster. A petty ignorant pretender to politicks.

> There are quacks of all sorts; as bullies, pedants, hypocrites, empiricks, law-jobbers and *politicasters*. L'Estrange.

politi'cian. (2) A man of artifice; one of deep contrivance.

> If a man succeeds in any attempt, though undertook with never so much rashness, his success shall vouch him a *politician*, and good luck shall pass for deep contrivance; for give any one fortune, and he shall be thought a wise man. South.

po'llard. (1) A tree lopped.

(2) A clipped coin.

po'llen. A fine powder, commonly understood by the word farina; as also a sort of fine bran. Bailey.

po'ller. (1) Robber; pillager; plunderer.

po'ltron. A coward; a nidgit; a scoundrel.

polysy'llable. A word of many syllables.

>Your high nonsense blusters and makes a noise; it stalks upon hard words, and rattles through *polysyllables.* Addison.

po'mpous. Splendid; magnificent; grand.

ponk. A nocturnal spirit; a hag.

pop. A small smart quick sound. It is formed from the sound.

>I have several ladies, who could not give a *pop* loud enough to be heard at the farther end of the room, who can now discharge a fan, that it shall make a report like a pocket-pistol. Addison's *Spectator*, No. 102.

po'peseye. The gland surrounded with fat in the middle of the thigh: why so called I know not.

po'pular. (1) Vulgar; plebeian.

(2) Suitable to the common people.

(3) Beloved by the people; pleasing to the people.

(4) Studious of the favour of the people.

>A *popular* man is, in truth, no better than a prostitute to common fame and to the people. Dryden.

(5) Prevailing or raging among the populace: as, a *popular* distemper.

po'rcupine. The *porcupine,* when full grown, is as large as a moderate pig: the quills, with which its whole body is covered, are black on the shoulders, thighs, sides and belly; on the back, hips and loins they are variegated with white and pale brown: the neck is short and thick, the nose blunt, the nostrils very large in form of slits; the upper lip is slit or cleft as in the hare, and it has whiskers like a cat: the eyes are small, and the ears very like those of the human species: the legs are short, and on the hinder feet are five toes, but only four upon the fore feet, and its tail is four or five inches long, beset with spines in an annular series round it: there is no other difference between the *porcupine* of Malacca and that of Europe, but that the former grows to a larger size. Hill.

po'reblind. (Commonly spoken and written *purblind.*) Nearsighted; shortsighted.

>*Poreblind* men see best in the dimmer light, and like-

wise have their sight stronger near at hand, than those
that are not *poreblind*, and can read and write smaller
letters; for that the spirits visual in those that are *poreblind* are thinner and rarer than in others, and therefore
the greater light disperseth them. Bacon's *Natural History.*

po'rpoise, po'rpus. The sea-hog.

> Parch'd with unextinguish'd thirst,
> Small beer I guzzle till I burst;
> And then I drag a bloated corpus
> Swell'd with a dropsy like a *porpus.* Swift.

po'rret. A scallion.

po'rridge. Food made by boiling meat in water; broth.

po'rridgepot. The pot in which meat is boiled for a family.

po'rringer. (1) A vessel in which broth is eaten.

> A physician undertakes a woman with sore eyes, who
> dawbs 'em quite up with ointment, and, while she was
> in that pickle, carries off a *porringer.* L'Estrange.

(2) It seems in Shakespeare's time to have been a word of
contempt for a headdress; of which perhaps the first of
these passages may show the reason.

> Here is the cap your worship did bespeak.
> —Why this was moulded on a *porringer.* Shakespeare.

po'rtable. (4) Sufferable; supportable.

> How light and *portable* my pains seem now,
> When that which makes me bend, makes the king bow.
> Shakespeare's *King Lear.*

porta'ss. A breviary; a prayer book.

> An old priest always read in his *portass* mumpsimus
> domine for sumpsimus; whereof when he was ad-
> monished, he said that he now had used mumpsimus
> thirty years, and would not leave his old mumpsimus
> for their new sumpsimus. Camden.

po'rtly. (1) Grand of mien.

> Rudely thou wrong'st my dear heart's desire,
> In finding fault with her too *portly* pride. Spenser.

po'rwigle. A tadpole or young frog not yet fully shaped.

po'snet. A little bason; a porringer; a skillet.

po'sse. An armed power; from *posse comitatus,* the power of the shires. A low word.

po'sset. Milk curdled with wine or any acid.

po'ster. A courier; one that travels hastily.

poste'riors. The hinder parts.

> To raise one hundred and ten thousand pounds, is as vain as that of Rabelais, to squeeze out wind from the *posteriors* of a dead ass. Swift.

to po'stil. To gloss; to illustrate with marginal notes.

po'sy. (1) A motto on a ring.

pot. (5) To go to pot. To be destroyed or devoured. A low phrase.

> John's ready money went into the lawyers pockets; then John began to borrow money upon the bank stock, now and then a farm went to *pot.* Arbuthnot's *History of John Bull.*

pota'to. (I suppose an American word.) An esculent root.

> Leek to the Welch, to Dutchmen butter's dear,
> Of Irish swains *potatoe* is the chear;
> Oats for their feasts the Scottish shepherds grind,
> Sweet turnips are the food of Blouzelind;
> While she loves turnips, butter I'll despise,
> Nor leeks, nor oatmeal, nor *potatoe* prize. Gay.

potbe'lly. A swelling paunch.

> He will find himself a forked stradling animal and a *potbelly.* Arbuthnot and Pope.

to potch. (1) To thrust; to push.

(2) To poach; to boil slightly.

po'tcompanion. A fellow drinker; a good fellow at carousals.

po'tgun. (By mistake or corruption used for *popgun.*) A gun which makes a small smart noise.

> An author, thus who pants for fame,
> Begins the world with fear and shame,
> When first in print, you see him dread
> Each *potgun* levell'd at his head. Swift's *Miscellanies.*

po'ther. (1) Bustle, tumult; flutter.

(2) Suffocating cloud.

> He suddenly unties the poke,
> Which from it sent out such a smoke,
> As ready was them all to choke,
> So grievous was the *pother*. Drayton.

to po'ther. To make a blustering ineffectual effort.

> He that loves reading and writing, yet finds certain seasons wherein those things have no relish, only *pothers* and wearies himself to no purpose. Locke.

potva'liant. Heated with courage by strong drink.

potu'lent. (1) Pretty much in drink.

(2) Fit to drink.

to pouch. (2) To swallow.

(3) To pout; to hang down the lip. Ainsworth.

to pounce. (1) To pierce; to perforate.

> Barbarous people, that go naked, do not only paint, but *pounce* and raise their skin, that the painting may not be taken forth, and make it into works. Bacon's *Natural History*.

(2) To pour or sprinkle through small perforations.

pou'ncetbox. A small box perforated.

> He was perfumed like a milliner,
> And, 'twixt his finger and his thumb, he held
> A *pouncetbox*, which ever and anon
> He gave his nose. Shakespeare, *Henry IV*.

pou'ndage. (1) A certain sum deducted from a pound; a sum paid by the trader to the servant that pays the money, or to the person who procures him customers.

pou'peton. A puppet or little baby.

pou'picts. In cookery, a mess of victuals made of veal stakes and slices of bacon. Bailey.

to po'wder. To come tumultuously and violently. A low corrupt word.

> Whilst two companions were disputing it at sword's point, down comes a kite *powdering* upon them, and gobbets up both. L'Estrange.

po'wdering-tub. (1) The vessel in which meat is salted.

(2) The place in which an infected lecher is physicked to preserve him from putrefaction.

> To the spital go,
> And from the *powd'ring-tub* of infamy
> Fetch forth the lazar kite Doll Tearsheet. Shakespeare.

po'wer. (13) A large quantity; a great number. In low language: as, *a* power *of good things.*

pox. (1) Pustules; efflorescencies; exanthematous eruptions.
(2) The venereal disease. This is the sense when it has no epithet.

> Wilt thou still sparkle in the box,
> Still ogle in the ring?
> Can'st thou forget thy age and *pox.* Dorset.

pra'ctick. (1) Relating to action; not merely theoretical.

> When he speaks,
> The air, a charter'd libertine, is still;
> And the mute wonder lurketh in men's ears,
> To steal his sweet and honied sentences;
> So that the act and *practick* part of life
> Must be the mistress to this theorick. Shakespeare.

(2) In Spenser it seems to signify, sly; artful.

> Thereto his subtile engines he doth bend,
> His *practick* wit, and his fair filed tongue,
> With thousand other sleights. *Fairy Queen.*

practi'tioner. (2) One who uses any sly or dangerous arts.

> There is some papistical *practitioners* among you. Whitgift.

pragma'tick, pragma'tical. Meddling; impertinently busy; assuming business without leave or invitation.

> He understands no more of his own affairs, than a child; he has got a sort of a *pragmatical* silly jade of a wife, that pretends to take him out of my hands. Arbuthnot.

prame. A flat bottomed boat. Bailey.

to prank. To decorate; to dress or adjust to ostentation.

> Some *prank* their ruffs, and others timely dight
> Their gay attire. *Fairy Queen.*

prank. A frolick; a wild flight; a ludicrous trick; a wicked act.

They caused the table to be covered and meat set on, which was no sooner set down, than in came the harpies, and played their accustomed *pranks*. Raleigh.

pra'son. A leek: also a sea weed as green as a leek. Bailey.

pra'vity. Corruption; badness; malignity.

More people go to the gibbet for want of timely correction, than upon any incurable *pravity* of nature. L'Estrange.

preca'rious. Dependent; uncertain, because depending on the will of another; held by courtesy; changeable or alienable at the pleasure of another. No word is more unskilfully used than this with its derivatives. It is used for *uncertain* in all its senses; but it only means uncertain, as dependent on others: thus there are authors who mention the *precariousness* of an *account*, of the *weather*, of a *die*.

preca'riousness. Uncertainty; dependence on others. The following passage from a book, otherwise elegantly written, affords an example of the impropriety mentioned at the word *precarious*.

Most consumptive people die of the discharge they spit up, which, with the *precariousness* of the symptoms of an oppressed diaphragm from a mere lodgement of extravasated matter, render the operation but little adviseable. Sharp's *Surgery*.

pre'cious. (3) Worthless. An epithet of contempt or irony.

More of the same kind, concerning these *precious* saints amongst the Turks, may be seen in Pietro della valle. Locke.

pre'cipice. A headlong steep; a fall perpendicular without gradual declivity.

Drink as much as you can get; because a good coachman never drives so well as when he is drunk; and then shew your skill, by driving to an inch by a *precipice*. Swift.

pre'dal. Robbing; practising plunder. This word is not countenanced from analogy.

to preen. To trim the feathers of birds, to enable them to glide

[306]

more easily through the air: for this use nature has furnished them with two peculiar glands, which secrete an unctuous matter into a perforated oil bag, out of which the bird, on occasion, draws it with its bill. Bailey.

to pre'face. (2) To face; to cover. A ludicrous sense.

> I love to wear cloaths that are flush,
> Not *prefacing* old rags with plush. Cleveland.

to prefi'ne. To limit beforehand.

> He, in his immoderate desires, *prefined* unto himself three years, which the great monarchs of Rome could not perform in so many hundreds. Knolles's *History of the Turks.*

to prefi'x. (1) To appoint beforehand.

> At the *prefix'd* hour of her awaking,
> Came I to take her from her kindred's vault. Shakespeare.

(2) To settle; to establish.

> These boundaries of species are as men, and not as nature makes them, if there are in nature any such *prefixed* bounds. Locke.

pre'gnancy. (2) Fertility; fruitfulness; inventive power; acuteness.

> This writer, out of the *pregnancy* of his invention, hath found out an old way of insinuating the grossest reflections under the appearance of admonitions. Swift's *Miscellanies.*

pre'gnant. (3) Full of consequence.

> These knew not the just motives and *pregnant* grounds, with which I thought myself furnished. King Charles.

pre'gnantly. (2) Fully; plainly; clearly.

> The dignity of this office among the Jews is so *pregnantly* set forth in holy writ, that it is unquestionable; kings and priests are mentioned together. South's *Sermons.*

to preju'dicate. To determine beforehand to disadvantage.

> Are you, in favour of his person, bent
> Thus to *prejudicate* the innocent? Sandys.

pre'judice. (1) Prepossession; judgment formed beforehand without examination. It is used for prepossession in favour of any thing or against it. It is sometimes used with *to* before that which the *prejudice* is against, but not properly.

> There is an unaccountable *prejudice to* projectors of all kinds, for which reason, when I talk of practising to fly, silly people think me an owl for my pains. Addison.

(2) Mischief; detriment; hurt; injury. This sense is only accidental or consequential; *a bad thing* being called a *prejudice*, only because *prejudice* is commonly *a bad thing*, and is not derived from the original or etymology of the word: it were therefore better to use it less; perhaps *prejudice* ought never to be applied to any mischief, which does not imply some partiality or prepossession. In some of the following examples its impropriety will be discovered.

> England and France might, through their amity,
> Breed him some *prejudice;* for from this league
> Peep'd harms that menac'd him. Shakespeare, *Henry VIII*.

to prejudi′ce. (3) To injure; to hurt; to diminish; to impair; to be detrimental to. This sense, as in the noun, is often improperly extended to meanings that have no relation to the original sense; who can read with patience of an ingredient that *prejudices* a medicine?

> To this is added a vinous bitter, warmer in the composition of its ingredients than the watry infusion; and, as gentian and lemon-peel make a bitter of so grateful a flavour, the only care required in this composition was to chuse such an addition as might not *prejudice* it. *London Dispensatory*.

prejudi′cial. (2) Contrary; opposite.

(3) Mischievous; hurtful; injurious; detrimental. This sense is improper. See *prejudice*, noun and verb.

> One of the young ladies reads, while the others are at work; so that the learning of the family is not at all *prejudicial* to its manufactures. Addison's *Guardian*.

prela′tion. Preference; setting of one above the other.

> In case the father left only daughters, they equally succeeded as in co-partnership, without any *prelation*

or preference of the eldest daughter to a double portion. Hale.

prelu'dious. Previous; introductory.

That's but a *preludious* bliss,

Two souls pickeering in a kiss. Cleveland.

pre'mises. (2) In low language, houses or lands: as, *I was upon the* premises.

prepe'nse, prepe'nsed. Forethought; preconceived; contrived beforehand: as, *malice* prepense.

prepo'sterous. (1) Having that first which ought to be last; wrong; absurd; perverted.

Put a case of a land of Amazons, where the whole government, publick and private, is in the hands of women: is not such a *preposterous* government against the first order of nature, for women to rule over men, and in itself void? Bacon.

(2) Applied to persons: foolish; absurd.

Preposterous ass! that never read so far

To know the cause why musick was ordain'd. Shakespeare.

presbyte'rian. An abettor of presbytery or calvinistical discipline.

pre'sence. (6) Room in which a prince shows himself to his court.

The lady Anne of Bretagne, passing through the *presence* in the court of France, and espying Chartier, a famous poet, leaning upon his elbow fast asleep, openly kissing him, said, we must honour with our kiss, the mouth from whence so many sweet verses have proceeded. Peacham.

pre'sent. (3) Ready at hand; quick in emergencies.

If a man write little, he had need have a great memory; if he confer little, he had need have a *present* wit; and if he read little, he had need have much cunning. Bacon.

to press. (11) To force into military service. This is properly *impress*.

pre'ssgang. A crew that strols about the streets to force men into naval service.

pre′ssmoney. Money given to a soldier when he is taken or forced into the service.

> Here Peascod, take my pouch, 'tis all I own,
> 'Tis my *pressmoney.*—Can this silver fail? Gay.

prest. (1) Ready; not dilatory. This is said to have been the original sense of the word *prest men;* men, not forced into the service, as now we understand it, but men, for a certain sum received, *prest* or ready to march at command.

> Grittus desired nothing more than, at his first entrance, to have confirmed the opinion of his authority in the minds of the vulgar people, by the *prest* and ready attendance of the Vayuod. Knolles's *History of the Turks.*

(2) Neat; tight. In both senses the word is obsolete.

prestiga′tion. A deceiving; a juggling; a playing legerdemain.

pre′sto. Quick; at once. A word used by those that show legerdemain.

> *Presto!* begone! 'tis here again;
> There's ev'ry piece as big as ten. Swift.

to prete′nd. (1) To hold out; to stretch forward. This is mere Latinity, and not used.

> Lucagus, to lash his horses, bends
> Prone to the wheels, and his left foot *pretends.* Dryden.

(2) To portend; to foreshow. Not in use.

> All these movements seemed to be *pretended* by moving of the earth in Sussex. Hayward.

(5) To hold out as a delusive appearance; to exhibit as a cover of something hidden. This is rather Latin.

> Warn all creatures from thee
> Henceforth; lest that too heav'nly form, *pretended*
> To hellish falshood, snare them. Milton's *Paradise Lost.*

(6) To claim. In this sense we rather say, *pretend to.*

> Are they not rich? what more can they *pretend?* Pope.

pre′ternatural. Different from what is natural; irregular.

pre′tty. (3) It is used in a kind of diminutive contempt in poetry, and in conversation: as, *a* pretty *fellow indeed!*

(4) Not very small. This is a very vulgar use.

> A weazle a *pretty* way off stood leering at him. L'Estrange.

to preva′ricate. To cavil; to quibble; to shuffle.

> He *prevaricates* with his own understanding, and cannot seriously consider the strength, and discern the evidence of argumentations against his desires. South.

to preve′nt. (1) To go before as a guide; to go before, making the way easy.

> Are we to forsake any true opinion, or to shun any requisite action, only because we have in the practice thereof been *prevented* by idolaters. Hooker, b. v, s. 12.

(2) To go before; to be before; to anticipate.

> The same officer told us, he came to conduct us, and that he had *prevented* the hour, because we might have the whole day before us for our business. Bacon.

(3) To preoccupy; to preengage; to attempt first.

> Thou hast *prevented* us with offertures of love, even when we were thine enemies. King Charles.

(4) To hinder; to obviate; to obstruct. This is now almost the only sense.

pri′apism. A preternatural tension.

> The person every night has a *priapism* in his sleep. Floyer.

prick. (1) A sharp slender instrument; any thing by which a puncture is made.

> The country gives me proof
> Of bedlam beggars, who, with roaring voices,
> Strike in their numb'd and mortified bare arms
> Pins, wooden *pricks*, nails, sprigs of rosemary. Shakespeare.

pri′cklouse. A word of contempt for a taylor. A low word.

> A taylor and his wife quarreling; the woman in contempt called her husband *pricklouse*. L'Estrange.

pride. (2) Insolence; rude treatment of others; insolent exultation.

> That witch
> Hath wrought this hellish mischief unawares;
> That hardly we escap'd the *pride* of France. Shakespeare.

(8) The state of a female beast soliciting the male.

It is impossible you should see this,
Were they as salt as wolves in *pride*. Shakespeare.

prie. I suppose an old name of privet.

Lop popler and sallow, elme, maple and *prie*,
Wel saved from cattel, till summer to lie. Tusser.

pri′estcraft. Religious frauds; management of wicked priests to
gain power.

Puzzle has half a dozen common-place topicks; though
the debate be about Doway, his discourse runs upon
bigotry and *priestcraft*. *Spectator*.

prie′stridden. Managed or governed by priests.

Such a cant of high-church and persecution, and being
priestridden. Swift.

prig. (A cant word derived perhaps from *prick*, as he *pricks* up,
he is *pert*; or from *prickeared*, an epithet of reproach be-
stowed upon the presbyterian teachers.) A pert, conceited,
saucy, pragmatical, little fellow.

There have I seen some active *prig*,
To shew his parts, bestride a twig. Swift's *Miscellanies*.

prill. A birt or turbot. Ainsworth.

prim. Formal; precise; affectedly nice.

A ball of new dropt horse's dung,
Mingling with apples in the throng,
Said to the pippin, plump and *prim*,
See, brother, how we apples swim. Swift's *Miscel-
lanies*.

prince. (4) The son of a king; in England only the eldest son;
the kinsman of a sovereign.

pri′ncock, pri′ncox. A coxcomb; a conceited person; a pert
young rogue.

You are a saucy boy;
This trick may chance to scathe you I know what;
You must contrary me! you are a *princox*, go. Shake-
speare.

to prink. To prank; to deck for show.

---

prill. Johnson defines *birt* as turbot.

Hold a good wager she was every day longer *prinking* in the glass than you was. *Art of Tormenting.*

pri′sonbase. A kind of rural play, commonly called *prisonbars.* The spachies of the court play every Friday at ciocho di canni, which is no other than *prisonbase* upon horseback, hitting one another with darts, as the others do with their hands. Sandys's *Travels.*

pri′thee. A familiar corruption of *pray thee*, or *I pray thee*, which some of the tragick writers have injudiciously used.

Alas! why com'st thou at this dreadful moment,
To shock the peace of my departing soul?
Away! I *prithee* leave me! Rowe's *Jane Shore.*

priva′tion. (1) Removal or destruction of any thing or quality.

So bounded are our natural desires,
That wanting all, and setting pain aside,
With bare *privation* sense is satisfy'd. Dryden.

(2) The act of the mind by which, in considering a subject, we separate it from any thing appendant.

(3) The act of degrading from rank or office.

pri′vity. (1) Private communication.

(2) Consciousness; joint knowledge; private concurrence. All the doors were laid open for his departure, not without the *privity* of the prince of Orange, concluding that the kingdom might better be settled in his absence. Swift.

(3) (In the plural.) Secret parts.

Few of them have any thing to cover their *privities.* Abbot.

pri′vy. Place of retirement; necessary house.

Your fancy
Would still the same ideas give ye,
As when you spy'd her on the *privy.* Swift.

pro. For; in defence of; *pro* and *con*, for *pro* and *contra*, for and against. Despicable cant.

proba′tion. (1) Proof; evidence; testimony.

---

prink. Jane Collier's *Essay on the Art of Ingeniously Tormenting* was published in 1753.

He was lapt in a most curious mantle, which, for more *probation,* I can produce. Shakespeare, *Cymbeline.*

probo'scis. A snout; the trunk of an elephant; but it is used also for the same part in every creature, that bears any resemblance thereunto.

pro'ceed. Produce: as, *the* proceeds *of an estate. Clarissa.* Not an imitable word, though much used in law writings.

proce'rity. Talness; height of stature.

We shall make attempts to lengthen out the human figure, and restore it to its ancient *procerity.* Addison.

to pro'ctor. To manage. A cant word.

I cannot *proctor* mine own cause so well

To make it clear. Shakespeare, *Antony and Cleopatra.*

to pro'cure. To bawd; to pimp.

Our author calls colouring, lena sorosis, in plain English, the bawd of her sister, the design or drawing: she cloaths, she dresses her up, she paints her, she makes her appear more lovely than naturally she is, she *procures* for the design, and makes lovers for her.

Dryden's *Dufresnoy.*

procu'rer. (1) One that gains; obtainer.

(2) Pimp; pandar.

prodi'giously. (1) Amazingly; astonishingly; portentously; enormously.

(2) It is sometimes used as a familiar hyperbole.

I am *prodigiously* pleased with this joint volume. Pope.

prodito'rious. (1) Trayterous; treacherous; perfidious.

(2) Apt to make discoveries.

Solid and conclusive characters are emergent from the mind, and start out of children when themselves least think of it; for nature is *proditorious.* Wotton, *On Education.*

to profa'ne. (2) To put to wrong use.

I feel me much to blame,

So idly to *profane* the precious time. Shakespeare.

profi'cuous. Advantageous; useful.

It is very *proficuous,* to take a good large dose. Harvey.

to profo'und. To dive; to penetrate. A barbarous word.

We cannot *profound* into the hidden things of nature,
nor see the first springs that set the rest a-going.
Glanvill.

to prog. (1) To rob; to steal.

(2) To shift meanly for provisions. A low word.

She went out *progging* for provisions as before.
L'Estrange.

prog. Victuals; provision of any kind. A low word.

Spouse tuckt up doth in pattens trudge it,

With handkerchief of *prog*, like trull with budget;

And eat by turns plumcake and judge it. Congreve.

to pro'gress. To move forward; to pass. Not used.

Let me wipe off this honourable dew,

That silverly doth *progress* on thy cheeks. Shakespeare.

to proin. (A corruption of *prune*.) To lop; to cut; to trim; to
prune.

I sit and *proin* my wings

After flight, and put new stings

To my shafts. Benj. Jonson.

proleta'rian. Mean; wretched; vile; vulgar.

Like speculators should foresee,

From pharos of authority,

Portended mischiefs farther than

Low *proletarian* tything-men. *Hudibras,* p. i.

prolu'sion. Entertainments; performance of diversion.

It is memorable, which Famianus Strada, in the first
book of his academical *prolusions,* relates of Suarez.
Hakewill.

promi'scuous. Mingled; confused; undistinguished.

A wild, where weeds and flow'rs *promiscuous* shoot.
Pope.

pro'misebreaker. Violator of promises.

He's an hourly *promisebreaker*, the owner of no one good
quality worthy your entertainment. Shakespeare.

pro'mptuary. A storehouse; a repository; a magazine.

prone. (1) Bending downward; not erect.

(2) Lying with the face downwards: contrary to supine.

Upon these three positions in man, wherein the spine

can only be at right lines with the thigh, arise those postures, *prone*, supine and erect. Browne's *Vulgar Errours*.

prong. A fork.

The cooks make no more ado, but slicing it into little gobbets, prick it on a *prong* of iron, and hang it in a furnace. Sandys's *Journey*.

to prope'nd. To incline to any part; to be disposed in favour of any thing.

pro'per. (9) Elegant; pretty.

Moses was a *proper* child. *Hebrews*, xi, 23.

(10) Tall; lusty; handsome with bulk.

At last she concluded with a sigh, thou wast the *properest* man in Italy. Shakespeare.

pro'perty. (2) Quality; disposition.

It is the *property* of an old sinner to find delight in reviewing his own villanies in others. South's *Sermons*.

(6) Nearness or right. I know not which is the sense in the following lines.

Here I disclaim all my paternal care,

Propinquity, and *property* of blood,

And as a stranger to my heart and me,

Hold thee. Shakespeare, *King Lear*.

propri'ety. (1) Peculiarity of possession; exclusive right.

You that have promis'd to yourselves *propriety* in love,

Know womens hearts like straws do move. Suckling.

to propu'gn. To defend; to vindicate.

pro'sody. The part of grammar which teaches the sound and quantity of syllables, and the measures of verse.

prosterna'tion. Dejection; depression; state of being cast down; act of casting down. A word not to be adopted.

Pain interrupts the cure of ulcers, whence are stirred up a fever, watching, and *prosternation* of spirits. Wiseman.

to pro'stitute. (1) To sell to wickedness; to expose to crimes for a reward. It is commonly used of women sold to whoredom by others or themselves.

(2) To expose upon vile terms.

[316]

pro'stitute. (1) A hireling; a mercenary; one who is set to sale.

At open fulsome bawdry they rejoice,

Base *prostitute!* thus dost thou gain thy bread. Dryden.

(2) A publick strumpet.

From every point they come,

Then dread no dearth of *prostitutes* at Rome. Dryden.

prostitu'tion. (1) The act of setting to sale; the state of being set to sale.

(2) The life of a publick strumpet.

An infamous woman, having passed her youth in a most shameless state of *prostitution*, now gains her livelihood by seducing others. Addison's *Spectator.*

prota'sis. (1) A maxim or proposition.

(2) In the ancient drama, the first part of a comedy or tragedy that explains the argument of the piece.

prote'rvity. Peevishness; petulance.

pro'tocol. The original copy of any writing.

An original is stiled the *protocol*, or scriptura matrix; and if the *protocol*, which is the root and foundation of the instrument, does not appear, the instrument is not valid. Ayliffe.

pro'toplast. Original; thing first formed as a copy to be followed afterwards.

The consumption was the primitive disease, which put a period to our *protoplasts*, Adam and Eve. Harvey.

proud. (1) Too much pleased with himself.

The *proudest* admirer of his own parts might find it useful to consult with others, though of inferior capacity. Watts.

(2) Elated; valuing himself. With *of* before the object.

In vain *of* pompous chastity you're *proud*,

Virtue's adultery of the tongue, when loud. Dryden.

(8) Salacious; eager for the male.

That camphire begets in men an impotency unto venery, observation will hardly confirm, and we have found it fail in cocks and hens, which was a more favourable tryal than that of Scaliger, when he gave it unto a bitch that was *proud*. Browne.

to pro′verb. Not a good word. (1) To mention in a proverb.

> Am I not sung and *proverb'd* for a fool
> In ev'ry street; do they not say, how well
> Are come upon him his deserts? Milton's *Agonistes.*

(2) To provide with a proverb.

pro′vince. (1) A conquered country; a country governed by a delegate.

provi′ncial. (3) Not of the mother country; rude; unpolished.

> A country 'squire having only the *provincial* accent upon his tongue, which is neither a fault, nor in his power to remedy, must marry a cast wench. Swift.

provoca′tive. Any thing which revives a decayed or cloyed appetite.

pro′vost. (1) The chief of any body: as, *the* provost *of a college.*

(2) The executioner of an army.

> Kingston, *provost* marshal of the king's army, was deemed not only cruel but inhuman in his executions. Hayward.

pro′ximately. Immediately; without intervention.

prude. A woman over nice and scrupulous, and with false affectation.

> Not one careless thought intrudes,
> Less modest than the speech of *prudes*. Swift.

pru′dish. Affectedly grave.

> I know you all expect, from seeing me,
> Some formal lecture, spoke with *prudish* face. Garrick.

to prune. To dress; to prink. A ludicrous word.

> Every scribbling man
> Grows a fop as fast as e'er he can,
> *Prunes* up, and asks his oracle the glass,
> If pink or purple best become his face. Dryden.

prune′llo. (1) A kind of stuff of which the clergymen's gowns are made.

> Worth makes the man, and want of it, the fellow;
> The rest is all but leather or *prunello*. Pope.

pru′rience, pru′riency. An itching or a great desire or appetite to any thing. Swift.

pshaw. An expression of contempt.

A peevish fellow has some reason for being out of humour, or has a natural incapacity for delight, and therefore disturbs all with pishes and *pshaws*.
Spectator, No. 438.

pube′rty. The time of life in which the two sexes begin first to be acquainted.

The cause of changing the voice at the years of *puberty* seemeth to be, for that when much of the moisture of the body, which did before irrigate the parts, is drawn down to the spermatical vessels, it leaveth the body more hot than it was, whence cometh the dilatation of the pipes. Bacon.

pu′blican. (1) A toll gatherer.

As Jesus sat at meat, many *publicans* and sinners came and sat down with him. *Matthew*, ix, 10.

(2) A man that keeps a house of general entertainment. In low language.

pu′dder. A tumult; a turbulent and irregular bustle.

to pu′dder. To perplex; to disturb; to confound.

He that will improve every matter of fact into a maxim, will abound in contrary observations, that can be of no other use but to perplex and *pudder* him. Locke.

pu′dding. (2) The gut of an animal.

As sure as his guts are made of *puddings*. Shakespeare.

(3) A bowel stuffed with certain mixtures of meal and other ingredients.

pu′ddingpie. A pudding with meat baked in it.

pu′ddingtime. (1) The time of dinner; the time at which pudding, anciently the first dish, is set upon the table.

(2) Nick of time; critical minute.

Mars that still protects the stout,
In *puddingtime* came to his aid. *Hudibras*.

pu′dency. Modesty; shamefacedness.

puefe′llow. A partner.

This carnal cur
Preys on the issue of his mother's body;
And makes her *puefellow* with others moan. Shakespeare.

pug. A kind name of a monkey, or any thing tenderly loved.

Upon setting him down, and calling him *pug,* I found
him to be her favourite monkey. Addison's *Spectator.*

pu′ggered. Crowded; complicated. I never found this word in
any other passage.

Nor are we to cavil at the red *puggered* attire of the
turkey, and the long excrescency that hangs down over
his bill, when he swells with pride. More's *Antidote
against Atheism.*

pugh. (Corrupted from *puff,* or borrowed from the sound.) A
word of contempt.

pu′gil. What is taken up between the thumb and two first
fingers.

pu′isne. (*Puis nè,* French. It is commonly spoken and written
puny. See *puny.*) (1) Young; younger; later in time.

(2) Petty; inconsiderable; small.

puke. Vomit; medicine causing vomit.

to puke. To spew; to vomit.

The infant

Mewling and *puking* in the nurse's arms. Shakespeare.

to pule. (1) To cry like a chicken.

(2) To whine; to cry; to whimper.

This *puling* whining harlot rules his reason,

And prompts his zeal for Edward's bastard brood. Rowe.

to pullu′late. To germinate; to bud.

pulse. (3) To feel one's pulse. To try to know one's mind artfully.

to pu′lvil. To sprinkle with perfumes in powder.

Have you *pulvilled* the coachman and postilion, that
they may not stink of the stable. Congreve's *Way of
the World.*

to pump. (2) To examine artfully by sly interrogatories, so
as to draw out any secrets or concealments.

punch. (2) (Cant word.) A liquour made by mixing spirit with
water, sugar, and the juice of lemons.

The West India dry gripes are occasioned by lime juice
in *punch.* Arbuthnot, *On Aliments.*

---

punch. No doubt a cant word, but Johnson's favorite alcoholic drink.

pu′nctually. Nicely; exactly; scrupulously.

pu′ndle. A short and fat woman. Ainsworth.

punk. A whore; a common prostitute; a strumpet.

> She may be a *punk;* for many of them are neither maid, widow, nor wife. Shakespeare, *Measure for Measure.*

pu′nster. A quibbler; a low wit who endeavours at reputation by double meaning.

pu′ny. (1) Young.

to pup. To bring forth whelps: used of a bitch bringing young.

to pu′rfle. To decorate with a wrought or flowered border; to border with embroidery; to embroider.

pu′rfle, pu′rflew. A border of embroidery.

pu′rgatory. A place in which souls are supposed by the papists to be purged by fire from carnal impurities, before they are received into heaven.

pu′rist. One superstitiously nice in the use of words.

pu′ritan. A sectary pretending to eminent purity of religion.

> The schism which the papists on the one hand, and the superstition which the *puritans* on the other, lay to our charge, are very justly chargeable upon themselves. Sanderson.

pu′rseproud. Puffed up with money.

pu′rsy. Shortbreathed and fat.

> An hostess dowager,
> Grown fat and *pursy* by retail
> Of pots of beer and bottl'd ale. *Hudibras,* p. iii.

pu′rtenance. The pluck of an animal.

> The shaft against a rib did glance,
> And gall'd him in the *purtenance. Hudibras,* p. i.

purve′yor. (2) A procurer; a pimp.

> The stranger, ravish'd at his good fortune, is introduced to some imaginary title; for this *purveyor* has her representatives of some of the finest ladies. Addison.

pu′shing. Enterprising; vigorous.

puss. (2) The sportsman's term for a hare.

to put. (46) To put out. To place at usury.

> To live retir'd upon his own,
> He call'd his money in;

But the prevailing love of pelf,
Soon split him on the former shelf,
   He *put* it *out* again. Dryden's *Horace*.

put. (1) An action of distress.

The stag's was a forc'd *put*, and a chance rather than a
choice. L'Estrange.

   (2) A rustick; a clown.

pu′tage. In law, prostitution on the woman's part.

pu′tid. Mean; low; worthless.

He that follows nature is never out of his way; whereas
all imitation is *putid* and servile. L'Estrange.

py′gmy. A dwarf; one of a nation fabled to be only three spans
high, and after long wars to have been destroyed by cranes.

py′romancy. Divination by fire.

Q

to quack. (1) To cry like a duck. This word is often written *quaake,* to represent the sound better.

(2) To chatter boastingly; to brag loudly; to talk ostentatiously.

> Believe mechanick virtuosi
> Can raise them mountains in Potosi,
> Seek out for plants with signatures,
> To *quack* of universal cures. *Hudibras,* p. iii.

quack. (1) A boastful pretender to arts which he does not understand.

> Some *quacks* in the art of teaching, pretend to make young gentlemen masters of the languages, before they can be masters of common sense. Felton, *On the Classicks.*

(2) A vain boastful pretender to physick; one who proclaims his own medical abilities in publick places.

(3) An artful tricking practitioner in physick.

> Despairing *quacks* with curses fled the place,
> And vile attorneys, now an useless race. Pope.

qua'cksalver. One who brags of medicines or salves; a medicaster; a charlatan.

quadru'ped. An animal that goes on four legs, as perhaps all beasts.

The king of brutes,
Of *quadrupeds* I only mean. Swift.

to qua'ffer. (A low word, I suppose, formed by chance.) To feel out. This seems to be the meaning.

Ducks, having larger nerves that come into their bills than geese, *quaffer* and grope out their meat the most. Derham.

quaid. (Of this participle I know not the verb, and believe it only put by Spenser, who often took great liberties, for *quailed,* for the poor convenience of his rhyme.) Crushed; dejected; depressed.

Therewith his sturdy courage soon was *quaid,*
And all his senses were with sudden dread dismaid.
Fairy Queen.

quaint. (1) Nice; scrupulously, minutely, superfluously exact; having petty elegance.

(2) Subtle; artful. Obsolete.

As clerkes been full subtle and *quaint.* Chaucer.

(3) Neat; pretty; exact.

Her mother hath intended,
That, *quaint* in green, she shall be loose enrob'd
With ribbands pendent, flaring 'bout her head. Shakespeare.

(4) Subtly excogitated; finespun.

I'll speak of frays,
Like a fine bragging youth, and tell *quaint* lies,
How honourable ladies sought my love,
Which I denying they fell sick and died. Shakespeare.

(5) *Quaint* is, in Spenser, quailed; depressed. I believe by a very licentious irregularity.

With such fair slight him Guyon fail'd:
Till at the last, all breathless, weary and faint,
Him spying, with fresh onset he assail'd,
And kindling new his courage, seeming *quaint,*
Struck him so hugely, that through great constraint
He made him stoop. *Fairy Queen,* b. ii.

(6) Affected; foppish. This is not the true idea of the word, which Swift seems not to have well understood.

To this we owe those monstrous productions, which under the name of trips, spies, amusements, and other conceited appellations, have overrun us; and I wish I could say, those *quaint* fopperies were wholly absent from graver subjects. Swift.

qualm. A sudden fit of sickness; a sudden seizure of sickly languor.

qua'ndary. A doubt; a difficulty; an uncertainty. A low word.

qua'rantain, qua'rantine. The space of forty days, being the time which a ship, suspected of infection, is obliged to forbear intercourse or commerce.

qua'rrel. (4) Something that gives a right to mischief or reprisal.

> Wives are young men's mistresses, companions for middle age, and old men's nurses; so a man may have a *quarrel* to marry when he will. Bacon's *Essays*.

to qua'rry. To prey upon. A low word not in use.

> With cares and horrors at his heart, like the vulture that is day and night *quarrying* upon Prometheus's liver. L'Estrange.

qua'rterday. One of the four days in the year, on which rent or interest is paid.

qua'rto. A book in which every sheet, being twice doubled, makes four leaves.

> Our fathers had a just value for regularity and systems; then folio's and *quarto's* were the fashionable sizes, as volumes in octavo are now. Watts.

quean. A worthless woman, generally a strumpet.

> This well they understand like cunning *queans,*
> And hide their nastiness behind the scenes. Dryden.

to queck. To shrink; to show pain; perhaps to complain.

> The lads of Sparta were accustomed to be whipped at altars, without so much as *quecking*. Bacon.

querimo'niously. Querulously; with complaint.

> To thee, dear Thom, myself addressing,
> Most *querimoniously* confessing. Denham.

que'rpo. A dress close to the body; a waistcoat.

> I would fain see him walk in *querpo*, like a cased rabbit, without his holy furr upon his back. Dryden.

que'stman, que'stmonger. Starter of lawsuits or prosecutions.

quib. A sarcasm; a bitter taunt. Ainsworth. The same perhaps with *quip*.

to qui′bble. To pun; to play on the sound of words.

qui′bble. A low conceit depending on the sound of words; a pun.

qui′bbler. A punster.

quick. (1) A live animal.

> Peeping close into the thick,
> Might see the moving of some *quick*,
>   Whose shape appeared not;
> But were it fairy, fiend or snake,
> My courage earned it to wake,
>   And manful thereat shot. Spenser.

(2) The living flesh; sensible parts.

>   Seiz'd with sudden smart,
> Stung to the *quick*, he felt it at his heart. Dryden.

(3) Living plants.

to qui′ckset. To plant with living plants.

qui′ddany. Marmalade; confection of quinces made with sugar.

qui′ddit. A subtilty; an equivocation. A low word.

> Why may not that be the skull of a lawyer? where be his *quiddits* now? his quillets? his cases? and his tricks? Shakespeare.

qui′llet. Subtilty; nicety; fraudulent distinction.

> Ply her with love letters and billets,
> And bait them well for quirks and *quillets. Hudibras.*

to quinch. To stir; to flounce as in resentment or pain.

qui′ntin. An upright post, on the top of which a cross post turned upon a pin, at one end of the cross post was a broad board, and at the other a heavy sand bag; the play was to ride against the broad end with a lance, and pass by before the sand bag coming round, should strike the tilter on the back.

quip. A sharp jest; a taunt; a sarcasm.

> Notwithstanding all her sudden *quips*,
> The least whereof would quell a lover's hope,
> Yet, spaniel like, the more she spurns my love,
> The more it grows, and fawneth on her still. Shakespeare.

quirk. (1) Quick stroke; sharp fit.

(2) Smart taunt.

> I may chance to have some odd *quirks* and remnants of wit broken on me. Shakespeare.

(3) Subtilty; nicety; artful distinction.

> There are a thousand *quirks* to avoid the stroke of the law. L'Estrange's *Fables*.

(4) Loose light tune.

> Now the chappel's silver bell you hear,
> That summons you to all the pride of pray'r;
> Light *quirks* of musick, broken and uneven. Pope.

quits. An exclamation used when any thing is repayed and the parties become even.

to quob. (A low word.) To move as the embrio does in the womb; to move as the heart does when throbbing.

quo'ndam. Having been formerly. A ludicrous word.

> This is the *quondam* king, let's seize upon him. Shakespeare.

R

ra′bbit. A furry animal that lives on plants, and burrows in the ground.

> A company of scholars, going to catch conies, carried one with them which had not much wit, and gave in charge, that if he saw any, he should be silent for fear of scaring of them; but he no sooner espied a company of *rabbits,* but he cried aloud, *ecce multi cuniculi;* which he had no sooner said, but the conies ran to their burrows; and he being checked by them for it, answered, who would have thought that the *rabbits* understood Latin? Bacon's *Apophthegms.*

rack-rent. Rent raised to the uttermost.

> Have poor families been ruined by *rack-rents,* paid for the lands of the church? Swift's *Miscellanies.*

ra′ckoon. The *rackoon* is a New England animal, like a badger, having a tail like a fox, being cloathed with a thick and deep furr: it sleeps in the day time in a hollow tree, and goes out a-nights, when the moon shines, to feed on the sea side, where it is hunted by dogs. Bailey.

to raff. To sweep; to huddle; to take hastily without distinction.

> Their causes and effects I thus *raff* up together. Carew.

ragamu′ffin. (From *rag* and I know not what else.)

> Attended with a crew of *ragamuffins,* she broke into his house, turned all things topsy-turvy, and then set it on fire. Swift.

rail. (4) A woman's upper garment. This is preserved only in the word *nightrail*.

rai'ment. Vesture; vestment; cloaths; dress; garment. A word now little used but in poetry.

rai'ndeer. A deer with large horns, which, in the northern regions, draws sledges through the snow.

rake. (2) A loose, disorderly, vicious, wild, gay, thoughtless fellow; a man addicted to pleasure.

> Men, some to bus'ness, some to pleasure take;
> But ev'ry woman is at heart a *rake*. Pope.

to rake. (1) To search; to grope. It has always an idea of coarseness or noisomness.

> One is for *raking* in Chaucer for antiquated words, which are never to be reviv'd, but when sound or significancy is wanting. Dryden.

ra'kehel. A wild, worthless, dissolute, debauched, sorry fellow.

> A *rakehell* of the town, whose character is set off with excessive prodigality, prophaneness, intemperance and lust, is rewarded with a lady of great fortune to repair his own, which his vices had almost ruined. Swift.

ra'kehelly. Wild; dissolute.

> I scorn the *rakehelly* rout of our ragged rhimers, which without learning boast, without judgment jangle, and without reason rage and foam. Spenser's *Pastorals*.

to ra'lly. (2) To treat with slight contempt; to treat with satirical merriment.

> If after the reading of this letter, you find yourself in a humour rather to *rally* and ridicule, than to comfort me, I desire you would throw it into the fire. Addison.

ra'mbooze, ra'mbuse. A drink made of wine, ale, eggs and sugar in the winter time; or of wine, milk, sugar and rosewater in the summer time. Bailey.

ra'mekin, ra'mequins. In cookery, small slices of bread covered with a farce of cheese and eggs. Bailey.

ra'mmish. Strong scented.

to ranch. (Corrupted from *wrench*.) To sprain; to injure with

___
ramekin. Johnson defines *to farce* as "to fill with mingled ingredients."

violent contortion. This is the proper sense, but, in Dryden, it seems to be to *tear*.

> Against a stump his tusk the monster grinds,
> And *ranch'd* his hips with one continu'd wound. Dryden.

rand. Border; seam: as, *the* rand *of a woman's shoe.*

range. (7) A kitchen grate.

> The buttery must be visible, and we need for our *ranges,* a more spacious and luminous kitchen.
> Wotton's *Architecture.*

ra'nny. The shrewmouse.

rant. High sounding language unsupported by dignity of thought.

> Dryden himself, to please a frantick age,
> Was forc'd to let his judgment stoop to rage,
> To a wild audience he conform'd his voice,
> Comply'd to custom, but not err'd through choice;
> Deem then the people's, not the writer's sin,
> Almansor's rage, and *rants* of Maximin. Granville.

ra'ntipole. (This word is wantonly formed from *rant.*) Wild; roving; rakish. A low word.

> What at years of discretion, and comport yourself at this *rantipole* rate! Congreve's *Way of the World.*

to ra'ntipole. To run about wildly. It is a low word.

> The eldest was a termagant imperious wench; she used to *rantipole* about the house, pinch the children, kick the servants, and torture the cats and dogs. Arbuthnot.

to rap. (1) To affect with rapture; to strike with extasy; to hurry out of himself.

> These are speeches of men, not comforted with the hope of that they desire, but *rapped* with admiration at the view of enjoyed bliss. Hooker.

(2) To snatch away.

to rap and rend. To seize by violence.

> Their husbands robb'd, and made hard shifts
> T' administer unto their gifts
> All they could *rap and rend* and pilfer,
> To scraps and ends of gold and silver. *Hudibras,* p. ii.

rape. (4) The juice of grapes is drawn as well from the *rape,* or whole grapes pluck'd from the cluster, and wine pour'd upon them in a vessel, as from a vat, where they are bruised. Ray.

ra'pport. Relation; reference; proportion. A word introduced by the innovator, Temple, but not copied by others.

'Tis obvious what *rapport* there is between the conceptions and languages in every country, and how great a difference this must make in the excellence of books. Temple.

ra'ptured. Ravished; transported. A bad word.

He drew
Such madning draughts of beauty to the soul,
As for a while cancell'd his *raptur'd* thought
With luxury too daring. Thomson's *Summer*.

rare. (5) Raw; not fully subdued by the fire. This is often pronounced *rear*.

New-laid eggs, with Baucis' busy care,
Turn'd by a gentle fire, and roasted *rare*. Dryden.

ra'reeshow. A show carried in a box.

The fashions of the town affect us just like a *rareeshow*, we have the curiosity to peep at them, and nothing more. Pope.

rasca'lion. One of the lowest people.

That proud dame
Us'd him so like a base *rascallion*,
That old pig—what d'ye call him—malion,
That cut his mistress out of stone,
Had not so hard a hearted one. *Hudibras*, p. i.

rasca'lity. The low mean people.

Jeroboam having procured his people gods, the next thing was to provide priests; hereupon, to the calves he adds a commission, for the approving, trying and admitting the *rascality* and lowest of the people to minister in that service. South.

ra'sure. (1) The act of scraping or shaving.

---

rapport. Sir William Temple was an innovator in that he tried to naturalize many French words into English. Johnson thought this absurd and unnecessary.

[331]

(2) A mark in a writing where something has been rubbed out.

rat. An animal of the mouse kind that infests houses and ships.

> If in despair he goes out of the way like a *rat* with a dose of arsenick, why he dies nobly. Dennis.

to smell a rat. To be put on the watch by suspicion as the cat by the scent of a rat; to suspect danger.

rata'fia. A fine liquor, prepared from the kernels of apricots and spirits. Bailey.

rath. Early; coming before the time.

> Bring the *rath* primrose that forsaken dies,
> The tufted crow-toe and pale jessamine. Milton.

ra'tsbane. Poison for rats; arsenick.

> Poor Tom! that hath laid knives under his pillow, and halters in his pew, set *ratsbane* by his porridge. Shakespeare.

to ra'ttle. (1) To make a quick sharp noise with frequent repetitions and collisions of bodies not very sonorous: when bodies are sonorous, it is called *jingling*.

ra'ttlesnake. A kind of serpent.

ra'ttoon. A West Indian fox, which has this peculiar property, that if any thing be offered to it that has lain in water, it will wipe and turn it about with its fore feet, before it will put it to its mouth. Bailey.

rau'city. Hoarseness; loud rough noise.

to rave. (3) To be unreasonably fond. With *upon* before the object of fondness. A colloquial and improper sense.

> Another partiality is a fantastical and wild attributing all knowledge to the ancients or the moderns: this *raving upon* antiquity, in matter of poetry, Horace has wittily exposed in one of his satires. Locke.

to ra'vel. (1) To fall into perplexity or confusion.

(2) To work in perplexity; to busy himself with intricacies.

> It will be needless to *ravel* far into the records of elder times; every man's memory will suggest many pertinent instances. *Decay of Piety*.

ra'vin. (1) Prey; food gotten by violence.

[332]

The lion strangled for his lionesses, and filled his holes
with prey, and his dens with *ravin. Nahum,* ii, 2.

(2) Rapine; rapaciousness.

They might not lie long in a condition exposed to the
ravin of any vermin that may find them, being unable to
escape. Ray, *On the Creation.*

ra'whead. The name of a spectre, mentioned to fright children.

Hence draw thy theme, and to the stage permit
Rawhead and bloody bones, and hands and feet,
Ragousts for Tereus or Thyestes drest. Dryden.

read. (1) Counsel.

The man is blest that hath not lent
To wicked *read* his ear. Sternhold.

(2) Saying; saw. This word is in both senses obsolete.

rea'dy. Ready money. A low word.

Lord Strutt was not flush in *ready,* either to go to law,
or clear old debts. Arbuthnot's *History of John Bull.*

to re'alize. (2) To convert money into land.

rear. (1) Raw; half roasted; half sodden.

(2) Early. A provincial word.

O'er yonder hill does scant the dawn appear,
Then why does Cuddy leave his cot so *rear?* Gay.

rea'rmouse. The leather-winged bat.

Of flying fishes, the wings are not feathers, but a thin
kind of skin, like the wings of a bat or *rearmouse.* Abbot.

rea'son. (8) Right; justice.

I was promis'd on a time,
To have *reason* for my rhyme:
From that time unto this season,
I receiv'd nor rhyme nor *reason.* Spenser.

to reave. (1) To take away by stealth or violence. An obsolete
word.

Dismounting from his lofty steed,
He to him leapt, in mind to *reave* his life. Spenser.

(2) It was used as well in a good as bad sense.

Each succeeding time addeth or *reaveth* goods and
evils, according to the occasions itself produceth. Carew.

to reba'te. To blunt; to beat to obtuseness; to deprive of keen-
ness.

> Their innocence unfeign'd long joys afford
> To the honest nuptial bed, and, in the wane
> Of life, *rebate* the miseries of age. Philips.

rebu'ff. Repercussion; quick and sudden resistance.

rebu'ke. (2) In low language, it signifies any kind of check.

> He gave him so terrible a *rebuke* upon the forehead
> with his heel, that he laid him at his length. L'Estrange.

rece'ss. (1) Retirement; retreat; withdrawing; secession.

> Fair Thames she haunts, and ev'ry neighb'ring grove,
> Sacred to soft *recess* and gentle love. Prior.

(2) Departure.

> We come into the world, and know not how; we live
> in it in a self-nescience, and go hence again, and are as
> ignorant of our *recess*. Glanvill's *Scepsis*.

(3) Place of retirement; place of secrecy; private abode.

(4) Perhaps an abstract of the proceedings of an imperial
diet.

> In the imperial chamber, the proctors have a florin taxed
> and allowed them for every substantial *recess*. Ayliffe.

(8) Privacy; secrecy of abode.

re'cipe. A medical prescription.

> Th' apothecary train is wholly blind,
> From files a random *recipe* they take,
> And many deaths of one prescription make. Dryden.

recita'tion. Repetition; rehearsal.

to reck. To care; to heed; to mind; to rate at much; to be in
care. Out of use. *Reck* is still retained in Scotland.

> Thou's but a lazy loorde,
> And *recks* much of thy swinke,
> That with fond terms and witless words,
> To bleer mine eyes do'st think. Spenser.

re'cklesness. (From *reck*. This word in the seventeenth article

---

recklesness. In the seventeenth of the "Articles of Religion" of the Church
of England, and of the Protestant Episcopal Church, the word is
still *wretchlessness*.

is erroneously written *wretchlessness*.) Carelessness; negligence.

to reclai′m. (1) To reform; to correct.

(2) To reduce to the state desired.

Much labour is requir'd in trees, to tame
Their wild disorder, and in ranks *reclaim*. Dryden.

(3) To recall; to cry out against.

The head-strong horses hurried Octavius, the trembling charioteer, along, and were deaf to his *reclaiming* them. Dryden.

(4) To tame.

Are not hawks brought to the hand, and lions, tygers and bears *reclaimed* by good usage? L'Estrange's *Fables*.

to recogni′se. (2) To review; to reexamine.

However their causes speed in your tribunals, Christ will *recognise* them at a greater. South.

re′creant. (1) Cowardly; meanspirited; subdued; crying out for mercy; recanting out of fear.

Thou
Must, as a foreign *recreant*, be led
With manacles along our street. Shakespeare.

(2) Apostate; false.

to re′create. (1) To refresh after toil; to amuse or divert in weariness.

(2) To delight; to gratify.

These ripe fruits *recreate* the nostrils with their aromatick scent. More's *Divine Dialogues*.

(3) To relieve; to revive.

recrea′tion. (1) Relief after toil or pain; amusement in sorrow or distress.

recta′ngle. A figure which has one angle or more of ninety degrees.

If all Athens should decree, that in *rectangle* triangles the square, which is made of the side that subtendeth the right angle, is equal to the squares which are made of the sides containing the right angle, geometricians

would not receive satisfaction without demonstration.
Browne's *Vulgar Errours.*

recu're. Recovery; remedy.

Whatsoever fell into the enemies hands, was lost without *recure:* the old men were slain, the young men led away into captivity. Knolles's *History of the Turks.*

re'dbreast. A small bird, so named from the colour of its breast.

No burial this pretty babe
Of any man receives,
    But robin *redbreast* painfully
Did cover him with leaves. *Children in the Wood.*

re'dcoat. A name of contempt for a soldier.

The fearful passenger, who travels late,
Shakes at the moon-shine shadow of a rush,
And sees a *redcoat* rise from ev'ry bush. Dryden.

reddi'tion. Restitution.

She is reduced to a perfect obedience, partly by voluntary *reddition* and desire of protection, and partly by conquest. Howell's *Vocal Forest.*

rede. Counsel; advice. Not used.

Do not as some ungracious pastors do,
Shew me the steep and thorny way to heav'n;
Whilst he a puft and reckless libertine,
Himself the primrose path of dalliance treads,
And recks not his own *rede.* Shakespeare, *Hamlet.*

redi'ntegrate. Restored; renewed; made new.

Charles VIII. received the kingdom of France in flourishing estate, being *redintegrate* in those principal members, which anciently had been portions of the crown, and were after dissevered: so as they remained only in homage, and not in sovereignty. Bacon's *Henry VII.*

re'dshank. (1) This seems to be a contemptuous appellation for some of the people of Scotland.

He sent over his brother Edward with a power of Scots and *redshanks* unto Ireland, where they got footing. Spenser.

(2) A bird. Ainsworth.

to ree. To riddle; to sift.

After malt is well rubbed and winnowed, you must then *ree* it over in a sieve. Mortimer's *Husbandry.*

ree'chy. Smoky; sooty; tanned.

Let him, for a pair of *reechy* kisses,
Make you to ravel all this matter out. Shakespeare, *Hamlet.*

reek. (2) A pile of corn or hay.

The covered *reek,* much in use westward, must needs prove of great advantage in wet harvests. Mortimer.

ree'ky. Smoky; tanned; black.

Shut me in a charnel house,
O'ercover'd quite with dead men's rattling bones,
With *reeky* shanks and yellow chapless skulls. Shakespeare.

to refe'l. To refute; to repress.

Friends not to *refel* ye,
Or any way quell ye,
Ye aim at a mystery,
Worthy a history. Benj. Jonson's *Gypsies.*

refi'nedly. With affected elegance.

Will any dog
Refinedly leave his bitches and his bones,
To turn a wheel? Dryden.

refocilla'tion. Restoration of strength by refreshment.

reforma'tion. (2) The change of religion from the corruptions of popery to its primitive state.

re'fragable. Capable of confutation and conviction.

to refu'nd. (3) Swift has somewhere the absurd phrase, *to* refund *himself,* for to *reimburse.*

to rego'rge. (1) To vomit up; to throw back.

It was scoffingly said, he had eaten the king's goose, and did then *regorge* the feathers. Hayward.

(2) To swallow eagerly.

Drunk with wine,
And fat *regorg'd* of bulls and goats. Milton's *Agonistes.*

---

refund. "The printer has a demand . . . to be fully refunded, both for his disgraces, his losses, and the apparent danger of his life." Swift, letter to Bishop Hort, 12 May 1736, cited by *O.E.D.*

to regra′te. (1) To offend; to shock.

> The cloathing of the tortoise and viper rather *regrateth*, than pleaseth the eye. Derham's *Physico-Theology*.

(2) To engross; to forestal.

> Neither should they buy any corn, unless it were to make malt thereof; for by such engrossing and *regrating*, the dearth, that commonly reigneth in England, hath been caused. Spenser.

regre′t. (3) Dislike; aversion. Not proper.

> Is it a virtue to have some ineffective *regrets* to damnation, and such a virtue too, as shall serve to balance all our vices. *Decay of Piety*.

re′gular. In the Romish church, all persons are said to be *regulars*, that do profess and follow a certain rule of life, in Latin stiled *regula;* and do likewise observe the three approved vows of poverty, chastity and obedience. Ayliffe's *Parergon*.

to regu′rgitate. To throw back; to pour back.

> The inhabitants of the city remove themselves into the country so long, until, for want of recept and encouragement, it *regurgitates* and sends them back. Graunt.

rein. (3) To give the reins. To give license.

> War to disorder'd rage let loose the *reins*. Milton.

re′levant. Relieving.

re′lickly. In the manner of relicks.

reli′gionist. A bigot to any religious persuasion.

rema′rkable. Observable; worthy of note.

remigra′tion. Removal back again.

> The Scots, transplanted hither, became acquainted with our customs, which, by occasional *remigrations*, became diffused in Scotland. Hale.

re′mora. (1) A let or obstacle.

(2) A fish or a kind of worm that sticks to ships, and retards their passage through the water.

> The *remora* is about three quarters of a yard long; his body before three inches and a half over, thence tapering to the tail end; his mouth two inches and a half over; his chops ending angularly; the nether a little

broader; and produced forward near an inch; his lips rough with a great number of little prickles. *Grew.*

remo'rse. (2) Tenderness; pity; sympathetick sorrow.

The rogues slighted me into the river, with as little *remorse* as they would have drowned a bitch's blind puppies. *Shakespeare.*

remo'tion. The act of removing; the state of being removed to distance.

All this safety were *remotion*, and thy defence absence. *Shakespeare.*

remo'ved. Remote; separate from others.

Your accent is something finer, than you could purchase in so *removed* a dwelling. *Shakespeare, As You Like It.*

rena'rd. The name of a fox in fable.

rende'zvous. (2) A sign that draws men together.

The philosophers-stone and a holy war are but the *rendezvous* of cracked brains, that wear their feather in their head instead of their hat. *Bacon.*

renega'de, renega'do. (1) One that apostatises from the faith; an apostate.

to rene'ge. To disown.

The design of this war is to make me *renege* my conscience and thy truth. *King Charles.*

to rent. (Now written *rant.*) To roar; to bluster: we still say, *a* tearing *fellow,* for *a noisy bully.*

He ventur'd to dismiss his fear,
That partings wont to *rent* and tear,
And give the desperatest attack
To danger still behind its back. *Hudibras,* p. iii.

repai'r. (1) Resort; abode.

So 'scapes th' insulting fire his narrow jail,
And makes small outlets into open air;
There the fierce winds his tender force assail;
And beat him downward to his first *repair. Dryden.*

repa'ndous. Bent upwards.

repercu'ssion. The act of driving back; rebound.

repercu'ssive. (1) Having the power of driving back or causing a rebound.

(2) Repellent.

Blood is stanched by astringent and *repercussive* medicines. Bacon's *Natural History*.

(3) Driven back; rebounding. Not proper.

Amid Carnarvon's mountains rages loud
The *repercussive* roar: with mighty crush
Tumble the smitten cliffs. Thomson.

repe′rtory. A treasury; a magazine; a book in which any thing is to be found.

repeti′tion. (4) Recital from memory, as distinct from reading.

replica′tion. (1) Rebound; repercussion. Not in use.

(2) Reply; answer.

This is a *replication* to what Menelaus had before offered, concerning the transplantation of Ulysses to Sparta. Broome.

to repo′rt. (4) To return; to rebound; to give back.

In Ticinum is a church with windows only from above, that *reporteth* the voice thirteen times, if you stand by the close end wall over against the door. Bacon.

reproa′chful. (1) Scurrilous; opprobrious.

An advocate may be punished for *reproachful* language, in respect of the parties in suit. Ayliffe's *Parergon*.

(2) Shameful; infamous; vile.

To make religion a stratagem to undermine government, is contrary to this superstructure, most scandalous and *reproachful* to christianity. Hammond's *Fundamentals*.

reproba′tion. (1) The act of abandoning or state of being abandoned to eternal destruction.

God, upon a true repentance, is not so fatally tied to the spindle of absolute *reprobation*, as not to keep his promise, and seal merciful pardons. Mayne.

(2) A condemnatory sentence.

You are empower'd to give the final decision of wit, to put your stamp on all that ought to pass for current, and set a brand of *reprobation* on clipt poetry and false coin. Dryden.

repti′le. An animal that creeps upon many feet.

Terrestial animals may be divided into quadrupeds or

reptiles, which have many feet, and serpents which have no feet. Locke's *Elements of Natural Philosophy*.

repu′blican. One who thinks a commonwealth without monarchy the best government.

These people are more happy in imagination than the rest of their neighbours, because they think themselves so; though such a chimerical happiness is not peculiar to *republicans*. Addison.

repu′gnance, repu′gnancy. (1) Inconsistency; contrariety.

It is no affront to omnipotence, if, by reason of the formal incapacity and *repugnancy* of the thing, we aver that the world could not have been made from all eternity. Bentley.

(2) Reluctance; unwillingness; struggle of opposite passion.

That which causes us to lose most of our time, is the *repugnance* which we naturally have to labour. Dryden.

repu′gnant. (1) Disobedient; not obsequious.

His antique sword,
Rebellious to his arm, lies where it falls,
Repugnant to command. Shakespeare, *Hamlet*.

(2) Contrary; opposite.

repu′lsive. Driving off; having the power to beat back or drive off.

repu′teless. Disreputable; disgraceful. A word not inelegant, but out of use.

Opinion, that did help me to the crown,
Had left me in *reputeless* banishment,
A fellow of no mark nor livelihood. Shakespeare, *Henry V*.

re′quiem. (2) Rest; quiet; peace. Not in use.

The midwife kneel'd at my mother's throes,
With pain produc'd, and nurs'd for future woes;
Else had I an eternal *requiem* kept,
And in the arms of peace for ever slept. Sandys.

re′remouse. A bat.

to rescri′be. (1) To write back.

(2) To write over again.

Calling for more paper to *rescribe* them, he shewed him the difference betwixt the ink-box and the sand-box. Howell.

rese′ntment. (1) Strong perception of good or ill.

He retains vivid *resentments* of the more solid morality. More's *Divine Dialogues*.

rese′rve. (5) Exception in favour.

Each has some darling lust, which pleads for a *reserve*, and which they would fain reconcile to the expectations of religion. Rogers's *Sermons*.

re′sidence. (3) That which settles at the bottom of liquours.

re′sin. The fat sulphurous parts of some vegetable, which is natural or procured by art, and will incorporate with oil or spirit, not an aqueous menstruum. Quincy.

resipi′scence. Wisdom after the fact; repentance.

to reso′lve. (1) To inform; to free from a doubt or difficulty.

I cannot brook delay, *resolve* me now;
And what your pleasure is, shall satisfy me. Shakespeare.

(6) To melt; to dissolve.

Resolving is bringing a fluid, which is new concreted, into the state of fluidity again. Arbuthnot, *On Aliments*.

respira′tion. (2) Relief from toil.

Till the day
Appear of *respiration* to the just,
And vengeance to the wicked. Milton's *Paradise Lost*, b. xii.

to respo′nd. (1) To answer. Little used.

(2) To correspond; to suit.

To ev'ry theme *responds* thy various lay;
Here rowls a torrent, there meanders play. Broome.

to rest. (2) To sleep the final sleep; to die.

Ἱερὸν ὕπνον
Κοιμᾶται· θνήσκειν μὴ λέγε τοὺς ἀγαθούς·

---

to rest. The lines from Callimachus, "He sleeps a holy sleep; say not that the good die" (tr. Courtney), are perhaps a private reference to Johnson's wife, who died in 1752.

restaura′tion. The act of recovering to the former state.

resti′ff. (1) Unwilling to stir; resolute against going forward; obstinate; stubborn. It is originally used of an horse, that, though not wearied, will not be driven forward.

> So James the drowsy genius wakes
> Of Britain, long entranc'd in charms,
> *Restiff*, and slumb'ring on its arms. Dryden.

(2) Being at rest; being less in motion. Not used.

resti′fness. Obstinate reluctance.

> That it gave occasion to some men's further *restiveness*, is imputable to their own depraved tempers. King Charles.

resti′nction. The act of extinguishing.

restora′tion. The act of replacing in a former state. This is properly *restauration*.

to restri′ct. To limit; to confine. A word scarce English.

to restri′nge. To limit; to confine.

re′sty. Obstinate in standing still. See *restiff*.

to resu′lt. (1) To fly back.

> With many a weary step, and many a groan,
> Up the high hill he heaves a huge round stone;
> The huge round stone, *resulting* with a bound,
> Thunders impetuous down, and smoaks along the
> ground.
> Pope's *Odyssey*.

resupina′tion. The act of lying on the back.

to retai′l. (1) To divide into small parcels.

> Bound with triumphant garlands will I come,
> And lead thy daughter to a conqueror's bed;
> To whom I will *retail* my conquest won,
> And she shall be sole victress, Caesar's Caesar. Shakespeare.

(2) To sell in small quantities.

(3) To sell at second hand.

> The sage dame,
> By names of toasts, *retails* each batter'd jade. Pope.

to retai′n. (1) To belong to; to depend on.

> These betray upon the tongue no heat nor corrosiveness,

but coldness mixed with a somewhat languid relish *retaining* to bitterness. Boyle.

to retch. To force up something from the stomach.

re′tchless. (Sometimes written *wretchless,* properly *reckless.* See *reckless.*) Careless.

> He struggles into breath, and cries for aid;
> Then helpless in his mother's lap is laid:
> He creeps, he walks, and issuing into man,
> Grudges their life, from whence his own began;
> *Retchless* of laws, affects to rule alone. Dryden.

rete′ntion. (4) Limitation.

> His life I gave him, and did thereto add
> My love without *retention* or restraint;
> All his. Shakespeare, *Twelfth Night.*

(5) Custody; confinement; restraint.

> I sent the old and miserable king
> To some *retention* and appointed guard. Shakespeare, *King Lear.*

re′ticence. Concealment by silence.

reti′culated. Made of network; formed with interstitial vacuities.

to retre′nch. (1) To cut off; to pare away.

> Nothing can be added to the wit of Ovid's Metamorphoses; but many things ought to have been *retrenched.* Dryden.

retrocopu′lation. Post-coition.

retromi′ngency. The quality of staling backwards.

> The last foundation was *retromingency,* or pissing backwards; for men observing both sexes to urine backwards, or aversly between their legs, they might conceive there were feminine parts in both. Browne's *Vulgar Errours.*

to retu′nd. To blunt; to turn.

> Covered with skin and hair keeps it warm, being naturally a very cold part, and also to quench and dissipate the force of any stroke that shall be dealt it, and *retund* the edge of any weapon. Ray, *On the Creation.*

reve. The bailiff of a franchise or manour.

The *reve,* the miller, and the mincing lady prioress speak in character. Dryden.

revel-rout. A mob; an unlawful assembly of a rabble. Ainsworth.

For this his minion, the *revel-rout* is done.

—I have been told, that you

Are frequent in your visitation to her. Rowe's *Jane Shore.*

revenue. (*Revenu,* Fr. Its accent is uncertain.) Income; annual profits received from lands or other funds.

revi'ction. Return to life.

If the Rabines prophecy succeed, we shall conclude the days of the phenix, not in its own, but in the last and general flames, without all hope of *reviction.* Browne.

revi'val. Recall from a state of languour, oblivion, or obscurity.

revivi'scency. Renewal of life.

Scripture makes mention of a restitution and *reviviscency* of all things at the end of the world. Burnet.

rha'bdomancy. Divination by a wand.

Of peculiar *rhabdomancy* is that which is used in mineral discoveries, with a forked hazel, commonly called Moses's rod, which, freely held forth, will stir and play if any mine be under it. Browne's *Vulgar Errours.*

rha'psody. Any number of parts joined together, without necessary dependence or natural connection.

The words slide over the ears, and vanish like a *rhapsody* of evening tales. Watts's *Improvement of the Mind.*

rhe'torick. (1) The act of speaking not merely with propriety, but with art and elegance.

We could not allow him an orator, who had the best thoughts, and who knew all the rules of *rhetorique,* if he had not acquired the art of using them. Dryden's *Dufresnoy.*

---

revenue. W. P. Courtney noted that in 1913 the accent was still uncertain, *rev'enue* in ordinary speech but *reven'ue* in British official circles. The second is no longer recognized in the *Concise Oxford Dictionary.*

to rheto′ricate. To play the orator; to attack the passions.

rhino′ceros. A vast beast in the East Indies armed with a horn in his front.

rhu′barb. A medicinal root slightly purgative, referred by botanists to the dock.

ri′bald. A loose, rough, mean, brutal wretch.

> That lewd *ribbald*, with vile lust advanced,
> Laid first his filthy hands on virgin clean,
> To spoil her dainty corse so fair and sheen. *Fairy Queen.*

ri′baldry. Mean, lewd, brutal language.

> Mr. Cowley asserts, that obscenity has no place in wit;
> Buckingham says, 'tis an ill sort of wit, which has nothing more to support it than bare-faced *ribaldry*. Dryden.

to ri′broast. To beat soundly. A burlesque word.

> That done, he rises, humbly bows,
> And gives thanks for the princely blows;
> Departs not meanly proud, and boasting
> Of his magnificent *ribroasting*. Butler.

ri′dgling, ri′dgil. A ram half castrated.

> Tend them well, and see them fed
> In pastures fresh, and to their watering led;
> And 'ware the *ridgling* with his butting head. Dryden.

rife. Prevalent; prevailing; abounding. It is now only used of epidemical distempers.

> This is the place,
> Whence ev'n now the tumult of loud mirth
> Was *rife*, and perfect in my list'ning ear. Milton.

to rift. (2) To belch; to break wind.

to rig. (1) To dress; to accoutre. Cloaths are proverbially said to be for the back, and victuals for the belly.

> Jack was *rigged* out in his gold and silver lace, with a feather in his cap; and a pretty figure he made in the world. L'Estrange.

ri′ggish. Wanton; whorish.

> Vilest things
> Become themselves in her, that the holy priests
> Bless her, when she is *riggish*. Shakespeare, *Antony and Cleopatra.*

to ri′ggle. (Properly to *wriggle.*) To move backward and forward, as shrinking from pain.

right. An expression of approbation.

>*Right,* cries his lordship, for a rogue in need
>To have a taste, is insolence indeed:
>In me 'tis noble, suits my birth and state. Pope.

ri′gol. A circle. Used in Shakespeare for a diadem.

>This sleep is sound; this is a sleep,
>That, from this golden *rigol,* hath divorc'd
>So many English kings. Shakespeare, *Henry IV.*

ri′gour. (2) A convulsive shuddering with sense of cold.

rime. (1) Hoar frost.

>(2) A hole; a chink.
>Though birds have no epiglottis, yet can they contract the *rime* or chink of their larinx, so as to prevent the admission of wet or dry indigested. Browne's *Vulgar Errours.*

ringlea′der. The head of a riotous body.

ri′ot. (1) Wild and loose festivity.

>(3) To run riot. To move or act without controll or restraint.
>One man's head *runs riot* upon hawks and dice. L'Estrange.

ri′otous. (1) Luxurious; wanton; licentiously festive.

to rise. (1) To change a jacent or recumbent, to an erect posture.

to ri′vel. To contract into wringles and corrugations.

>Alum stipticks, with contracting pow'r,
>Shrink his thin essence like a *rivel'd* flow'r. Pope.

ri′ver. A land current of water bigger than a brook.

river-dragon. A crocodile. A name given by Milton to the king of Egypt.

>Thus with ten wounds
>The *river-dragon* tam'd at length, submits
>To let his sojourners depart. Milton's *Paradise Lost.*

river-horse. Hippopotamus.

roach. A *roach* is a fish of no great reputation for his dainty taste: his spawn is accounted much better than any other part of him: he is accounted the water sheep, for his simplicity and foolishness; and it is noted, that *roaches* recover strength, and grow in a fortnight after spawning. Walton's *Angler.*

roa′ry. Dewy.

On Lebanon his foot he set,
And shook his wings with *roary* May dews wet. Fairfax.

to rule the roast. To govern; to manage; to preside. It was perhaps originally *roist,* which signified a tumult, to direct the populace.

Alma slap-dash, is all again
In ev'ry sinew, nerve, and vein;
Runs here and there, like Hamlet's ghost,
While every where she *rules the roast.* Prior.

to rob. (1) To deprive of any thing by unlawful force, or by secret theft; to plunder. To be *robbed,* according to the present use of the word, is to be injured by theft secret or violent; to *rob,* is to take away by unlawful violence; and to *steal,* is to take away privately.

robe. A gown of state; a dress of dignity.

Through tatter'd cloaths small vices do appear;
Robes and furr'd gowns hide all. Shakespeare, *King Lear.*

to robe. To dress pompously; to invest.

robe′rsman, robe′rtsman. In the old statutes, a sort of bold and stout robbers or night thieves, said to be so called from Robinhood, a famous robber.

rock. (3) A distaff held in the hand, from which the wool was spun by twirling a ball below.

A learned and a manly soul
I purpos'd her; that should with even powers,
The *rock,* the spindle, and the sheers, controul
Of destiny, and spin her own free hours. Benj. Jonson.

rogue. (1) A wandering beggar; a vagrant; a vagabond.
(2) A knave; a dishonest fellow; a villain; a thief.
(3) A name of slight tenderness and endearment.
(4) A wag.

to rogue. (1) To wander; to play the vagabond.

(2) To play knavish tricks.

ro'guy. Knavish; wanton. A bad word.

> A shepherd's boy had gotten a *roguy* trick of crying a wolf, and fooling the country with false alarms. L'Estrange.

to roll. (1) To be moved by the successive application of all parts of the surface to the ground.

roll. (10) (*Role,* Fr.) Part; office. Not in use.

> In human society, every man has his *roll* and station assigned him. L'Estrange.

ro'mage. A tumult; a bustle; an active and tumultuous search for any thing.

roma'nce. (1) A military fable of the middle ages; a tale of wild adventures in war and love.

(2) A lie; a fiction. In common speech.

roma'ntick. (1) Resembling the tales of romances; wild.

> Philosophers have maintained opinions, more absurd than any of the most fabulous poets or *romantick* writers. Keill.

(2) Improbable; false.

(3) Fanciful; full of wild scenery.

ro'mish. Popish.

romp. (1) A rude, awkward, boisterous, untaught girl.

> She was in the due mean between one of your affected courtesying pieces of formality, and your *romps* that have no regard to the common rules of civility. Arbuthnot.

(2) Rough rude play.

to romp. To play rudely, noisily, and boisterously.

> A stool is the first weapon taken up in a general *romping* or skirmish. Swift's *Rules to Servants.*

ro'ndeau. A kind of ancient poetry, commonly consisting of thirteen verses; of which eight have one rhyme and five another: it is divided into three couplets, and at the end of the second and third, the beginning of the rondeau is repeated in an equivocal sense, if possible. Trevoux.

[349]

ro′nion. (I know not the etymology, nor certainly the meaning of this word.) A fat bulky woman.

> Give me, quoth I,
> Aroint the witch! the rump fed *ronyon* cries. Shakespeare.

ront. An animal stinted in the growth.

rook. (3) A cheat; a trickish rapacious fellow.

> I am, like an old *rook*, who is ruined by gaming, forced to live on the good fortune of the pushing young men. Wycherley.

ro′pery. Rogue's tricks. See *ropetrick.*

> What saucy merchant was this, that was so full of his *ropery.* Shakespeare, *Merchant of Venice.*

ro′petrick. Probably rogue's tricks; tricks that deserve the halter.

ro′py. Viscous; tenacious; glutinous.

> Ask for what price thy venal tongue was sold;
> Tough, wither'd truffles, *ropy* wine, a dish
> Of shotten herrings, or stale stinking fish. Dryden's *Juvenal.*

ro′sary. A bunch of beads, on which the Romanists number their prayers.

ro′scid. Dewy; abounding with dew; consisting of dew.

to speak under the rose. To speak any thing with safety, so as not afterwards to be discovered.

> By desiring a secrecy to words *spoke under the rose,* we mean, in society and compotation, from the ancient custom in symposiack meetings, to wear chaplets of roses about their heads. Browne's *Vulgar Errours.*

ro′sier. A rosebush.

ro′sin. (1) Inspissated turpentine; a juice of the pine.

(2) Any inspissated matter of vegetables that dissolves in spirit.

> Tea contains little of a volatile spirit; its *rosin* or fixed oil, which is bitter and astringent, cannot be extracted but by rectified spirit. Arbuthnot, *On Aliments.*

---

ronion. "An abusive term applied to a woman," *O.E.D.*

ro′strum. (1) The beak of a bird.

(2) The beak of a ship.

(3) The scaffold whence orators harangued.

rote. (1) A harp; a lyre. Obsolete.

Wele couthe he sing, and playen on a *rote*. Chaucer.

(2) Words uttered by mere memory without meaning; memory of words without comprehension of the sense.

to rote. To fix in the memory, without informing the understanding.

ro′tgut. Bad beer.

They overwhelm their panch daily with a kind of flat *rotgut*, we with a bitter dreggish small liquor. Harvey.

rough. (8) Not polished; not finished by art: as, *a* rough *diamond*.

to rou′ghcast. (1) To mould without nicety or elegance; to form with asperities and inequalities.

(2) To form any thing in its first rudiments.

In merriment they were first practised, and this *roughcast* unhewn poetry was instead of stage plays for one hundred and twenty years. Dryden's Dedication to *Juvenal*.

rought. (Commonly written by Spenser *raught*.) Reached.

The moon was a month old, when Adam was no more, And *rought* not to five weeks, when he came to fivescore. Shakespeare, *Love's Labour Lost*.

round. (7) Plain; clear; fair; candid; open.

Round dealing is the honour of man's nature; and a mixture of falsehood is like allay in gold and silver, which may make the metal work the better, but it embaseth it. Bacon.

(9) Plain; free without delicacy or reserve; almost rough.

Let his queen mother all alone intreat him,

To shew his griefs; let her be *round* with him. Shakespeare.

to round. (2) To whisper.

Cicero was at dinner, where an ancient lady said she was but forty: one that sat by *rounded* him in the ear, she is far more out of the question: Cicero answered, I must believe her, for I heard her say so any time these ten years. Bacon.

rou'ndhead. A puritan, so named from the practice once prevalent among them of cropping their hair round.

rou'ndhouse. The constable's prison, in which disorderly persons, found in the street, are confined.

rouse. A dose of liquor rather too large.

> They have given me a *rouse* already.
>
> —Not past a pint as I am a soldier. Shakespeare, *Othello*.

rout. (1) A clamorous multitude; a rabble; a tumultuous croud.

> The mad ungovernable *rout*,
>
> Full of confusion and the fumes of wine,
>
> Lov'd such variety and antick tricks. Roscommon.

to rove. To ramble; to range; to wander.

ro'ver. (4) At rovers. Without any particular aim.

> Men of great reading show their talents on the meanest subjects; this is a kind of shooting *at rovers*. Addison.

ro'ynish. Paltry; sorry; mean; rude.

> The *roynish* clown, at whom so oft
>
> Your grace was wont to laugh, is also missing. Shakespeare.

ru'brick. Directions printed in books of law and in prayer books; so termed, because they were originally distinguished by being in red ink.

ructa'tion. A belching arising from wind and indigestion.

to rud. To make red.

> Her cheeks, like apples, which the sun had *rudded*. Spenser.

ru'desby. An uncivil turbulent fellow. A low word, now little used.

> I must be forced
>
> To give my hand, opposed against my heart,
>
> Unto a mad-brain *rudesby*, full of spleen. Shakespeare.

ruff. (1) A puckered linen ornament, formerly worn about the neck. See *ruffle*.

> You a captain; for what? for tearing a whore's *ruff* in a bawdy house? Shakespeare, *Henry IV*, p. ii.

(4) New state. This seems to be the meaning of this cant word.

> How many princes that, in the *ruff* of all their glory, have been taken down from the head of a conquering army to the wheel of the victor's chariot. L'Estrange.

ru'ffle. (1) Plaited linnen used as an ornament.

rug. (1) A coarse, nappy, woollen cloath.

(2) A coarse nappy coverlet used for mean beds.

(3) A rough woolly dog.

> Mungrels, spaniels, curs,
> Shoughes, water *rugs*, and demy wolves are cleped
> All by the name of dogs. Shakespeare, *Macbeth*.

ru'gin. A nappy cloth.

rum. (1) A country parson. A cant word.

> I'm grown a mere mopus; no company comes,
> But a rabble of tenants and rusty dull *rums*. Swift.

(2) A kind of spirits distilled from molosses.

ru'mmer. A glass; a drinking cup.

rump. (1) The end of the backbone.

> If his holiness would thump
> His reverend bum 'gainst horse's *rump*,
> He might b'equipt from his own stable. Prior.

ru'nagate. A fugitive; rebel; apostate.

ru'ndlet. A small barrel.

ru'nnet. A liquor made by steeping the stomach of a calf in hot water, and used to coagulate milk for curds and cheese. It is sometimes written *rennet*.

ru'nnion. A paltry scurvy wretch.

> You witch! you poulcat! you *runnion!* Shakespeare.

ruse. Cunning; artifice; little stratagem; trick; wile; fraud; deceit. A French word neither elegant nor necessary.

rush. (2) Any thing proverbially worthless.

> What occasion hast thou to give up, John Bull's friendship is not worth a *rush*. Arbuthnot's *History of John Bull*.

rush-candle. A small blinking taper, made by stripping a rush, except one small stripe of the bark which holds the pith together, and dipping it in tallow.

ru′sset. (3) Coarse; homespun; rustick. It is much used in
descriptions of the manners and dresses of the country, I
suppose, because it was formerly the colour of rustick dress:
in some places, the rusticks still die cloaths spun at home
with bark, which must make them *russet*.

> Taffata phrases, silken terms precise,
> Figures pedantical: these summer flies
> Have blown me full of maggot ostentation:
> Henceforth my wooing mind shall be exprest
> In *russet* yeas, and honest kersy noes. Shakespeare.

ru′stical. Rough; savage; boisterous; brutal; rude.

to ru′sticate. To banish into the country.

> I was deeply in love with a milliner, upon which I was
> sent away, or, in the university phrase, *rusticated* for
> ever. *Spectator.*

ru′stick. (3) Brutal; savage.

> My soul foreboded I should find the bow'r
> Of some fell monster, fierce with barb'rous pow'r;
> Some *rustick* wretch, who liv'd in heav'n's despight,
> Contemning laws, and trampling on the right. Pope.

to rut. To desire to come together. Used of deer.

ruth. Mercy; pity; tenderness; sorrow for the misery of another.

> All *ruth*, compassion, mercy he forgot. Fairfax.

ru′ttish. Wanton; libidinous; salacious; lustful; lecherous.

> That is an advertisement to one Diana, to take heed of
> the allurement of count Rousillon, a foolish idle boy; but
> for all that very *ruttish*. Shakespeare, *All's well that ends
> well.*

S

sa′bbatism. Observance of the sabbath superstitiously rigid.

sa′chel. A small sack or bag.

sack. (2) A kind of sweet wine, now brought chiefly from the Canaries.

sa′ckposset. A posset made of milk, sack, and some other ingredients.

sad. (5) Bad; inconvenient; vexatious. A word of burlesque complaint.

> These qualifications make him a *sad* husband. Addison.

saga′cious. (1) Quick of scent.

> With might and main they chas'd the murd'rous fox,
> Nor wanted horns t' inspire *sagacious* hounds. Dryden.

(2) Quick of thought; acute in making discoveries.

sagi′ttary. A centaur; an animal half man half horse, armed with a bow and quiver.

sail. (5) To strike sail. To lower the sail.

(6) A proverbial phrase for abating of pomp or superiority.

> Margaret
> Must *strike* her *sail*, and learn a while to serve
> Where kings command. Shakespeare, *Henry VI*.

saim. Lard. It still denotes this in Scotland: as swine's *saim*.

to saint. To act with a shew of piety.

> Whether the charmer sinner it or *saint* it,
> If folly grows romantick, I must paint it. Pope.

salama′nder. An animal supposed to live in the fire, and imagined to be very poisonous. Ambrose Parey has a picture of the salamander, with a receipt for her bite; but there is no such creature, the name being now given to a poor harmless insect.

sale. (5) It seems in Spenser to signify a wicker basket; perhaps from *sallow,* in which fish are caught.

> To make baskets of bulrushes was my wont;
> Who to entrap the fish in winding *sale*
> Was better seen? Spenser.

sa′lesman. One who sells cloaths ready made.

sa′lework. Work for sale; work carelessly done.

sali′va. Every thing that is spit up; but it more strictly signifies that juice which is separated by the glands called salival. Quincy.

saliva′tion. A method of cure much practised of late in venereal, scrophulous, and other obstinate causes, by promoting a secretion of spittle. Quincy.

sa′llow. A tree of the genus of willow. See *willow.*

sa′lmagundi. A mixture of chopped meat and pickled herrings with oil, vinegar, pepper, and onions.

salt. (4) Lecherous; salacious.

> Be a whore still:
> Make use of thy *salt* hours, season the slaves
> For tubs and baths; bring down the rose-cheek'd youth
> To the tub-fast, and the diet. Shakespeare, *Timon.*

salta′tion. (1) The act of dancing or jumping.

> The locusts being ordained for *saltation,* their hinder legs do far exceed the others. Browne's *Vulgar Errours.*

(2) Beat; palpitation.

salti′nbanco. A quack or mountebank.

> *Saltinbancoes,* quacksalvers, and charlatans deceive them: were Aesop alive, the Piazza and Pont-neuf could not speak their fallacies. Browne's *Vulgar Errours.*

sa′lvage. Wild; rude; cruel. It is now spoken and written *savage.*

sa′lvo. An exception; a reservation; an excuse.

> It will be hard if he cannot bring himself off at last with some *salvo* or distinction, and be his own confessor. L'Estrange.

sane. Sound; healthy. Baynard wrote a poem on preserving the body in a *sane* and sound state.

sa′pid. Tasteful; palatable; making a powerful stimulation upon the palate.

> Thus camels, to make the water *sapid,* do raise the mud with their feet. Browne's *Vulgar Errours.*

sa′ppy. (2) Young; not firm; weak.

> This young prince was brought up among nurses, 'till he arrived to the age of six years: when he had passed this weak and *sappy* age, he was committed to Dr. Cox. Hayward.

sarco′phagy. The practice of eating flesh.

> There was no *sarcophagy* before the flood; and, without the eating of flesh, our fathers preserved themselves unto longer lives than their posterity. Browne's *Vulgar Errours.*

sark. (1) A shark or shirk. Bailey.

(2) In Scotland it denotes a shirt.

> Flaunting beaus gang with their breasts open, and their *sarks* over their waistcoats. Arbuthnot, *History of John Bull.*

sarn. A British word for pavement, or stepping stones, still used in the same sense in Berkshire and Hampshire.

sa′tire. A poem in which wickedness or folly is censured. Proper *satire* is distinguished, by the generality of the reflections, from a *lampoon* which is aimed against a particular person; but they are too frequently confounded.

sa′ucebox. An impertinent or petulant fellow.

sa′usage. A roll or ball made commonly of pork or veal, and sometimes of beef, minced very small, with salt and spice; sometimes it is stuffed into the guts of fowls, and sometimes only rolled in flower.

to sa′vage. To make barbarous, wild, or cruel. A word not well authorised.

> Friends, relations, love himself,
> *Savag'd* by woe, forget the tender tie. Thomson.

sa′vanna. An open meadow without wood; pasture ground in America.

say. (2) Sample.

So good a *say* invites the eye,
A little downward to espy
The lively clusters of her breasts. Sidney.

scab. (3) A paltry fellow, so named from the itch often incident
to negligent poverty.

I would thou did'st itch from head to foot, and I had the
scratching of thee, I would make thee the loathsom'st
scab in Greece. Shakespeare, *Troilus and Cressida.*

scald. Paltry; sorry.

Saucy lictors
Will catch at us like strumpets, and *scald* rhymers
Ballad us out o' tune. Shakespeare.

scale. (3) The small shells or crusts which lying one over another make the coats of fishes.

scalp. (1) The scull; the cranium; the bone that incloses the
brain.

to sca'mble. (1) To be turbulent and rapacious; to scramble; to
get by struggling with others.

Scambling, out-facing, fashion-mong'ring boys,
That lie, and cog, and flout, deprave and slander. Shakespeare.

(2) To shift aukwardly.

Some *scambling* shifts may be made without them.
More.

sca'mbler. (Scottish.) A bold intruder upon one's generosity or
table.

sca'ntlet. (Corrupted, as it seems, from *scantling.*) A small pat-
tern; a small quantity; a little piece.

While the world was but thin, the ages of mankind were
longer; and as the world grew fuller, so their lives were
successively reduced to a shorter *scantlet,* 'till they came
to that time of life which they now have. Hale.

sca'ntling. (1) A quantity cut for a particular purpose.

(2) A certain proportion.

(3) A small quantity.

A *scantling* of wit lay gasping for life, and groaning beneath a heap of rubbish. Dryden.

scape. (1) Escape; flight from hurt or danger; the act of declin-
ing or running from danger; accident of safety.

(2) Means of escape; evasion.

(3) Negligent freak.

> No natural exhalation in the sky,
> No *scape* of nature, no distemper'd day,
> But they will pluck away its nat'ral cause,
> And call them meteors, prodigies, and signs. Shakespeare.

(4) Loose act of vice or lewdness.

> A bearne! a very pretty bearne! sure some *scape*: though I am not bookish, yet I can read waiting-gentlewoman in the *scape*. Shakespeare, *Winter's Tale*.

sca′ramouch. A buffoon in motly dress.

sca′recrow. An image or clapper set up to fright birds: thence any vain terrour.

> No eye hath seen such *scarecrows*: I'll not march through Coventry with them, that's flat. Shakespeare, *Henry IV*.

sca′refire. A fright by fire; a fire breaking out so as to raise terrour.

to scarf. (1) To throw loosely on.

(2) To dress in any loose vesture.

> Come, seeling night,
> *Scarf* up the tender eye of pitiful day. Shakespeare, *Macbeth*.

sca′rfskin. The cuticle; the epidermis; the outer scaly integuments of the body.

to sca′rify. To let blood by incisions of the skin, commonly after the application of cupping-glasses.

sca′tches. Stilts to put the feet in to walk in dirty places. Bailey.

scate. A kind of wooden shoe, with a steel plate underneath, on which they slide over the ice.

scath. Waste; damage; mischief; depopulation. *Scath* in Scotland denotes spoil or damage: as, he bears the *scath* and the scorn. A proverb.

> Still preserv'd from danger, harm, and *scath*,
> By many a sea and many an unknown shore. Fairfax.

sca′tterling. A vagabond; one that has no home or settled habitation.

> Such losels and *scatterlings* cannot easily, by any ordi-

nary officer, be gotten, when challenged for any such fact. Spenser.

sca'venger. A petty magistrate, whose province is to keep the streets clean.

sce'lerat. A villain; a wicked wretch. A word introduced unnecessarily from the French by a Scottish author.

sce'nick. Dramatick; theatrical.

sce'nography. The art of perspective.

sche'dule. (1) A small scroll.

    (2) A little inventory.

> I will give out *schedules* of my beauty: it shall be inventoried, and every particle and utensil label'd to my will. Shakespeare.

schola'stick. (2) Befitting the school; suitable to the school; pedantick; needlessly subtle.

> Both sides charge the other with idolatry, and that is a matter of conscience, and not a *scholastick* nicety. Stillingfleet.

scho'ly. An explanatory note. This word, with the verb following, is, I fancy, peculiar to the learned Hooker.

> He therefore, which made us to live, hath also taught us to pray, to the end, that speaking unto the Father in the Son's own prescript form, without *scholy* or gloss of ours, we may be sure that we utter nothing which God will deny. Hooker.

sci'olous. Superficially or imperfectly knowing.

> I could wish these *sciolous* zelotists had more judgment joined with their zeal. Howell.

scio'machy. Battle with a shadow. This should be written *skiamachy*.

> To avoid this *sciomachy*, or imaginary combat of words, let me know, sir, what you mean by the name of tyrant? Cowley.

sci'ssure. A crack; a rent; a fissure.

to scoat, to scotch. To stop a wheel by putting a stone or piece of wood under it before. Bailey.

scold. A clamourous, rude, mean, low, foul-mouthed woman.

> Sun-burnt matrons mending old nets;

Now singing shrill, and scolding oft between;
Scolds answer foul-mouth'd *scolds*. Swift.

scomm. A buffoon. A word out of use, and unworthy of revival.
The *scomms,* or buffoons of quality, are wolvish in conversation. L'Estrange.

sconce. (2) The head: perhaps as being the *acropolis,* or citadel
of the body. A low word.

Why does he suffer this rude knave now to knock him
about the *sconce* with a dirty shovel, and will not tell
him of his action of battery? Shakespeare, *Hamlet.*

to sconce. (A word used in the universities, and derived plausibly by Skinner, whose etymologies are generally rational,
from *sconce,* as it signifies the head; to *sconce* being to fix a
fine on any one's head.) To mulct; to fine. A low word
which ought not to be retained.

score. (8) Twenty. I suppose, because twenty, being a round
number, was distinguished on tallies by a long score.
(9) A song in score. The words with the musical notes of a
song annexed.

sco'rpion. (1) A reptile much resembling a small lobster, but
that his tail ends in a point with a very venomous sting.
(3) A scourge so called from its cruelty.

scot. (1) Shot; payment.
(2) Scot and lot. Parish payments.
The chief point that has puzzled the freeholders, as well
as those that pay *scot and lot,* for about these six months,
is, whether they would rather be governed by a prince
that is obliged by law to be good, or by one who, if he
pleases, may plunder or imprison. Addison.

to scotch. To cut with shallow incisions.

scotch hoppers. A play in which boys hop over lines or scotches
in the ground.

sco'ttering. A provincial word which denotes, in Herefordshire,
a custom among the boys of burning a wad of pease-straw
at the end of harvest. Bailey.

to scourse. To exchange one thing for another; to swap. Ainsworth. It seems a corruption of *scorsa,* Ital. exchange; and
hence a *horse scourser.*

sco′vel. A sort of mop of clouts for sweeping an oven; a maulkin. Ainsworth and Bailey.

to scra′bble. To paw with the hands.

scrag. Any thing thin or lean.

scra′gged. (This seems corrupted from *cragged*.) Rough; uneven; full of protuberances or asperities.

scra′mble. (1) Eager contest for something, in which one endeavours to get it before another.

to scranch. To grind somewhat crackling between the teeth. The Scots retain it.

scra′nnel. (Of this word I know not the etymology, nor any other example.) Vile; worthless. Perhaps grating by the sound.

> When they list, their lean and flashy songs
>
> Grate on their *scrannel* pipes of wretched straw. Milton.

scrape. Difficulty; perplexity; distress. This is a low word.

scrat. An hermaphrodite. Skinner and Junius.

scraw. Surface or scurf.

> Neither should that odious custom be allowed of cutting *scraws*, which is flaying off the green surface of the ground to cover their cabins, or make up their ditches. Swift.

scree′chowl. An owl that hoots in the night, and whose voice is supposed to betoken danger, misery, or death.

scrine. A place in which writings or curiosities are reposited.

> Help then, O holy virgin,
>
> Thy weaker novice to perform thy will;
>
> Lay forth, out of thine everlasting *scrine*,
>
> The antique rolls which there lie hidden still. *Fairy Queen.*

scri′vener. (1) One who draws contracts.

> (2) One whose business is to place money at interest.
> I am reduced to beg and borrow from *scriveners* and usurers, that suck the heart and blood. Arbuthnot, *History of John Bull.*

scroyle. (This word I remember only in Shakespeare: it seems derived from *escrouelle*, French, a scrofulous swelling; as he

[362]

calls a mean fellow a *scab* from his itch, or a *patch* from his raggedness.) A mean fellow; a rascal; a wretch.

> The *scroyles* of Angiers flout you kings,
> And stand securely on their battlements,
> As in a theatre. Shakespeare's *King John.*

scrub. (1) A mean fellow, either as he is supposed to scrub himself for the itch, or as he is employed in the mean offices of scouring away dirt.

(2) Any thing mean or despicable.

(3) A worn out broom. Ainsworth.

scru′ple. (1) Doubt; difficulty of determination; perplexity: generally about minute things.

scru′tinous. Captious; full of inquiries. A word little used.

> Age is froward, uneasy, *scrutinous,*
> Hard to be pleas'd, and parcimonious. Denham.

to scruze. (Perhaps from *screw.* This word, though now disused by writers, is still preserved, at least in its corruption, *to scrouge,* in the London jargon.) To squeeze; to compress.

to scu′ddle. To run with a kind of affected haste or precipitation. A low word.

scu′rrilous. Grossly opprobrious; using such language as only the license of a buffoon can warrant; loudly jocular; vile; low.

scu′rvily. Vilely; basely; coarsely. It is seldom used but in a ludicrous sense.

scut. The tail of those animals whose tails are very short, as a hare.

to scu′ttle. (From *scud* or *scuddle.*) To run with affected precipitation.

sea. (5) Half seas over. Half drunk.

> The whole magistracy was pretty well disguised before I gave 'em the slip: our friend the alderman was *half seas over* before the bonfire was out. *Spectator.*

se′acalf. The seal.

> The *seacalf,* or seal, is so called from the noise he makes like a calf: His head comparatively not big, shaped rather like an otter's, with teeth like a dog's, and mus-

taches like those of a cat: his body long, and all over hairy: his forefeet, with fingers clawed, but not divided, yet fit for going: his hinder feet, more properly fins, and fitter for swimming, as being an amphibious animal. The female gives suck, as the porpess, and other viviparous fishes. Grew's *Musaeum*.

seacoa'l. Coal, so called not because found in the sea, but because brought to London by sea; pitcoal.

se'acow. The manatee.

The *seacow* is a very bulky animal, of the cetaceous kind. It grows to fifteen feet long, and to seven or eight in circumference: its head is like that of a hog, but longer, and more cylindrick: its eyes are small, and it has no external ears, but only two little apertures in the place of them; yet its sense of hearing is very quick. Its lips are thick, and it has two long tusks standing out. It has two fins, which stand forward on the breast like hands, whence the Spaniards first called it manatee. The female has two round breasts placed between the pectoral fins. The skin is very thick and hard, and not scaly, but hairy. This creature lives principally about the mouths of the large rivers in Africa, the East Indies, and America, and feeds upon vegetables. Its flesh is white like veal, and very well tasted. The lapis manati, which is of a fine clean white colour, and bony texture, is properly the os petrosum of this animal. This stone has been supposed to be a powerful amulet, but is now neglected. Hill's *Materia Medica*.

seado'g. Perhaps the shark.

se'ahog. The porpus.

se'ahorse. (1) The *seahorse* is a fish of a very singular form, as we see it dried, and of the needlefish kind. It is about four or five inches in length, and nearly half an inch in diameter in the broadest part. Its colour, as we see it dried, is a deep reddish brown; and its tail is turned round under the belly. It is found about the Mediterranean, and has been celebrated for medicinal virtues; but is at present wholly neglected. Hill's *Materia Medica*.

(2) The morse.

(3) The medical and the poetical *seahorse* seem very different. By the seahorse Dryden means probably the hippopotamus.

> By 'em
> *Seahorses*, flound'ring in the slimy mud,
> Toss'd up their heads, and dash'd the ooze about 'em.
> Dryden.

se′amaid. Mermaid.

se′aman. (2) Merman; the male of the mermaid.

seal. The seacalf. See *seacalf*.

> The *seal* or soyle is in make and growth not unlike a pig, ugly faced, and footed like a moldwarp: he delighteth in musick, or any loud noise, and thereby is trained to shew himself above water: they also come on land. Carew.

seam. (5) Tallow; grease; hog's lard.

searce. A sieve; a bolter.

se′archer. (2) Officer in London appointed to examine the bodies of the dead, and report the cause of death.

> The *searchers*, who are ancient matrons sworn to their office, repair to the place where the dead corps lies, and by view of the same, and by other inquiries, examine by what disease the corps died. Graunt's *Bills of Mortality*.

sect. (1) A body of men following some particular master, or united in some settled tenets. Often in a bad sense.

se′ctarism. Disposition to petty sects in opposition to things established.

> Nothing hath more marks of schism and *sectarism* than this presbyterian way. King Charles.

see′ksorrow. One who contrives to give himself vexation.

see′ly. (1) Lucky; happy.

(2) Silly; foolish; simple. Spenser.

se′lcouth. Uncommon. Spenser. The same with *uncouth*.

sell. *Sell* is retained in Scotland for self, and *sells* in the plural for selves.

> They turn round like grindle-stones,
> Which they dig out fro' the dells,

For their bairns bread, wives and *sells*. Ben. Jonson.

se'minary. (1) The ground where any thing is sown to be afterwards transplanted.

(2) The place or original stock whence any thing is brought.

(3) Seminal state.

> The hand of God, who first created the earth, hath wisely contrived them in their proper *seminaries*, and where they best maintain the intention of their species. Browne's *Vulgar Errours*.

(4) Original; first principles.

> Nothing subministrates apter matter to be converted into pestilent *seminaries*, sooner than steams of nasty folks and beggars. Harvey, *On the Plague*.

(5) Breeding place; place of education, from whence scholars are transplanted into life.

se'nsible. (7) Convinced; persuaded. A low use.

> They are very *sensible* that they had better have pushed their conquests on the other side of the Adriatick; for then their territories would have lain together. Addison.

(8) In low conversation it has sometimes the sense of reasonable; judicious; wise.

> I have been tired with accounts from *sensible* men, furnished with matters of fact, which have happened within their own knowledge. Addison.

se'nsual. (1) Consisting in sense; depending on sense; affecting the senses.

> Far as creation's ample range extends,
> The scale of *sensual*, mental pow'rs ascends. Pope.

se'nsuous. Tender; pathetick; full of passion.

> To this poetry would be made precedent, as being less subtile and fine; but more simple, *sensuous*, and passionate. Milton.

se'ntence. (3) A maxim; an axiom, generally moral.

sente'ntious. Abounding with short sentences, axioms, and maxims, short and energetick.

---

seminary (3,4). Johnson has apparently transposed the examples for these.

se′ntiment. (2) The sense considered distinctly from the language or things; a striking sentence in a composition.

sequa′cious. (1) Following; attendant.

> Orpheus could lead the savage race,
> And trees uprooted left their place,
> *Sequacious* of the lyre;
> But bright Cecilia rais'd the wonder higher:
> When to her organ vocal breath was giv'n,
> An angel heard and straight appear'd,
> Mistaking earth for heav'n. Dryden.

(2) Ductile; pliant.

to seque′ster. (1) To separate from others for the sake of privacy.

(2) To put aside; to remove.

(3) To withdraw; to segregate.

(4) To set aside from the use of the owner to that of others.

(5) To deprive of possessions.

> It was his taylor and his cook, his fine fashions and his French ragou's, which *sequestered* him; and, in a word, he came by his poverty as sinfully as some usually do by their riches. South.

sera′glio. A house of women kept for debauchery.

> There is a great deal more solid content to be found in a constant course of well living, than in the voluptuousness of a *seraglio.* Norris.

sere′ne. A calm damp evening.

to sere′ne. (1) To calm; to quiet.

(2) To clear; to brighten. Not proper.

> Take care
> Thy muddy bev'rage to *serene,* and drive
> Precipitant the baser ropy lees. Philips.

sermocina′tor. A preacher; a speechmaker.

se′rpent. An animal that moves by undulation without legs. They are often venomous. They are divided into two kinds; the *viper,* which brings young, and the *snake,* that lays eggs.

to serr. To drive hard together; to crowd into a little space. Not received into use, nor deserving reception.

> The frowning and knitting of the brows is a gathering or *serring* of the spirits, to resist in some measure; and also

this knitting will follow upon earnest studying, though it
be without dislike. Bacon's *Natural History*.

to se'rry. To press close; to drive hard together. For *serry* Bacon
uses *serr;* but neither *serr* nor *serry* are received.

With them rose
A forest huge of spears; and thronging helms
Appear'd, and *serried* shields in thick array,
Of death immeasurable. Milton's *Paradise Lost*.

se'rvant. (3) A word of civility used to superiours or equals.
This subjection, due from all men to all men, is something more than the compliment of course, when our
betters tell us they are our humble *servants,* but understand us to be their slaves. Swift.

sess. Rate; cess charged; tax.

sette'e. A large long seat with a back to it.

se'tter. (3) A man who performs the office of a setting dog, or
finds out persons to be plundered.

Another set of men are the devil's *setters,* who continually beat their brains how to draw in some innocent unguarded heir into their hellish net, learning his humour,
prying into his circumstances, and observing his weak
side. South.

se'vennight. (2) We use still the word *sevennight* or *se'nnight*
in computing time: as, it happened on Monday was *sevennight*, that is, *on the Monday before last Monday;* it will be
done on Monday *sevennight*, that is, *on the Monday after
next Monday*.

se'veral. (3) Any inclosed or separate place.
They had their *several* for heathen nations, their *several*
for the people of their own nation, their *several* for men,
their *several* for women, their *several* for their priests,
and for the high priest alone their *several*. Hooker.
(4) Inclosed ground.
There was a nobleman that was lean of visage, but immediately after his marriage he grew pretty plump and
fat. One said to him, your lordship doth contrary to other
married men; for they at first wax lean, and you wax fat.
Sir Walter Raleigh stood by and said, there is no beast,

that if you take him from the common, and put him into the *several*, but will wax fat. Bacon.

se'veralty. State of separation from the rest.

se'vocation. The act of calling aside.

sewer. (1) An officer who serves up a feast.

(2) A passage for water to run through, now corrupted to *shore*.

Men suffer their private in judgment to be drawn into the common *sewer*, or stream of the present vogue. King Charles.

sex. (2) Womankind; by way of emphasis.

Shame is hard to be overcome; but if the *sex* once get the better of it, it gives them afterwards no more trouble. Garth.

to shab. To play mean tricks; a low barbarous cant word.

sha'bbily. Meanly; reproachfully; despicably; paltrily. A cant word.

sha'bby. (A word that has crept into conversation and low writing; but ought not to be admitted into the language.) Mean; paltry.

The dean was so *shabby*, and look'd like a ninny,

That the captain suppos'd he was curate to Jenny. Swift.

shagre'en. The skin of a kind of fish, or skin made rough in imitation of it.

to sha'green. To irritate; to provoke. Both should be written *chagrin*.

to shail. To walk sideways; a low word.

Child, you must walk strait, without skiewing and *shailing* to every step you set. L'Estrange.

shale. (Corrupted, I think, for *shell*.) A husk; the case of seeds in siliquous plants.

sha'llowbrained. Foolish; futile; trifling; empty.

It cannot but be matter of just indignation to all good men to see a company of lewd *shallowbrained* huffs making atheism, and contempt of religion, the sole badge of wit. South.

to sham. (1) To trick; to cheat; to fool with a fraud; to delude with false pretences. A low word.

sha′mbling. Moving aukwardly and irregularly. A low bad word.

> So when nurse Nokes to act young Ammon tries,
> With *shambling* legs, long chin, and foolish eyes,
> With dangling hands he strokes th′ imperial robe,
> And with a cuckold′s air commands the globe. Smith.

sha′mefaced. Modest; bashful; easily put out of countenance.

> A man may be *shamefaced*, and a woman modest, to the degree of scandalous. L′Estrange.

sha′mmer. A cheat; an impostor. A low word.

sha′mrock. The Irish name for three leaved grass.

> If they found a plot of watercresses, or *shamrocks*, there they flocked as to a feast for the time. Spenser, *On Ireland*.

sha′nker. A venereal excrescence.

sha′pesmith. One who undertakes to improve the form of the body. A burlesque word.

> No *shapesmith* yet set up and drove a trade,
> To mend the work that providence had made. Garth.

sha′rdborn. Born or produced among broken stones or pots. Perhaps *shard* in Shakespeare may signify the sheaths of the wings of insects.

> Ere to black Hecat′s summons
> The *shardborn* beetle with his drowsy hums
> Hath rung night′s yawning peal, there shall be done
> A deed of dreadful note. Shakespeare.

sha′rded. Inhabiting shards.

to share. (3) To cut; to separate; to sheer.

> Scalp, face, and shoulders the keen steel divides,
> And the *shar′d* visage hangs on equal sides. Dryden.

sha′rebone. The os pubis; the bone that divides the trunk from the limbs.

shark. (1) A voracious sea-fish.

(2) A greedy artful fellow; one who fills his pockets by sly tricks.

(3) Trick; fraud; petty rapine.

to shark. To pick up hastily or slily.

sha′rper. A tricking fellow; a petty thief; a rascal.

sha′tterbrained, sha′tterpated. Inattentive; not consistent. A low word.

sha′veling. A man shaved; a friar, or religious. Used in contempt.

sha′ver. (2) A man closely attentive to his own interest.

> My lord
> Was now dispos'd to crack a jest,
> And bid friend Lewis go in quest;
> This Lewis is a cunning *shaver.* Swift.

(3) A robber; a plunderer.

shaw. A thicket; a small wood. A tuft of trees near Lichfield is called Gentle *shaw.*

she. (2) It is sometimes used for a woman absolutely, with some degree of contempt.

> Lady, you are the cruell'st *she* alive,
> If you will lead these graces to the grave,
> And leave the world no copy. Shakespeare's *Twelfth Night.*

to sheal. To shell. See *shale.*

> Thou art a *shealed* peascod. Shakespeare, *King Lear.*

shear, shears. (1) An instrument to cut, consisting of two blades moving on a pin, between which the thing cut is intercepted. *Shears* are large, and *scissars* a smaller instrument of the same kind.

> When the fleece is shorn,
> Then their defenceless limbs the brambles tear;
> Short of their wool, and naked from the *sheer.* Dryden.

(2) The denomination of the age of sheep.

> When sheep is one *shear,* they will have two broad teeth before; when two *shear,* four; when three, six; when four, eight: and after that, their mouths break. Mortimer.

she′cklaton. He went to fight against the giant in his robe of *shecklaton,* which is that kind of gilded leather with which they use to embroider the Irish jackets. Spenser.

sheen, shee′ny. (This was probably only the old pronunciation of shine.) Bright; glittering; shewy. A word now not in use.

sheep. (1) The animal that bears wool: remarkable for its usefulness and innocence.

(2) In contempt. A foolish silly fellow. Ainsworth.

shee′pbiter. A petty thief.

> There are political *sheepbiters* as well as pastoral; betrayers of publick trusts, as well as of private.
> L'Estrange.

sheeps eye. A modest diffident look, such as lovers cast at their mistresses.

sheet. (5) A single complication or fold of paper in a book.

to shend. (1) To ruin; to spoil; to mischief.

> Such a dream I had of dire portent,
> That much I fear my body will be *shent:*
> It bodes I shall have wars. Dryden.

(2) To disgrace; to degrade; to blame.

(3) To overpower; to crush; to surpass.

> She pass'd the rest as Cynthia doth *shend*
> The lesser stars. Spenser.

she′rbet. The juice of lemons or oranges mixed with water and sugar.

> They prefer our beer above all other drinks; and considering that water is with the rarest, especially in this clime, the dearest of *sherbets,* and plenty of barley, it would prove infinitely profitable to such as should bring in the use thereof. Sandys.

shift. (1) Expedient found or used with difficulty; difficult means.

(5) A woman's linen.

shi′fter. One who plays tricks; a man of artifice.

> 'Twas such a *shifter*, that, if truth were known,
> Death was half glad when he had got him down. Milton.

shill-I-shall-I. A corrupt reduplication of *shall I?* The question of a man hesitating. To stand *shill-I-shall-I*, is to continue hesitating and procrastinating.

> I am somewhat dainty in making a resolution, because when I make it, I keep it: I don't stand *shill-I-shall-I* then; if I say't, I'll do't. Congreve's *Way of the World.*

ship. A ship may be defined a large hollow building, made to pass over the sea with sails. Watts.

shive. (1) A slice of bread.

> Easy it is
> Of a cut loaf to steal a *shive*. Shakespeare, *Titus Andronicus*.

(2) A thick splinter, or lamina cut off from the main substance.

shock. (6) A rough dog.

> I would fain know why a *shock* and a hound are not distinct species. Locke.

shoe′ing-horn. (2) Any thing by which a transaction is facilitated; any thing used as a medium. In contempt.

> I have been an arrant *shoeing-horn* for above these twenty years. I served my mistress in that capacity above five of the number before she was shod. Though she had many who made their applications to her, I always thought myself the best shoe in her shop. *Spectator*.

to shog. To shake; to agitate by sudden interrupted impulses.

> After it is washed, they put the remnant into a wooden dish, the which they softly *shog* to and fro in the water, until the earthy substance be flitted away. Carew.

shore. (2) The bank of a river. A licentious use.

> Beside the fruitful *shore* of muddy Nile,
> Upon a sunny bank outstretched lay,
> In monstrous length a mighty crocodile. Spenser.

(3) A drain; properly *sewer*.

sho′rling. The felt or skin of a sheep shorn.

to sho′rten. (4) To cut off; to defeat.

> The Irish dwell altogether by their septs, so as they may conspire what they will; whereas if there were English placed among them, they should not be able to stir but that it should be known, and they *shortened* according to their demerits. Spenser.

shot. (4) A sum charged; a reckoning.

> A man is never welcome to a place, 'till some certain *shot* be paid, and the hostess say welcome. Shakespeare.

sho'tfree. Clear of the reckoning.

> Though I could 'scape *shotfree* at London, I fear the shot here: here's no scoring but upon the pate. Shakespeare, *Henry IV*.

sho'tten. (From *shoot*.) Having ejected the spawn.

sho'vel. An instrument consisting of a long handle and broad blade with raised edges.

shrew. A peevish, malignant, clamorous, spiteful, vexatious, turbulent woman. (It appears in Robert of Gloucester, that this word signified anciently any one perverse or obstinate of either sex.)

> Every one of them, who is a *shrew* in domestick life, is now become a scold in politicks. Addison, *Freeholder*.

shrewd. (1) Having the qualities of a shrew; malicious; troublesome; mischievous.

> Her eldest sister is so curst and *shrewd*,
> That 'till the father rids his hands of her,
> Your love must live a maid. Shakespeare.

(2) Maliciously sly; cunning; more artful than good.
> It was a *shrewd* saying of the old monk, that two kind of prisons would serve for all offenders, an inquisition and a bedlam: if any man should deny the being of a God, and the immortality of the soul, such a one should be put into the first, as being a desperate heretick; but if any man should profess to believe these things, and yet allow himself in any known wickedness, such a one should be put into bedlam. Tillotson.

(3) Bad; ill-betokening.

(4) Painful; pinching; dangerous; mischievous.
> When a man thinks he has a servant, he finds a traitor that eats his bread, and is readier to do him a mischief, and a *shrewd* turn, than an open adversary. South's *Sermons*.

shre'wmouse. A mouse of which the bite is generally supposed venomous, and to which vulgar tradition assigns such malignity, that she is said to lame the foot over which she runs. I am informed that all these reports are calumnious, and that her feet and teeth are equally harmless with those of any other little mouse. Our ancestors however looked on her with such terrour, that they are supposed to have given her name to a scolding woman, whom for her venom they call a *shrew*.

shrift. Confession made to a priest. A word out of use.

The duke's commands were absolute,
Therefore my lord, address you to your *shrift*,
And be yourself; for you must die this instant. Rowe.

shrimp. (2) A little wrinkled man; a dwarf. In contempt.

He hath found,
Within the ground,
At last, no *shrimp*,
Whereon to imp
His jolly club. Ben. Jonson.

to shrink. To make to shrink. Not in use.

The sixth age shifts
Into the lean and slipper'd pantaloon.
His youthful hose well sav'd, a world too wide
For his *shrunk* shank. Shakespeare.

shrub. (2) (A cant word.) Spirit, acid, and sugar mixed.

to shuffle. (2) To play mean tricks; to practise fraud; to evade fair questions.

If a steward be suffered to run on, without bringing him to a reckoning, such a sottish forbearance will teach him to *shuffle*, and strongly tempt him to be a cheat. South.

shu'fflecap. A play at which money is shaken in a hat.

to si'ccate. To dry.

si'cker. Surely; certainly.

Sicker thou's but a lazy loord,
And rekes much of thy swink,
That with fond terms and witless words,
To bleer mine eyes do'st think. Spenser.

si'debox. Seat for the ladies on the side of the theatre.

sidera'tion. A sudden mortification, or, as the common people call it, a blast; or a sudden deprivation of sense, as in an apoplexy.

si′gnature. (2) A mark upon any matter, particularly upon plants, by which their nature or medicinal use is pointed out.

> Herbs are described by marks and *signatures,* so far as to distinguish them from one another. Baker, *On Learning.*

(3) Proof; evidence.

> Some rely on certain marks and *signatures* of their election, and others on their belonging to some particular church or sect. Rogers's *Sermons.*

si′lent. (4) Wanting efficacy. I think an Hebraism.

> Second and instrumental causes, together with nature itself, without that operative faculty which God gave them, would become *silent,* virtueless and dead.
> Raleigh's *History.*

silk. (1) The thread of the worm that turns afterwards to a butterfly.

> The worms were hallow'd that did breed the *silk;*
> And it was dy'd in mummy, which the skilful
> Conserv'd of maiden's hearts. Shakespeare's *Othello.*

(2) The stuff made of the worms thread.

si′llabub. Curds made by milking upon vinegar.

> Joan takes her neat rubb'd pail, and now
> She trips to milk the sand-red cow;
> Where, for some sturdy foot-ball swain,
> Joan strokes a *sillabub* or twain. Wotton.

si′lly. (1) Harmless; innocent; inoffensive; plain; artless.

(2) Weak; helpless.

> After long storms,
> In dread of death and dangerous dismay,
> With which my *silly* bark was tossed sore,
> I do at length descry the happy shore. Spenser.

simoni′ack. One who buys or sells preferment in the church.

> If the bishop alleges that the person presented is a *simoniac,* or unlearned, they are to proceed to trial. Ayliffe.

simple. A single ingredient in a medicine; a drug. It is popularly used for an *herb.*

to simple. To gather simples.

>   As once the foaming boar he chas'd,
>   Lascivious Circe well the youth survey'd,
>   As *simpling* on the flow'ry hills he stray'd. Garth.

simple′r. A simplist. An herbarist.

si′mpleton. A silly mortal; a trifler; a foolish fellow. A low word.

si′mular. One that counterfeits.

>   Hide thee, thou bloody hand,
>   Thou perjurer, thou *simular* of virtue,
>   That art incestuous. Shakespeare's *King Lear*.

simula′tion. That part of hypocrisy which pretends that to be which is not.

> For distinction sake, a deceiving by word is commonly called a lie; and deceiving by actions, gestures, or behaviour, is called *simulation* or hypocrisy. South's *Sermons*.

since′re. (1) Unhurt; uninjured.

>   He try'd a tough well chosen spear;
>   Th' inviolable body stood *sincere*. Dryden.

(2) Pure; unmingled.

> The pleasures of sense beasts taste *sincere* and pure always, without mixture or allay, without being distracted in the pursuit, or disquieted in the use of them. Atterbury.

si′ndon. A fold; a wrapper.

> There were found a book and a letter, both written in fine parchment, and wrapped in *sindons* of linen. Bacon.

si′ngle. (7) Pure; uncorrupt; not double minded; simple. A scriptural sense.

> The light of the body is the eye: if thine eye be *single*, thy whole body shall be full of light. *Matthew*, vi, 22.

to si′ngle. (2) To sequester; to withdraw.

> Yea simply, saith Basil, and universally, whether it be in works of nature, or of voluntary choice, I see not any thing done as it should be, if it be wrought by an agent *singling* itself from consorts. Hooker.

(3) To take alone.

> Many men there are, than whom nothing is more commendable when they are *singled;* and yet, in society

with others, none less fit to answer the duties which are
looked for at their hands. Hooker.

si′nister. (1) Being on the left hand; left; not right; not dexter.
Captain Spurio, with his cicatrice, an emblem of war,
here on his *sinister* cheek. Shakespeare, *All's well that
ends well.*

si′nistrous. Absurd; perverse; wrong-headed.
A knave or fool can do no harm, even by the most *sinis-
trous* and absurd choice. Bentley.

si′nistrously. (1) With a tendency to the left.
(2) Perversely; absurdly.

to sink. (10) To suppress; to conceal; to intervert.
If sent with ready money to buy any thing, and you happen to be out of pocket, *sink* the money, and take up the
goods on account. Swift's *Rules to Servants.*

sink. (1) A drain; a jakes.
Returning home at night, you'll find the *sink*
Strike your offended sense with double stink. Swift.
(2) Any place where corruption is gathered.

si′nworm. A vile sinful creature.
I would not soil these pure ambrosial weeds,
With the rank vapours of the *sin-worm* mould. Milton.

sir. (2) The title of a knight or baronet. This word was anciently so much held essential, that the Jews in their ad-
dresses expressed it in Hebrew characters.
(3) It is sometimes used for *man.*
(4) A title given to the loin of beef, which one of our kings
knighted in a fit of good humour.
He lost his roast-beef stomach, not being able to touch
a *sir*-loin which was served up. Addison.

si′ren. A goddess who enticed men by singing, and devoured
them; any mischievous enticer.

si′rrah. A compellation of reproach and insult.
Guess how the goddess greets her son,
Come hither, *sirrah;* no, begone. Prior.

---

sir. (4) Fuller said that Henry VIII did the knighting (*Church History,*
vi, ii, 299) but the *sir* comes from *sur, over.*

si′rop, si′rup. The juice of vegetables boiled with sugar.

site. (2) It is taken by Thomson for posture, or situation of a
thing with respect to itself: but improperly.

> And leaves the semblance of a lover fix'd
> In melancholy *site*, with head declin'd,
> And love-dejected eyes. Thomson's *Spring*.

si′thence. Since; in latter times.

six and seven. To be *at six and seven*, is to be in a state of disorder and confusion.

> In 1588, there sat in the see of Rome a fierce thundring
> friar, that would set all *at six and seven*, or at six and
> five, if you allude to his name. Bacon.

size. (2) A settled quantity. In the following passage it seems
to signify the allowance of the table: whence they say a *sizer*
at Cambridge.

> 'Tis not in thee
> To cut off my train, to scant my *sizes*,
> And, in conclusion, to oppose the bolt
> Against my coming in. Shakespeare's *King Lear*.

to size. (1) To adjust, or arrange according to size.

> Two troops so match'd were never to be found,
> Such bodies built for strength, of equal age,
> In stature *siz'd*. Dryden's *Knights Tale*.

(2) To settle; to fix.

> There was a statute for dispersing the standard of the
> exchequer throughout England; thereby to *size* weights
> and measures. Bacon's *Henry VII*.

ska′ddle. Hurt; damage.

skai′nsmate. (I suppose from *skain*, or *skean*, a knife, and *mate*,
a messmate.) It is remarkable that *mes*, Dutch, is a knife.

> Scurvy knave, I am none of his flirt gills;
> I am none of his *skainsmates*. Shakespeare's *Romeo and
> Juliet*.

skean. A short sword; a knife.

ske′gger. Little salmons called *skeggers*, are bred of such sick
salmon that might not go to the sea, and though they
abound, yet never thrive to any bigness. Walton's *Angler*.

ske′llum. A villain; a scoundrel. Skinner.

skep. (1) *Skep* is a sort of basket, narrow at the bottom, and wide at the top to fetch corn in.

(2) In Scotland, the repositories where the bees lay their honey is still called *skep*.

to skill. (1) To be knowing in; to be dextrous at.

> The overseers were all that could *skill* of instruments of musick. *2 Chronicles*, xxxiv, 12.

(2) To differ; to make difference; to interest; to matter. Not in use.

ski'llet. A small kettle or boiler.

to skim. (4) To cover superficially. Improper.

> Dang'rous flats in secret ambush lay,
> Where the false tides *skim* o'er the cover'd land,
> And seamen with dissembled depths betray. Dryden.

ski'mbleskamble. (A cant word formed by reduplication from *scamble*.) Wandering; wild.

skink. (1) Drink; any thing potable.

(2) Pottage.

> Scotch *skink*, which is a pottage of strong nourishment, is made with the knees and sinews of beef, but long boiled: jelly also of knuckles of veal. Bacon's *Natural History*.

ski'nker. One that serves drink.

> Hang up all the poor hop-drinkers,
> Cries old Sym, the king of *skinkers*. Ben. Jonson.

ski'pjack. An upstart.

> The want of shame or brains does not presently entitle every little *skipjack* to the board's end in the cabinet. L'Estrange.

ski'pkennel. A lackey; a footboy.

to skirre. To scour; to ramble over in order to clear.

skue. Oblique; sidelong. It is most used in the adverb *askue*.

slab. (A word, I suppose, of the same original with *slabber*, or *slaver*.) Thick; viscous; glutinous.

> Nose of Turk, and Tartar's lips;
> Finger of birth-strangl'd babe,
> Ditch-deliver'd by a drab;
> Make the gruel thick and *slab*. Shakespeare, *Macbeth*.

to sla'bber. (1) To let the spittle fall from the mouth; to drivel.

(2) To shed or pour any thing.

sla'bby. (1) Thick; viscous.

(2) Wet; floody.

> When waggish boys the stunted besom ply,
> To rid the *slabby* pavements, pass not by. Gay.

to slam. To slaughter; to crush. A word not used but in low conversation.

sla'pdash. All at once: as any thing broad falls with a *slap* into the water, and *dashes* it about. A low word.

to slash. (2) To lash. *Slash* is improper.

> Daniel, a sprightly swain, that us'd to *slash*
> The vig'rous steeds that drew his lord's calash,
> To Peggy's side inclin'd. King.

sla'ttern. A woman negligent, not elegant or nice.

> We may always observe, that a gossip in politicks is a *slattern* in her family. Addison's *Freeholder*.

sleave. (Of this word I know not well the meaning: *sleave* silk is explained by Gouldman *floccus sericus*, a lock of silk; and the women still say *sleave the silk*, for *untwist* it. Ainsworth calls a weaver's shuttle or reed a *slay*. *To sley* is to part a twist into single fibres.)

> I on a fountain light,
> Whose brim with pinks was platted,
> The banks with daffadillies dight
> With grass like *sleave* was matted. Drayton's *Cynthia*.

sleazy. (Often written *sleezy*.) Weak; wanting substance. This seems to be of the same race with *sleave*, or from to *sley*.

to sleek. (1) To comb smooth and even.

sleeve. (2) *Sleeve*, in some provinces, signifies a knot or skein of silk, which is by some very probably supposed to be its meaning in the following passage. (See *sleave*.)

> Methought I heard a voice cry, sleep no more!
> Macbeth doth murder sleep; the innocent sleep;
> Sleep that knits up the ravell'd *sleeve* of care,
> The birth of each day's life. Shakespeare.

(3) *Sleeve*, Dutch, signifies a cover; any thing spread over;

which seems to be the sense of *sleeve* in the proverbial phrase.

> John laughed heartily in his *sleeve* at the pride of the esquire. Arbuthnot's *History of John Bull*.

(4) To hang on a *sleeve;* to make dependent.

slee′veless. (2) Wanting reasonableness; wanting propriety; wanting solidity. (This sense, of which the word has been long possessed, I know not well how it obtained; Skinner thinks it properly *liveless* or *lifeless:* to this I cannot heartily agree, though I know not what better to suggest. Can it come from *sleeve*, a knot, or *skein,* and so signify *unconnected, hanging ill together?* or from *sleeve,* a cover; and therefore means *plainly absurd;* foolish without palliation?)

> My landlady quarrelled with him for sending every one of her children on a *sleeveless* errand, as she calls it. *Spectator.*

to sley. (See *to sleave.*) To part or twist into threads.

slice. (3) A broad head fixed in a handle; a peel; a spatula.

> The pelican hath a beak broad and flat, much like the *slice* of apothecaries, with which they spread plaisters. Hakewill.

to sli′dder. To slide with interruption.

slim. (A cant word as it seems, and therefore not to be used.) Slender; thin of shape.

> I was jogg'd on the elbow by a *slim* young girl of seventeen. Addison.

to slink. To cast; to miscarry of. A low word.

> To prevent a mare's *slinking* her foal, in snowy weather keep her where she may have good spring-water to drink. Mortimer.

sli′pper. A shoe without leather behind, into which the foot slips easily.

sli′ppy. Slippery; easily sliding. A barbarous provincial word.

> The white of an egg is ropy, *slippy*, and nutritious. Floyer.

sli′pslop. Bad liquor. A low word formed by reduplication of *slop*.

slish. A low word formed by reduplicating *slash*.

> What! this a sleeve?
> Here's snip and nip, and *slish* and slash,
> Like to a censor in a barber's shop. Shakespeare.

to slop. To drink grossly and greedily.

slop. Mean and vile liquor of any kind. Generally some nauseous or useless medicinal liquor.

to slot. To strike or clash hard.

slouch. (1) A downcast look; a depression of the head. In Scotland, an ungainly gait, as also the person whose gait it is.

(2) A man who looks heavy and clownish.

to slouch. To have a downcast clownish look.

slo′wworm. The blind worm; a small viper, venomous, but scarcely mortal.

to slu′bber. (1) To do any thing lazily, imperfectly, or with idle hurry.

(2) To stain; to daub. (This seems to be from *slobber, slabber,* or *slaver.*)

(3) To cover coarsely or carelessly.

slu′bberdegullion. (I suppose a cant word without derivation.) A paltry, dirty, sorry wretch.

to slu′mber. (2) To stupify; to stun.

> To honest a deed after it was done, or to *slumber* his conscience in the doing, he studied other incentives. Wotton.

to slur. (1) To sully; to soil; to contaminate.

(2) To pass lightly; to balk; to miss.

> Studious to please the genius of the times,
> With periods, points, and tropes he *slurs* his crimes;
> He robb'd not, but he borrow'd from the poor,
> And took but with intention to restore. Dryden.

(3) To cheat; to trick.

slut. (1) A dirty woman.

(2) A word of slight contempt to a woman.

> The frogs were ready to leap out of their skins for joy, 'till one crafty old *slut* in the company advised them to consider a little better on't. L'Estrange.

slu'ttery. The qualities or practice of a slut.

> These make our girls their *sluttery* rue,
> By pinching them both black and blue;
> And put a penny in their shoe,
> The house for cleanly sweeping. Drayton.

slu'ttish. Nasty; not nice; not cleanly; dirty; indecently negligent of cleanliness.

> The nastiness of that nation, and *sluttish* course of life, hath much promoted the opinion, occasioned by their servile condition at first, and inferior ways of parsimony ever since. Browne.

slu'ttishness. The qualities or practice of a slut; nastiness; dirtiness.

> I look on the instinct of this noisome and troublesome creature, the louse, of searching out foul and nasty clothes to harbour and breed in, as an effect of divine providence, designed to deter men and women from *sluttishness* and sordidness, and to provoke them to cleanliness and neatness. Ray, *On the Creation.*

small. (5) Little in the principal quality, as *small* beer; not strong; weak.

sma'llcoal. Little wood coals used to light fires.

sma'ragdine. Made of emerald; resembling emerald.

smart. A fellow affecting briskness and vivacity. A cant word.

smatch. (Corrupted from *smack.*) (1) Taste; tincture; twang.

> Some nations have a peculiar guttural or nasal *smatch* in their language. Holder's *Elements of Speech.*

to smeeth, or smutch. To smoke; to blacken with smoke.

sme'llfcast. A parasite; one who haunts good tables.

> The ant lives upon her own, honestly gotten; whereas the fly is an intruder, and a common *smellfeast* that spunges upon other people's trenchers. L'Estrange.

to smerk. To smile wantonly.

sme'rky, smirk. Nice; smart; jaunty.

smi'cket. (Diminutive of *smock, smocket, smicket.*) The under garment of a woman.

smock. (1) The under garment of a woman; a shift.

(2) *Smock* is used in a ludicrous kind of composition for any thing relating to women.

Plague on his *smock*-loyalty!

I hate to see a brave bold fellow sotted,

Made sour and senseless, turn'd to whey by love.
Dryden.

smockfa'ced. Palefaced; maidenly.

Old chiefs reflecting on their former deeds,

Disdain to rust with batter'd invalids;

But active in the foremost ranks appear,

And leave young *smockfac'd* beaux to guard the rear.
Fenton.

smoke. The visible effluvium, or sooty exhalation from any thing burning.

to smoke. (2) To smell out; to find out.

Tom Tattle passes for an impertinent, and Will. Trippet begins to be *smoked*, in case I continue this paper. Addison, *Spectator*.

(3) To sneer; to ridicule to the face.

Smoke the fellow there. Congreve.

smo'ther. (1) A state of suppression.

A man were better relate himself to a statue, than suffer his thoughts to pass in *smother*. Bacon.

(2) Smoke; thick dusk.

The greater part enter only like mutes to fill the stage, and spend their taper in smoke and *smother*. Collier, *On Fame*.

smug. Nice; spruce; dressed with affectation of niceness, but without elegance.

He who can make your visage less horrid, and your person more *smug*, is worthy some good reception. *Spectator*.

smu'ggler. A wretch, who, in defiance of justice and the laws, imports or exports goods either contraband or without payment of the customs.

snack. A share; a part taken by compact.

All my demurs but double his attacks;

At last he whispers, "Do, and we go *snacks*." Pope.

snake. A serpent of the oviparous kind, distinguished from a viper. The snake's bite is harmless. *Snake* in poetry is a general name for a viper.

sna′kewood. What we call *snakewood* is properly the smaller branches of the root of a tall strait tree growing in the island of Timor, and other parts of the East. It has no remarkable smell; but is of an intensely bitter taste. The Indians are of opinion, that it is a certain remedy for the bite of the hooded serpent, and from thence its name of *lignum colubrinum*, or *snakewood*. We very seldom use it. Hill's *Materia Medica*.

to snap. (4) To catch suddenly and unexpectedly.

> Did I not see you, rascal, did I not!
> When you lay snug to *snap* young Damon's goat?
> Dryden.

snap. (2) A greedy fellow.

(4) A catch; a theft.

sna′pdragon. (2) A kind of play, in which brandy is set on fire, and raisins thrown into it, which those who are unused to the sport are afraid to take out; but which may be safely snatched by a quick motion, and put blazing into the mouth, which being closed, the fire is at once extinguished.

to snarl. To intangle; to embarrass. I know not that this sense is well authorized.

> Confused *snarled* consciences render it difficult to pull out thread by thread. *Decay of Piety*.

snast. The snuff of a candle.

sne′aker. A large vessel of drink.

> I have just left the right worshipful and his myrmidons about a *sneaker* of five gallons. *Spectator*.

sneap. A reprimand; a check.

> My lord, I will not undergo this *sneap* without reply: you call honourable boldness impudent sauciness: if a man will court'sy and say nothing, he is virtuous. Shakespeare, *Henry IV*.

to sneb. (Properly to *snib*. See *sneap*.) To check; to chide; to reprimand.

to sneeze. To emit wind audibly by the nose.

snick and snee. A combat with knives.

> Among the Dunkirkers, where *snick and snee* was in fashion, a boatswain with some of our men drinking to-

gether, became quarrelsome: one of our men beat him down; then kneeling upon his breast, he drew out a knife, sticking in his sash, and cut him from the ear towards the mouth. Wiseman's *Surgery*.

to sni'cker. To laugh slily, wantonly, or contemptuously; to laugh in one's sleeve.

to sni'ggle. *Sniggling* is thus performed: in a warm day, when the water is lowest, take a strong small hook, tied to a string about a yard long; and then into one of the holes, where an eel may hide herself, with the help of a short stick put in your bait leisurely, and as far as you may conveniently: if within the sight of it, the eel will bite instantly, and as certainly gorge it: pull him out by degrees. Walton's *Angler*.

snip. (3) A share; a snack. A low word.

He found his friend upon the mending hand, which he was glad to hear, because of the *snip* that he himself expected upon the dividend. L'Estrange.

sni'psnap. (A cant word formed by reduplication of *snap*.) Tart dialogue.

Dennis and dissonance, and captious art,
And *snipsnap* short, and interruption smart. Pope's *Dunciad*.

to snite. To blow the nose.

sni'vel. Snot; the running of the nose.

snot. The mucus of the nose.

Thus, when a greedy sloven once has thrown
His *snot* into the mess, 'tis all his own. Swift.

snout. (2) The nose of a man, in contempt.

Charm'd with his eyes, and chin, and *snout*,
Her pocket-glass drew slily out;
And grew enamour'd with her phiz,
As just the counterpart of his. Swift.

sno'wbroth. Very cold liquor.

to snudge. To lie idle, close, or snug.

snuff. (1) Snot. In this sense it is not used.

(2) The useless excrescence of a candle: whence *moucher la chandelle*.

(5) Resentment expressed by snifting; perverse resentment.

> Jupiter took *snuff* at the contempt, and punished him: he sent him home again. L'Estrange.

to soak. (2) To drain; to exhaust. This seems to be a cant term.

> A greater sparer than a saver; for though he had such means to accumulate, yet his forts, and his garrisons, and his feastings, wherein he was only sumptuous, could not but *soak* his exchequer. Wotton.

to sob. To soak. A cant word.

> The tree being *sobbed* and wet, swells. Mortimer.

soci'ety. (1) Union of many in one general interest.

sock. (2) The shoe of the ancient comick actors, taken in poems for comedy, and opposed to buskin or tragedy.

so'dden. Boiled; seethed.

> *Sodden* business! there's a stew'd phrase indeed. Shakespeare.

soe. (*Sae,* Scottish.) A large wooden vessel with hoops, for holding water; a cowl.

so'fa. (I believe an eastern word.) A splendid seat covered with carpets.

soft. Hold; stop; not so fast.

> But *soft,* my muse, the world is wide,
> And all at once was not descry'd. Suckling.

soho. A form of calling from a distant place.

soi'lure. Stain; pollution.

> He merits well to have her,
> Not making any scruple of her *soilure.* Shakespeare.

to so'journ. To dwell any where for a time; to live as not at home; to inhabit as not in a settled habitation. Almost out of use.

> He who *sojourns* in a foreign country, refers what he sees abroad to the state of things at home. Atterbury.

sold. Military pay; warlike entertainments.

so'lemn. (1) Anniversary; observed once a year with religious ceremonies.

to soli'cit. (5) To disturb; to disquiet. A Latinism.

> I find your love, and would reward it too;

But anxious fears *solicit* my weak breast. Dryden, *Spanish Fryar*.

soli'citor. (2) One who does in Chancery the business which is done by attorneys in other courts.

solidu'ngulous. Whole-hoofed.

It is set down by Aristotle and Pliny, that an horse and all *solidungulous* or whole-hoofed animals have no gall, which we find repugnant unto reason. Browne's *Vulgar Errours*.

solifi'dian. One who supposes only faith, not works, necessary to justification.

so'lipede. An animal whose feet are not cloven.

so'llar. A garret.

solu'tion. (1) Disruption; breach; disjunction; separation.

sona'ta. A tune.

song. (6) An old song. A trifle.

A hopeful youth, newly advanced to great honour, was forced by a cobler to resign all for an *old song*. Addison.

so'ngish. Containing songs; consisting of songs. A low word.

so'ngster. A singer. Used of human singers, it is a word of slight contempt.

so'nnet. (1) A short poem consisting of fourteen lines, of which the rhymes are adjusted by a particular rule. It is not very suitable to the English language, and has not been used by any man of eminence since Milton.

A book was writ of late call'd Tetrachordon,
And woven close, both matter, form, and stile;
The subject new: it walk'd the town a-while,
Numb'ring good intellects, now seldom por'd on:
Cries the stall-reader, Bless us, what a word on
A title-page is this! and some in file
Stand spelling false, while one might walk to Mile-
End-green. Why is it harder, sirs, than Gordon,
Colkitto, or Macdonnel, or Galasp?
Those rugged names to our like mouths grow sleek,

---

sonnet. Johnson illustrates with Milton's least characteristic sonnet.

That would have made Quintilian stare and gasp:
　　Thy age like ours, soul of sir John Cheek,
Hated not learning worse than toad or asp,
　　When thou taught'st Cambridge and king Edward
　　Greek. Milton.

(2) A small poem.

sonnette′er. A small poet, in contempt.

There are as many kinds of gardening as of poetry: your
makers of parterres and flower-gardens are epigram-
matists and *sonnetteers* in this art. *Spectator.*

soonly. Quickly; speedily. This word I remember in no other
place; but if *soon* be, as it seems once to have been, an
adjective, *soonly* is proper.

A mason meets with a stone that wants no cutting, and,
soonly approving of it, places it in his work. More.

so′oterkin. A kind of false birth fabled to be produced by the
Dutch women from sitting over their stoves.

When Jove was, from his teeming head,
Of wit's fair goddess brought to-bed,
There follow'd at his lying-in,
For after-birth, a *sooterkin.* Swift.

sooth. Truth; reality. Obsolete.

sop. (1) Any thing steeped in liquour to be eaten.

(2) Any thing given to pacify, from the *sop* given to
Cerberus.

To Cerberus they give a *sop,*
His tripple barking mouth to stop. Swift.

to sophi′sticate. To adulterate; to corrupt with something spuri-
ous.

sophistica′tion. Adulteration; not genuineness.

sorbi′tion. The act of drinking or sipping.

sore. (5) The buck is called the first year a fawn; the second,
a pricket; the third, a sorel; and the fourth year, a *sore.*
Shakespeare.

so′rtilege. The act or practice of drawing lots.

to soss. (A cant word.) To sit lazily on a chair; to fall at once
into a chair.

The winter sky began to frown,

Poor Stella must pack off to town;
From wholesome exercise and air,
To *sossing* in an easy chair. Swift.

sot. (1) A blockhead; a dull ignorant stupid fellow; a dolt.

(2) A wretch stupified by drinking.

A surly ill-bred lord,
That chides and snaps her up at every word:
A brutal *sot;* who while she holds his head,
With drunken filth bedaubs the nuptial bed. Granville.

sough. A subterraneous drain.

sou'lshot. Something paid for a soul's requiem among the Romanists.

soup. Strong decoction of flesh for the table.

Let the cook daub the back of the footman's new livery, or, when he is going up with a dish of *soup*, let her follow him softly with a ladle-full. Swift.

souse. (1) Pickle made of salt.

(2) Any thing kept parboiled in salt-pickle.

to souse. (1) To parboil, and steep in pickle.

(2) To throw into water. A ludicrous sense.

Who those were that run away,
And yet gave out th' had won the day;
Although the rabble *sous'd* them for't,
O'er head and ears in mud and dirt. Butler.

so'uvenance. Remembrance; memory.

so'wins. Flummery, somewhat sour'd and made of oatmeal.

to sowl. To pull by the ears.

spa'ddle. A little spade.

spa'gyrist. A chymist.

span. (1) The space from the end of the thumb to the end of the little finger extended.

spa'ncounter, spa'nfarthing. A play at which money is thrown within a span or mark.

spa'niel. (2) A low, mean, sneaking fellow; a courtier; a dedicator; a pensioner; a dependant; a placeman.

spa'nker. A small coin.

spark. (4) A lively, showy, splendid, gay man. It is commonly used in contempt.

[391]

spa'rkish. (1) Airy; gay. A low word.

(2) Showy; well dressed; fine.

to spa'tiate. To rove; to range; to ramble at large.

to spawl. To throw moisture out of the mouth.

> What mischief can the dean have done him,
> That Traulus calls for vengeance on him?
> Why must he sputter, *spawl*, and slaver it,
> In vain against the people's fav'rite. Swift.

spawl. Spittle; moisture ejected from the mouth.

specula'tor. (3) A spy; a watcher.

to spelt. To split; to break. A bad word.

spe'rable. Such as may be hoped.

to spet. To bring or pour abundantly. (*Spet* in Scotland is a superabundance of water: as, that tide or fresh was a high *spet*.)

to spew. To vomit; to ease the stomach.

> He could have haul'd in
> The drunkards, and the noises of the inn;
> But better 'twas that they should sleep or *spew*,
> Than in the scene to offend or him or you. Ben. Jonson.

sphinx. The *sphinx* was a famous monster in Egypt, that remained by conjoined Nilus, having the face of a virgin, and the body of a lion. Peacham, *On Drawing*.

spick and span. (This word I should not have expected to have found authorised by a polite writer. *Span-new* is used by Chaucer, and is supposed to come from *spannan,* to stretch, Sax. *expandere,* Lat. whence *span. Span-new* is therefore originally used of cloath new extended or dressed at the clothiers, and *spick and span* is newly extended on the *spikes* or tenters: it is however a low word.) Quite new; now first used.

> While the honour, thou hast got,
> Is *spick and span* new, piping hot,
> Strike her up bravely. Butler.

spill. (2) A small quantity of money. I know not whence derived.

> The bishops, who consecrated this ground, were wont to have a *spill* or sportule from the credulous laity. Ayliffe.

to spill. (2) To destroy; to mischief.

> Be not angry with these fires;
> For then their threats will kill me:
> Nor look too kind on my desires;
> For then my hopes will *spill* me. Ben. Jonson.

spilth. Any thing poured out or wasted.

spi'ndle. (3) Any thing slender. In contempt.

> The marriage of one of our heiresses with an eminent
> courtier gave us *spindle* shanks and cramps. *Tatler.*

spi'nny. I suppose *small, slender.* A barbarous word.

spi're. (1) A curve line; any thing wreathed or contorted; a
curl; a twist; a wreath.

spi'ssitude. Grossness; thickness.

to spi'tchcock. To cut an eel in pieces and roast him. Of this
word I find no good etymology.

> No man lards salt pork with orange peel,
> Or garnishes his lamb with *spitchcockt* eel. King.

spi'ttal. (Corrupted from *hospital.*) A charitable foundation.
In use only in the phrases, *a spittal sermon,* and *rob not the
spittal.*

spi'ttle. (Corrupted from *hospital,* and therefore better written *spital,* or *spittal.*) Hospital. It is still retained in Scotland.

spi'tvenom. Poison ejected from the mouth.

> The *spitvenom* of their poisoned hearts breaketh out to
> the annoyance of others. Hooker.

to splash. To daub with dirt in great quantities.

spla'ymouth. Mouth widened by design.

> All authors to their own defects are blind:
> Had'st thou but Janus-like a face behind,
> To see the people when *splaymouths* they make,
> To mark their fingers pointed at thy back,
> Their tongues loll'd out a foot. Dryden.

spleen. (2) Anger; spite; ill-humour.

> In noble minds some dregs remain,
> Not yet purg'd off, of *spleen* and sour disdain. Pope.

splu'tter. Bustle; tumult. A low word.

spoil. (4) The slough; the cast-off skin of a serpent.

sponge. A soft porous substance supposed by some the nidus of animals. It is remarkable for sucking up water.

spo'ngy. (2) Wet; drenched; soaked; full like a sponge.

When their drenched natures lie as in a death,
What cannot you and I perform upon
Th' unguarded Duncan? What not put upon
His *spungy* officers, who shall bear the guilt. Shakespeare.

sponk. A word in Edinburgh which denotes a match, or any thing dipt in sulphur that takes fire: as, any *sponks* will ye buy? Touchwood.

spo'nsor. A surety; one who makes a promise or gives security for another.

to spoom. (Probably from *spume*, or *foam*, as a ship driven with violence spumes, or raises a foam.)

When virtue *spooms* before a prosperous gale,
My heaving wishes help to fill the sail. Dryden.

spo'onmeat. Liquid food; nourishment taken with a spoon.

spot. (3) I know not well the meaning of *spot* in this place, unless it be a scandalous woman; a disgrace to her sex.

Let him take thee,
And hoist thee up to the shouting plebeians;
Follow his chariot, like the greatest *spot*
Of all thy sex. Shakespeare's *Antony and Cleopatra*.

spraints. The dung of an otter.

to sprawl. (1) To struggle as in the convulsions of death.

Hang the child, that he may see it *sprawl*;
A sight to vex the father's soul. Shakespeare.

spray. (2) The foam of the sea, commonly written *spry*.

spright. (Contraction of *spirit, spiritus*, Latin: it was anciently written *sprete* or *spryte*; and *spirit*, as now written, was long considered in verse as a monosyllable: this word should therefore be spelled *sprite*, and its derivatives *spritely, spriteful*; but custom has determined otherwise.) (1) Spirit; shade; soul; incorporeal agent.

(2) Walking spirit; apparition.

The ideas of goblins and *sprights* have no more to do with darkness than light; yet let but a foolish maid

inculcate these often on the mind of a child, possibly he
shall never be able to separate them again. Locke.

(3) Power which gives cheerfulness or courage.

to spright. To haunt as a spright. A ludicrous use.

I am *sprighted* with a fool. Shakespeare's *Cymbeline*.

spri'ngal. A youth. Spenser.

to sprit. To throw out; to eject with force. Commonly *spirt*.

Toads sometimes exclude or *sprit* out a dark and liquid
matter behind, and a venomous condition there may be
perhaps therein; but it cannot be called their urine.
Browne.

sprunt. Any thing that is short and will not easily bend.

to spunge. (Rather *to sponge*.) To hang on others for maintenance.

spu'nginghouse. A house to which debtors are taken before
commitment to prison, where the bailiffs sponge upon them,
or riot at their cost.

spu'rway. A horseway; a bridle-road; distinct from a road for
carriages.

squab. A kind of sofa or couch; a stuffed cushion.

On her large *squab* you find her spread,
Like a fat corpse upon a bed. Swift.

to squab. To fall down plump or flat; to squelch or squash.

to squa'bble. To quarrel; to debate peevishly; to wrangle; to
fight. A low word.

Drunk? and speak parrot? and *squabble?* swagger? oh,
thou invincible spirit of wine! Shakespeare's *Othello*.

to squall. To scream out as a child or woman frighted.

In my neighbourhood, a very pretty prattling shoulder
of veal *squalls* out at the sight of a knife. *Spectator*.

square. (4) Parallel; exactly suitable.

She's a most triumphant lady, if report be *square* to her.
Shakespeare.

(5) Strong; stout; well set. As, a *square* man.

(6) Equal; exact; honest; fair. As, *square* dealing.

squash. (1) Any thing soft and easily crushed.

(3) Any thing unripe; any thing soft. In contempt.

How like I then was to this kernel,

This *squash,* this gentleman. Shakespeare's *Winter's Tale.*

(4) A sudden fall.

Since they will overload my shoulders, I shall throw down the burden with a *squash* among them. Arbuthnot.

squat. (1) The posture of cowering or lying close.

A stitch-fall'n cheek that hangs below the jaw;
Such wrinkles as a skilful hand would draw
For an old grandam ape, when with a grace
She sits at *squat,* and scrubs her leathern face. Dryden.

(2) A sudden fall.

to squeal. To cry with a shrill sharp voice; to cry with pain. *Squeak* seems a short sudden cry, and *squeal* a cry continued.

squelch. Heavy fall. A low ludicrous word.

So soon as the poor devil had recovered the *squelch,* away he scampers, bawling like mad. L'Estrange.

squib. (1) A small pipe of paper filled with wildfire. Used in sport.

(2) Any petty fellow.

The *squibs,* in the common phrase, are called libellers. *Tatler.*

squintife'go. Squinting. A cant word.

The timbrel and the *squintifego* maid
Of Isis awe thee; lest the gods for sin,
Should, with a swelling dropsy stuff thy skin. Dryden.

to squi'ny. To look asquint. A cant word.

I remember thine eyes well enough:
Do'st thou *squiny* at me? Shakespeare's *King Lear.*

squi'rrel. A small animal that lives in woods, remarkable for leaping from tree to tree.

to squirt. To prate; to let fly. Low cant.

You are so given to *squirting* up and down, and chattering, that the world would say, I had chosen a jack-pudding for a prime minister. L'Estrange.

sta'dle. (1) Any thing which serves for support to another.

(2) A staff; a crutch.

(3) A tree suffered to grow for coarse and common uses, as posts or rails. Of this meaning I am doubtful.

Coppice-woods, if you leave in them *staddles* too thick, will run to bushes and briars, and have little clean underwood. Bacon.

staff. (6) A stanza; a series of verses regularly disposed, so as that, when the stanza is concluded, the same order begins again.

sta'ffish. Stiff; harsh. Obsolete.

sta'ger. (1) A player.

(2) One who has long acted on the stage of life; a practitioner; a person of cunning.

> Be by a parson cheated!
> Had you been cunning *stagers*,
>   You might yourselves be treated
> By captains and by majors. Swift.

stale. (1) Something exhibited or offered as an allurement to draw others to any place or purpose.

> The trumpery in my house bring hither,
> For *stale* to catch these thieves. Shakespeare, *Tempest*.

(2) In Shakespeare it seems to signify a prostitute.

> I stand dishonour'd, that have gone about
> To link my dear friend to a common *stale*. Shakespeare.

(3) Urine; old urine.

(4) Old beer; beer somewhat acidulated.

(5) A handle.

> It hath a long *stale* or handle, with a button at the end for one's hand. Mortimer's *Husbandry*.

to stale. To make water.

> Having ty'd his beast t' a pale,
> And taken time for both to *stale*. Hudibras.

to stalk. (1) To walk with high and superb steps. It is used commonly in a sense of dislike.

stal'kinghorse. A horse either real or fictitious by which a fowler shelters himself from the sight of the game; a mask; a pretence.

sta'mmel. Of this word I know not the meaning.

---

stammel. "A coarse woollen cloth; . . . the shade of red in which the cloth was commonly dyed." *O.E.D.*

Reedhood, the first that doth appear
In *stammel:* scarlet is too dear. Ben. Jonson.

sta′ndish. A case for pen and ink.

A grubstreet patriot does not write to secure, but get something: should the government be overturned he has nothing to lose but an old *standish.* Addison.

stang. A perch.

These fields were intermingled with woods of half a *stang*, and the tallest tree appeared to be seven feet high. Swift.

stank. Weak; worn out.

sta′nza. A number of lines regularly adjusted to each other; so much of a poem as contains every variation of measure or relation of rhyme. *Stanza* is originally a room of a house, and came to signify a subdivision of a poem; a staff.

sta′ple. (1) A settled mart; an established emporium.

The customs of Alexandria were very great, it having been the *staple* of the Indian trade. Arbuthnot, *On Coins.*

star. (1) One of the luminous bodies that appear in the nocturnal sky.

(3) Configuration of the planets supposed to influence fortune.

From forth the fatal loins of these two foes,
A pair of *star* crost lovers take their life. Shakespeare.

sta′rfish. A fish branching out into several points.

starga′zer. An astronomer, or astrologer. In contempt.

stark. Is used to intend or augment the signification of a word: as *stark mad*, mad in the highest degree. It is now little used but in low language.

Who, by the most cogent arguments, will disrobe himself at once of all his old opinions, and turn himself out *stark* naked in quest of new notions? Locke.

sta′tary. Fixed; settled.

The set and *statary* times of pairing of nails, and cutting of hair, is but the continuation of ancient superstition. Browne.

state. (12) A canopy; a covering of dignity.

> Over the chair is a *state* made round of ivy, somewhat whiter than ours; and the *state* is curiously wrought with silver and silk. Bacon.

sta′teswoman. A woman who meddles with publick affairs. In contempt.

sta′ticks. The science which considers the weight of bodies.

sta′tist. A statesman; a politician; one skilled in government.

to stave and tail. To part dogs by interposing a staff, and by pulling the tail.

> The conquering foe they soon assail'd,
> First Trulla *stav'd*, and Cerdon *tail'd*. Hudibras.

stays. Without singular. (1) Boddice; a kind of stiff waistcoat made of whalebone, worn by ladies.

steak. A slice of flesh broiled or fried; a collop.

> The surgeon protested he had cured him very well, and offered to eat the first *stake* of him. *Tatler*.

stea′lth. (1) The act of stealing; theft.

(2) The thing stolen.

stegano′graphy. The art of secret writing by characters or cyphers, intelligible only to the persons who correspond one with another. Bailey.

to stench. (1) To make to stink.

stercora′ceous. Belonging to dung; partaking of the nature of dung.

> Green juicy vegetables, in a heap together, acquire a heat equal to that of a human body; then a putrid *stercoraceous* taste and odour, in taste resembling putrid flesh, and in smell human faeces. Arbuthnot, *On Aliments*.

ste′ven. A cry, or loud clamour.

> Ne sooner was out, but swifter than thought,
> Fast by the hide, the wolf Lowder caught;
> And had not Roffy renne to the *steven*,
> Lowder had been slain thilke same even. Spenser.

stew. (1) A bagnio; a hot-house.

(2) A brothel; a house of prostitution. (This signification is by some imputed to this, that there were licensed brothels near the *stews* or fishponds in Southwark; but probably *stew*, like bagnio, took a bad signification from bad use.)

> Her, though seven years she in the *stews* had laid,
> A nunnery durst receive and think a maid
> And though in childbirth's labour she did lie,
> Midwives would swear 'twere but a tympany. Donne.

(3) A storepond; a small pond where fish are kept for the table.

to stick. (15) To stick out. To be unemployed.

to sti'ckle. (1) To take part with one side or other.

(2) To contest; to altercate; to contend rather with obstinacy than vehemence.

(3) To trim; to play fast and loose; to act a part between opposites.

sti'ckler. (1) A sidesman to fencers; a second to a duellist; one who stands to judge a combat.

> Our former chiefs, like *sticklers* of the war,
> First fought t' inflame the parties, then to poise:
> The quarrel lov'd, but did the cause abhor;
> And did not strike to hurt, but made a noise. Dryden.

(2) An obstinate contender about any thing.

sti'ngo. (From the sharpness of the taste.) Old beer. A cant word.

sti'ngy. (A low cant word. In this word, with its derivatives, the *g* is pronounced as in *gem*.) Covetous; niggardly; avaricious.

to stink. To emit an offensive smell, commonly a smell of putrefaction.

> Chloris, this costly way to *stink* give o'er,
> 'Tis throwing sweet into a common shore;
> Not all Arabia would sufficient be,
> Thou smell'st not of thy sweets, they *stink* of thee.
> Granville.

sti'nkard. A mean stinking paltry fellow.

sti'nker. Something intended to offend by the smell.

The air may be purified by burning of stinkpots or
stinkers in contagious lanes. Harvey.

sti′nkpot. An artificial composition offensive to the smell.

sti′rious. Resembling icicles.

stitch. (3) In Chapman it seems to mean furrows or ridges,
and perhaps has the same meaning in the following passage of Dryden, which otherwise I do not understand.

> A *stitch*-fall'n cheek, that hangs below the jaw,
> Such wrinkles as a skilful hand would draw,
> For an old grandam ape. Dryden.

sti′thy. (1) An anvil; the iron body on which the smith forges
his work.

to stive. (1) To stuff up close.
(2) To make hot or sultry.

> His chamber was commonly *stived* with friends or
> suitors of one kind or other. Wotton.

stoat. A small stinking animal.

sto′cah. An attendant; a walletboy; one who runs at a horse-
man's foot; a horseboy.

to stock. (4) To stock up. To extirpate.

> The wild boar not only spoils her branches, but *stocks
> up* her roots. *Decay of Piety.*

sto′ckfish. Dried cod, so called from its hardness.

sto′ckjobber. A low wretch who gets money by buying and sell-
ing shares in the funds.

> The *stockjobber* thus from 'Change-alley goes down,
> And tips you the freeman a wink;
>
> Let me have but your vote to serve for the town,
> And here is a guinea to drink. Swift.

sto′cklock. Lock fixed in wood.

stoli′dity. Stupidity; want of sense.

to sto′mach. To resent; to remember with anger and malignity.

> The lion began to shew his teeth, and to *stomach* the
> affront. L'Estrange's *Fables.*

sto′machful. Sullen; stubborn; perverse.

> A *stomachful* boy put to school, the whole world could
> not bring to pronounce the first letter. L'Estrange.

stone. (7) Testicle.

(9) Stone is used by way of exaggeration.

She had got a trick of holding her breath, and lying at her length for *stone* dead. L'Estrange.

sto′nehorse. A horse not castrated.

stool. (3) Stool of repentance, or cutty stool, in the kirks of Scotland, is somewhat analogous to the pillory. It is elevated above the congregation. In some places there may be a seat in it; but it is generally without, and the person stands therein who has been guilty of fornication, for three Sundays in the forenoon; and after sermon is called upon by name and surname, the beadle or kirkofficer bringing the offender, if refractory, forwards to his post; and then the preacher proceeds to admonition. Here too are set to publick view adulterers; only these are habited in a coarse canvas, analogous to a hairy or monastick vest, with a hood to it, which they call the sack or sackcloth, and that every Sunday throughout a year, or longer.

stork. A bird of passage famous for the regularity of its departure.

sto′ryteller. One who relates tales; an historian. In contempt.

In such a satire all would seek a share,
And every fool will fancy he is there;
Old *storytellers* too must pine and die,
To see their antiquated wit laid by;
Like her, who miss'd her name in a lampoon,
And griev'd to find herself decay'd so soon. Dryden.

stound. (1) Sorrow; grief; mishap. Out of use. The Scots retain it.

(2) Astonishment; amazement.

(3) Hour; time; season. Spenser.

stout. A cant name for strong beer.

stove. (1) A hot house; a place artificially made warm.

stra′ppado. Chastisement by blows.

stra′pping. Vast; large; bulky. Used of large men or women in contempt.

stre′perous. Loud; noisy.

strappado. Wrong. It is raising a man by the arms with a rope and then letting him fall the length of the rope.

stre'wment. Any thing scattered in decoration.

> Her death was doubtful.—For charitable prayers,
> Shards, flints, and pebbles should be thrown on her;
> Yet here she is allow'd her virgin chants,
> Her maiden *strewments,* and the bringing home
> Of bell and burial. Shakespeare, *Hamlet.*

strick. A bird of bad omen.

> The ill fac'd owl, death's dreadful messenger,
> The hoarse night-raven, trump of doleful drere,
> The leather-winged bat, day's enemy,
> The rueful *strick,* still waiting on the bier. *Fairy Queen.*

stri'dulous. Making a small noise.

strike. A bushel; a dry measure of capacity.

string. (9) To have two strings to the bow. To have two views or two expedients; to have double advantage, or double security.

stro'nghand. Force; violence.

> They wanting land wherewith to sustain their people, and the Tuscans having more than enough, it was their meaning to take what they needed by *stronghand.* Raleigh.

stro'ngwater. Distilled spirits.

to strout. To swell out; to puff out; to enlarge by affectation.

strude, or strode. A stock of breeding mares. Bailey.

to strut. (2) To swell; to protuberate.

> The goats with *strutting* dugs shall homeward speed. Dryden.

strut. An affectation of stateliness in the walk.

> Certain gentlemen of the gown, by smirking countenances and an ungainly *strut* in their walk, have got preferment. Swift.

stud. (1) A post; a stake. In some such meaning perhaps it is to be taken in the following passage, which I do not understand.

> A barn in the country, that hath one single *stud,* or one height of *studs* to the roof, is two shillings a foot. Mortimer.

to stum. To renew wine by mixing fresh wine and raising a new fermentation.

stu'mpy. Full of stumps; hard; stiff; strong. A bad word.

stupe. Cloath or flax dipped in warm medicaments, and applied to a hurt or sore.

stupra'tion. Rape; violation.

stu'rdy. (1) Hardy; stout; brutal; obstinate. It is always used of men with some disagreeable idea of coarseness or rudeness.

sturk. A young ox or heifer. Bailey.

sty. (2) Any place of bestial debauchery.

subderiso'rious. Scoffing or ridiculing with tenderness and delicacy.

> This *subderisorious* mirth is far from giving any offence to us: it is rather a pleasant condiment of our conversation. More.

subditi'tious. Put secretly in the place of something else.

su'bdolous. Cunning; subtle; sly.

subdu'ement. Conquest. A word not used, nor worthy to be used.

su'blapsary. Done after the fall of man.

subli'me. The grand or lofty stile. *The sublime* is a Gallicism, but now naturalized.

subme'rsion. The act of drowning; state of being drowned.

su'btly. (1) Slily; artfully; cunningly.

succi'nct. (1) Tucked or girded up; having the cloaths drawn up to disengage the legs.

> His vest *succinct* then girding round his waist,
> Forth rush'd the swain. Pope.

to succu'mb. To yield; to sink under any difficulty. Not in use, except among the Scotch.

succu'ssation. A trot.

> They move two legs of one side together, which is tolutation or ambling, or lift one foot before and the cross foot behind, which is *succussation* or trotting. Browne's *Vulgar Errours*.

su'cket. A sweet meat.

> Nature's confectioner, the bee,

Whose *suckets* are moist alchimy;
The still of his refining mold,
Minting the garden into gold. Cleveland.

su'ckingbottle. A bottle which to children supplies the want of a pap.

sudori'fick. Provoking or causing sweat.

suds. (1) A lixivium of soap and water.

(2) To be in the suds. A familiar phrase for being in any difficulty.

sug. Many have sticking on them *sugs*, or trout-lice, which is a kind of worm like a clove or pin, with a big head, and sticks close to him and sucks his moisture. Walton.

sugge'stion. Private hint; intimation; insinuation; secret notification.

to su'ggilate. To beat black and blue; to make livid by a bruise.

suit. (5) (*Suite*, French.) Retinue; company. Obsolete.

Plexirtus's ill-led life, and worse gotten honour, should have tumbled together to destruction, had there not come in Tydeus and Telenor, with fifty in their *suite* to his defence. Sidney.

su'llens. (Without singular.) Morose temper; gloominess of mind. A burlesque word.

su'mmer. (2) The principal beam of a floor.

Oak, and the like true hearty timber, may be better trusted in cross and transverse works for *summers*, or girders, or binding beams. Wotton.

to su'mmer. To keep warm.

Maids well *summer'd*, and warm kept, are like flies at Bartholomew-tide, blind, though they have their eyes. Shakespeare.

sun. (1) The luminary that makes the day.

to sup. To drink by mouthfuls; to drink by little at a time; to sip.

supersa'liency. The act of leaping upon any thing.

Their coition is by *supersaliency*, like that of horses. Browne.

superse'rviceable. Over officious; more than is necessary or required.

supersti′tion. (1) Unnecessary fear or scruples in religion; observance of unnecessary and uncommanded rites or practices; religion without morality.

(2) False religion; reverence of beings not proper objects of reverence; false worship.

(3) Over-nicety; exactness too scrupulous.

supi′ne. (1) Lying with the face upward.

(2) Leaning backwards with exposure to the sun.

(3) Negligent; careless; indolent; drousy; thoughtless; inattentive.

to suppla′nt. (1) To trip up the heels.

His legs entwining
Each other, till *supplanted* down he fell;
A monstrous serpent on his belly prone. Milton.

supple. (3) Flattering; fawning; bending.

There is something so *supple* and insinuating in this absurd unnatural doctrine, as makes it extremely agreeable to a prince's ear. Addison.

to surba′te. To bruise and batter the feet with travel; to harrass; to fatigue.

Their march they continued all that night, the horsemen often alighting, that the foot might ride, and others taking many of them behind them; however they could not but be extremely weary and *surbated*. Clarendon.

surd. (1) Deaf; wanting the sense of hearing.

(2) Unheard; not perceived by the ear.

(3) Not expressed by any term.

surpri′sal, surpri′se. (2) A dish, I suppose, which has nothing in it.

Few care for carving trifles in disguise,
Or that fantastick dish some call *surprise*. King's *Cookery*.

to su′scitate. To rouse; to excite.

susurra′tion. Whisper; soft murmur.

to swa′ddle. (2) To beat; to cudgel. A low ludicrous word.

Great on the bench, great in the saddle,
That could as well bind o'er as *swaddle*. Hudibras.

swa'ggy. Dependent by its weight.

> The beaver is called animal ventricosum, from his *swaggy* and prominent belly. Browne's *Vulgar Errours*.

to swale, to sweal. To waste or blaze away; to melt: as, *the candle* swales.

swa'llow. The throat; voracity.

> Had this man of merit and mortification been called to account for his ungodly *swallow*, in gorging down the estates of helpless widows and orphans, he would have told them that it was all for charitable uses. South.

swap. Hastily; with hasty violence; as, he did it *swap*. A low word.

to swap. To exchange. See *to swop*.

sward. (1) The skin of bacon.

to swash. To make a great clatter or noise: whence *swashbuckler*.

swe'arer. A wretch who obtests the great name wantonly and profanely.

swee'pstake. A man that wins all.

to swelt. To puff in sweat, if that be the meaning.

> Chearful blood in faintness chill did melt,
> Which like a fever fit through all his body *swelt*. *Fairy Queen*.

to swerve. (4) To climb on a narrow body.

> Ten wildings have I gather'd for my dear
> Upon the topmost branch, the tree was high,
> Yet nimbly up from bough to bough I *swerv'd*. Dryden.

to swig. To drink by large draughts.

to swill. (1) To drink luxuriously and grossly.

> The wretched, bloody, and usurping boar
> That spoil'd your summer fields and fruitful vines,
> *Swills* your warm blood like wash, and makes his trough
> In your embowel'd bosoms. Shakespeare's *Richard III*.

swi'mmingly. Smoothly; without obstruction. A low word.

> John got on the battlements, and called to Nick, I hope the cause goes on *swimmingly*. Arbuthnot.

to swinge. (1) To whip; to bastinade; to punish.

This very rev'rend letcher, quite worn out
With rheumatisms, and crippled with his gout,
Forgets what he in youthful times has done,
And *swinges* his own vices in his son. Dryden, jun.,
Juvenal.

(2) To move as a lash. Not in use.

He, wroth to see his kingdom fail,
Swinges the scaly horror of his folded tail. Milton.

swi'ngebuckler. A bully; a man who pretends to feats of arms.

swi'nging. Great; huge. A low word.

A good *swinging* sum of John's readiest cash went towards building of Hocus's countryhouse. Arbuthnot.

to swi'ngle. (1) To dangle; to wave hanging.

(2) To swing in pleasure.

swink. Labour; toil; drudgery. Obsolete.

swo'bber. (1) A sweeper of the deck.

(2) Four privileged cards that are only incidentally used in
betting at the game of whist.

to swop. To change; to exchange one thing for another. A low
word.

When I drove a thrust home, he put it by,
And cried, as in derision, spare the stripling;
Oh that insulting word! I would have *swopp'd*
Youth for old age, and all my life behind,
To have been then a momentary man.
Dryden's *Cleomenes.*

swo'rder. A cut-throat; a soldier. In contempt.

syb. Related by blood. The Scottish dialect still retains it.

If what my grandsire to me said be true,
Siker I am very *syb* to you. Spenser's *Pastorals.*

to sy'cophant. To play the sycophant. A low bad word.

sympo'siack. Relating to merry makings; happening where company is drinking together.

synthe'tick. Conjoining; compounding; forming composition.

T

ta'bby. A kind of waved silk.

ta'bid. Wasted by disease; consumptive.

ta'ble. (10) Draughts; small pieces of wood shifted on squares.

> Monsieur the nice,
> When he plays at *tables*, chides the dice. Shakespeare.

(11) To turn the tables. To change the condition or fortune of two contending parties: a metaphor taken from the vicissitude of fortune at gaming tables.

to ta'ble. To board; to live at the table of another.

> You will have no notion of delicacies if you *table* with them; they are all for rank and foul feeding. Felton.

ta'chygraphy. The art or practice of quick writing.

tack. (3) To hold tack. To last; to hold out. *Tack* is still retained in Scotland, and denotes hold or persevering cohesion.

> If this twig be made of wood
> That will hold *tack*, I'll make the fur
> Fly 'bout the ears of that old cur. *Hudibras*, p. i.

ta'ckle. (1) An arrow.

(2) Weapons; instruments of action.

> She to her *tackle* fell,
> And on the knight let fall a peal
> Of blows so fierce, and press'd so home
> That he retir'd. *Hudibras*, p. i.

ta′dpole. A young shapeless frog or toad, consisting only of a
body and a tail; a porwiggle.

tag. (1) A point of metal put to the end of a string.

(2) Any thing paltry and mean.

He invited *tag*, rag, and bob-tail, to the wedding.
L'Estrange.

to tag. (1) To fit any thing with an end: as, *to* tag *a lace.*

(2) To append one thing to another.

(3) The word is here improperly used.

Compell'd by you to *tag* in rhimes

The common slanders of the times. Swift.

(4) To join: this is properly *to tack.*

Resistance, and the succession of the house of Hanover,
the whig writers perpetually *tag* together. Swift's *Miscellanies.*

tail. (1) That which terminates the animal behind; the continuation of the vertebrae of the back hanging loose behind.

tale. (1) A narrative; a story. Commonly a slight or petty account of some trifling or fabulous incident: as, *a* tale *of a
tub.*

ta′lent. (3) Quality; nature. An improper and mistaken use.

It is the *talent* of human nature to run from one extreme
to another. Swift.

to ta′mper. (1) To be busy with physick.

He tried washes to bring him to a better complexion,
but there was no good to be done; the very *tampering*
cast him into a disease. L'Estrange's *Fables.*

tang. (2) Relish; taste. A low word.

(3) Something that leaves a sting or pain behind it.

She had a tongue with a *tang*,

Would cry to a sailor, go hang. Shakespeare, *Tempest.*

(4) Sound; tone: this is mistaken for *tone* or *twang.*

to tang. To ring with.

Be opposite with a kinsman, surly with thy servants; let
thy tongue *tang* arguments of state; put thyself into the
trick of singularity. Shakespeare, *Twelfth Night.*

---

tale. Johnson told Boswell that he thought *A Tale of a Tub* too brilliant
to have been written by Swift.

ta'ntling. One seized with hopes of pleasure unattainable.

tar. A sailor; a seaman in contempt.

to tar. (2) To teaze; to provoke.

> Two curs shall tame each other; pride alone
> Must *tar* the mastiffs on, as 'twere the bone. Shakespeare.

tara'ntula. An insect whose bite is only cured by musick.

ta'rdy. (4) Unwary. A low word.

> Yield, scoundrel base, quoth she, or die,
> Thy life is mine, and liberty:
> But if thou think'st I took thee *tardy*,
> And dar'st presume to be so hardy,
> To try thy fortune o'er a-fresh,
> I'll wave my title to thy flesh. *Hudibras*, p. i.

(5) Criminal; offending. A low word.

tarpa'wling. (2) A sailor in contempt.

> Was any thing wanting to the extravagance of this age, but the making a living *tarpawlin* and a swabber the hero of a tragedy. Dennis.

ta'rriance. Stay; delay; perhaps sojourn.

tatterdema'lion. (*Tatter* and *I know not what.*) A ragged fellow.

> As a poor fellow was trudging along in a bitter cold morning with never a rag, a spark that was warm clad called to this *tatterdemalion*, how he could endure this weather? L'Estrange.

ta'wdry. Meanly shewy; splendid without cost; fine without grace; shewy without elegance. It is used both of things and of persons wearing them.

tea. A Chinese plant, of which the infusion has lately been much drunk in Europe.

> The fear of being thought pedants hath taken many young divines off from their severer studies, which they have exchanged for plays, in order to qualify them for *tea* tables. Swift.

teague. A name of contempt used for an Irishman.

te'chy. Peevish; fretful; irritable; easily made angry; froward.

> When it did taste the wormwood on the nipple, and felt

it bitter, pretty fool, to see it *techy*, and fall out with the dug. Shakespeare's *Romeo and Juliet.*

to teem. (2) To pour. A low word, imagined by Skinner to come from *tommen*, Danish, *to draw out; to pour.* The Scots retain it: **as,** teem *that water out;* hence Swift took this word.

Teem out the remainder of the ale into the tankard, and fill the glass with small beer. Swift's *Directions to the Butler.*

teen. Sorrow; grief.

Eighty odd years of sorrow have I seen,
And each hour's joy wreck'd with a week of *teen.* Shakespeare.

to teen. To excite; to provoke to do a thing. Spenser.

to teh-he. (A cant word made from the sound.) To laugh with a loud and more insolent kind of cachinnation; to titter.

to tell. (2) To tell on. To inform of. A doubtful phrase.

David saved neither man nor woman alive, to bring tidings to Gath, saying, lest they should *tell on* us, saying, so did David. *I Samuel*, xxvii, 11.

temperame'ntal. Constitutional.

Intellectual representations are received with as unequal a fate upon a bare *temperamental* relish or disgust. Glanvill.

te'mpest. (1) The utmost violence of the wind; the names by which the wind is called according to the gradual encrease of its force seems to be, a breeze; a gale; a gust; a storm; a tempest.

te'mplar. (From the Temple, an house near the Thames, anciently belonging to the knights templars, originally from the temple of Jerusalem.) A student in the law.

to te'mporize. (3) To comply: this is improper.

The dauphin is too wilful opposite,
And will not *temporize* with my entreaties:
He flatly says, he'll not lay down his arms. Shakespeare.

temse bread, temsed bread. Bread made of flower better sifted than common.

te'mulent. Inebriated; intoxicated as with strong liquors.

te'nderling. (1) The first horns of a deer.

(2) A fondling; one who is made soft by too much kindness.

te'nement. Any thing held by a tenant.

> What reasonable man will not think that the *tenement*
> shall be made much better, if the tenant may be drawn
> to build himself some handsome habitation thereon, to
> ditch and inclose his ground? Spenser, *On Ireland.*

te'nter. (1) A hook on which things are stretched.

(2) To be on the tenters. To be on the stretch; to be in difficulties; to be in suspense.

> In all my past adventures,
> I ne'er was set so on the *tenters;*
> Or taken tardy with dilemma,
> That ev'ry way I turn does hem me. *Hudibras,* p. ii.

to te'rebrate. To bore; to perforate; to pierce.

te'rmagant. A scold; a brawling turbulent woman. It appears in Shakespeare to have been anciently used of men.

> She threw his periwig into the fire: well, said he, thou
> art a brave *termagant. Tatler,* No. 54.

terre'strial. (2) Consisting of earth; terreous. Improper.

> I did not confine these observations to land or *terrestrial*
> parts of the globe, but extended them to the fluids.
> Woodward.

terse. (1) Smooth.

(2) Cleanly written; neat; elegant without pompousness.

> These accomplishments in the pulpit appear by a quaint,
> *terse,* florid style, rounded into periods without propriety
> or meaning. Swift's *Miscellanies.*

te'ster. (1) A sixpence.

testudi'neous. Resembling the shell of a tortoise.

te'tchy. Froward; peevish: a corruption of *testy* or *touchy.*

te'trical, te'tricous. Froward; perverse; sour.

to te'wtaw. To beat; to break.

> The method and way of watering, pilling, breaking, and
> *tewtawing,* of hemp and flax, is a particular business.
> Mortimer.

te'xtman. A man ready in quotation of texts.

tharm. Intestines twisted for several uses.

thew. (1) Quality; manners; customs; habit of life; form of behaviour.

> From mother's pap I taken was unfit,
> And streight deliver'd to a fairy knight,
> To be upbrought in gentle *thewes* and martial might.
> *Fairy Queen*, b. i.

(2) In Shakespeare it seems to signify brawn, or bulk, from the Saxon *theow, the thigh*, or some such meaning.

> Will you tell me, master Shallow, how to chuse a man? Care I for the limbs, the *thewes*, the stature, bulk and big semblance of a man? give me the spirit, master Shallow. Shakespeare's *Henry IV*.

the'wed. Educated; habituated; accustomed.

thick. (4) Thick and threefold. In quick succession; in great numbers.

> They came *thick and threefold* for a time, till one experienced stager discovered the plot. L'Estrange's *Fables*.

thi'ckskin. A coarse gross man; a numskul.

thief. (2) An excrescence in the snuff of a candle.

> Their burning lamps the storm ensuing show,
> Th' oil sparkles, *thieves* about the snuff do grow. May.

to thole. To wait awhile. Ainsworth.

thoroughpa'ced. Perfect in what is undertaken; complete; thoroughsped. Generally in a bad sense.

thoroughsti'tch. Completely; fully. A low word.

to thou. To treat with familiarity.

> Taunt him with the licence of ink; if thou *thou'st* him some thrice, it shall not be amiss. Shakespeare.

thra'pple. The windpipe of any animal. They still retain it in the Scottish dialect.

thraso'nical. Boastful; bragging.

> His humour is lofty, his discourse peremptory, his general behaviour vain, ridiculous, and *thrasonical*. Shakespeare.

thrave. (1) A herd; a drove. Out of use.

(2) The number of two dozen.

to threap. A country word denoting to argue much or contend. Ainsworth.

thre'epenny. Vulgar; mean.

to thrid. To slide through a narrow passage.

thrift. (1) Profit; gain; riches gotten; state of prospering.

> He came out with all his clowns, horst upon such cart jades, and so furnished, as I thought with myself if that were *thrift*, I wisht none of my friends or subjects ever to thrive. Sidney, b. ii.

thro'atpipe. The weason; the windpipe.

thu'nder. (1) *Thunder* is a most bright flame rising on a sudden, moving with great violence, and with a very rapid velocity, through the air, according to any determination, upwards from the earth, horizontally, obliquely, downwards, in a right line, or in several right lines, as it were in serpentine tracts, joined at various angles, and commonly ending with a loud noise or rattling. Muschenbroek.

(2) In popular and poetick language *thunder* is commonly the noise, and *lightning* the flash; though *thunder* is sometimes taken for both.

thu'nderbolt. (1) Lightning; the arrows of heaven.

thu'nderstone. A stone fabulously supposed to be emitted by thunder; thunderbolt.

to thu'nderstrike. To blast or hurt with lightning.

thurifica'tion. The act of fuming with incense; the act of burning incense.

> The several acts of worship which were required to be performed to images are processions, genuflections, *thurifications*, deosculations, and oblations. Stillingfleet.

tick. (1) Score; trust.

> You would see him in the kitchen weighing the beef and butter, paying ready money, that the maids might not run a *tick* at the market. Arbuthnot's *History of John Bull*.

(2) The louse of dogs or sheep.

ti'ckle. (I know not whence to deduce the sense of this word.) Tottering; unfixed; unstable; easily overthrown.

> Thy head stands so *tickle* on thy shoulders, that a milkmaid, if she be in love, may sigh it off. Shakespeare.

tid. Tender; soft; nice.

to ti'ddle, to ti'dder. To use tenderly; to fondle.

ti'dewaiter. An officer who watches the landing of goods at the customhouse.

ti'dy. (1) Seasonable.

> If weather be faire and *tidie*, thy grain
> Make speedilie carriage, for feare of a raine. Tusser.

(3) It seems to be here put by mistake for *untidy*.

> Thou whorson *tidy* Bartholomew boar pig, when wilt thou leave fighting. Shakespeare, *Henry IV*.

tiff. (A low word, I suppose without etymology.) (1) Liquor; drink.

> I, whom griping penury surrounds,
> And hunger, sure attendant upon want,
> With scanty offals, and small acid *tiff*,
> Wretched repast! my meagre corps sustain. Philips.

(2) A fit of peevishness or sullenness; a pet.

ti'ger. A fierce beast of the leonine kind.

tight. (2) Free from fluttering rags; less than neat.

> Drest her again genteel and neat,
> And rather *tight* than great. Swift.

ti'ghter. A ribband or string by which women straiten their cloaths.

tike. (1) The louse of dogs or sheep. See *tick*.

(2) It is in Shakespeare the name of a dog, in which sense it is used in Scotland.

> Avaunt, you curs!
> Hound or spaniel, brache or hym,
> Or bobtail *tike*, or trundle tail. Shakespeare, *King Lear*.

ti'llyfally, ti'llyvalley. A word used formerly when any thing said was rejected as trifling or impertinent.

> *Tillyfally*, sir John, never tell me; your ancient swaggerer comes not in my doors. Shakespeare, *Henry IV*, p. ii.

tilt. (1) A tent; any covering over head.

> The roof of linnen
> Intended for a shelter!
> But the rain made an ass
> Of *tilt* and canvas,
> And the snow which you know is a melter. Denham.

(2) The cover of a boat.

to ti'mber. To light on a tree. A cant word.

> The one took up in a thicket of brush-wood, and the other *timbered* upon a tree hard by. L'Estrange's *Fables*.

ti'mbersow. A worm in wood.

> Divers creatures, though they be somewhat loathsome to take, are of this kind; as earth worms, *timbersows*, snails. Bacon's *Natural History*, No. 692.

ti'meless. (1) Unseasonable; done at an improper time.

(2) Untimely; immature; done before the proper time.

> Noble Gloster's death,
> Who wrought it with the king, and who perform'd
> The bloody office of his *timeless* end. Shakespeare, *Richard II*.

ti'mepleaser. One who complies with prevailing notions whatever they be.

tin. (1) One of the primitive metals called by the chemists jupiter.

to tind. To kindle; to set on fire.

tine. (2) Trouble; distress.

> The root whereof, and tragical effect,
> Vouchsafe, O thou the mournful'st muse of nine,
>   That wont'st the tragick stage for to direct,
> In funeral complaints and wailful *tine*.
> Spenser's *Muipotmos*.

to tine. (1) To kindle; to light; to set on fire.

(2) To shut.

to ti'ngle. (1) To feel a sound, or the continuance of a sound, in the ears. This is perhaps rather *tinkle*.

> When our ear *tingleth*, we usually say that somebody is talking of us; which is an ancient conceit. Browne.

(2) To feel a sharp quick pain with a sensation of motion.

> The pale boy senator yet *tingling* stands. Pope.

(3) To feel either pain or pleasure with a sensation of motion.

> They suck pollution through their *tingling* veins. Tickell.

to tink. To make a sharp shrill noise.

to ti'nkle. (2) It seems to have been improperly used by Pope.

The wand'ring streams that shine between the hills,
The grots that echo to the *tinkling* rills. Pope.
(3) To hear a low quick noise.

With deeper brown the grove was overspread,
A sudden horrour seiz'd his giddy head,
And his ears *tinkled*, and the colour fled. Dryden.

ti'ny. Little; small; puny. A burlesque word.

When that I was a little *tiny* boy,
A foolish thing was but a toy. Shakespeare, *Twelfth Night*.

to ti'pple. To drink luxuriously; to waste life over the cup.

ti'pple. Drink; liquor.

ti'ppled. Tipsy; drunk.

ti'ppler. A sottish drunkard; an idle drunken fellow.

ti'sick. (Corrupted from *phthisick*.) Consumption; morbid waste.

ti'ssue. Cloth interwoven with gold or silver.

tit. (1) A small horse: generally in contempt.

Thou might'st have ta'en example
From what thou read'st in story;
  Being as worthy to sit
  On an ambling *tit*,
As thy predecessor Dory. Denham.

(2) A woman: in contempt.

What does this envious *tit*, but away to her father with a tale. L'Estrange.

(3) A *titmouse* or *tomtit*. A bird.

ti'tter. (2) I know not what it signifies in Tusser.

From wheat go and rake out the *titters* or tine,
If eare be not forth, it will rise again fine. Tusser.

ti'ttletattle. Idle talk; prattle; empty gabble.

tituba'tion. The act of stumbling.

toad. An animal resembling a frog; but the frog leaps, the toad crawls: the toad is accounted venomous, I believe truly.

In the great plague there were seen, in divers ditches about London, many *toads* that had tails three inches

---

titter. (2) "Some kind of weed found in cornfields," *O.E.D.*

long, whereas *toads* usually have no tails. Bacon's *Natural History.*

to′adstone. A concretion supposed to be found in the head of a toad.

tod. (1) A bush; a thick shrub.

(2) A certain weight of wool, twenty eight pounds.

to′gcd. Gowned; dressed in gowns.

to toil. (2) To weary; to overlabour.

Then, *toil'd* with works of war, retir'd himself
To Italy. Shakespeare's *Richard II.*

toil. (2) Any net or snare woven or meshed.

A fly falls into the *toil* of a spider. L'Estrange.

to tole. (This seems to be some barbarous provincial word.) To train; to draw by degrees.

Whatever you observe him to be more frighted at than he should, *tole* him on to by insensible degrees, till at last he masters the difficulty. Locke.

to′llbooth. A prison.

to′lsey. The same with *tolbooth.*

to′mboy. A mean fellow; sometimes a wild coarse girl.

to′nguepad. A great talker.

She who was a celebrated wit at London is, in that dull part of the world, called a *tonguepad. Tatler.*

too. (1) Over and above; overmuch; more than enough. It is used to augment the signification of an adjective or adverb to a vicious degree.

to toot. To pry; to peep; to search narrowly and slily. It is still used in the provinces, otherwise obsolete.

I cast to go a shooting,
Long wand'ring up and down the land,
With bow and bolts on either hand,
For birds and bushes *tooting.* Spenser's *Pastorals.*

tooth. (8) In spite of the teeth. Notwithstanding threats expressed by shewing teeth; notwithstanding any power of injury or defence.

to top. (6) To perform eminently: as, *he* tops *his part.* This word, in this sense, is seldom used but on light or ludicrous occasions.

to′pman. The sawer at the top.

> The pit-saw enters the one end of the stuff, the *topman*
> at the top, and the pitman under him, the *topman* ob-
> serving to guide the saw exactly in the line. Moxon's
> *Mechanical Exercises.*

to′pping. Fine; noble; gallant. A low word.

> The *topping* fellow I take to be the ancestor of the fine
> fellow. *Tatler.*

tore. (Of this word I cannot guess the meaning.)

> Proportion according to rowen or *tore* upon the ground;
> the more *tore* the less hay will do. Mortimer's *Hus-
> bandry.*

torpe′do. A fish which while alive, if touched even with a long
stick, benumbs the hand that so touches it, but when dead
is eaten safely.

to′rpent. Benumbed; struck motionless; not active; incapable
of motion.

to′rtoise. (1) An animal covered with a hard shell: there are
tortoises both of land and water.

(2) A form into which the ancient soldiers used to throw
their troops, by bending down and holding their bucklers
above their heads so that no darts could hurt them.

to′ry. (A cant term, derived, I suppose, from an Irish word
signifying a savage.) One who adheres to the antient constitution of the state, and the apostolical hierarchy of the
church of England, opposed to a whig.

> The knight is more a *tory* in the country than the town,
> because it more advances his interest. Addison.

touch. (18) A cant word for a slight essay.

> Print my preface in such a form as, in the booksellers
> phrase, will make a sixpenny *touch.* Swift.

to′uchy. Peevish; irritable; irascible; apt to take fire. A low
word.

to touse. To pull; to tear; to haul; to drag: whence *touser* or
towzer, the name of a mastiff.

---

tore. "Long coarse grass remaining in the field in winter or spring,"
O.E.D.

Take him hence; to th' rack with him: we'll *towze* you
Joint by joint, but we will know his purpose. Shakespeare.

to'wer. (3) A high head-dress.

Lay trains of amorous intrigues
In *towers*, and curls, and perriwigs. *Hudibras,* p. iii.

town. (3) In England, any number of houses to which belongs a regular market, and which is not a city or see of a
bishop.

(4) The court end of London.

A virgin whom her mother's care
Drags from the *town* to wholesome country air. Pope.

(5) The people who live in the capital.

(6) It is used by the inhabitants of every town or city: as
we say, *a new family is come to* town.

toy. (6) Odd story; silly tale.

I never may believe
These antick fables, nor these fairy *toys.* Shakespeare.

(7) Frolick; humour; odd fancy.

Shall that which hath always received this construction,
be now disguised with a *toy* of novelty. Hooker, b. v.

tra'desman. A shopkeeper. A merchant is called a *trader,* but
not a tradesman; and it seems distinguished in Shakespeare
from a man that labours with his hands.

I live by the awl, I meddle with no *tradesmen's* matters.
Shakespeare.

to tradu'ce. (2) To propagate; to encrease by deriving one
from another.

From these only the race of perfect animals were propagated and *traduced* over the earth. Hale.

trainba'nds. The militia; the part of a community trained to
martial exercise.

traino'il. Oil drawn by coction from the fat of the whale.

tra'iny. Belonging to train oil. A bad word.

Here steams ascend,
Where the huge hogsheads sweat with *trainy* oil. Gay.

to traipse. (A low word, I believe, without any etymology.)

To walk in a careless or sluttish manner.

Two slip-shod muses *traipse* along,

In lofty madness, meditating song. Pope.

trait. A stroke; a touch. Scarce English.

By this single *trait* Homer marks an essential difference between the Iliad and Odyssey; that in the former the people perished by the folly of their kings; in this by their own folly. Broome's Notes on the *Odyssey*.

traje′ct. A ferry; a passage for a water-carriage.

What notes and garments he doth give thee,

Bring to the *traject*, to the common ferry,

Which trades to Venice. Shakespeare, *Merchant of Venice*.

tra′ngram. (A cant word.) An odd intricately contrived thing.

What's the meaning of all these *trangrams* and gim-cracks? what are you going about, jumping over my master's hedges, and running your lines cross his grounds? Arbuthnot.

to transla′te. (6) To explain. A low colloquial use.

There's matter in these sighs, these profound heaves You must *translate;* 'tis fit we understand them. Shakespeare.

to transpi′re. (2) To escape from secrecy to notice: a sense lately innovated from France, without necessity.

transubstantia′tion. A miraculous operation believed in the Romish church, in which the elements of the eucharist are supposed to be changed into the real body and blood of Christ.

to trape. To run idly and sluttishly about. It is used only of women.

trapes. An idle slatternly woman.

He found the sullen *trapes*

Possest with th' devil, worms, and claps. *Hudibras*, p. iii.

trash. (2) A worthless person.

(3) Matter improper for food, frequently eaten by girls in the green sickness.

(4) I believe that the original signification of *trash* is the loppings of trees, from the verb.

to trash. (1) To lop; to crop.

(2) To crush; to humble.

to tra'vail. To harrass; to tire.

> As if all these troubles had not been sufficient to *travail* the realm, a great division fell among the nobility. Hayward.

to tra'vel. (4) To labour; to toil. This should be rather *travail.*

> I've watch'd and *travell'd* hard;
> Some time I shall sleep out; the rest I'll whistle. Shakespeare.

tra'veltainted. Harrassed; fatigued with travel.

tra'verse. (2) Something that thwarts, crosses, or obstructs; cross accident; thwarting obstacle. This is a sense rather French than English.

> He sees no defect in himself, but is satisfied that he should have carried on his designs well enough, had it not been for unlucky *traverses* not in his power. Locke.

tra'vesty. Dressed so as to be made ridiculous; burlesqued.

tra'ytrip. A kind of play, I know not of what kind.

> Shall I play my freedom at *traytrip,* and become thy bond slave. Shakespeare's *Twelfth Night.*

tre'acle. (1) A medicine made up of many ingredients.

(2) Molosses; the spume of sugar.

tre'adle. (2) The sperm of the cock.

> At each end of the egg is a *treadle,* formerly thought to be the cock's sperm. Derham.

tre'atable. Moderate; not violent.

> The heats or the colds of seasons are less *treatable* than with us. Temple.

tree. (1) A large vegetable rising, with one woody stem, to a considerable height.

treme'ndous. Dreadful; horrible; astonishingly terrible.

tre'ncherfly. One that haunts tables; a parasite.

> He found all people came to him promiscuously, and he tried which of them were friends, and which only *trencherflies* and spungers. L'Estrange.

---

traytrip. "A game at dice, or with dice, in which success probably depended on the casting of a trey or three." *O.E.D.*

tre′nchermate. A table companion; a parasite.

tre′ndle. Any thing turned round. Now improperly written *trundle*.

trepa′n. (2) A snare; a stratagem by which any one is ensnared. (Of this signification Skinner assigns for the reason, that some English ships in queen Elizabeth's reign being invited, with great shew of friendship, into Trapani, a part of Sicily, were there detained.)

tre′things. Taxes; imposts.

tri′cksy. Pretty. This is a word of endearment.

> All this service have I done since I went.
> —My *tricksy* spirit! Shakespeare's *Tempest*.

to trim. To balance; to fluctuate between two parties.

> If such by *trimming* and time-serving, which are but two words for the same thing, betray the church by nauseating her pious orders, this will produce confusion. South's *Sermons*.

trim. Dress; geer; ornaments.

> The goodly London in her gallant *trim*,
> The phoenix daughter of the vanquish'd old,
> Like a rich bride does to the ocean swim,
> And on her shadow rides in floating gold. Dryden.

tri′mmer. One who changes sides to balance parties; a turn-coat.

trio′bolar. Vile; mean; worthless.

> Turn your libel into verse, and then it may pass current amongst the balladmongers for a *triobolar* ballad. Cheynell.[*]

tripe. (1) The intestines; the guts.

(2) It is used in ludicrous language for the human belly.

tripu′diary. Performed by dancing.

> Claudius Pulcher underwent the like success when he continued the *tripudiary* augurations. Browne's *Vulgar Errours*.

tri′stful. Sad; melancholy; gloomy; sorrowful. A bad word.

tri′vial. (1) Vile; worthless; vulgar; such as may be picked up in the highway.

---

[*] An error for Dr. Jasper Mayne (*O.E.D.*).

Be subjects great, and worth a poet's voice,
For men of sense despise a *trivial* choice. Roscommon.
(2) Light; trifling; unimportant; inconsiderable. This use is
more frequent, though less just.

to troll. (1) To roll; to run round.

How pleasant on the banks of Styx,
To *troll* it in a coach and six. Swift.

tro'lmydames. (Of this word I know not the meaning.)

A fellow I have known to go about with *trolmydames:*
I knew him once a servant of the prince. Shakespeare,
Winter's Tale.

trot. (2) An old woman. In contempt. I know not whence derived.

Give him gold enough, and marry him to an old *trot*
with ne'er a tooth in her head: why, nothing comes
amiss, so money comes withal. Shakespeare, *Taming of
the Shrew.*

to tro'uble. (9) (In low language.) To sue for a debt.

tro'uble-state. Disturber of a community; publick makebate.

to troul. (1) To move volubly.

(2) To utter volubly.

to trounce. To punish by an indictment or information.

trout. (2) A familiar phrase for an honest, or perhaps for a
silly fellow.

Here comes the *trout* that must be caught with tickling.
Shakespeare.

to trow. To think; to imagine; to conceive. A word now disused, and rarely used in ancient writers but in familiar language.

trow. An exclamation of enquiry.

Well, if you be not turn'd Turk, there is no more sailing
by the star.
—What means the fool, *trow?* Shakespeare.

tru'btail. A short squat woman. Ainsworth.

to truck. To give in exchange; to exchange.

Go, miser! go; for lucre sell thy soul,

---

trolmydames. "A game played by ladies, resembling bagatelle," *O.E.D.*,
under *troll-madam.*

>   *Truck* wares for wares, and trudge from pole to pole;
>   That men may say, when thou art dead and gone,
>   See, what a vast estate he left his son. Dryden.

to tru'ckle. To be in a state of subjection or inferiority; to yield;
to creep.

>   His zeal was not to lash our crimes,
>   But discontent against the times:
>   For had we made him timely offers,
>   To raise his post or fill his coffers:
>   Perhaps he might have *truckled* down,
>   Like other brethren of his gown. Swift.

tru'culent. (1) Savage; barbarous.

(2) Terrible of aspect.

(3) Destructive; cruel.

>   Pestilential seminaries, according to their grossness or
>   subtilty, cause more or less *truculent* plagues, some of
>   such malignity, that they enecate in two hours.
>   Harvey, *On the Plague.*

truebre'd. Of a right breed.

>   Bauble do you call him? he's a substantial *truebred*
>   beast, bravely forehanded. Dryden's *Don Sebastian.*

truepe'nny. A familiar phrase for an honest fellow.

trull. (1) A low whore; a vagrant strumpet.

>   So Maevius, when he drain'd his skull,
>   To celebrate some suburb *trull;*
>   His similies in order set,
>   And ev'ry crambo he cou'd get;
>   Before he could his poem close,
>   The lovely nymph had lost her nose. Swift.

(2) It seems to have had first at least a neutral sense: a
girl; a lass; a wench.

>   Among the rest of all the route
>   A passing proper lasse,
>   A white-hair'd *trull*, of twenty years,
>   Or neere about there was:
>   In stature passing all the rest,
>   A gallant girl for hewe;
>   To be compar'd with townish nymphs,
>   So fair she was to viewe. Turberville.

trump. (3) To put to or upon the trumps. To put to the last
    expedient.

        We are now put *upon* our last *trump;* the fox is earth'd,
        but I shall send my two terriers in after him. Dryden.

tru'mpery. (1) Something fallaciously splendid; something of
    less value than it seems.

tr'umpet-tongued. Having tongues vociferous as a trumpet.

trunk-hose. Large breeches formerly worn.

        The short *trunk-hose* shall show thy foot and knee
        Licentious, and to common eye-sight free;
        And with a bolder stride, and looser air,
        Mingl'd with men, a man thou must appear. Prior.

tub. (2) A state of salivation. I know not well why so called.

tuck. (1) A long narrow sword.

        If he by chance escape your venom'd *tuck,*
        Our purpose may hold there. Shakespeare, *Hamlet.*

    (2) A kind of net.

        The *tuck* is narrower meashed, and therefore scarce law-
    ful with a long bunt in the midst. Carew.

tu'cker. A small piece of linen that shades the breast of women.

to tuft. To adorn with a tuft; a doubtful word, not authorised
    by any competent writer.

                Sit beneath the shade
        Of solemn oaks, that *tuft* the swelling mounts,
        Thrown graceful round. Thomson.

tu'fty. Adorned with tufts. A word of no authority.

        Let me strip thee of thy *tufty* coat,
        Spread thy ambrosial stores. Thomson's *Summer.*

tu'mbrel. A dungcart.

        My corps is in a *tumbril* laid, among
        The filth and ordure, and inclos'd with dung;
        That cart arrest, and raise a common cry,
        For sacred hunger of my gold I die. Dryden.

tu'mour. (2) Affected pomp; false magnificence; puffy gran-
    deur; swelling mien; unsubstantial greatness.

        His stile was rich of phrase, but seldom in bold meta-
    phors; and so far from the *tumour,* that it rather wants
    a little elevation. Wotton.

to tump. Among gardeners, to fence trees about with earth.

tun. (2) A pipe; the measure of two hogsheads.

(3) Any large quantity proverbially.

> I have ever follow'd thee with hate,
> Drawn *tuns* of blood out of thy country's breast. Shakespeare.

(4) A drunkard. In burlesque.

(7) Dryden has used it for a perimetrical measure, I believe without precedent or propriety.

> A *tun* about was every pillar there;
> A polish'd mirrour shone not half so clear. Dryden.

tu'nnel. (2) A funnel; a pipe by which liquor is poured into vessels.

> For the help of the hearing, make an instrument like a *tunnel*, the narrow part of the bigness of the hole of the ear, and the broader end much larger. Bacon.

to tu'nnel. (2) To catch in a net.

(3) This word is used by Derham for to make net-work; to reticulate.

> Some birds not only weave the fibrous parts of vegetables, and curiously *tunnel* them into nests, but artificially suspend them on the twigs of trees. Derham.

tup. A ram. This word is yet used in Staffordshire, and in other provinces.

to tup. To but like a ram.

t'urcism. The religion of the Turks.

> Methinks I am at Mecca, and hear a piece of *turcism* preached to me by one of Mahomet's priests. Dr. Mayne.

tu'rkey. A large domestick fowl brought from Turkey.

tu'rkois. A blue stone numbered among the meaner precious stones, now discovered to be a bone impregnated with cupreous particles.

tu'rmoil. Trouble; disturbance; harrassing uneasiness; tumultuous molestation. Little in use.

turn. (11) A step off the ladder at the gallows.

> They, by their skill in palmistry,
> Will quickly read his destiny;
> And make him glad to read his lesson,
> Or take a *turn* for it at the session. Butler.

turnpi′ke. (1) A cross of two bars armed with pikes at the end, and turning on a pin, fixed to hinder horses from entering.

(2) Any gate by which the way is obstructed.

tu′rnsick. Vertiginous; giddy.

> If a man see another turn swiftly and long; or if he look upon wheels that turn, himself waxeth *turnsick*. Bacon.

tu′rnspit. He that anciently turned a spit, instead of which jacks are now generally used.

> I give you joy of the report
> That he's to have a place at court;
> Yes, and a place he will grow rich in,
> A *turnspit* in the royal kitchen. Swift's *Miscellanies*.

tu′rtle. It is used among sailors and gluttons for a tortoise.

to tu′tor. (2) To treat with superiority or severity.

> I hardly yet have learn'd
> T' insinuate, flatter, bow, and bend my knee:
> Give sorrow leave a while to *tutor* me
> To this submission. Shakespeare, *Richard II*.

tuz. (I know not whether it is not a word merely of cant.) A lock or tuft of hair.

> With odorous oil thy head and hair are sleek;
> And then thou kemp'st the *tuzzes* on thy cheek;
> Of these thy barbers take a costly care. Dryden.

twain. Two. An old word, not now used but ludicrously.

twang. A word making a quick action, accompanied with a sharp sound. Little used, and little deserving to be used.

> There's one, the best in all my quiver,
> *Twang!* thro' his very heart and liver. Prior.

twa′ngling. Contemptibly noisy.

> She did call me rascal, fidler,
> And *twangling* jack, with twenty such vile terms. Shakespeare.

to twa′ttle. To prate; to gabble; to chatter.

tweague, tweak. Perplexity; ludicrous distress. A low word.

---

turtle. A curious example of Johnson's conservatism: the better classes would speak of "tortoise steak or soup;" vulgarians like sailors or gluttons would talk of "turtle soup".

to twidle. (This is commonly written *tweedle*.) To touch
lightly. A low word.

twi'ster. One who twists; a ropemaker. To this word I have
annexed some remarkable lines, which explain twist in all
its senses.

> When a *twister* a-twisting will twist him a twist,
> For the twisting of his twist, he three twines doth in-
>   twist;
> But if one of the twines of the twist do untwist,
> The twine that untwisteth untwisteth the twist.
> Untwirling the twine that untwisteth between,
> He twirls with his *twister* the two in a twine;
> Then twice having twisted the twines of the twine,
> He twitcheth the twine he had twined in twain.
> The twain that in twining before in the twine,
> As twins were intwisted, he now doth untwine,
> 'Twixt the twain intertwisting a twine more between,
> He, twirling his *twister,* makes a twist of the twine.
> Wallis.

to twi'tter. (2) To be suddenly moved with any inclination.
A low word.

> A widow which had a *twittering* toward a second hus-
> band, took a gossipping companion to manage the jobb.
> L'Estrange.

twittletwa'ttle. Tattle; gabble. A vile word.

> Insipid *twittletwatles,* frothy jests, and jingling wit-
> ticisms, inure us to a misunderstanding of things.
> L'Estrange.

two'handed. Large; bulky; enormous of magnitude.

> If little, then she's life and soul all o'er;
> An Amazon, the large *twohanded* whore. Dryden.

u

u'mbles. A deer's entrails.

un. A Saxon privative or negative particle answering to *in* of the Latins, and *a* of the Greeks, *on*, Dutch. It is placed almost at will before adjectives and adverbs. All the instances of this kind of composition cannot therefore be inserted; but I have collected a number sufficient, perhaps more than sufficient, to explain it.

unane'led. Without the bell rung. This sense I doubt.

> Thus was I, sleeping, by a brother's hand
> Cut off ev'n in the blossoms of my sin,
> Unhousel'd, unanointed, *unanel'd*. Shakespeare, *Hamlet*.

unassu'red. (2) Not to be trusted.

> The doubts and dangers, the delays and woes;
> The feigned friends, the *unassured* foes,
> Do make a lover's life a wretch's hell. Spenser.

unba'cked. (1) Not tamed; not taught to bear the rider.

> A well wayed horse will safely convey thee to thy journey's end, when an *unbacked* filly may give thee a fall. Suckling.

unba'thed. Not wet.

to unbege't. To deprive of existence.

> Wishes each minute he could *unbeget*
> Those rebel sons, who dare t' usurp his seat. Dryden.

---

un. We have omitted several hundred definitions and examples of words beginning with *un*. Johnson collected more than enough.

[431]

unblen′ched. Not disgraced; not injured by any soil.

> There, where every desolation dwells,
> She may pass on with *unblench′d* majesty:
> Be it not done in pride, or in presumption. Milton.

unco′meatable. Inaccessible; unattainable. A low, corrupt word.

unconco′cted. Not digested; not matured.

> We swallow cherry-stones, but void them *unconcocted.* Browne's *Vulgar Errours.*

unco′nscionable. (3) Enormous; vast. A low word.

> His giantship is gone somewhat crest-fall′n,
> Stalking with less *unconscionable* strides,
> And lower looks, but in a sultry chafe. Milton's *Agonistes.*

uncontro′ulable. (2) Indisputable; irrefragable.

> This makes appear the error of those, who think it an *uncontroulable* maxim, that power is always safer lodged in many hands, than in one; those many are as capable of enslaving as a single person. Swift.

unco′uth. Odd; strange; unusual.

underfe′llow. A mean man; a sorry wretch.

> They carried him to a house of a principal officer, who with no more civility, though with much more business than those *underfellows* had shewed, in captious manner put interrogatories unto him. Sidney.

underso′ng. Chorus; burthen of a song.

understra′pper. A petty fellow; an inferior agent.

> Every *understrapper* perk′d up, and expected a regiment, or his son must be a major. Swift.

to unhe′le. To uncover; to expose to view. Spenser.

unhi′debound. Lax of maw; capacious.

> Though plenteous, all too little seems
> To stuff this maw, this vast, *unhidebound* corps. Milton.

unhou′selled. Having not the sacrament.

u′nicorn. (1) A beast, whether real or fabulous, that has only one horn.

(2) A bird.

> Of the *unicorn* bird, the principal marks are these;

headed and footed like the dunghill cock, tailed like a
goose, horned on his forehead, with some likeness, as
the unicorn is pictured; spur'd on his wings, bigger than
a swan. Grew.

u'nion. (3) A pearl. Not in use.

The king shall drink to Hamlet's better breath;
And in the cup an *union* shall he throw,
Richer than that which four successive kings
In Denmark's crown have worn. Shakespeare, *Hamlet.*

unke'mpt. Not combed. Obsolete.

to unke'nnel. (1) To drive from his hole.

(2) To rouse from its secrecy, or retreat.

If his occult guilt
Do not itself *unkennel* in one speech,
It is a damned ghost that we have seen. Shakespeare.

unke'nt. Unknown. Obsolete.

Go, little book, thyself present,
As child whose parent is *unkent,*
To him, that is the president
Of nobleness and chivalrie. Spenser.

unki'ndly. (1) Unnatural; contrary to nature.

They, with their filthiness,
Polluted this same gentle soil long time,
That their own mother loath'd their beastliness,
And 'gan abhor her brood's *unkindly* crime,
All were they born of her own native slime. *Fairy
Queen.*

to unkno'w. To cease to know.

It's already known;
Oh! can you keep it from yourselves, *unknow* it? Smith.

unli'cked. Shapeless; not formed: from the opinion that the
bear licks her young to shape.

Shape my legs of an unequal size,
To disproportion me in every part,
Like to a chaos, or *unlick'd* bear-whelp. Shakespeare.

unlu'cky. (3) Slightly mischievous; mischievously waggish.

A lad, th' *unluckiest* of his crew,
Was still contriving something bad, but new. King.

unobno′xious. Not liable; not exposed to any hurt.

> In fight they stood
> Unwearied, *unobnoxious* to be pain′d. Milton's *Paradise Lost.*

to unpa′y. To undo. A low ludicrous word.

> Pay her the debt you owe her, and *unpay* the villainy you have done her: the one you may do with sterling money, and the other with current repentance. Shakespeare.

to unphilo′sophize. To degrade from the character of a philosopher. A word made by Pope.

unpla′usive. Not approving.

> 'Tis like he'll question me,
> Why such *unplausive* eyes are bent on him. Shakespeare.

unpreve′nted. (2) Not preceded by any thing.

> Thy grace
> Comes *unprevented*, unimplor'd, unsought. Milton.

to unprovi′de. To divest of resolution or qualifications.

> I'll not expostulate with her, lest
> Her beauty *unprovide* my mind again. Shakespeare, *Othello.*

unque′stionable. (2) Such as cannot bear to be questioned without impatience; this seems to be the meaning here.

> What were his marks? —
> — A lean cheek, which you have not; an *unquestionable* spirit, which you have not. Shakespeare.

to unra′vel. (2) To disorder; to throw out of the present constitution.

> So prophane and sceptical an age, takes a pride in *unravelling* all the received principles of reason and religion. Tillotson.

unre′ady. (3) Awkward; ungain.

> Young men, in the conduct of actions, use extreme remedies at first, and, that which doubleth all errors, will not acknowledge or retract them; like an *unready* horse, that will neither stop nor turn. Bacon.

unrecu′ring. Irremediable.

[434]

I found her straying in the park,
Seeking to hide herself; as doth the deer,
That hath received some *unrecuring* wound. Shakespeare.

unsha'keable. Not subject to concussion. Not in use.

to unsho'ut. To annihilate, or retract a shout.
Unshout the noise that banish'd Marcius;
Repeal him, with the welcome of his mother. Shakespeare.

unsi'fted. (2) Not tried.
Affection! puh! you speak like a green girl,
Unsifted in such perilous circumstance. Shakespeare.

unsi'ght. Not seeing. A low word, used only with *unseen*, as in the example following. Probably formed by corruption of *unsighted*.
They'll say our business to reform
The church and state is but a worm;
For to subscribe, *unsight*, unseen,
To an unknown church discipline. *Hudibras.*

unsophi'sticated. Not adulterated.

to unspe'ak. To retract; to recant.
I put myself to thy direction, and
Unspeak mine own detraction; here abjure
The taints and blames I laid upon myself. Shakespeare.

unspe'd. Not dispatched; not performed.
Venutus withdraws,
Unsped the service of the common cause. Garth.

unsta'id. Not cool; not prudent; not settled into discretion; not steady; mutable.
Wo to that land,
Which gasps beneath a child's *unstaid* command.
Sandys.

unthri'ft. An extravagant; a prodigal.
The curious *unthrift* makes his cloaths too wide,
And spares himself, but would his taylor chide. Herbert.

unthri'fty. (2) Not easily made to thrive or fatten. A low word.
Grains given to a hide-bound or *unthrifty* horse, recover him. Mortimer's *Husbandry.*

to untre′ad. To tread back; to go back in the same steps.

unwa′yed. Not used to travel; not seasoned in the road.

> Beasts, that have been rid of their legs, are as much for a man's use, as colts that are *unwayed,* and will not go at all. Suckling.

unwee′ting. Ignorant; unknowing.

unwri′ting. Not assuming the character of an author.

> The peace of the honest *unwriting* subject was daily molested. Arbuthnot.

upho′lder. (3) An undertaker; one who provides for funerals.

> Where the brass knocker wrapt in flannel band,
> Forbids the thunder of the footman's hand;
> Th' *upholder,* rueful harbinger of death,
> Waits with impatience for the dying breath. Gay.

upho′lsterer. One who furnishes houses; one who fits up apartments with beds and furniture.

u′ppish. Proud; arrogant. A low word.

u′pspring. This word seems to signify upstart; a man suddenly exalted.

u′pstart. One suddenly raised to wealth, power, or honour; what suddenly rises and appears.

> Mushrooms have two strange properties; the one, that they yield so delicious a meat; the other, that they come up so hastily, even in a night, and yet they are unsown: and therefore such as are *upstarts* in state, they call in reproach mushrooms. Bacon's *Natural History.*

u′rchin. (1) A hedge-hog.

> (2) A name of slight anger to a child.

ure. Practice; use; habit. Obsolete.

> He would keep his hand in *ure* with somewhat of greater value, till he was brought to justice. L'Estrange.

u′rinal. A bottle, in which water is kept for inspection.

> This hand, when glory calls,
> Can brandish arms, as well as *urinals.* Garth.

urina′tor. A diver; one who searches under water.

> The precious things that grow there, as pearl, may be much more easily fetched up by the help of this, than

by any other way of the *urinators*. Wilkins's *Mathematicall Magick*.

u'rine. Animal water.

Drink, Sir, is a great provoker of nose-painting, sleep, and *urine*. Shakespeare.

to u'rine. To make water.

Places where men *urine* commonly, have some smell of violets. Bacon's *Natural History*.

u'sager. One who has the use of any thing in trust for another.

u'sance. (1) Use; proper employment.

(2) Usury; interest paid for money.

He lends out money gratis, and brings down
The rate of *usance*. Shakespeare, *Merchant of Venice*.

usqueba'ugh. (An Irish and Erse word, which signifies the water of life.) It is a compounded distilled spirit, being drawn on aromaticks; and the Irish sort is particularly distinguished for its pleasant and mild flavour. The Highland sort is somewhat hotter; and, by corruption, in Scottish they call it *whisky*.

u'stion. The act of burning; the state of being burned.

u'tis. A word which probably is corrupted, at least, is not now understood.

Then here will be old *utis*: it will be an excellent stratagem. Shakespeare's *Henry IV*.

to u'tter. (3) To sell; to vend.

They bring it home, and *utter* it commonly by the name of Newfoundland fish. Abbot's *Description of the World*.

u'tterer. (3) A seller; a vender.

---

utis. "A period of festivity," *O.E.D.*

V

to va'cate. (3) To defeat; to put an end to.

> He *vacates* my revenge;
> For while he trusts me, 'twere so base a part
> To fawn, and yet betray. Dryden.

va'ccary. A cow-house; a cow-pasture. Bailey.

vacilla'tion. The act or state of reeling or staggering.

> The muscles keep the body upright, and prevent its falling, by readily assisting against every *vacillation*. Derham.

to vade. To vanish; to pass away. Spenser. A word useful in poetry, but not received.

vague. (1) Wandering; vagrant; vagabond.

> Gray encouraged his men to set upon the *vague* villains, good neither to live peaceably, nor to fight. Hayward.

vail. (3) Money given to servants. It is commonly used in the plural. See *vale*.

to vail. To yield; to give place; to shew respect by yielding. In this sense, the modern writers have ignorantly written *veil*.

> Thy convenience must *veil* to thy neighbour's necessity; and thy very necessities must yield to thy neighbour's extremity. South.

vale. (2) Money given to servants.

> Since our knights and senators account

To what their sordid, begging *vails* amount;
Judge what a wretched share the poor attends,
Whose whole subsistence on those alms depends.
Dryden.

va'llancy. A large wig that shades the face.

But you, loud Sirs, who through your curls look big,
Criticks in plume and white *vallancy* wig. Dryden.

to vamp. To piece an old thing with some new part.

I had never much hopes of your *vampt* play. Swift.

va'ncourier. A harbinger; a precursor.

va'porer. A boaster; a braggart.

This shews these *vaporers*, to what scorn they expose
themselves. *Government of the Tongue.*

va'porish. Vaporous; splenetick; humoursome.

va'porous. (2) Windy; flatulent.

If the mother eat much beans, or such *vaporous* food,
it endangereth the child to become lunatick. Bacon.

va'pour. (5) (In the plural.) Diseases caused by flatulence,
or by diseased nerves; hypochondriacal maladies; melancholy; spleen.

to va'pour. (2) To bully; to brag.

va'rlet. (1) Anciently a servant or footman.

to va'rnish. (3) To palliate; to hide with colour of rhetorick.

Speak the plain truth, and *varnish* not your crimes!
Philips.

vasta'tion. Waste; depopulation.

vasti'dity. Wideness; immensity. A barbarous word.

Perpetual durance,
Through all the world's *vastidity*. Shakespeare.

va'ticide. A murderer of poets.

The caitiff *vaticide* conceiv'd a prayer. Pope's *Dunciad.*

va'udevil. A song common among the vulgar, and sung about
the streets. Trevoux. A ballad; a trivial strain.

va'ulty. Arched; concave. A bad word.

I will kiss thy detestable bones,
And put my eye-balls in thy *vaulty* brows,
And ring these fingers with thy houshold worms. Shake-
speare.

to vaunt. (2) I scarcely know in what sense Dryden has used this word, unless it be miswritten for *vaults*.

> 'Tis he: I feel him now in ev'ry part;
> Like a new world he *vaunts* about my heart. Dryden.

ve′getable. Any thing that has growth without sensation, as plants.

vege′te. Vigorous; active; spritely.

> The faculties in age must be less *vegete* and nimble than in youth. Wallis.

to ve′llicate. To twitch; to pluck; to act by stimulation.

vendita′tion. Boastful display.

> Some, by a cunning protestation against all reading, and *venditation* of their own naturals, think to divert the sagacity of their readers from themselves, and cool the scent of their own fox-like thefts; when yet they are so rank as a man may find whole pages together usurped from one author. B. Jonson.

ve′ney. A bout; a turn.

> I bruis'd my shin with playing at sword and dagger, three *veneys* for a dish of stewed prunes. Shakespeare.

ve′ngeance. (2) It is used in familiar language. *To do with a vengeance, is to do with vehemence; what a vengeance,* emphatically what?

ventri′loquist. One who speaks in such a manner as that the sound seems to issue from his belly.

ve′rdant. Green. This word is so lately naturalized, that Skinner could find it only in a dictionary.

> Each odorous bushy shrub
> Fenc'd up the *verdant* wall. Milton.

verge. (1) A rod, or something in form of a rod, carried as an emblem of authority. The mace of a dean.

ve′rjuice. Acid liquor expressed from crab-apples. It is vulgarly pronounced *varges*.

> Hang a dog upon a crab-tree, and he'll never love *verjuice*. L'Estrange.

vermice′lli. A paste rolled and broken in the form of worms.

> With oysters, eggs, and *vermicelli,*
> She let him almost burst his belly. Prior.

verna′cular. Native; of one's own country.

> London weekly bills number deep in consumptions; the same likewise proving inseparable accidents to most other diseases; which instances do evidently bring a consumption under the notion of a *vernacular* disease to England. Harvey.

ve′rsion. (1) Change; transformation.

> Springs, the antients thought to be made by the *version* of air into water. Bacon's *Natural History*.

(2) Change of direction.

(3) Translation.

vice. (3) The fool, or punchinello of old shows.

> I'll be with you again
> In a trice, like to the old *vice*,
>   Your need to sustain;
> Who with dagger of lath, in his rage and his wrath,
>   Cries, ah, ha! to the devil. Shakespeare.

(5) Gripe; grasp.

> If I but fist him once; if he come but within my *vice*. Shakespeare.

vi′cety. Nicety; exactness. A word not used.

vidu′ity. Widowhood.

to vinde′miate. To gather the vintage.

> Now *vindemiate*, and take your bees towards the expiration of this month. Evelyn.

vira′go. (1) A female warriour; a woman with the qualities of a man.

(2) It is commonly used in detestation for an impudent turbulent woman.

to vi′rgin. (A cant word.) To play the virgin.

vi′rginal. (More usually *virginals*.) A musical instrument so called, because commonly used by young ladies.

to vi′rginal. To pat; to strike as on the virginal. A cant word.

> Still *virginalling* upon thy palm. Shakespeare.

vi′rtual. Having the efficacy without the sensible or material part.

virtuo′so. A man skilled in antique or natural curiosities; a man studious of painting, statuary, or architecture.

vi'sion. (4) A dream; something shewn in a dream. A dream
happens to a sleeping, a vision may happen to a waking
man. A dream is supposed natural, a vision miraculous; but
they are confounded.

vitupera'tion. Blame; censure.

viva'cious. (1) Long-lived.

viz. (This word is *videlicet,* written with a contraction.) To
wit; that is. A barbarous form of an unnecessary word.

> That which so oft by sundry writers
> Has been apply'd t' almost all fighters,
> More justly may b' ascrib'd to this,
> Than any other warrior, *viz.*
> None ever acted both parts bolder,
> Both of a chieftain and a soldier. *Hudibras.*

vo'ider. A basket, in which broken meat is carried from the
table.

> A *voider* for the nonce,
> I wrong the devil should I pick their bones. Cleveland.

vo'lant. (1) Flying; passing through the air.

> The *volant,* or flying automata, are such mechanical
> contrivances as have a self-motion, whereby they are
> carried aloft in the air, like birds. Wilkins's *Mathemati-*
> *call Magick.*

(2) Nimble; active.

vole. A deal at cards, that draws the whole tricks.

> Past six, and not a living soul!
> I might by this have won a *vole.* Swift.

vo'lery. A flight of birds.

volubi'lity. (1) The act or power of rolling.

> *Volubility,* or aptness to roll, is the property of a bowl,
> and is derived from its roundness. Watts's *Logick.*

vo'lume. (1) Something rolled, or convolved.

(2) As much as seems convolved at once; as a fold of a serpent, a wave of water.

> Behind the gen'ral mends his weary pace,

---

volant. (1) Johnson was interested in aviation before there were aviators.
There is a flying machine in his *Rasselas,* and in the last year of his
life he contributed to the expenses of a balloon ascent.

And silently to his revenge he sails:
    So glides some trodden serpent on the grass,
And long behind his wounded *volume* trails. Dryden.
(3) A book; so called, because books were antiently rolled
upon a staff.

to voluntee'r. To go for a soldier. A cant word.

vo'wel. A letter which can be uttered by itself.

vowfe'llow. One bound by the same vow.

vu'lture. A large bird of prey remarkable for voracity.

W

to wa'bble. (A low, barbarous word.) To shake; to move from side to side.

waft. (1) A floating body.

(2) Motion of a streamer. Used as a token or mean of information at sea.

waid. Crushed.

His horse *waid* in the back, and shoulder shotten. Shakespeare.

waif. Goods found, but claim'd by no body; that of which every one waves the claim. Commonly written *weif*. Ainsworth.

wake. (1) The feast of the dedication of the church, formerly kept by watching all night.

The droiling peasant scarce thinks there is any world beyond his village, nor gaiety beyond that of a *wake*. *Government of the Tongue.*

(2) Vigils; state of forbearing sleep.

to walk. (7) To be in motion. Applied to a clamorous or abusive female tongue; and is still in low language retain'd.

As she went, her tongue did *walk*

In foul reproach, and terms of vile despight;

Provoking him by her outragious talk. Spenser.

wall. (3) To take the wall. To take the upper place; not to give place.

When once the poet's honour ceases,

From reason far his transports rove:
    And Boileau, for eight hundred pieces,
Makes Louis *take the wall* of Jove. Prior.

wa'llet. (1) A bag, in which the necessaries of a traveller are put; a knapsack.

(2) Any thing protuberant and swagging.
    Who would believe, that there were mountaineers
    Dew-lapt like bulls, whose throats had hanging at them
    Wallets of flesh. Shakespeare.

walle'yed. Having white eyes.

to wa'llop. To boil.

wa'ltron. The morse, or *waltron*, is called the sea-horse. Woodward.

to wa'mble. To roll with nausea and sickness. It is used of the stomach.
    A covetous man deliberated betwixt the qualms of a *wambling* stomach, and an unsettled mind. L'Estrange.

wa'ntwit. A fool; an idiot.

wa'ped. Dejected; crushed by misery.
    This makes the *waped* widow wed again. Shakespeare.

war'ling. This word is I believe only found in the following adage, and seems to mean, one often quarrelled with.
    Better be an old man's darling than a young man's *warling*. Camden's *Remains*.

wa'rlock, wa'rluck. (*Vardlookr*, Islandick, a charm; *werlog*, Saxon, an evil spirit. This etymology was communicated by Mr. Wise.) A male witch; a wizzard.

to warp. (3) It is used by Shakespeare to express the effect of frost.
    Freeze, freeze, thou bitter sky,
    Thou do'st not bite so nigh
        As benefits forgot:
    Though thou the waters *warp*,
    Thy sting is not so sharp

---

warlock. A rare example of Johnson's naming a correspondent who helped him in the *Dictionary*. Perhaps not many did. The Rev. Francis Wise was Radclivian Librarian and Keeper of the Archives at Oxford. He also helped get Johnson an honorary M.A. in time to have the degree on the title-page of the *Dictionary*.

As friends remember'd not. Shakespeare, *As You Like It*.

to warra'y. To make war upon.

Six years were run since first in martial guise
The Christian lords *warraid* the eastren land. Fairfax.

wa'rren. A kind of park for rabits.

The coney convenes a whole *warren*, tells her story, and advises upon a revenge. L'Estrange.

wash. (6) The feed of hogs gathered from washed dishes.

wasp. A brisk stinging insect, in form resembling a bee.

wa'ssail. (1) A liquour made of apples, sugar, and ale, anciently much used by English goodfellows.
(2) A drunken bout.

wa'tching. Inability to sleep.

to wa'ter. (3) The mouth *waters*. The man longs; there is a vehement desire. From dogs who drop their slaver when they see meat which they cannot get.

wa'termelon. A plant. It hath trailing branches, as the cucumber or melon, and is distinguished from other cucurbitaceous plants, by its leaf deeply cut and jagged, and by its producing uneatable fruit. Miller.

to wawl. To cry; to howl.

The first time that we smell the air,
We *wawle* and cry. Shakespeare's *King Lear*.

wea'nel, wea'nling. (1) An animal newly weaned.
(2) A child newly weaned.

wea'ponsalve. A salve which was supposed to cure the wound, being applied to the weapon that made it.

wea'sel. A small animal that eats corn and kills mice.

we'sand. The windpipe; the passage through which the breath is drawn and emitted.

weatherspy'. A star-gazer; an astrologer; one that foretels the weather.

And sooner may a gulling *weatherspy*,
By drawing forth heav'n's scheme tell certainly,

---

wesand. This word is out of alphabet because Johnson originally used *weasand*, as do two of his examples. But while correcting proof, he changed his mind, and forgot to put the word in its proper order.

What fashion'd hats or ruffs, or suits next year,
Our giddy-headed antick youth will wear. Donne.

wee. Little; small: whence the word *weasle* or *weesel* is used for little; as a *weesel* face. In Scotland it denotes small or little; as *wee* ane, a little one, or child; a *wee* bit, a little bit.

weel. (1) A whirlpool.

(2) A twiggen snare or trap for fish, (perhaps from willow.)

we'erish. This old word is used by Ascham in a sense which the lexicographers seem not to have known. Applied to tastes, it means insipid; applied to the body, weak and washy: here it seems to mean sour; surly.

A voice not soft, weak, piping, womanish; but audible, strong, and manlike: a countenance not *weerish* and crabbed, but fair and comely. Ascham's *Schoolmaster.*

weft. (1) That of which the claim is generally waved; any thing wandering without an owner, and seized by the lord of the manour.

(2) It is in Bacon for *waft*, a gentle blast.

The smell of violets exceedeth in sweetness that of spices, and the strongest sort of smells are best in a *weft* afar off. Bacon.

to weld. To beat one mass into another, so as to incorporate them.

we'lder. A term perhaps merely Irish; though it may be derived from *to wield*, to *turn* or *manage:* whence *wielder*, welder.

Such immediate tenants have others under them, and so a third and fourth in subordination, 'till it comes to the *welder*, as they call him, who sits at a rack-rent, and lives miserably. Swift.

we'lked. Wrinkled; wreathed.

Methought his eyes
Were two full moons: he had a thousand noses,
Horns *welk'd* and wav'd like the enridged sea. Shakespeare.

we'lkin. (1) The visible regions of the air. Out of use, except in poetry.

(2) Welkin eye, is, I suppose, blue eye; skycoloured eye.
>   Yet were it true
>   To say this boy were like me! Come, sir page,
>   Look on me with your *welkin eye*, sweet villain. Shakespeare.

to we'lter. (1) To roll in water or mire.

(2) To roll voluntarily; to wallow.

>   If a man inglut himself with vanity, or *welter* in filthiness like a swine, all learning, all goodness is soon forgotten. Ascham.

wemm. A spot; a scar.

we'nnel. An animal newly taken from the dam.

>   Pinch never thy *wennels* of water or meat,
>   If ever ye hope for to have them good neat. Tusser.

whale. The largest of fish; the largest of the animals that inhabit this globe.

wha'ly. Marked in streaks.

>   A bearded goat, whose rugged hair,
>   And *whaly* eyes, the sign of jealousy,
>   Was like the person's self, whom he did bear. *Fairy Queen.*

to whee'dle. To entice by soft words; to flatter; to persuade by kind words.

>   He that first brought the word sham, or *wheedle*, in use, put together as he thought fit, ideas he made it stand for. Locke.

to whe'rret. (1) To hurry; to trouble; to teaze. A low colloquial word.

(2) To give a box on the ear. Ainsworth.

whey. (1) The thin or serous part of milk, from which the oleose or grumous part is separated.

(2) It is used of any thing white and thin.

>   Those linnen cheeks of thine
>   Are counsellors to fear. What, soldiers *whey* face!
>   Shakespeare.

to whi'ffle. To move inconstantly, as if driven by a puff of wind.

whi'ffler. (1) One that blows strongly.

(2) One of no consequence; one moved with a whiff or puff.

> Every *whiffler* in a laced coat, who frequents the chocolate-house, shall talk of the constitution. Swift.

whig. (1) Whey.

(2) The name of a faction.

> The southwest counties of Scotland have seldom corn enough to serve them round the year; and the northern parts producing more than they need, those in the west come in the summer to buy at Leith the stores that come from the north; and from a word, whiggam, used in driving their horses, all that drove were called the whiggamors, and shorter the *whiggs*. Now in that year before the news came down of duke Hamilton's defeat, the ministers animated their people to rise and march to Edinburgh; and they came up marching on the head of their parishes with an unheard-of fury, praying and preaching all the way as they came. The marquis of Argyle and his party came and headed them, they being about six thousand. This was called the whiggamor's inroad; and ever after that, all that opposed the court came in contempt to be called *whigs*: and from Scotland the word was brought into England, where it is now one of our unhappy terms of disunion. Burnet.

> Whoever has a true value for church and state, should avoid the extremes of *whig* for the sake of the former, and the extremes of tory on the account of the latter. Swift.

to while. To loiter.

> Men guilty this way never have observed that the *whiling* time, the gathering together, and waiting a little before dinner, is the most aukwardly passed away of any. *Spectator*.

whi′nyard. A sword, in contempt.

whi′pster. A nimble fellow.

whi′rlbat. Any thing moved rapidly round to give a blow. It is frequently used by the poets for the ancient cestus.

At *whirlbat* he had slain many, and was now himself
slain by Pollux. L'Estrange.

whist. A game at cards, requiring close attention and silence.

whi'stle. (3) The mouth; the organ of whistling.

Let's drink the other cup to wet our *whistles,* and so
sing away all sad thoughts. Walton's *Angler.*

whi'temcat. Food made of milk.

whi'tewash. A wash to make the skin seem fair.

The clergy, during Cromwell's usurpation, were very
much taken up in reforming the female world; I have
heard a whole sermon against a *whitewash.* Addison.

whi'tleather. Leather dressed with alum, remarkable for tough-
ness.

Nor do I care much, if her pretty snout

Meet with her furrow'd chin, and both together

Hem in her lips, as dry as good *whitleather.* Suckling.

whi'tsul. A provincial word.

Their meat was *whitsul,* as they call it, namely, milk,
sour milk, cheese, curds, butter. Carew.

whi'ttle. (1) A white dress for a woman. Not in use.

(2) A knife.

to whi'ttle. To cut with a knife; to edge; to sharpen. Not in use.

who'reson. A bastard. It is generally used in a ludicrous dislike.

to whurr. To pronounce the letter *r* with too much force.

whyno't. A cant word for violent or peremptory procedure.

Capoch'd your rabbins of the synod,

And snap'd their canons with a *whynot. Hudibras.*

wi'cked. (2) It is a word of ludicrous or slight blame.

That same *wicked* bastard of Venus, that blind rascally
boy, that abuses every one's eyes because his own are
out, let him be judge how deep I am in love. Shakespeare.

width. Breadth; wideness. A low word.

wife. (2) It is used for a woman of low employment.

Strawberry *wives* lay two or three great strawberries at
the mouth of their pot, and all the rest are little ones.
Bacon.

wildgo'osechase. A pursuit of something as unlikely to be
caught as the wildgoose.

Let a man consider the time, money, and vexation, that this *wildgoosechace* has cost him, and then say what have I gotten to answer all this expence, but loose, giddy frolick? L'Estrange.

wi'llow. A tree worn by forlorn lovers.

to wince. To kick as impatient of a rider, or of pain.

> The angry beast did straight resent
> The wrong done to his fundament,
> Began to kick, and fling, and *wince*,
> As if h' had been beside his sense. *Hudibras*.

to winch. To kick with impatience; to shrink from any uneasiness.

wind. (9) Down the wind. To decay.

> A man that had a great veneration for an image in his house, found that the more he prayed to it to prosper him in the world, the more he went *down the wind* still. L'Estrange.

wi'ndegg. An egg not impregnated; an egg that does not contain the principles of life.

wi'ndward. Towards the wind.

to wipe. (5) To cheat; to defraud.

> The next bordering lords commonly incroach one upon another, as one is stronger, or lie still in wait to *wipe* them out of their lands. Spenser, *On Ireland*.

wipe. (2) A blow; a stroke; a jeer; a gybe; a sarcasm.

> To statesmen would you give a *wipe*,
> You print it in Italick type:
> When letters are in vulgar shapes,
> 'Tis ten to one the wit escapes;
> But when in capitals exprest,
> The dullest reader smoaks the jest. Swift.

wisea'cre. (1) A wise, or sententious man. Obsolete.

(2) A fool; a dunce.

wi'stful. (1) Attentive; earnest; full of thought.

(2) It is used by Swift, as it seems, for *wishful*.

> Lifting up one of my sashes, I cast many a *wistful* melancholy look towards the sea. *Gulliver's Travels*.

wi'stly. Attentively; earnestly.

> Speaking it, he *wistly* look'd on me;

As who shall say,—I would thou wert the man. Shakespeare.

wit. (2) Imagination; quickness of fancy.

witch. (2) A winding sinuous bank.

wi'tcracker. A joker; one who breaks a jest.

to wite. To blame; to reproach.

> The palmer 'gan most bitterly
> Her to rebuke, for being loose and light;
> Which not abiding, but more scornfully
> Scoffing at him, that did her justly *wite*,
> She turn'd her boat about. *Fairy Queen*, c. xii.

wi'tness. (3) With a witness. Effectually; to a great degree, so as to leave some lasting mark or testimony behind. A low phrase.

> Now gall is bitter *with a witness;*
> And love is all delight and sweetness. Prior.

witsna'pper. One who affects repartee.

> Go in, sirrah; bid them prepare for dinner.—
> —That is done, sir; they have all stomachs.—
> —What a *witsnapper* are you! Shakespeare.

wi'tticism. A mean attempt at wit.

> We have a libertine fooling even in his last agonies, with a *witticism* between his teeth, without any regard to sobriety and conscience. L'Estrange.

wi'ttol. A man who knows the falsehood of his wife and seems contented; a tame cuckold.

wi'tworm. One that feeds on wit; a canker of wit.

wo'lf. (1) A kind of wild dog that devours sheep.

(2) An eating ulcer.

wont. Custom; habit; use. Out of use.

> 'Tis not his *wont* to be the hindmost man,
> Whate'er occasion keeps him from us now. Shakespeare.

wood. Mad; furious; raging. Obsolete.

> Winds do rage, as winds were *wood*,
> And cause spring tides to raise great flood. Tusser.

woo'dcock. A bird of passage with a long bill; his food is not known. It is a word ludicrously used for a dunce.

woo'dlouse. An insect.

The millepes or *woodlouse* is a small insect of an oblong figure, about half an inch in length, and a fifth of an inch in breadth; of a dark blueish or livid grey colour, and having its back convex or rounded: notwithstanding the appellation of millepes, it has only fourteen pair of short legs; it is a very swift runner, but it can occasionally roll itself up into the form of a ball, which it frequently does, and suffers itself to be taken. They are found in great plenty under old logs of wood or large stones, or between the bark and wood of decayed trees. Millepedes are aperient, attenuant, and detergent; and the best way of taking them is swallowing them alive, which is easily and conveniently done; and they are immediately destroyed on falling into the stomach. Hill's *Materia Medica*.

to word. To dispute.

He that descends not to *word* it with a shrew, does worse than beat her. L'Estrange.

world. (16) For all the world. Exactly. A ludicrous sense; now little used.

worm. (1) A small harmless serpent that lives in the earth.

(2) A poisonous serpent.

to worm. (1) To drive by slow and secret means.

(2) To deprive a dog of something, nobody knows what, under his tongue, which is said to prevent him, nobody knows why, from running mad.

wo'rnil. In the backs of cows in the summer, are maggots generated, which in Essex we call *wornils,* being first only a small knot in the skin. Derham's *Physico-Theology*.

worth. To be. This word is only now retained in *wo worth*, or *wurth; wo* be

Wo *worth* the man

That first did teach the cursed steel to bite
In his own flesh, and make way to the living sp'rit.
Fairy Queen.

would. (8) It has the signification of I wish, or I pray; this, I believe, is improper; and formed by a gradual corruption of the phrase, *would God;* which originally imputed, *that*

God would, might God will, might God decree; from this phrase ill understood came, *would to God;* thence, *I would to God:* And thence *I would,* or elliptically, *would* come to signify, *I wish:* and so it is used even in good authours, but ought not to be imitated.

> Wise men will do it without a law; I *would* there might be a law to restrain fools. Bacon's *Advice to Villiers.*

wou'lding. Motion of desire; disposition to any thing; propension; inclination; incipient purpose.

> It will be every man's interest to join good performances to spiritual purposes, to subdue the exorbitancies of the flesh, as well as to continue the *wouldings* of the spirit. Hammond.

wou'ndy. Excessive. A low bad word.

> These stockings of Susan's cost a *woundy* deal of pains the pulling on. Gay.

wri'tative. A word of Pope's coining; not to be imitated.

> Increase of years makes men more talkative, but less *writative;* to that degree, that I now write no letters but of plain how d'ye's. Pope to Swift.

to wri'thle. To wrinkle; to corrugate.

> Her *writhled* skin, as rough as maple rind,
> So scabby was, that would have loathed all womankind. Spenser.

X Is a letter, which, though found in Saxon words, begins no
word in the English language.

Y

yare. Ready; dextrous; eager.

> I do desire to learn, Sir; and I hope, if you have occasion
> to use me for your turn, you shall find me *yare*. Shake-
> speare.

to yean. To bring young. Used of sheep.

> The skilful shepherd peel'd me certain wands;
> He struck them up before the fulsome ewes,
> Who, then conceiving, did in *yeaning* time
> Fole party-colour'd lambs. Shakespeare.

yea′nling. The young of sheep.

to yearn. To grieve; to vex.

> She laments for it, that it would
> *Yern* your heart to see it. Shakespeare.

yest. (1) The foam, spume, or flower of beer in fermentation;
barm.

(2) The spume on a troubled sea.

yelk. The yellow part of the egg. It is commonly pronounced,
and often written *yolk*.

ye′llowboy. A gold coin. A very low word.

> John did not starve the cause; there wanted not *yellow-
> boys* to fee council. Arbuthnot's *John Bull*.

to yerk. To throw out or move with a spring.

---

yest. Out of alphabetical order because Johnson changed his mind about
the spelling, as he had with *wesand*.

Their wounded steeds
Fret fetlock deep in gore, and with wild rage
Yerk out their armed heels at their dead masters. Shakespeare.

yond. Mad; furious: perhaps transported with rage; under alienation of mind, in which sense it concurs with the rest.

Then like a lion, which hath long time sought
His robbed whelps, and at the last them found
Amongst the shepherd swains, then waxeth wood and
yond;
So fierce he laid about him. *Fairy Queen.*

you'ngster, you'nker. A young person. In contempt.

youth. (1) The part of life succeeding to childhood and adolescence; the time from fourteen to twenty eight.

you'thy. Young; youthful. A bad word.

The scribler had not genius to turn my age, as indeed
I am an old maid, into raillery, for affecting a *youthier*
turn than is consistent with my time of day. *Spectator.*

yux. The hiccough.

Z

Z is found in the Saxon alphabets, set down by grammarians, but is read in no word originally Teutonick: its sound is uniformly that of an hard *s*.

za'ffar, za'ffir. *n.s.* Powder the calx of cobalt, very fine, and mix it with three times its weight of powdered flints, this being wetted with common water, the whole concretes into a solid mass called *zaffre*, which from its hardness has been mistaken for a native mineral. Hill, *On Fossils*.

> Cobalt being sublimed, the flowers are of a blue colour; these, German mineralists call *zaffir*. Woodward.

> The artificers in glass tinge their glass blue with that dark mineral *zaphara*. Boyle, *On Colours*.

za'ny. *n.s.* (Probably of *zanei*.) The contraction of Giovanni or sanna, a scoff, according to Skinner. One employed to raise laughter by his gestures, actions and speeches; a merry Andrew; a buffoon.

> Some carrytale, some pleaseman, some slight *zany*,
> Some mumblenews, some trencher knight, some Dick,
> Told our intents before. Shakespeare.

> Then write that I may follow, and so be
> Thy echo, thy debtor, thy foil, thy *zany*,
> I shall be thought, if mine like thine I shape,
> All the world's lion, though I be thy ape. Donne.

> Oh, great restorer of the good old stage,
> Preacher at once, and *zany* of thy age. Pope's *Dunciad*.

za'rnich. *n.s.* *Zarnich* is a solid substance in which orpiment is frequently found; and it approaches to the nature of orpiment, but without its lustre and foliated texture. The common kinds of *zarnich* are green and yellow; and to this we owe the distinction of orpiment into these colours, though there is no such substance as green orpiment. *Zarnich* contains a large quantity of arsenick in it. Hill's *Materia Medica*.

zeal. *n.s.* (ζῆλος, *zelus,* Latin.) Passionate ardour for any person or cause.

> This present age, wherein *zeal* hath drowned charity and skill; meekness will not now suffer any man to marvel, whatsoever he shall hear reproved by whomsoever. Hooker.

> If I had had time to have made new liveries, I would have bestowed the thousand pound I borrowed of you: but it is no matter, this poor show doth better; this doth infer the *zeal* I had to see him. Shakespeare's *Henry IV*.

> O Cromwell, Cromwell!
> Had I but serv'd my God with half the *zeal*
> I serv'd my king, he would not in mine age
> Have left me naked to mine enemies. Shakespeare.

> Among the seraphims
> Abdiel, than whom none with more *zeal* ador'd
> The Deity, and divine commands obey'd,
> Stood up, and in a flame of *zeal* severe,
> The current of his fury thus oppos'd. Milton's *Paradise Lost*.

> *Zeal*, the blind conductor of the will. Dryden.

> She with such a *zeal* the cause embrac'd,
> As women, where they will, are all in haste;
> The father, mother, and the kin beside,
> Were overborne by the fury of the tide. Dryden.

> The princes applaud with a furious joy,
> And the king seiz'd a flambeau with *zeal* to destroy. Dryden.

> Seriousness and *zeal* in religion is natural to the English. Tillotson's *Sermons*.

Good men often blemish the reputation of their piety by over-acting some things in their religion; by an indiscreet *zeal* about things wherein religion is not concerned. Tillotson.

True *zeal* seems not to be any one single affection of the soul; but rather a strong mixture of many holy affections; rather a gracious constitution of the whole mind, than any one particular grace, swaying a devout heart, and filling it with all pious intentions; all not only uncounterfeit, but most fervent. Sprat's *Sermons.*

When the sins of a nation have provoked God to forsake it, he suffers those to concur in the most pernicious counsels for enslaving conscience, who pretend to the greatest *zeal* for the liberty of it. Stillingfleet.

This rebellion has discovered to his majesty, who have espoused his interests with *zeal* or indifference. Addison's *Freeholder.*

A scorn of flattery and a *zeal* for truth. Pope.

zea′lot. *n.s.* (*zeloteur*, French; ζηλωτης.) One passionately ardent in any cause. Generally used in dispraise.

The fury of *zealots*, intestine bitterness and division were the greatest occasion of the last fatal destruction of Jerusalem. King Charles.

Are not those men too often the greatest *zealots* who are most notoriously ignorant? true zeal should always begin with true knowledge, and thence proceed to an unwearied passion, for what it once knows to be worthy of such passion. Sprat.

No wonder that so many of these deluded *zealots* have been engaged in a cause which they at first abhorred, and have wished or acted for the success of an enterprize, that might have ended in the extirpation of the protestant religion. Addison.

zea′lous. *adj.* (from *zeal.*) Ardently passionate in any cause.

Our hearts are right with God, and our intentions pious, if we act our temporal affairs with a desire no greater than our necessity, and in actions of religion we be *zealous,* active, and operative, so far as prudence will permit. Taylor.

This day, at height of noon, came to my sphere,
A spirit, *zealous,* as he seem'd to know
More of the Almighty's works. Milton's *Paradise Lost.*

We should be not only devout towards God, but *zealous* towards men; endeavouring by all prudent means to recover them out of those snares of the devil, whereby they are taken captive. *Decay of Piety.*

It is not at all good to be *zealous* against any person, but only against their crimes. It is better to be *zealous* for things than for persons: but then it should be only for good things; a rule that does certainly exclude all manner of zeal for ill things, all manner of zeal for little things. Sprat's *Sermons.*

Being instructed only in the general, and *zealous* in the main design; and as finite beings, not admitted into the secrets of government, the last resorts of providence, or capable of discovering the final purposes of God, they must be sometimes ignorant of the means conducing to those ends in which alone they can oppose each other. Dryden.

zea′lously. *adv.* (from *zealous.*) With passionate ardour.
Thy care is fixt, and *zealously* attends,
To fill thy odorous lamp with deeds of light,
And hope that reaps not shame. Milton.

To enter into a party as into an order of friars, with so resigned an obedience to superiors, is very unsuitable with the civil and religious liberties we so *zealously* assert. Swift.

zea′lousness. *n.s.* (from *zealous.*) The quality of being zealous.

ze′chin. *n.s.* (So named from *zecha,* a place in Venice where the mint is settled for coinage.) A gold coin worth about nine shillings sterling.

zedo′ary. *n.s.* (*zedoaire,* French.) A spicy plant, somewhat like ginger in its leaves, but of a sweet scent.

zed. *n.s.* The name of the letter *z.*

Thou whoreson *zed,* thou unnecessary letter. Shakespeare.

ze′nith. *n.s.* (Arabick.) The point over head opposite to the nadir.

> Fond men! if we believe that men do live
> Under the *zenith* of both frozen poles,
> Though none come thence, advertisement to give,
> Why bear we not the like faith of our souls? Davies.

> These seasons are designed by the motions of the sun, when that approaches nearest our *zenith,* or vertical point, we call it summer. Browne's *Vulgar Errours.*

ze′phyr, ze′phyrus. *n.s.* (*zephyrus,* Latin.) The west wind; and poetically any calm soft wind.

> They are as gentle
> As *zephyrs* blowing below the violet. Shakespeare's *Cymbeline.*

> *Zephyr,* you shall see a youth with a merry countenance, holding in his hand a swan with wings displayed, as about to sing. Peacham, *On Drawing.*

> Forth rush the levent and the ponent winds,
> Eurus and *Zephyr.* Milton.

> Mild as when *Zephyrus* on Flora breathes. Milton.

> Their every musick wakes,
> Whence blending all the sweeten'd *zephyr* springs. Thomson.

zest. *n.s.* (1) The peel of an orange squeezed into wine.
(2) A relish; a taste added.

to zest. *v.a.* To heighten by an additional relish.

zete′tick. *adj.* (from ζητέω.) Proceeding by enquiry.

zeu′gma. *n.s.* (from ζεῦγμα.) A figure in grammar, when a verb agreeing with divers nouns, or an adjective with divers substantives, is referred to one expresly, and to the other by supplement, as lust overcame shame, boldness fear, and madness reason.

zoc′le. *n.s.* (In architecture.) A small sort of stand or pedestal, being a low square piece or member, serving to support a busto, statue, or the like, that needs to be raised; also a low square member serving to support a column, instead of a pedestal, base, or plinth. *Dict.*

zo'diack. *n.s.* (*zodiaque*, French; ζωδιακὸς, ἐκ τῶν ζώων, the living creatures, the figures of which are painted on it in globes.) The track of the sun through the twelve signs; a great circle of the sphere, containing the twelve signs.

> The golden sun salutes the morn,
> And having gilt the ocean with his beams,
> Gallops the *zodiack* in his glist'ring coach. Shakespeare.

> Years he number'd scarce thirteen,
> When fates turn'd cruel;
> Yet three fill'd *zodiacks* had he seen
> The stage's jewel. Ben. Jonson.

> By his side,
> As in a glist'ring *zodiack* hung the sword,
> Satan's dire dread; and in his hand the spear. Milton.

> It exceeds even their absurdity to suppose the *zodiack* and planets to be efficient of, and antecedent to themselves, or to exert any influences before they were in being. Bentley.

> Here in a shrine that cast a dazling light,
> Sat fixt in thought the mighty Stagyrite;
> His sacred head a radiant *zodiack* crown'd,
> And various animals his sides surround. Pope.

zone. *n.s.* (ζωνή; *zona*, Latin.) (1) A girdle.

> The middle part
> Girt like a starry *zone* his waist, and round
> Skirted his loins, and thighs, with downy gold
> And colours dipp'd in heav'n. Milton's *Paradise Lost.*

> An embroider'd *zone* surrounds her waist. Dryden.

> Thy statues, Venus, though by Phidias' hand
> Design'd immortal, yet no longer stand;
> The magick of thy shining *zone* is past,
> But Salisbury's garter shall for ever last. Granville.

> Scarce could the goddess from her nymph be known,
> But by the crescent and the golden *zone.* Pope.

(2) A division of the earth.

The whole surface of the earth is divided into five *zones:* the first is contained between the two tropicks, and is called the torrid *zone*. There are two temperate *zones,* and two frigid *zones*. The northern temperate *zone* is terminated by the tropick of Cancer and the artick polar circle: the southern temperate *zone* is contained between the tropick of Capricorn and the polar circle: the frigid *zones* are circumscribed by the polar circles, and the poles are in their centers.

> True love is still the same: the torrid *zones,*
> And those more frigid ones,
> > It must not know:
> For love grown cold or hot,
> Is lust or friendship, not
> > The thing we show;
> For that's a flame would die,
> Held down or up too high:
> Then think I love more than I can express,
> And would love more, could I but love thee less.
> Suckling.

> As five *zones* th' etherial regions bind,
> Five correspondent are to earth assign'd:
> The sun, with rays directly darting down,
> Fires all beneath, and fries the middle *zone*. Dryden.

(3) Circuit; circumference.

> > Scarce the sun
> Hath finish'd half his journey, and scarce begins
> His other half in the great *zone* of heav'n. Milton.

zoo′grapher. *n.s.* (ζωὴ and γράφω.) One who describes the nature, properties, and forms of animals.

> One kind of locust stands not prone, or a little inclining upward; but a large erectness, elevating the two fore legs, and sustaining itself in the middle of the other four, by *zoographers* called the prophet and praying locust. Browne's *Vulgar Errours*.

zoo′graphy. *n.s.* (of ζωὴ and γράφω.) A description of the forms, natures, and properties of animals.

If we contemplate the end of the effect, its principal final cause being the glory of its maker, this leads us into divinity; and for its subordinate, as it is designed for alimental sustenance to living creatures, and medicinal uses to man, we are thereby conducted into *zoography.* Glanvill, *Scepsis Scientifica.*

zoo′logy. *n.s.* (of ζῶον and λόγος.). A treatise concerning living creatures.

zoo′phyte. *n.s.* (ζώοφυτον, of ζωός and φυτὸν.) Certain vegetables or substances which partake of the nature both of vegetables and animals.

zoopho′rick column. *n.s.* (In architecture.) A statuary column, or a column which bears or supports the figure of an animal. *Dict.*

zoo′phorus. *n.s.* (ζωοφορὸς.) A part between the architraves and cornice, so called on account of the ornaments carved on it, among which were the figures of animals. *Dict.*

zoo′tomist. *n.s.* (of ζωοτομία.) A dissector of the bodies of brute beasts.

zoo′tomy. *n.s.* (ζωοτομία, of ζῶον and τεμνω.) Dissection of the bodies of beasts.